SUNDAR SANKARAN is founder-director of Advantage-India Consulting Pvt. Ltd. (www.advantage-india.com) a 20-year old strategy consulting and knowledge incubation boutique. He has also founded finberry academy pvt ltd (www.finberry.org) and Stratberry Publishing (www.stratberry.com).

Sundar is renowned as an effective trainer, who can simplify concepts, and catalyse learning through linkages with day-to-day examples. He operates with equal ease at macro-level perspective programs as well as micro-drill-down programs. His programs, which cover the entire range from leadership to product to selling, are not merely for knowledge dissemination; they seek to bring change within participants, so that they are enthusiastic about the desired behaviour.

Wide experience across geographies, markets and products have helped Sundar conceptualise several unique seminars and workshops in the areas of strategy, economics, finance and financial markets. Within mutual funds, financial planning and wealth management, his programs span products, business development, selling skills, legalities and high-end data analytics.

Over the years, Sundar has trained over 20,000 participants belonging to leading mutual funds, including Kotak Mahindra, Fidelity, Standard Chartered, Canbank, Tata, LIC, UTI, SBI, HDFC, Optimix and BOB; banks, including Kotak Mahindra Bank, SBI, ICICI, HDFC, Citi, Deutsche, Standard Chartered, ABN Amro, Corporation Bank, Bank of Rajasthan, Bank of Baroda, Bank of India, PNB and State Bank of Hyderabad; financial product distributors, including Kotak Securities, JM Morgan Stanley Distribution, ICICI Capital, Cholamandalam Distribution, NJ IndiaInvest, Birla Sunlife Distribution, Integrated Finance and Bajaj Capital; and the media, including The Times of India, The Economic Times, Financial Express, Business Line, CNBC, across a range of innovative programs.

Sundar is a prolific writer. He has developed the courseware and examinations for over twenty certifications offered by apex education bodies such as SEBI's National Institute of Securities Market (NISM), National Stock Exchange's NCFM and Indian Institute of Banking and Finance.

Sundar provides consulting and research inputs to leading corporations on their corporate structure, business plan, financial structure, performance management systems, product portfolio, channel management, customer insights, learning models and technology strategies.

Sundar has worked in senior capacities at Bajaj Auto and Kotak Mahindra. His hands-on feel of financial markets and industry is well complemented by his academic qualifications from IIM Ahmedabad (1988), IIT Bombay, RA Podar College, Mumbai, Associate of the Institute of Company Secretaries of India (1992) and Associate of the Institute of Cost Accountants of India (1988).

His other passions include reading, Indian classical music and travel.

Praise for Sundar Sankaran's, *Indian Mutual Funds Handbook*

"A comprehensive guide to the world of Indian mutual funds, its operational and regulatory mechanisms, the advantages and limitations of investing in them, along with a practical approach to personal financial planning. It highlights the finer nuances. . . ." *The Economic Times*

"From his experience as a trainer in strategic management and financial markets, Sundar Sankaran visits the subject of mutual funds in a no-nonsense manner . . . *Indian Mutual Funds Handbook* is ideal for investors looking for a deeper understanding of mutual funds . . . Sankaran simplifies concepts for the layman." *Business World*

"The best book that I have come across for understanding mutual funds. Will be useful for employees of asset management companies, marketing intermediaries, investors and students — any one who wants insights into mutual funds in India."

M. Subramanian, former CEO India, Barclays Bank plc.

"The common sense approach to mutual funds makes interesting reading."

C. Jayaram, former Joint Managing Director, Kotak Mahindra Asset Management Co Ltd.

"I congratulate you for a genuine effort at demystification and to make understanding of mutual funds crisp and simple."

P.G.R. Prasad, former Managing Director, SBI Funds Management Pvt Ltd.

"If you think you know everything about mutual funds, read the book to find out how much you do not know!"

Prof. G. Sethu, former Dean, UTI Institute of Capital Markets

"Very comprehensive. Covers every topic relating to the mutual fund industry in simple language."

M.V. Suryanarayana, former Chief Executive, Jeevan Bima Sahayog Asset Management Company Limited (Asset Manager for LIC Mutual Fund)

"An attempt to unfold various facets of mutual fund industry."

Manubhai Parekh, former Managing Director, BOB Asset Mgt Co. Ltd.

"The chapter on financial planning may catalyse several new business models in mutual fund distribution."

Niraj Chokshi & Jignesh Desai, Directors, NJ IndiaInvest

"For those who are joining the mutual funds show, Sundar Sankaran has just the right book for you. . . . And Sundar is confident you'd make money in mutual funds." *The Hindu Business Line*

5th Edition

INDIAN MUTUAL FUNDS HANDBOOK

A Guide for Industry Professionals and Intelligent Investors

Sundar Sankaran

VISION BOOKS

www.visionbooksindia.com

www.visionbooksindia.com

Disclaimer

The author and the publisher disclaim all legal or other responsibilities for any losses which investors may suffer by investing or trading using the methods described in this book. Readers are advised to seek professional guidance before making any specific investments. This book is meant purely for the purpose of investor and trader education.

First Published, 2003
Reprinted, 2004 (Twice), 2005 (Twice), 2006 (Twice)
2nd Revised and Expanded Edition, 2007
Reprinted, 2007, 2008 (Thrice), 2009, 2010
3rd Revised Edition, 2012
4th Revised Edition, 2016
Reprinted, 2017
5th Revised Edition, 2018
Reprinted, 2019, 2020, 2021, 2022, 2023

ISBN 10: 93-86268-19-1
ISBN 13: 978-93-86268-19-8

Published by
Vision Books Pvt. Ltd.
(Incorporating Orient Paperbacks and CARING Imprints)
24 Feroze Gandhi Road, Lajpat Nagar 3
New Delhi 110024, India.
Phone: (+91-11) 2984 0821 / 22
e-mail: visionbooks@gmail.com

Printed at
Ashim Print Line
38/2, 35 & 36 Sahibabad Industrial Area, Ghaziabad
Uttar Pradesh 201010, India.

DEDICATED TO

My departed parents

Shri C. D. Sankaran

and

Smt. Lalitha Sankaran.

Dream what you dare to dream

Be what you wish to be

Do what you like to do.

Contents

Foreword to the Second Edition

by

Shekhar Sathe

The mutual fund industry has entered a new era in India. The so-called second phase of reforms has slowly crept in and is almost half way through without any formal say-so. Total mutual fund assets under management at the end of December 2006 were above ₹ 3.5 lakh crore, which is more than 10% of total deposits in the banking system. Close to ₹ 2 lakh crore of those assets were invested in debt and money market instruments; the rest being equity assets. Clearly, the mutual fund industry has grown to be an important part of the Indian financial system. The main significance of this development is the increased disintermediation of risk from banks to investors in mutual funds themselves.

SEBI, the principal regulator of the industry, has admirably kept pace with the developments in the market. On the one hand, the regulator has paved the way for introduction of structured products, such as capital guarantied portfolios and dramatically different risk / reward pay-off products; on the other hand, it has restrained asset management companies from issuing open-end fund products which are merely old wine in new bottles. This will pave the way for dramatic growth in close-ended products.

The main challenges before the asset management industry are to design new products, communicate about them with precision and simplicity, and deliver the product design with professional meticulousness.

The challenges before investors are to understand these products, the precise nature of the risk they are undertaking and be discerning in apportioning their allocation between the multitude of products on offer.

The challenge for the distributors, as always, will be how not to "mis-sell".

My foreword to the first edition of this book had talked about "RESTFULness." Now I think it is time for restlessness. Which means we all have to be wary of our investment choices.

Sundar's book will guide us by reinforcing our fundamental understanding about mutual funds.

January 2007

Shekhar Sathe
Director,
Kotak Mahindra Trustee Company Ltd.

Foreword to the First Edition

by

Shekhar Sathe

This handbook will act as a catalyst for demystifying mutual funds. Each chapter addresses complex issues in a very simple and entertaining way to make mutual fund investing common sense.

Like banks, mutual funds will eventually become a significant part of the Indian financial system and, therefore, a part and parcel of the life of the common investor. I dare say that to manage personal savings is not an easy role for people uninitiated into the complexities of today's markets. In India, the financial system is entering the next stage of reforms, where individuals will have to decide for themselves what is good and safe for them, or what is risky but rewarding. This handbook holds the reader's hand and walks her through the world of funds.

Mutual funds are mistakenly equated with stock markets. Past few years have decisively proven that debt schemes are also capable of producing handsome returns. It is important for investors to correctly gauge the risk/reward relationship for any investment proposal. One of the glaring mistakes people make is the assumption that equity schemes have high risk and, therefore, give a high reward. The correct relationship is that higher the risk, higher should be the reward for justifying that risk; and that along with the potential of high reward there is the possibility of high loss as well.

Another misunderstanding about equity schemes is that they are long-term investments. What it means is that given the high volatility of the stock market, it may take a long time for you to earn the high return (to justify the high risk you take) you are looking for. Sundar vividly brings out the right perspectives in each of the chapters.

In my view the quality of a mutual fund is best described by the acronym, RESTFUL. Each letter of the word stands for a performance parameter:

R represents the risk reward relationship. The return generated by a fund needs to be adjusted for the risk the fund takes.
E represents ease or convenience in transacting.
S represents service standards of a fund-house.
T represents transparency or the quality of disclosures to investors.
F represents familiarity of the fund house about their customers' needs.
U represents utility of a particular scheme to meet investors' financial planning needs.
L represents liquidity. Is the fund delivering the liquidity it promises at the right price to the investor?

Anyone who studies this handbook will be able to judge investment propositions offered by any fund on each of these parameters and be able to take the first step towards making worry-free investments. I wholeheartedly recommend this book to everyone who wants to make informed investment decisions.

SHEKHAR SATHE
Director,
Kotak Mahindra Trustee Company Ltd.

Preface to the Fifth Edition

Mutual funds can be a conundrum for people who are not closely associated with the industry. Even many who have been part of the industry for several years continue to have some misconceptions. This book aims to unravel some of the mysteries and clear the typical confusions I have noticed among participants in my workshops, and other people I interact with.

There are so many inter-linked concepts on the subject, that the sequencing of topics was a challenge. I hope my experience of handling several hundred workshops has ensured a reader-friendly sequence. Readers can supplement the learning with my companion publication, *Wealth Engine: Indian Financial Planning & Wealth Management Handbook* [Vision Books, 2012]. Appropriate references to chapters in *Wealth Engine* have been provided at relevant places.

Readers who wish to understand the *raison d'etre* and mechanics of mutual funds, a powerful investment avenue, will treasure the book. You can read the chapters in any sequence. The index can be referred to access terms that are explained in chapters you may have skipped. Chapters 10, 11 and 13 are a synthesis of advanced statistics and the financial markets. I hope the complex subject has been explained lucidly. Readers who are uncomfortable with advanced quantitative techniques can skim through the non-quantitative sections of these chapters.

The subject of taxation is discussed in Chapter 17.*

Books, like people, need to evolve. That is how they become thought-leaders in the space. As with earlier editions of this book, I not only explain whatever exists in the Indian mutual funds arena, but also introduce concepts that will find their way in due course. It is gratifying that issues highlighted in earlier editions were followed by regulatory changes on matters such as intermediary roles and commission structures, scheme classification and determination of distributable reserves. The previous edition of this book introduced the concept of smart-beta to the do-

* This chapter has been updated with tax provision applicable in Assessment Year 2019-20.

mestic reader. This edition explores the potential of big data, artificial intelligence and block-chain technology for mutual funds and unit-holders.

Needless to say, this book is not a recommendation to buy or sell any financial products. Some of the examples provided are illustrative. Kindly consult your investment advisor before taking any decisions related to your investment portfolio.

The content in the book is updated till 15 April 2018. The mutual fund industry is dynamic. For a few months after the launch of the book, important subsequent changes will be highlighted at www.imfh.info. However, as suggested by my solicitor, I need to clarify that this is purely a gesture of goodwill. I retain the right to discontinue such updates any time — or offer such updates only as a paid service.

Happy reading! Happy investing! Happy living!

SUNDAR SANKARAN

Mumbai
April 2018

Acknowledgements

My exposure to mutual funds happened through a series of chance occurrences, rather than by design. I clearly recall four such:

- Seeking approval of the Securities and Exchange Board of India (SEBI) for a mutual fund that never saw the light of the day.
- Joint venture discussions for another proposed mutual fund that was never formed.
- Handling investments and accounting for a USD50mn international fund based outside India.
- Seminars and workshops for employees and distributors of Kotak Mahindra Asset Management Company (KMAMC).

These four accidents provided me an opportunity to understand different facets of the mutual funds industry, namely setting up a fund house; fund management, accounting and operations; and marketing and sales.

I am thankful to Kotak Mahindra Mutual Fund, LIC Mutual Fund, Canbank Mutual Fund, Tata Mutual Fund, Fidelity Mutual Fund, Standard Chartered Mutual Fund, Optimix Mutual Fund and SBI Mutual Fund for engaging me as a trainer. Seminars and workshops on their behalf over the last 16 years have taken me to all parts of the country, meeting distributors and agents of all sizes and shapes. It has been a truly exhilarating learning experience. My association with Unit Trust of India's S&P's CNX Nifty UTI Notional Depository Receipts ("SUNDER") provided useful perspectives on exchange traded funds.

Mr. Shekhar Sathe formerly with Kotak Mahindra, and Mr. Prakash Dalal of Kotak Mahindra were instrumental in launching my deep involvement with the industry in India. Mr. M. R. Murali, Mr. Punathara and Mr. R. K. Jain who were with Jeevan Bima Sahayog AMC (JBSAMC) introduced me to the functioning of their agency network. Mr. Manoj Jain, Mr. Ajay Mishra, and Mr. Chaitanya Nayak of SBI Mutual Fund and Mr. Ajay Mittal (earlier with SBI Mutual Fund) gave me opportunities to understand their agency network.

Mr. Srikar Baljekar (formerly with Kotak and Fidelity) and Mr. Ramesh (then with JBSAMC) helped clarify various accounting and operational aspects. Mr. Atul Monga who was with Kotak Mahindra provided useful insights into the psyche of distributors that got reinforced and refined in the course of my interactions in the market. Mr. Pitambar Chowdhury of Tata Mutual Fund provided me the platform to interact with the younger generation and understand their approach to learning about mutual funds. Mr. Krishnan Sitaraman and Mr. Vijay Krishnamurthy of CRISIL were kind to share some aspects of their ranking and rating methodology. Mr. V. Ramesh, Managing Director and CEO of MF Utilities India Pvt. Ltd. clarified various aspects of MF Utilities.

Mr. Paritosh Sharma and Ms. Gargi Dutta of National Institute of Securities Market (NISM) were involved in the content that I developed for the NISM certification that replaced AMFI certification in June 2010. Mr. Rohit Jain was involved in developing other mutual fund and investment adviser certifications for NISM.

Mr. Arup Mukherjee gave me the opportunity of developing an entire range of post-graduate certifications for National Stock Exchange's NCFM. This included capital markets, derivatives, project finance, mutual funds, financial planning, wealth management, treasury management, risk management and mergers and acquisitions.

Mr. R. H. Sarma who was with Indian Institute of Banking & Finance (IIBF), offered me an opportunity to develop a module on financial planning. Mr. P. Balachandran of IIBF kept me engaged through content development for their programs on financial advising and wealth management.

The book also reflects some of the thought processes of Mr. N. R. Ramanujam and Mr. Ramesh Nayak (ex-Canbank), Mr. Vijay Venkatram, Mr. Arjun Inamdar and Mr. Arindam Ghosh (ex-Fidelity), Mr. Sandesh Kirkire (ex-Kotak) as well as Mr. Neeraj Chokshi and Mr. Jignesh Desai of NJ IndiaInvest. Arun Ohri, who was Chief, Marketing at IL&FS Mutual Fund, helped brainstorm on various business issues in the mutual fund industry.

Prof. G. Sethu of IIM Tiruchi provided excellent academic perspectives and also motivated me to get this book published. Dr. (Ms.) Rachana Baid, of Indian Institute of Capital Markets (IICM) and Dr. (Ms.) Poonam Mehra of NISM provided significant value, in particular on the statistical concepts. Dr. (CA) Varadraj Bapat of IIT, Bombay has been a pillar of support in my endeavours in academic research, which will continue embellishing future editions of this book.

The book also benefited from the bed-time reading of Mr. Jayen Shah (now with IDFC), when he fractured his leg.

Sudhir Bansal of Applied Media put me in touch with Mr. Kapil Malhotra of Vision Books, the publisher of this book. Mr. Suhayl Abidi's deep knowledge of the publishing industry provided the comfort and helped me sign up with Vision Books. I am indebted to my friend from college days, Mr. Murali Aiyer formerly with CRISIL, but for whom I would never have known Suhayl.

My colleagues and former colleagues at Advantage-India Consulting Pvt. Ltd. and Finberry Academy Pvt. Ltd, put up with my idiosyncrasies and supported the book through its various editions.

My wife and coffee-partner, Shashi Surana helped chisel many newer thoughts through her incessant and incisive questioning of the fundamentals. Most of all, acknowledgements are due to all the accidents that contributed to this book!

Chapter 1

Introduction

On my way to the office of Opportunistic Mutual Fund, I decided to visit the No Promises Laundry. There was this white shirt, which had a stain that remained after my regular wash.

I checked with the owner of the laundry — should I opt for "ordinary wash" or "dry cleaning?" The owner said I could try either, but suggested dry cleaning. She clarified that she would try her best but there was no guarantee that the stain would go. I had other options, but I left the shirt at the laundry for dry cleaning.

On my way out, I overheard a conversation:

Lady: But my sari was not torn when I gave it to you for washing. I should have given it to some other laundry.

Laundry boy: Madam, your sari material is defective. Your sari would have been torn in any other laundry as well. We washed your sari along with other saris. Only yours got torn.

I finally reached the offices of Opportunistic Mutual Fund. There was this ₹ 100,000 I had received from one of the seminars. I thought I'd invest it in a mutual fund.

I checked with the front desk — should I opt for an equity scheme or a debt scheme? The girl said I could invest in either, but suggested equity scheme if I wanted to invest for the longer term. She clarified that the fund manager would try her best, but there was no assured return. I had other options, but I handed over my cheque and application for a diversified equity scheme.

On my way out, I overheard a conversation:

Man: But I invested ₹ 1 lakh in the debt scheme expecting you to give me a good return. I should have invested with another mutual fund.

Front desk: Sir, the debt market turned adverse. We tried our best. You would have lost money even if you had invested in any other debt mutual fund. The problem was your timing. Investors who invested in our debt scheme before you did, or afterwards, earned a good return. The same fund manager managed your investment in the scheme as well as theirs. But only you lost money.

It is logical to surmise from this fictional account that "A mutual fund is like a laundry." Perhaps, the only difference is that in a laundry when you give one shirt, you will certainly not get two shirts back. In a mutual fund, you can double your investment — or lose your shirt in the market!

To what extent is a mutual fund, a laundry? Can investors avoid losing their shirt? Read on for a better understanding of mutual funds.

1.1 What is a Mutual Fund?

1.1.1 Pooled Vehicle

A mutual fund (MF) is a vehicle to pool money from investors, with a promise that the money would be invested in a particular manner, by professional managers who are expected to honour the promise.

In India mutual funds are governed by the regulations of Securities and Exchange Board of India (SEBI).

1.1.2 Professional Management

The idea behind a mutual fund is that individual investors generally lack the time, the inclination or the skills to manage their own investments. Thus, mutual funds appoint an Asset Management Company (AMC) that hires professional fund managers to manage the investments for the benefit of their investors. In return, the AMC earns a management fee from the investors. This is payable irrespective of whether or not the investor earns a return.

1.1.3 Schemes

You might wonder — why does the investor go to an AMC that in turn will appoint a professional fund manager? Why does the investor not approach a professional fund manager directly?

Indeed, an individual investor could choose to hire a professional fund manager to manage her money as per her investment and risk preferences. Such personal treatment, often referred to as Portfolio Management Scheme (PMS) in India, entails significant demands on the time of the managers; this increases the costs for the investor. Further, PMS can be offered only to clients having investment portfolio above ₹ 25 lakh. Many PMS providers operate with a higher minimum investment requirement.

It is possible to balance the time and cost required to manage investments by grouping investors together based on their preferences. In this manner, the focus of the investment activity can be shifted from a single investor (as in the case of PMS) to a group of investors having similar expectations (as in the case of a mutual fund).

For ease of management and reporting, such a group of investors is identified with a "mutual fund scheme". In commercial terminology, the investors invest in a scheme — and the professional managers manage the scheme. A mutual fund can, and typically does, have several schemes to cater to different investor preferences.

1.1.4 Money in Trust

The AMC manages investments of the scheme for the benefit of its investors. Every scheme has an:

- Investment portfolio (Portfolio Statement);
- Account of income and expenditure (Revenue Account); and
- Account of assets and liabilities (Balance Sheet).

In order to ensure fairness to investors, SEBI regulates the expenditure that can be charged to a scheme (borne by investors in that scheme), whether as management fees or as other expenses.

The gains of any scheme (after accounting for income, permitted expenses, profits and losses from the investment activity) belong to its investors. Similarly losses, if any, would need to be borne by its investors, up to the amount invested. Thus, the mutual fund manages the scheme's money in trust for the benefit of its investors.

1.1.5 Legal Framework

Across the world, the mutual fund sector is viewed as a critical mechanism to channel investor funds into the capital market. Since these investors are often not so well qualified to invest, the mutual fund business is highly regulated. Regulations vary from country to country. But, broadly, they provide for:

- Checks and balances in the legal structure;
- Pre-qualifications to start a mutual fund;
- Permissible schemes and investments;
- Control over marketing process;
- Level of operational flexibility to the professional investors; and
- Valuation of securities, etc.

Association of Mutual Funds in India (AMFI) is a body that represents the interests of the industry. All mutual funds in India are members of AMFI.

The legal framework governing mutual funds in India is discussed in detail in Chapter 3.

1.2 Who are the Parties Involved?

1.2.1 Investors

Every investor, given her financial position and personal disposition, has a certain inclination to take risk (risk appetite). The hypothesis is that by taking an incremental risk (of losing capital, wholly or partly), it would be possible for the investor to earn an incremental return.

But assuming risk without regularly monitoring it is foolhardy. Therefore, it would be prudent for investors who take a risk to be able to manage this risk.

A mutual fund is the solution for investors who lack the time, the inclination or the skills to actively manage their investment risk in individual securities. They can delegate this role to the mutual fund, while retaining the right and the obligation to monitor their investments in the scheme (which, in turn, invests in individual securities).

In the absence of a mutual fund option, the moneys of such "passive" investors would lie either in bank deposits or other "safe" investment options, thus depriving them of the possibility of earning a better return.

Investing through a mutual fund would make economic sense for an investor if her investment, over the medium to long term, fetches a return (net of all costs, expenses and taxes) that is higher than what she would otherwise have earned by investing directly, or parking the funds in the bank.

As Bogle succinctly puts it, "Because the goal of investing is to accumulate real wealth — an enhanced ability to pay for goods and services — the ultimate focus of the long-term investor must be on real, not nominal, returns."[1] (Nominal Returns *minus* Inflation = Real Returns).

1.2.2 Trustees

Trustees are the people within a mutual fund organization who are responsible for ensuring that investors' interests in a scheme are properly taken care of.

In return for their services, they are paid trustee fees, which are normally charged to the scheme. Their roles and responsibilities are discussed in detail in Chapter 3.

1.2.3 Asset Management Company (AMC)

AMCs manage the investment portfolios of schemes and handle various other routine activities incidental to the mutual fund business. An AMC's income comes from the management fees it charges the schemes it manages. The management fee is calculated as a percentage of net assets managed. Some countries provide for performance based management fees as well.

In order to earn the management fee, an AMC has naturally to employ people and bear all the establishment costs that are related to its activity, such as for premises, furniture, computers and other assets, software development, communication costs, etc. These are to be met out of the management fee earned.

Expenses such as on distributor commission, marketing, etc. can be directly borne by the mutual fund scheme. However, in some cases competition in the marketplace could force an AMC to bear some of these costs, which would otherwise have been borne by investors in the schemes.

So long as the income earned through management fees more than covers its expenses, an AMC is economically viable.

Given the nature of its activity, a certain minimum establishment and infrastructure is necessary for an AMC's functioning. Since costs cannot be reduced below a base level, every AMC needs to have a reasonable corpus of assets under management (AUM), below which it may not be viable.

The break-even level of AUM is a function of cost structure of the AMC and distribution of assets between its different types of schemes. It may be noted that debt schemes and index schemes generally yield a lower management fee. As a thumb-rule, in the Indian context it is difficult for an AMC to break-even if its AUM is below ₹ 10,000 crore.

1.2.4 Distributors

Distributors earn a commission for bringing investors into the schemes of a mutual fund. This commission is an expense for the scheme, although there are occasions when an AMC may choose to bear the cost, wholly or partly.

Depending on the financial and physical resources at their disposal, the distributors could be:

- Tier 1 distributors who have their own or franchised network reaching out to investors all across the country; or
- Tier 2 distributors who are generally regional players with some reach within their region; or
- Tier 3 distributors who are small and marginal players with limited reach.

1.2.5 Registrars

An investor's holding in mutual fund schemes is typically recorded by the scheme's Registrar and Transfer Agent (RTA). Some AMCs prefer to handle this role in-house, i.e. on their own instead of appointing an RTA. The registrar or the AMC as the case may be, maintains an account of the investor's investments in and disinvestments (redemptions) from the schemes and handles corporate actions such as dividend payments.

1.2.6 Custodian

The custodian maintains custody of the securities in which the scheme invests — as distinct from the RTA who records the investment by investors in the scheme. Thus, for investment transactions of the mutual fund, it is the Custodian who receives or gives delivery. This ensures an ongoing independent record of the investments of the scheme. The custodian also follows up on various corporate actions, such as rights, bonus and dividends declared by investee companies.

In one of the securities market scams, a large provident fund investor parted with some of its funds without gaining custody of the securities where they were supposed to have invested. When the scam broke out, they realized that the money was gone, but they did not have the securities. The custodian in the mutual fund structure is in a position to prevent such risks.

1.3 Capital Flow in the Economy

As noted earlier, mutual funds make it possible for investors to assume risks, in the expectation of higher returns. This increases the level of risk capital that is available in the economy for funding enterprise.

The mutual funds also add depth to the security markets where they invest, thus contributing to liquidity and price discovery. This again is a significant factor in channelling more money into the markets, instead of this being locked up in unproductive physical capital, like gold, real estate, etc.

1.4 Corporate Governance

As large and informed investors, mutual funds can perform an active role in ensuring that their investee companies operate with the highest standards of corporate governance. This benefits all investors in those companies.

Lately, the regulators have enhanced the responsibility of mutual funds in this regard. Mutual funds are expected to report on their website, details of how they voted in their investee companies' meetings of shareholders.

1.5 Schemes and Units

Investment in a company is normally represented by a certain number of shares. People invest in a company by acquiring its shares; they disinvest by selling its shares. The total outstanding shares of a company multiplied by the face value of each share, constitutes the share capital of a company.

What shares are for a company, units are for a mutual fund scheme. Thus, investors invest in a scheme by buying its units; they disinvest by selling its units. The total outstanding units of a scheme multiplied by the face value of its units, constitutes the unit capital of the scheme.

Every scheme has an investment objective or philosophy, i.e. a promise by the AMC on how the funds would be managed. Investors in a scheme are essentially buying into this investment objective or philosophy.

1.6 Net Asset Value (NAV)

The NAV indicates the intrinsic worth of a scheme. NAV per unit represents the worth of each unit that investors hold in that scheme. For this purpose, all investments that the scheme owns are marked to market (MTM), i.e. they are valued at the prevailing market price. Details of how NAV is calculated are covered in Chapter 5.

1.7 Benefits of Investing in Mutual Funds

1.7.1 Legal Comfort

The legal structure, which is a source of comfort for investors, is discussed in detail in Chapter 3.

1.7.2 Tax Efficiency

In general, investors pay tax on a year-to-year basis. So if they were to earn and then re-invest any income, what they would re-invest is the amount that is available after paying tax.

Mutual fund schemes, on the other hand, do not pay any tax on their income. So the same earning in a mutual fund scheme could facilitate a higher re-investment.

This differential tax treatment offers an opportunity to investors to multiply their money within a scheme, without paying tax in the interim. The incidence of taxation can be postponed until the investor needs the money — at which point of time the income can be structured as a long-term capital gain (through re-purchase, i.e. sale of units by the investor to the scheme), with the incidental tax efficiencies discussed in Chapter 17.

1.7.3 Choice of Risk Position

There are as many risk-level options among mutual fund schemes as the water-level options in the milk sold by the unorganised milk sector in India! The choice of water level is entirely that of the buyer. The investor can either savour the water (risk) or drown in it!

Each mutual fund scheme promises a certain water (risk) level, and is expected to stick to it. Mutual fund schemes that do not stick to their promise are not worth investing in.

In the case of milk, the buyer would be happy with a water level that is lower than what was promised. However, with mutual funds, variation from promised risk level is unethical, irrespective of whether it is higher or lower than the promise. The trustees are responsible for ensuring that the AMC invests as per its committed investment objective, and maintains the promised risk character of the scheme.

1.7.4 Professional Management

Investment is a specialised and full-time activity. AMCs are expected to have the professional people and the establishment to carry out this specialized work. Further, professional managers can take more dispassionate decisions, such as selling in a stop-loss situation, which investors find difficult on emotional grounds.

1.7.5 Investment Convenience

The facility of making investments through Investor Service Centres as well as through the Internet, a facility offered by most AMCs and large distributors, ensures convenience. Similarly, it is possible for investors to benefit from various facilities that mutual fund schemes offer, as discussed in Chapter 15. Mutual funds that permit switches between schemes without any cost, help investors to manage their exposures economically.

1.7.6 Liquidity

Most mutual fund schemes in the market offer liquidity by letting investors buy or sell units directly from the scheme. This is unlike direct investment in the securities market, where it is possible that the investor does not find a counter-party for her trade.

Some categories of mutual fund schemes do not offer investors the facility of such direct transactions. However, these are listed in a stock exchange and can be traded like other listed securities.

1.7.7 Investment Lot

Direct investment in the securities market often comes with a stiff minimum investment requirement. This is particularly so in the Indian debt market, where realistic options for retail investors are only now emerging.

On the other hand, mutual fund schemes give investors the option of investing as little as ₹ 5,000 with the added assurance of liquidity. Minimum investment is as low as ₹ 500 for some schemes. Obtaining wide exposure across a range of sectors and companies, through investment of such small amounts in a mutual fund scheme is a unique benefit that the industry offers.

1.7.8 Cost Economies

Given its size, an AMC would be in a position to negotiate better brokerage terms for the sales and purchases of its investments. No doubt the operating costs get loaded to its schemes, and thus charged to the scheme's investors. But there are regulations on the extent of such loading.

So long as the incremental returns through professional management and tax efficiencies are more than the costs charged to the schemes, investors gain by investing through mutual funds.

1.8 Limitations of Mutual Funds

1.8.1 Shared Investment Portfolio

All investors in a mutual fund scheme share its investment portfolio. In other words, the portfolio is not customised for each investor. An investor looking for a customised portfolio can opt for PMS, where the cost structure is higher, and regulatory protection is not so strong.

1.8.2 Intermediation Cost

An investor in a mutual fund scheme is exposed to two kinds of intermediation cost — one is the fund management cost; and the second is the distribution cost.

Fund management cost needs to be viewed in the context of value added through investment convenience, professional management and investor protection. Further, investors do benefit from economies of scale, when these costs are distributed over a large base of investors.

Mutual fund schemes do offer investors the facility of buying units directly from the scheme, i.e. without using the services of a distributor. On such direct investments, investors do not need to incur the distribution cost.

1.8.3 Problem of Choice

The mutual fund industry offers investors a wide range of schemes to choose from. This makes it difficult for many investors to decide what to buy. Investors facing such a challenge can use the services of a mutual fund distributor. For the others, a lot of scheme and performance information is easily available for free. Thus, informed investment decisions can be taken.

1.9 Indian Mutual Fund Industry (Size)

As per Hindu religion, an auspicious start to any event would be an invocation to the Lord Ganesha. So also, any discussion on the mutual fund sector in India has to start with Unit Trust of India (UTI)!

UTI was constituted under the UTI Act, 1963. It commenced operations in July 1964 "with a view to encouraging savings and investment and participation in the income, profits and gains accruing to the Corporation from the acquisition, holding, management and disposal of securities".

UTI remained the monopoly player in the mutual fund sector until 1987, when public sector banks and insurance companies were permitted to promote mutual fund business. Finally, in 1993, the Securities and Exchange Board of India (SEBI) came up with comprehensive mutual fund regulations, that permitted the private sector to start mutual fund operations. These were later replaced by the SEBI (Mutual Fund) Regulations, 1996.

Let's look at some highlights of the Indian mutual fund industry, based on data sourced from AMFI (as on 31 March 2018):

- Assets under management (AUM) which were ₹ 24.67 crore as on 31 March 1965 had grown to ₹ 21,36,036 crore as on 31 March 2018 (Average AUM during the quarter, Jan-Mar 2018 was ₹ 23,05,212 crore). The progress year-wise from 1965 to 2018 is shown in Annexure 1.1.

- There were 39 active mutual fund AMCs in India and 3 Infrastructure Debt Funds (IDFs). The distribution of their average assets under management is given in Annexure 1.2. The top 5 AMCs manage over 57% of the assets under management in the industry; the next 5 control a further 24%. Thus, almost 81% of the assets are with 10 AMCs. The bottom half (21 AMCs) control about 4% of the industry. Some mutual funds have chosen to move out of the space on account of difficulties in scaling up or other reasons. Further, SEBI has increased the minimum capital requirements for AMCs. On account of these factors, the next few years are likely to see significant mergers and acquisitions action in the industry.

Annexure 1.1: Assets under Management (1965-2018)

As on 31st March	*AUM (₹ Crore)*	*CAGR #*
1965	25	
1970	88	29.1%
1975	170	14.0%
1980	455	21.8%
1985	2,210	37.2%
1990	19,131	54.0%
1995	72,967	30.7%
2000	113,005	9.1%
2005	149,600	5.8%
2010	613,979	32.6%
2015	10,82,757	12.0%
2018	21,36,036	25.4%

1 crore = 10 million

Compounded Annual Growth Rate — calculated with respect to the previous row, for instance CAGR shown against row 1970, is the CAGR from 1965 to 1970 and so on.

Source: www.AMFIIndia.com

Annexure 1.2: Mutual Funds and Average AUM

(Average for quarter ended 31 March 2018)

Name of Mutual Fund	*Average AUM (₹ Crore)*	*Market Share*	*Cumulative Share*	*Rank*
ICICI Prudential Mutual Fund	305,739	13.3%	13.3%	1
HDFC Mutual Fund	300,549	13.0%	26.3%	2
Aditya Birla Sun Life Mutual Fund	247,529	10.7%	37.0%	3
Reliance Mutual Fund	244,904	10.6%	47.7%	4
SBI Mutual Fund	217,649	9.4%	57.1%	5
UTI Mutual Fund	154,939	6.7%	63.8%	6
Kotak Mahindra Mutual Fund	124,691	5.4%	69.2%	7
Franklin Templeton Mutual Fund	103,152	4.5%	73.7%	8
DSP BlackRock Mutual Fund	86,326	3.7%	77.5%	9
Axis Mutual Fund	77,325	3.4%	80.8%	10
IDFC Mutual Fund	69,919	3.0%	83.8%	11

(Contd . . .)

Name of Mutual Fund	*Average AUM (₹ Crore)*	*Market Share*	*Cumulative Share*	*Rank*
L&T Mutual Fund	65,932	2.9%	86.7%	12
Tata Mutual Fund	46,977	2.0%	88.7%	13
Sundaram Mutual Fund	34,306	1.5%	90.2%	14
Invesco Mutual Fund	26,203	1.1%	91.4%	15
DHFL Pramerica Mutual Fund	23,595	1.0%	92.4%	16
LIC Mutual Fund	20,118	0.9%	93.3%	17
Motilal Oswal Mutual Fund	17,735	0.8%	94.0%	18
JM Financial Mutual Fund	16,365	0.7%	94.7%	19
Mirae Asset Mutual Fund	15,756	0.7%	95.4%	20
Baroda Pioneer Mutual Fund	13,022	0.6%	96.0%	21
Canara Robeco Mutual Fund	12,496	0.5%	96.5%	22
Edelweiss Mutual Fund	12,100	0.5%	97.1%	23
IDBI Mutual Fund	10,760	0.5%	97.5%	24
Indiabulls Mutual Fund	10,714	0.5%	98.0%	25
HSBC Mutual Fund	10,261	0.4%	98.4%	26
BNP Paribas Mutual Fund	8,159	0.4%	98.8%	27
PRINCIPAL Mutual Fund	7,196	0.3%	99.1%	28
BOI AXA Mutual Fund	5,802	0.3%	99.3%	29
Union Mutual Fund	4,305	0.2%	99.5%	30
Mahindra Mutual Fund	3,368	0.1%	99.7%	31
Essel Mutual Fund	1,540	0.1%	99.7%	32
IL&FS Mutual Fund (IDF)	1,274	0.1%	99.8%	33
Quantum Mutual Fund	1,203	0.1%	99.9%	34
PPFAS Mutual Fund	1,010	0.0%	99.9%	35
IIFL Mutual Fund	793	0.0%	99.9%	36
IIFCL Mutual Fund (IDF)	650	0.0%	100.0%	37
Taurus Mutual Fund	509	0.0%	100.0%	38
Escorts Mutual Fund	231	0.0%	100.0%	39
Sahara Mutual Fund	64	0.0%	100.0%	40
Shriram Mutual Fund	43	0.0%	100.0%	41
SREI Mutual Fund (IDF)	0	0.0%	100.0%	42
	2,305,212			

Source: www.AMFIIndia.com

Note: Names and addresses of SEBI registered mutual funds are available at SEBI's website on ongoing basis.

Chapter 2

Mutual Fund Schemes and Comparable Products

Mutual fund schemes can be offered with any of a range of investment objectives, each corresponding to a certain point in the risk-return matrix. In a broad sense, schemes can be categorised based on tenor, asset class, position philosophy, or geography.

2.1 Types of Schemes by Tenor

2.1.1 Open-end Schemes

These are schemes that do not have a fixed maturity. The mutual fund announces sale and re-purchase prices for the units of such a scheme on an ongoing basis.

Sale price is the price at which an open-end scheme will sell new units to an investor; *Re-purchase price* is the price at which an investor can return her units to an open-end scheme. As per current SEBI guidelines, the Sale Price is equal to the NAV.

Post-NFO, the date of allotment of units is called "inception date". Sale and Re-purchase prices are announced from the following day, which marks the commencement of the continuous offer period.

Every sale or re-purchase transaction results in a change in the unit capital of the scheme. The unit capital increases, when additional units are sold; and decreases if existing units are re-purchased. This is elaborated in Chapter 6.

In general, open-end schemes are not listed. However, a mutual fund can choose to provide liquidity by listing the scheme in the stock market. In such a scenario, investors can either trade in the stock market, in which case there is no change in unit capital of the scheme; or opt for a sale or re-purchase, in which case unit capital of the scheme is impacted.

As can be expected, arbitrage opportunities come up when there are two alternative options for dealing in the same units.

In Chapter 15 mutual fund transaction engines in the stock market are discussed. This is not the same as "listing" of the schemes in the stock market. The transaction engines are only a platform to facilitate transactions (sale or re-purchase) between the investor and the scheme. Such transactions do affect the unit capital of the scheme.

2.1.2 Closed-end Schemes

These are schemes that have a fixed maturity. Liquidity in such schemes is available through listing in the stock market. Trades in the market entail change in the ownership of the units, but do not alter the scheme's unit capital.

Occasionally, closed-end schemes provide a re-purchase option to investors, either for a specified period or after a specified period. Such a re-purchase facility in a closed-end scheme is normally offered up to a total annual limit for all investors together, or a limit per investor. Such re-purchase would reduce the unit capital of the scheme.

It is not normal for closed-end schemes to sell new units on an ongoing basis, though they could make a rights offering to existing investors. In a rights offering, existing investors can choose to acquire new units from the scheme. The rights offer will specify the number of such units an investor is entitled to, and the price that would need to be paid for acquiring those units.

2.1.3 Interval Schemes

These are schemes that are largely closed-end. However, they become open-end during pre-specified time periods (known as *transaction periods*). For instance, the specified transaction period may be the first week of every quarter, or the second week of every month. Under SEBI regulations, each transaction period has to be a minimum of two working days.

The period between two successive transaction periods is called *interval period.* This has to be a minimum of 15 days.

Listing of interval funds is mandatory. Therefore, investors will normally be able to trade their units in the stock exchange. However, the limited periods of openness ensures liquidity for investors, if the units do not get traded in the stock exchange.

The stock exchanges have stipulated that (except for certain small value transactions) anyone who wishes to trade in the stock exchange should have a trading account with a broker and a demat account. This is equally applicable to all listed mutual fund units including those of interval funds. The transaction period in an interval fund, when the investor can deal directly with the scheme, is especially useful for those who do not have a trading or demat account, or do not prefer to transact through a stock exchange broker.

Interval schemes are permitted to invest only in such securities that mature on or before the opening of the next transaction period.

2.2 Types of Schemes by Asset Class

2.2.1 Securities

2.2.1.1 Equity Schemes

Equity schemes invest primarily in equity shares of companies. Depending on the scheme objective, investments could be in:

- *Growth stocks* where earnings growth is expected to be attractive,
- *Momentum stocks* that go up or down in line with the market and set the tone of the market,
- *Contrarian stocks* where investment is made contrary to the general tone of the market,
- *Value stocks* where the fund manager is of the view that current valuations in the market do not fully capture the intrinsic value of the company, or
- *Income stocks* that earn high returns through dividends.

In order to standardise categories and characteristics of each scheme category SEBI has mandated the following classification of open-end equity schemes: [Source: SEBI Circular SEBI/HO/IMD/DF3/CIR/P/2017/114 dt October 6, 2017].

MULTI-CAP FUND

An equity scheme investing across large cap, mid cap, small cap stocks. Minimum investment in equity and equity related instruments must be at least 65% of total assets.

LARGE CAP FUND

An equity scheme predominantly investing in large cap stocks. Minimum investment in equity and equity related instruments of large cap companies must be 80% of total assets.

LARGE & MID CAP FUND

An equity scheme investing in both large cap and mid cap stocks. Minimum investment in equity and equity related instruments of large cap companies must be 35% of total assets; minimum investment in equity and equity related instruments of mid cap stocks upto 35% of total assets.

MID CAP FUND

An equity scheme predominantly investing in mid cap stocks. Minimum investment in equity and equity related instruments of mid cap companies must be 65% of total assets.

SMALL CAP FUND

An equity scheme predominantly investing in small cap stocks. Minimum investment in equity and equity related instruments of small cap companies must be 65% of total assets.

DIVIDEND YIELD FUND

An equity scheme predominantly investing in dividend yielding stocks, with minimum investment in equity of 65% of total assets.

VALUE FUND

An equity scheme following a value investment strategy. Minimum investment in equity and equity related instruments must be 65% of total assets.

CONTRA FUND

An equity scheme following contrarian investment strategy. Minimum investment in equity and equity related instruments must be 65% of total assets.

FOCUSED FUND

An equity scheme investing in a maximum of 30 stocks; the focus, viz. multi cap, large cap, mid cap, small cap needs to be stated with a minimum investment in equity and equity related instruments of 65% of total assets.

SECTORAL / THEMATIC FUND

An equity scheme investing in a sector or a theme, with a minimum investment in equity and equity related instruments of the specified sector / theme of 80% of total assets. This category of funds is discussed later in this chapter.

ELSS

An equity linked saving scheme with a statutory lock in of three years and tax benefit. A minimum investment in equity and equity related instruments of 80% of total assets.

SEBI has categorised the investment universe of listed companies as follows, to ensure uniformity in the industry:

- Large Cap: The top 100 listed companies in terms of full market capitalization.
- Mid Cap: Companies ranked from 101 to 250 in terms of full market capitalization.
- Small Cap: Listed companies ranked 251 onwards in terms of full market capitalization.

The capitalisation is to be computed as the average across all the stock exchanges where the company is listed. AMFI is responsible to put together the list and upload it on their website every six months. The list, based on data as at the end of June and December each year, is to be uploaded within 5 calendar days from the end of each six-month period.

2.2.1.2 Debt Schemes

Debt schemes, as the name suggests, invest only in debt securities. Their risk, as is elaborated in Chapter 4, is primarily driven by the following:

- Credit Risk: Companies with sound financials are unlikely to default on the debt securities they issue. So, schemes that invest only in debt securities of such companies are subject to a lower credit risk, as compared to schemes that invest in debt securities issued by companies whose financials are weak. Since the government of the country is least likely to default, securities issued by the government (*Gilt Securities*) are considered to be lowest in credit risk. Lower the credit risk of a debt security, higher would be its credit rating.
- Interest Risk / Price Risk: Market value of debt securities change value in the market in synch with changes in overall yields in the debt market. Debt securities that are due for maturity very soon (say, a day) fluctuate in value a lot lesser than those that will mature a long time into the future (say, 10 years). Macaulay duration is the weighted average time in which a debt instrument will be repaid. Low Macaulay duration indicates that the debt security or debt scheme portfolio is expected to be less volatile as compared to an alternative that has high Macaulay duration. The concept is discussed further in Chapter 10.

SEBI has adopted the following classification for open-end debt schemes:

OVERNIGHT FUND

Debt scheme that invests in overnight securities having maturity of 1 day.

LIQUID FUND

Debt scheme that invests in debt and money market securities with maturity of upto 91 days only.

ULTRA SHORT-DURATION FUND

Debt scheme that maintains the Macaulay duration of its portfolio between 3 months and 6 months.

LOW DURATION FUND

Debt scheme that maintains the Macaulay duration of its portfolio between 6 months and 12 months.

MONEY MARKET FUND

Debt scheme that invests in instruments that will mature within 12 months.

SHORT DURATION FUND

Debt scheme that maintains the Macaulay duration of its portfolio between 1 year and 3 years.

MEDIUM DURATION FUND

Debt scheme that maintains the Macaulay duration of its portfolio between 3 years and 4 years.

MEDIUM TO LONG DURATION FUND

Debt scheme that maintains the Macaulay duration of its portfolio between 4 years and 7 years.

LONG DURATION FUND

Debt scheme that maintains the Macaulay duration of its portfolio greater than 7 years.

DYNAMIC BOND FUND

Debt scheme that invests across duration, depending on the call it takes on future direction of yields in the debt market.

CORPORATE BOND FUND

Debt scheme that invests in excess of 80% of its assets in the highest rated debt securities.

CREDIT RISK FUND

Debt scheme that invests in excess of 65% of its assets in debt securities that are below the highest in credit rating.

BANKING & PSU FUND

Debt scheme that invests at least 80% of its assets in debt securities of banks, public sector undertakings (PSU), and public financial institutions.

GILT FUND

Debt scheme that invests at least 80% of its assets in government securities across maturities. Apart from being the most liquid securities in the debt market, government securities are eligible for liquidity support, as explained in Chapter 4.

GILT FUND WITH 10-YEAR CONSTANT DURATION

Debt scheme that invests at least 80% of its assets in government securities, such that its Macaulay duration is maintained at 10 years.

FLOATER FUND

Debt scheme that invests at least 65% of its assets in debt securities with floating rate of interest, i.e. interest rate that goes up or down in line with the interest rate or yield on some benchmark in the debt market. For example, the benchmark could be the State Bank of India 3-year fixed deposit rate.

The SEBI classification scheme is a good beginning to bring some order to Indian mutual fund offerings. It can be argued that too many categories have been created for debt schemes. Further, the logic for pegging the duration of the medium duration fund at 3 to 4 years is not clear. It could have been kept at 3 to 5 years, in synch with the 1 to 3 year duration for short-duration fund; consequently, the medium to long duration fund could have been at 5 to 7 years, thus ensuring a 2-year window across these three categories of debt schemes.

Conservative investors need to note that, by definition, gilt funds can now have upto 20% of non-gilt securities. Thus, gilt funds could have an element of credit risk.

Besides these schemes which are part of the SEBI classification scheme for open-end debt schemes, investors come across the following terms in the market.

INCOME SCHEMES

These schemes invest in bond securities issued by the government or any other issuer. They have considerable flexibility in deciding on the maturity of their investment portfolio. Corporate Bond Fund and Credit Risk Fund are examples of income schemes.

JUNK BOND SCHEMES

Junk bond schemes invest in securities that are below investment grade. The hope is that attractive returns in such poor-quality investments would more than make up for the higher risk of losing the entire investment in some cases.

"High yield" bonds is a politically correct way of referring to junk bonds.

According to Benjamin Graham, "A junk bond could be appropriate if you are retired, are looking for extra monthly income to supplement your pension, and can tolerate temporary tumbles in value . . . A junk-bond fund, though, is only a minor option — not an obligation — for the intelligent investor."[2]

SEBI guidelines limit investment in unrated securities and securities that are below investment grade to 25 per cent of the net assets of any scheme. Therefore, currently it is not yet possible to have a full-fledged junk bond mutual fund scheme in India.

FIXED MATURITY PLAN (FMP)

An investor in a debt security gets her expected yield if she holds a fixed coupon debt security until maturity, and the issuer honours its commitment. But if she sells her security earlier, then what she recovers would depend on the market situation at the time of sale. She could equally end up with a capital gain or a capital loss.

A FMP seeks to replicate a similar pay-off structure for the investor by investing exclusively in debt securities of the pre-specified maturity. Thus, if an investor is desirous of investing for four years, she can invest in a fund that will invest in debt securities of 4-year maturity.

FMPs are closed-end in nature. Therefore, as per SEBI Guidelines, these need to be listed in a stock exchange.

On maturity, the scheme would redeem the securities in its portfolio and pay the investor. The investor, however, can exit earlier by selling the units in a stock exchange. But what she would recover in an early exit would depend on the market situation at her time of exit.

Thus, an investor is reasonably certain of the return if she stays invested in the scheme for the period originally envisaged, and the companies where the FMP has invested fulfil their obligations. But she also has an earlier exit option.

Normally, an assured returns scheme can be offered only if there is a named guarantor who offers the guarantee. An FMP operates like an assured returns scheme through the back door since the investor is reasonably assured of the expected return (subject to credit risk and re-investment risk) if she holds the units for the originally envisaged period — but there is no named guarantor for the return. It must be noted that the trade practice of informally mentioning an "indicative return" for such schemes is illegal.

Another benefit of FMP is its tax efficiency. The income accrued in the scheme would not bear a tax on year to year basis. Therefore, annual interest earned by the scheme would be re-invested on "gross basis". If the same income were to be received directly by the investor, it would be subject to tax each year, thus reducing the amount available for re-investment.

When a series of FMPs are issued for different maturities, they are called "Serial Funds". These funds can choose to invest exclusively in government securities, in which case they become "Serial Gilts". Alternatively, they can invest in non-government securities, in which case they become "Serial Income Schemes."

The suffix "Gilt" to any of the above categories means that the portfolio will not take much exposure to non-Government securities.

2.2.1.3 Hybrid Schemes

Hybrid schemes invest in a mix of equity and debt. The debt investments ensure a basic interest income, which the fund manager hopes to top up with capital gains on the equity portfolio. However, losses can eat into the basic interest income and capital.

As John Bogle, a legendary figure in the mutual fund industry, puts it: "The greatest benefit of a balanced investment programme is that it makes risk more palatable. An allocation to bonds moderates the short-term volatility of stocks, giving the risk averse long-term investor the courage and confidence to sustain a heavy allocation to equities. Choose a balance of stocks and bonds according to your unique circumstances — your investment objectives, your time horizon, your level of comfort with risk, and your financial resources”.[3]

According to Hall, one of the common allocations used in these types of funds is known as the robot mix:

- 55 per cent in stock,
- 35 per cent in bonds, and
- 10 per cent in cash equivalents.[4]

The golden balance is a 50:50 ratio between debt and equity. Balanced schemes of Indian mutual funds tend to have at least 65% equity exposure, keeping in mind existing tax laws, which are discussed in detail in Chapter 17.

SEBI has proposed a classification system for hybrid schemes as follows:

CONSERVATIVE HYBRID FUND

A scheme that invests 10% to 25% of its assets in equity, the balance being in debt.

BALANCED HYBRID FUND

A scheme that invests 40% to 60% of its assets in equity; the balance in debt.

AGGRESSIVE HYBRID FUND

A scheme that invests 60% to 80% of its assets in equity, the balance in debt.

DYNAMIC ASSET ALLOCATION FUND OR BALANCED ADVANTAGE FUND

A scheme that manages its exposure to the asset classes dynamically. It has the mandate to vary its allocation between asset classes depending on its market view.

MULTI ASSET ALLOCATION FUND

A scheme that invests in at least three asset classes, e.g. equity, debt and gold with a minimum allocation of 10% to each asset class. Foreign securities are not treated as a separate asset class for this purpose.

ARBITRAGE FUND

A scheme that seeks to earn risk-neutral income by taking opposite positions in different markets — e.g. buying a share in the cash market, and reversing the position, i.e. hedging the risk in the futures market]. Such schemes need to invest at least 65% of their assets in equity and equity related securities.

EQUITY SAVINGS FUND

A scheme that invests in equity, debt and arbitrage. A minimum of 65% of total assets need to be equity, while debt needs to be at least 10% of the total assets. The scheme has to specify its minimum expected levels of hedged and unhedged position.

Investors will also come across the following types of schemes which are in the nature of closed-end hybrid schemes.

MONTHLY INCOME PLAN (MIP)

A MIP is a special case of hybrid fund that invests largely in debt. However, a small component of 15%-20% is invested in equity.

This is a good product for investors who are less oriented to taking investment risk, but would like some exposure to equity. The debt component in the portfolio ensures that the NAV of MIP does not fluctuate as widely as the equity market.

Investors should not get misled by the name. A "Monthly Income Plan" does not assure any monthly income. If the scheme does not earn a profit, then the scheme will not be able to distribute a dividend.

MIPs are taxed as debt schemes. So the favourable tax treatment that equity schemes enjoy is not available.

CAPITAL PROTECTION ORIENTED SCHEMES

A capital protection oriented scheme is a kind of hybrid scheme, where a part of the initial issue proceeds is invested in gilts that would accumulate interest and mature to a value equivalent to the amount invested by the investor. Thus, the investors' capital is protected. The remaining issue proceeds, namely the excess over what is required to be invested in gilts for capital protection, are invested in risky investments.

Suppose an investment in gilts for 5 years yields 7% return. In that case, a 5-year closed-end scheme that collects ₹ 100 from investors can invest as follows:

- ₹ 71.30 in gilt of 5-year maturity,
- Balance ₹ 28.70 in shares.

At the end of 5 years, the investment in gilt, including accumulated interest, would grow to ₹ 100 which would be adequate to cover the amount collected from investors. Thus, even if the investment in shares were completely wiped out, an extremely very remote possibility, the investor's capital is still protected. The illustration assumes no costs are charged to the portfolio.

The above approach to capital protection is called Constant Proportion Portfolio Insurance (CPPI). An alternate is Option-based Portfolio Insurance (OBPI). Here, the capital protection is built through purchase of suitable derivative products. Derivatives are contracts whose value depends on some underlying, such as an equity index or a stock or interest rate.

Under SEBI regulations, capital protection oriented schemes can only be structured as closed-end schemes; re-purchase of units before maturity is not permitted.

Since capital protection depends on the portfolio, SEBI has provided that:

- The proposed portfolio structure has to be rated by a SEBI-registered credit rating agency from the point of view of assessing the degree of certainty of achieving the objective of capital protection.
- The debt component in the portfolio can be invested only in securities that have the highest investment grade rating.
- Trustees would have to monitor the portfolio structure and report on it in their half-yearly trustees' report.

2.2.2 Physical (Real) Assets

Technically, mutual funds can invest in any asset. This includes real estate, precious metals (gold, silver), other metals (aluminium, steel), oil and other commodities. However, in India, mutual funds are not permitted to invest in physical assets other than real estate and gold.

2.2.2.1 Real Estate Mutual Fund Schemes

In April 2008, SEBI announced guidelines for Real Estate Mutual Funds. These were aimed at wider retail participation.

In September 2014, SEBI announced a new set of regulations for Real Estate Investment Trusts (REIT). Under the regulations, the minimum amount for any investor in a REIT is ₹ 2 lakh.

Industry is yet to launch a Real Estate Mutual Fund scheme; REITs are yet to gain importance in India.

2.2.2.2 Gold Funds

Industry offers Gold Funds in two formats:

GOLD EXCHANGE TRADED FUNDS

An exhaustive discussion on Exchange Traded Funds (ETFs) is featured later in this Chapter. At this stage, it would suffice to note that Gold ETFs invest in physical gold or gold-related securities. Thus, investors earn returns that are linked to the performance of gold. Investors need to have a demat account in order to invest in any ETF.

GOLD SAVINGS SCHEMES

The structure of ETFs imposes two constraints on investors — firstly, every investors needs to have a demat account; secondly, investors cannot invest in a Gold ETF through SIP.

Gold Savings Schemes are an Indian innovation that addresses these constraints of Gold ETF. The Gold Savings Scheme is a fund that invests in Gold ETFs. It allows investors to invest through SIP and without the requirement of a demat account.

A limitation of gold savings schemes is that there is one more layer of cost, in addition to the costs built into the ETF transactions. This pulls down the returns for investors in Gold Savings Schemes, as compared to Gold ETF.

2.3 Types of Schemes by Position Philosophy

Investors tend to expect mutual fund schemes to perform in all market conditions. This would require fund managers to have the flexibility to take a long or short position in any kind of asset class, without any limitations. "Unconstrained mutual funds" operate with that kind of flexibility. It must be noted that even such funds can take investment decisions that may not work out, and lead to losses.

Indian mutual fund schemes with the exception of Dynamic Asset Allocation / Balanced Advantage funds are typically "constrained", i.e. they are committed to invest in specific asset classes; the indicative distribution of the portfolio between various asset classes is defined in the Scheme Information Document. The following scheme categories have a distinctive position philosophy that has not been adequately discussed so far in this chapter:

2.3.1 Sector Funds

Regular equity funds invest in a mix of equities that are spread across different sectors. Therefore they are often referred to as diversified equity funds.

Sector funds, on the other hand, are expected to invest in only a specific sector. For instance, an energy fund would only invest in energy companies. Thus, an investor who is bullish about energy and wants an upside that is linked entirely to this sector (without a dilution arising out of exposure to other sectors) would invest in such a fund. If a sector runs into trouble, then the NAV of sector funds that are based on that sector take a steep hit.

As discussed as part of the SEBI classification scheme, at least 80 per cent of the investible money of any fund needs to be invested in the concerned sector or type of security, as the case may be.

In India, on account of a mix of legal slackness, fund managers' lack of guts and investors' lack of understanding of the concept, we faced situations where a few sector funds ended up becoming diversified equity funds with a bias towards the identified sector! We also saw diversified equity funds managed as if they were sector funds during the dotcom boom of the late 1990s. The recent SEBI measures should address these issues.

2.3.2 Thematic Funds

These are funds that invest as per a specific investment theme. For instance, a scheme might invest in all sectors where technology has a significant role. Thus, the portfolio of companies of such a fund would be wider than that of a software sector fund (that would invest primarily in software companies) to cover sectors such as education, telecom, financial services retail, etc. Similarly, a real estate sector fund might invest only in real estate companies; an infrastructure theme fund would invest in several sectors of relevance for infrastructure including construction, cement, steel, power, telecom, roads, etc.

On account of the broader spectrum of sectors that they invest in, thematic funds are less risky than sector funds, though they are more risky than diversified equity funds.

The core of an average investor's mutual fund equity portfolio is meant to be diversified equity funds; sector funds and thematic funds are add-ons that might constitute a minor part of the portfolio of only those investors who can digest the additional risk.

2.3.3 Index Funds

Index funds seek to have a position that replicates an identified index, say, S&P BSE Sensex or CNX Nifty. SEBI insists that 95% of the total assets should be in such replicating investment for index funds and ETFs.

Patrons of Indian classical music would be aware that the violinist or harmonium player seeks to track the tunes and raga of the Carnatic or Hindustani music vocalist. On similar lines, the index fund manager seeks to track the tone and trajectory of the index.

The replicating position in an index fund can be created through either of two methods:

1. It can either be done by maintaining an investment portfolio that replicates the composition of the chosen index. Thus, the stocks in such a fund's portfolio would be the same as those that are used in calculating the index. The proportion of each stock in the portfolio, too, would be the same as the weight of the stock in the calculation of that index.
2. This replicating style of investment is called passive investing. Index funds are therefore often called "passive funds". Funds that are not passive, on the other hand, are often called "managed funds", or "active funds".

Index schemes are also referred to as "unmanaged schemes", since they are passive, or "tracker schemes", since they seek to track a specific index.

Passive investment places lower demands on the time and efforts of the AMC. All that is required is a good system that would integrate the valuation of securities (from the market) and information of sales and re-purchases of units (from the registrar) and generate the requisite buy and sell orders. Management fees for index funds are, therefore, lower than for managed schemes.

Alternately, a mutual fund, through its research can identify a basket of securities and / or derivatives whose movement is similar to that of the index. Schemes that invest in such baskets can be viewed as "active index funds".

Internationally, mutual funds have proprietary models that help create baskets that seek to outperform the market during a boom, while falling comparatively less in a bearish market.

Globally, there are more equity index funds than debt index funds.

2.3.4 Enhanced Index Funds

According to Hall, "The enhanced index fund is a managed index fund that seeks to beat the performance of its benchmark index by at least 0.1 per cent, but no more than 2 per cent. If the index fund's performance were to exceed this 2 per cent cap, it would then be considered an equity mutual fund."[5]

In India, there are mutual fund schemes that invest 80-90% of the portfolio as per a pre-specified index. Fund managers have flexibility in investing the balance.

2.3.5 Exchange Traded Funds (ETFs)

Exchange traded funds are open-end funds that trade on the exchange. Like index funds, ETFs are normally benchmarked to a stock exchange index, although globally, these days, synthetic ETFs have gone well beyond indices.

ETFs differ from index funds in the following respects:

- Post-New Fund Offer (NFO), the ETF only receives securities (for sale of new units) or releases securities (for units redeemed). The securities are received or released in the same mix as the index that the scheme is tracking. This is completely different from open-end index schemes, which receive and pay cash for their transactions with investors.
- An ETF does not offer sale and re-purchase prices for the units since it only receives or releases a basket of securities comprising the index. Such transactions in the index basket are a realistic option only for large investors. In order to offer liquidity for small investors, the AMC appoints designated market intermediaries (market makers) who buy from or sell units to the investors for cash. This constitutes the secondary market for the ETF.

  Thus, a small investor who wants to invest in an ETF would go to a market maker who is expected to offer two-way quotes at all times. She would know precisely how many units in the ETF she will get against her investment.

  The market maker can transfer its own holding of ETF units to the investor. Alternatively, the money collected from investors will have to be invested in the index basket by the market maker, and transferred to the ETF. The ETF will issue units against this investment, which can be given to the investor.

  Similarly, based on the market makers' two-way quotes, the small investor would know how much she can recover if she were to exit from the ETF. The market maker can choose to hold these units purchased from the investor. Alternatively, the market maker can offer the ETF units for re-purchase. In that case, the ETF will cancel the units and release index scrips from its portfolio, which the market maker would sell to pay the investor.

- The market maker makes money based on the spread in the two-way quote. Competition between market makers is expected to keep the bid-ask spread low. "Bid price" is the maximum price at which the market maker is prepared to buy the ETF unit from the investor; "Ask price" is the minimum price at which the market maker is prepared to sell ETF units to the investor.

  The ETF structure also ensures that the AMC does not need to pay a commission to market intermediaries for bringing investors into the fund on an ongoing basis. Similarly, there are no loads recovered by the AMC (the concept of loads is discussed in Chapter 5). Thus, a significant element of cost is eliminated for the investors. Investors only bear a cost that is implicit in the bid-ask spread and the normal cost associated with stock exchange transactions. Low expense ratio is an attraction for any investor. Absence of commission income is a reason why mutual fund distributors do not promote ETFs.

- Returns in an open-end fund can be affected by significant churning of unit holding. Suppose, for example, that many large applications are received in the fund on a particular day, followed by several large redemptions the following day. The fund manager would then be under pressure to buy and sell securities in the market to match such sudden inflows and outflows. Besides, most open-end funds maintain 5-10% of corpus in liquid assets to meet the cash flow requirements for possible redemptions. Extreme flows can pull down returns in an open-end index fund.

  ETFs only receive securities (if an investor invests) and give securities (if an investor disinvests). Since such transactions are effected in kind, short-term investments and disinvestments do not affect the performance of the fund. Long-term investors appreciate this feature in ETFs.

- A single NAV is applicable for the day in the case of open-end funds. Therefore, a single price would be applicable for all investors who buy units of an open-end index fund on any particular day. Similarly, a single price would be received by all investors who exit from an open-end index fund on any particular day (subject to cut-off timing, discussed in Chapter 15).

  An ETF, on the other hand, is traded in the stock market. Therefore its unit price keeps changing during the day. This intra-day fluctuation in ETF's unit price appeals to short-term investors.

An investor desirous of taking an exposure to an index has the following options:

- Invest directly in the basket of securities representing the index. But, this will entail a large outlay of funds.
- Invest in an index fund. But management expenses and liquidity maintenance could lead to gaps in tracking the market (tracking error).

- Invest in the index using futures and options that are traded in the derivatives segment of the stock exchange. These are, however, short duration instruments. The actively traded derivative contracts are for periods up to 3 months in India. Repeated rolling over of positions would increase the cost and uncertainty of creating a long term position.
- Invest in ETFs which do not suffer from the above noted weaknesses of direct investment, index funds and derivatives. It is for this reason that ETFs have taken off in a big way in the United States. In India, although ETFs have been in existence for over a decade, they are yet to emerge as a frontline investment vehicle for any class of investors.

2.3.6 Hedge Funds or Leveraged Funds

While the name "hedge fund" gives a psychological comfort of a fund being low on risk, nothing can be further away from the truth.

A feature of hedge funds is the extreme risk they take in the market, including shorting of stocks, i.e. selling stocks that they do not own, with the hope of buying them back later at a lower price. Shorting is an extremely risky investment strategy because the short-seller has an unlimited downside.

Many hedge funds are leveraged funds where the fund manager invests a mix of funds belonging to its investors (unit capital and reserves) and funds from lenders (borrowed funds). A leveraging of two would mean that for every ₹ 1 of unit capital, an additional ₹ 2 is borrowed, thus investing ₹ 3 in the market.

Borrowed funds have interest and repayment obligations that are independent of how the market performs. Thus, in bad market conditions, a non-leveraged fund only needs to bear a loss; a leveraged fund would also need to generate additional resources to meet the interest and repayment obligations on its borrowed funds.

However, when the returns on the investment portfolio are higher than the cost of borrowed funds, investors in a leveraged fund earn super-normal returns.

The following illustration will explain the concept better:

Table 2.1

Scheme	*A*	*B*	*C*
Leverage	Nil	1 time	2 times
Unit Capital (₹)	100	100	100
Loans (₹)	0	100	200
Investible Funds (₹)	100	200	300
Interest Rate on Loan	N/A	15%	15%
Portfolio Return	20%	20%	10%
Earning before Interest (₹)	20	40	30
Interest (₹)	0	15	30
Profit (₹)	20	25	-
Return on Unit Capital	**20%**	**25%**	**0%**

Hedge funds are, therefore, extremely risky funds; the level of risk being a function of the extent of leveraging and the nature of exposure taken. They are also less regulated, across the globe. Why then the name "hedge fund"? Why, indeed?

Suppose an investor has a short-sold position of ₹ 100 in the market. If the market goes up by 20%, then the investor effectively loses ₹ 20.

If such an investor wanted to neutralise this short-sold position, she can purchase shares worth ₹ 100. Or, if she invests in Scheme B in the above example, she only needs to invest ₹ 80 to fully reverse her short-sold position of ₹ 100. The 25% gain on ₹ 80 invested in Scheme B will give her ₹ 20 — precisely the amount she would lose in her earlier short-sold position.

Thus, a hedge fund can help a person to reverse her existing exposure with minimum capital outlay (and therefore cost). Hence the name "hedge funds".

As seen in Scheme C, it is also easy for hedge funds to wipe out their profits or even report significant losses.

David Faber states that "The average hedge fund charges a 1% management fee, just as a mutual fund does, but also takes 20% of any profits it generates within the funds in a given year."[6]

In the words of Lawrence Cunningham — Warren Buffett is a conservative decision maker. Explaining Berkshire's conservative financial policy of using little debt, Buffett says that if there were a 99% probability that higher leverage would produce something good and a 1% chance of a surprise that would produce something between anguish and default, he would not bite that bullet: "We wouldn't have liked those 99:1 odds — and never will. A small chance of distress or disgrace cannot, in our view, be offset by a large chance of extra returns."[7]

SEBI regulations have limited the right of mutual fund schemes to borrow. This has kept out hedge funds in the mutual fund sector. They are however available as Alternate Investment Funds (AIF) for large investors.

2.3.7 Option Income Fund

Let us consider a situation where you would like the right but not the obligation (an option), to buy 100 shares of Company Z from me at a price of ₹ 15 sometime in the future. I will give you that option only if you pay me an option premium. In option market terminology, I would be the writer of that option.

The option premium would be my income, because it is not refundable to you. There are two implications for me as the option writer:

- If the stock of Company Z rises above ₹ 15 in the market, you would exercise your option, in which case I would lose out on the opportunity of gaining from that appreciation (opportunity loss).
- If I operate on a fully hedged basis, then I will retain 100 shares of Company Z in my portfolio, so that I can offer them if you exercise your option. Thus, I

effectively lose my right to sell the shares (dead asset). During the period that I hold the share, the dividend would belong to me (holding income).

A typical option income fund will earn option premium through writing options on securities where the holding income is attractive enough to retain the security as a dead asset. The underlying view of the fund is that holding income plus option premium more than covers for the opportunity loss.

Since mutual funds in India are not permitted to write options, there are no option income funds in India yet.

2.4 Types of Schemes by Solution Orientation

The SEBI classification scheme envisages two types of such funds:

2.4.1 Retirement Fund

This is a scheme that has a lock-in period of 5 years or till retirement age, whichever is earlier.

2.4.2 Children's Fund

This is a scheme that has a lock-in period of 5 years or till the child attains the age of majority, whichever is earlier.

Such schemes facilitate emotive selling. They will have one of the portfolio structures discussed earlier.

2.5 Types of Schemes by Geography

2.5.1 Country or Region Funds

Country funds invest in securities issued by issuers from a specific country or region. The underlying belief is that the chosen country or region will demonstrate superior performance which, in turn, would be favourable for the securities (equity or debt) of that country.

For instance, funds that invested in Japan between 1980 and 1981 would have nearly doubled their assets in the boom that followed — and lost a similar amount if they had not sold in time. Funds that were invested in South East Asia during 1997-98, and later in Russia and Brazil, bit the dust.

The returns on country funds are affected not only by the performance of the market where they are invested, but also by changes in exchange rates.

While making international investments, the tax implication and risk of restrictions on taking sale proceeds out of the country need to be considered. For instance, Malaysia imposed restrictions on withdrawals during the South East Asian crisis. It is bad enough to see your investments shrink in value in a market; it gets worse when you cannot pull out your money, thus exposing yourself to further loss for an uncertain and extended period.

Example 2.1

Suppose a US$ asset earned a return of 20%, and the US$ itself appreciated by 10%, what is the return in rupee terms?

Say, ₹ 50,000 were invested in a dollar asset.

At exchange rate of ₹ 50 / $1, the investment is $1,000.

This would have appreciated to $1,200.

US$ has appreciated by 10%, i.e. each $ now fetches ₹ 55. So on sale of investments, the investor would receive $1,200 × ₹ 55 / $, i.e. ₹ 66,000.

Gain is (66,000 – 50,000) ÷ 50,000, i.e. 32%

An alternate approach to the calculations:

$(1 + R_{Rs}) = (1 + R_{US\$}) \times (1 + R_{ER})$

where,

R_{Rs} refers to returns in ₹

$R_{US\$}$ refers to returns in $

R_{ER} refers to change in exchange rate

$$\begin{aligned}(1 + R_{Rs}) &= (1 + 0.2) \times (1 + 0.1)\\ &= 1.2 \times 1.1\\ &= 1.32\end{aligned}$$

$R_{Rs} = 1.32 - 1$, i.e. 32%.

2.5.2 Offshore Funds

Offshore funds mobilise moneys from investors for investment outside their country. Unlike a country / region fund, they do not restrict their investment to any specific country / region.

A number of AMCs in India have launched *feeder schemes*, which collect money from domestic investors to invest in a *host scheme* abroad. The host scheme in turn, would have an investment charter that defines the kind of investments it would make. The host scheme may have a charter to invest in only a single country, in which case it would be like any country fund. Alternatively, the host scheme can be a globally diversified fund investing in any country where an opportunity is seen. In either case, the investor is exposed to foreign currency risk.

The benefits of a feeder scheme are:

- A feeder scheme in India will give Indian investors the convenience of transacting in Indian Rupees (although the value of the underlying investment in the host scheme is subject to the foreign currency risk).
- The investment in feeder scheme will not eat into the foreign investment limits to which the domestic investor may be subject.
- At times, the minimum investment amount for a feeder scheme is much lower than the limit applicable for direct investment in the host scheme.

- Further, the feeder scheme in India will comply with all the SEBI Mutual Fund regulations, i.e. the Indian investor gets all the protection that is available under those regulations.

2.6 Fund of Funds (FoF) Schemes

"Fund of funds schemes" invest primarily in other schemes of the same mutual fund or other mutual funds. The schemes in which the FoF invests may be domestic or overseas. FoF are subject to the following investment restrictions as per SEBI Regulations:

- They shall not invest in any other fund of funds scheme.
- They shall not invest their assets other than in schemes of mutual funds, except to the extent of funds required for meeting the liquidity requirements for the purpose of re-purchases or redemptions, as disclosed in the offer document of the fund of funds scheme.
- At least 95% of the total assets should be invested in the underlying scheme.

Native wisdom tell us that if the investor invests in a Fund of Funds scheme, which in turn invests in a mutual fund scheme, then the costs charged by the Fund of Funds scheme become a drag on the investors' return. The mutual fund industry, driven by a marketing objective to increase assets under management, has unfortunately come out with too many confusing schemes that have left the investors confounded. Therefore, investors find value even in incurring that additional cost of the Fund of Funds scheme. What next? Fund of Fund of Funds scheme?!!!

2.7 Schemes *versus* Options or Plans

As seen earlier, investors in a mutual fund scheme are essentially buying into the scheme's investment philosophy. Therefore, a scheme is the notional entity for which books of accounts are maintained. Every scheme has an investment portfolio.

At times there is a need to differentiate between investors within the same scheme. Such instances are described below.

2.7.1 Dividend, Growth, and Dividend Re-investment Option

Among the investors who subscribe to a scheme's investment philosophy, some might prefer a regular flow of income (dividend option), while others might prefer their income from the scheme to grow in the scheme itself (growth option). Among those who opt for Dividend option, some may like the dividend to be paid out to them (Payout sub-option under the Dividend option); others may like the dividend to be re-invested in the same scheme (Re-investment sub-option under the Dividend option).

To the extent that an investor has been paid out a dividend, her investment in the scheme would be worth less than that of an investor who has let her dividend grow in the scheme. The tax implications too vary with the option selected. The three options are compared in greater detail in Chapter 5.

2.7.2 Direct Plan *versus* Distributor Plan

Investors in the Direct Plan do not use the services of a distributor, i.e. they invest directly with the fund. So, distributor commissions are not charged to them Distributor commissions are charged only to investors in the Distributor Plan. The higher cost results in Distributor Plan NAV being lower than the Direct Plan NAV. Although Direct Plan NAV is higher in absolute value, since distributor commissions will not be charged, the future growth / income in Direct Plan will be higher than in the case of Distributor Plan.

2.7.3 Wholesale *versus* Retail

There is a significant difference in time and cost implications between servicing a single investor who invests ₹ 1 crore and servicing 1,000 investors who have each invested ₹ 10,000, although assets under management are the same in both cases. Accordingly, a mutual fund may choose not to penalise a large investor with the costs associated with servicing the small investor.

On the other hand, a wholesale-oriented investor base makes the fund corpus volatile. A fund manager of such a scheme would need to maintain higher cash positions and an extremely liquid portfolio at all times. A fund manager of a retail-oriented scheme does not need to be obsessed with liquidity; it would be possible to prioritise return over liquidity.

A mutual fund may choose to differentiate between classes of investors on the above grounds. Similarly, there may be a case to either offer a facility (say, easy liquidity) or impose a dis-incentive (e.g., longer notice period or a specific charge) on specific identified classes of investors.

In such situations, a mutual fund can theoretically offer different schemes to meet each such need. But this would lead to too many schemes of sub-optimal sizes making the activity administratively cumbersome. Therefore, instead of different schemes, mutual funds often choose to offer different options or plans under the same scheme.

The books of accounts and investment portfolio are kept at the scheme level, and pro-rata adjustments and transaction differences are made to reflect the differences between the different options or plans.

For instance, there would be a single revenue account, based on which the amount to be distributed as dividend under the scheme is decided. This dividend amount would be apportioned between the dividend and growth options based on value of assets under each option.

The dividend amount that is apportioned to "dividend option" is distributed among investors who have chosen that option. It is paid out to investors who have opted for Dividend payout sub-option; it will be re-invested in the same scheme for those who have selected the Dividend re-investment sub-option. Thus, the retained earnings for the various options would be different.

After certain mutual funds misutilised such flexibility, SEBI grew more cautious in permitting different options or plans under the same scheme, unless these are in the nature of dividend and growth options.

SEBI has laid down that any ongoing open-end scheme proposing to launch additional plans, other than dividend and growth plans (and distributor plan, separate from the regular plan), which differ from the main scheme in terms of portfolio, maturity or any other characteristics, must launch them as separate schemes. In such a case, disclosure requirements, minimum amount, investment restrictions, etc. would apply separately for each of the schemes.

2.8 Comparison with Other Products

The mutual fund sector operates under stricter regulations as compared to most other investment avenues. Apart from offering investors tax efficiency and legal comfort (which will be discussed in detail in Chapters 17 and 3 respectively), how do mutual funds compare with other products?

2.8.1 Company Fixed Deposits *versus* Mutual Funds

Fixed deposits are unsecured borrowings by the company accepting the money. Credit rating of the fixed deposit programme is an indication of the inherent default risk in the investment.

The moneys of investors in a mutual fund scheme are invested by the fund manager in specific investments under that scheme. These investments are held and managed in trust for the benefit of the scheme's investors. On the other hand, there is no such direct correlation between a company's fixed deposit mobilisation, and the avenues where it deploys these resources.

A corollary of such linkage between mobilisation and investment is that the gains and losses of the mutual fund scheme (after deducting costs) entirely flow through to the investors. Therefore, there can be no certainty of yield, unless a named guarantor assures a return or, to a lesser extent, if the investment is in a FMP type of structure. On the other hand, the return under a fixed deposit is certain, subject only to the default risk of the borrower.

Both fixed deposits and mutual funds offer liquidity, but subject to some differences:

- The provider of liquidity in the case of fixed deposits is the borrowing company. In mutual funds, the liquidity provider is the scheme itself for open-end schemes, or the market in the case of closed-end schemes.
- The basic value at which fixed deposits are encashable is not subject to market risk. However, the value at which units of a scheme are redeemed entirely de-

pends on the market. If securities have gained in value during the period, then the investor can even earn a return that is higher than what she anticipated when she invested. Conversely, she could also end up with a loss.

- Early encashment of fixed deposits is always subject to a penalty charged by the company that accepted the fixed deposit. Mutual fund schemes also have the option of charging a penalty on "early" redemption of units (by way of an "exit load" described in Chapter 5). If the NAV has appreciated adequately, then despite the exit load, the investor could earn a capital gain on her investment.

2.8.2 Bank Fixed Deposits *versus* Mutual Funds

Bank fixed deposits are similar to company fixed deposits. The major difference is that banks are more stringently regulated than are non-bank companies. They even operate under stricter requirements regarding Statutory Liquidity Ratio (SLR) and Cash Reserve Ratio (CRR) mandated by RBI.

While the above are causes for comfort, bank deposits too are subject to default risk. However, given the political and economic impact of bank defaults, the government as well as Reserve Bank of India (RBI) try to ensure that banks — at least the public sector banks — do not fail.

Further, bank deposits up to ₹ 1 lakh (including interest) are protected by the Deposit Insurance and Credit Guarantee Corporation (DICGC), so long as the bank has paid the required insurance premium of 10 paise per annum for every ₹ 100 of deposits. The monetary ceiling of ₹ 1 lakh is for all the deposits in all the branches of a bank, held by the depositor in the same capacity and right.

Suppose an investor's dues (principal plus interest) from two failed banks are as follows:

- Bank A, Branch 1 on own account ₹ 70,000.
- Bank A, Branch 2 on own account ₹ 40,000.
- Bank A as legal guardian for minor ₹ 80,000.
- Bank B on own account ₹ 90,000.

The benefit through DICGC would be as follows:

- Bank A on own account: ₹ 100,000 (as compared to the dues of ₹ 70,000 plus ₹ 40,000, i.e. ₹ 110,000 from both branches put together).
- Bank A as legal guardian of minor: ₹ 80,000 (since it is in a different capacity and within the ₹ 100,000 limit).
- Bank B: ₹ 90,000, since it is within the ₹ 100,000 limit in a different bank.

2.8.3 Bonds and Debentures *versus* Mutual Funds

As in the case of fixed deposits, credit rating of a bond or debenture is an indication of the inherent default risk in the investment. However, unlike fixed deposits, bonds and debentures are transferable securities.

While an investor may have an early encashment option from the issuer (for instance through a "put" option), liquidity is generally through a listing in the market. Implications of this are:

- If the security does not get traded in the market, then the liquidity remains on paper. In this respect, an open-end scheme offering continuous sale / repurchase option is superior.
- The value that the investor would realise in an early exit is subject to market risk. The investor could have a capital gain or a capital loss. This aspect is similar to a mutual fund scheme.

It is possible for an astute investor to earn attractive returns by directly investing in the debt market, and actively managing the positions. Given the market realities in India, however, it is difficult for most investors to actively manage their debt portfolio. Further, at times it is difficult to execute trades in the debt market even when the transaction size is as high as ₹ 1 crore. In this respect, investment in a debt scheme would be beneficial.

Debt securities could be backed by a hypothecation or mortgage of identified fixed and / or current assets, e.g. secured bonds or debentures. In such a case, if there is a default, the identified assets become available for meeting redemption requirements. An unsecured bond or debenture is for all practical purposes like a fixed deposit, as far as access to assets is concerned.

The investments of a mutual fund scheme are held by a custodian for the benefit of investors in the scheme. Thus, the securities that relate to a scheme are ring-fenced for the benefit of its investors.

2.8.4 Equity *versus* Mutual Funds

Investment in both equity and mutual funds is subject to market risk.

An investor holding an equity security that is not traded in the market place has a problem in realising value from it. But investment in an open-end mutual fund eliminates this direct risk of not being able to sell the investment in the market. An indirect risk remains, because the scheme has to realise its investments to pay investors. The AMC is, however, in a better position to handle the situation. Further, on account of various SEBI regulations discussed in Chapter 4, such illiquid securities are likely to be only a part of the scheme's portfolio.

Another benefit of equity mutual fund schemes is that they give investors the benefit of portfolio diversification through a small investment. For instance, an investor can take an exposure to the index by investing a mere ₹ 5,000 in an index fund.

2.8.5 Life Insurance *versus* Mutual Fund

Life insurance is a hedge against risk — and not really an investment option. So, it would be wrong to compare life insurance against any other financial product.

Various insurance policies are available to meet different needs of investors. Broadly, there are policies that offer only risk cover (term plans) and others which have an element of savings accumulation (endowment). Some insurance plans give the impression of being mutual funds in nature, on account of the choice of portfolio given to the insured, and quantification in the form of units (unit-linked insurance plans).

High front-end costs, largely on account of distribution expenses, impact the net return on the savings component of endowment policies and unit linked insurance plans.

Transparency levels in the insurance industry, although improving, are still below the standards set by mutual funds. For instance, an insurance plan may say that NAV is protected or that you will get the highest NAV over 7 years. Such statements cannot be taken at face value.

Suppose out of ₹ 100 invested by you, ₹ 40 is taken away towards various insurance, selling and administrative costs. Then, only the balance ₹ 60 will be part of the savings portion. You may be allotted 6 units at ₹ 10 against this. NAV protection / highest NAV would be only on this savings portion, i.e. after 40% (in this illustration) has been taken away towards costs. In comparison, the costs in the mutual fund industry are restricted to 2.5%, plus a small element on amounts mobilised from locations other than the Top 15 in the country.

2.8.6 Pension Fund *versus* Mutual Fund

Pension, as we all know, is a sum of money that some people (pensioners) are entitled to after they retire from regular employment. Pension schemes can be:

- Defined benefit schemes, where the pensioner gets a benefit that is linked to the average salary she was drawing around the time of retirement. The benefit may also be inflation indexed. People who worked for the Indian government and public sector companies traditionally earned pension in the form of a defined benefit.
- Defined contribution schemes, where the pensioner contributes a stipulated percentage of salary during her working years. The post-retirement corpus then depends on the contribution during the working years, and the return that those contributions earned. Provident fund schemes in the organised sector in India are of this nature.
- The National Pension System (NPS) offers an alternative defined contribution scheme, where the investor has the option of varying the investment amount each year. The minimum annual investment is ₹ 6,000. This corpus created

over a period is used to buy an annuity from an annuity provider. This annuity is the pension that will be received post-retirement.

In a defined benefit scheme, the organisation paying the pension takes a huge risk. Its liability is committed, irrespective of how much there is in the kitty. As the kitty dwindles, the organisation seeks to cover its liability to past employees, by recovering correspondingly higher amounts from current employees. Thus current employees end up subsidising the pension of past employees.

When the number of current employees in organisations reduces (with rationalisation, automation, etc.) while the number of retired employees increases (with higher life expectancy), the former take up increasing burdens. Over a period of time, the entire pension system becomes inequitable and risky.

People in India can subscribe to the NPS, which is a defined contribution scheme. Dedicated pension fund managers (PFM) are responsible for investing on behalf of the scheme. Investors have a choice regarding mix of debt and equity for their portfolio, and the PFM(s) who should manage it for them.

NPS is a good vehicle for the accumulation of long-term savings. The government has enforced an extremely low cost structure for NPS. This cost-effectiveness can be the basis for better returns for NPS subscribers as compared to insurance and mutual funds (it also depends on how well the portfolios are managed). Fewer product choices make it easier for investors to compare and decide between schemes and pension fund managers. Centralised record keeping and Points of Presence (POPs) all across the country add to the convenience for NPS subscribers.

Despite recent increases in the cost structure, NPS continues to be a cost-effective product. Persistence charge was recently introduced. Although the amount is nominal, its recovery through cancellation of units is rather non-transparent. Investors who track the performance of their NPS fund manager through NAV may miss out on the impact of the levy. Hopefully, such measures are not a harbinger of a switch towards the high cost and low transparency insurance model.

Under the Income Tax Act, 1961, a separate deduction of ₹ 50,000 from income is available for contributions in NPS. Withdrawals from the NPS are tax-exempt upto 40% of the corpus, provided the pensioner has attained the age of 60.

2.9 Indian Mutual Fund Industry (Schemes)

Let's look at some highlights of the Indian mutual fund industry:

- As on 31 March 2018, about 38% of the assets under management came from equity schemes, including 4% through ELSS schemes; a further 8% was contributed by balanced schemes and Gold ETF. A staggering 53% of the assets continue to be in debt schemes. Close-end and interval schemes comprise only 9% of the total AUM [*See* Annexure 2.1].

- The distribution of investor accounts and net assets as on 31 March 2018 reveals the following highlights (*See also:* Annexures 2.2 and 2.3):
    - The number of investor accounts at 6.65 crore is a significant jump from 4.17 crore as on 31 March 2015.
    - Retail represents 94.1% of the 6.65 crore investor accounts; however, it accounted for only 25.3% of the AUM. High net worth individuals (HNIs), investing above ₹ 5 lakh and retail together represent 54.9% of the AUM. Thus, a massive 45.1% of the AUM comes from non-individuals, namely corporates, banks, financial institutions and foreign institutional investors.
    - Equity oriented funds and balanced funds account for 82.1% of investor accounts, but only 44.1% of AUM.
    - For a country that invests so much in gold, ETF Gold contributes only 0.2% of the AUM, coming from 3.45 lakh investor accounts.
    - For a long term equity class like equity, only 32.3% of the equity fund AUM is held for more than 24 months. This number is down from 43.6% on 31 March 2018. Almost half the equity fund AUM was held for less than 12 months.

Despite the recent rise in the number of folios, there are a mere 6.65 crore (66.5 million) investor accounts (which includes non-individual accounts) in a country that has a population well in excess of 135 crore (1,351 million). In the context of India's capital market, the Indian mutual fund industry is much below the size and stature it deserves. It is hoped that in the years to come the industry will grow manifold and live up to the role originally envisaged when UTI was set up, namely to channelize the savings of retail investors into the capital market.

A single state, Maharashtra accounts for almost 45% of total mutual fund AUM in the country. Almost 77% comes from five states. Over 80% is accounted by just the top 15 geographical locations in the country. Thus, the mutual fund industry in India has a long way to go before it achieves the kind of reach that telecom companies and fast moving consumer goods companies have achieved.

On the positive side, the number of SIP accounts stood at 2.11 crore on 31 March 2018, contributing ₹ 7,119 crore in March 2018 alone. This does indicate that the flows into equity mutual fund schemes are likely to remain robust.

Annexure 2.1: Assets under Management (Category and Type-wise)

(as on 31 March 2018)

(₹ Cr)

Scheme Type	*Open End Funds*	*Close End Funds*	*Interval Funds*	*Total*	*% of Total*
INCOME	631,197	149,927	4,429	785,553	36.8%
INFRASTRUCTURE DEBT FUND	-	2,468	-	2,468	0.1%
EQUITY	639,195	30,012	-	669,207	31.3%
BALANCED	172,151	-	-	172,151	8.1%
LIQUID/MONEY MARKET	335,525	-	-	335,525	15.7%
GILT	11,404	-	-	11,404	0.5%
ELSS — EQUITY	75,598	4,985	-	80,583	3.8%
GOLD ETF	4,806	-	-	4,806	0.2%
OTHER ETFs	72,888	-	-	72,888	3.4%
FUND OF FUNDS INVESTING OVERSEAS	1,451	-	-	1,451	0.1%
TOTAL	**1,944,215**	**187,392**	**4,429**	**2,136,036**	100.0%
% of Total	91.0%	8.8%	0.2%		

1 crore = 10 million

Source: www.AMFIIndia.com

Annexure 2.2: Distribution of Investor Accounts

(As on 31 March 2018)

Scheme Type	*Number of Investor Accounts*						
	Corpo-rates	*Banks / FIs*	*FIIs*	*High Net-worth Individuals**	*Retail*	***Total***	*%*
Liquid / Money Market	33,717	963	13	120,873	854,130	**1,009,696**	1.5%
Gilt	3,152	52	11	9,575	70,797	**83,587**	0.1%
Debt-oriented	124,772	2,545	55	1,058,008	8,389,321	**9,574,701**	14.4%
Equity Oriented	188,417	762	100	1,706,525	47,402,657	**49,298,461**	74.1%
Balanced	32,210	95	12	631,729	4,653,108	**5,317,154**	8.0%
Gold ETF	2,609	6	1	6,950	335,440	**345,006**	0.5%
Other ETF	9,635	36	14	9,024	743,285	**761,994**	1.1%
Fund of Funds investing overseas	635	0	0	4,072	91,067	**95,774**	0.1%
Total	**395,147**	**4,459**	**206**	**3,546,756**	**62,539,805**	**66,486,373**	**100.0%**
%	0.6%	0.0%	0.0%	5.3%	94.1%	**100.0%**	

Scheme Type	*AUM (₹ Crore)*						
	Corporates	*Banks / FIs*	*FIIs*	*High Net-worth Individuals**	*Retail*	*Total*	*%*
Liquid / Money Market	238,256.63	9,603.31	49.75	30,864.11	7,530.53	**286,304.33**	13.5%
Gilt	9,519.04	195.12	331.35	3,214.43	1,332.86	**14,592.80**	0.7%
Debt-oriented	466,778.37	15,976.79	7,296.21	244,216.67	76,260.15	**810,528.19**	38.1%
Equity Oriented	116,346.36	1,005.79	4,977.03	260,390.40	388,414.93	**771,134.51**	36.3%
Balanced	20,407.30	195.32	911.12	88,416.87	57,454.40	**167,385.01**	7.9%
Gold ETF	1,690.62	1.34	0.79	999.62	2,162.93	**4,855.30**	0.2%
Other ETF	61,771.09	1,376.28	1,912.66	1,920.35	3,372.27	**70,352.65**	3.3%
Fund of Funds investing overseas	354.02	0.00	0.00	625.85	531.97	**1,511.84**	0.1%
Total	**915,123.43**	**28,353.95**	**15,478.91**	**630,648.30**	**537,060.04**	**2,126,664.63**	**100.0%**
%	43.0%	1.3%	0.7%	29.7%	25.3%	**100.0%**	

* Defined as individuals investing ₹ 5 lakh and above.

Source: www.AMFIIndia.com

Annexure 2.3: Age-wise Analysis of Investor Accounts

(As on 31 December 2017)

Holding Period	*Equity Funds*						
	Corporates	*Banks/FIs*	*FIIs*	*High Net-worth Individuals**	*Retail*	*Total*	*%*
0 -1 month	24,170.16	253.31	468.79	24,554.15	18,981.70	**68,428.11**	6.8%
1 -3 months	23,705.60	237.25	810.79	36,346.04	34,801.75	**95,901.43**	9.5%
3 - 6 months	59,305.83	266.03	872.35	49,082.15	40,690.21	**150,216.57**	14.9%
6 - 12 months	35,670.67	295.80	1,169.50	80,175.89	68,506.17	**185,818.03**	18.4%
12 - 24 months	30,477.32	1,330.37	82.92	70,989.04	79,254.24	**182,133.89**	18.1%
More than 24 months	26,907.44	218.74	3,116.83	88,459.81	206,300.55	**325,003.37**	32.3%
Total	**200,237.02**	**2,601.50**	**6,521.18**	**349,607.08**	**448,534.62**	**1,007,501.40**	**100.0%**
%	19.9%	0.3%	0.6%	34.7%	44.5%	**100.0%**	

* Defined as individuals investing ₹ 5 lakh and above.

Source: www.AMFIIndia.com

Holding Period	*Non-Equity Funds*						
	Corporates	*Banks / FIs*	*FIIs*	*High Net-worth Individuals**	*Retail*	*Total*	*%*
0 -1 month	162,845.56	8,792.93	799.05	20,094.82	4,541.78	197,074.14	17.6%
1 -3 months	94,979.04	4,538.86	4,240.83	26,711.58	6,220.84	136,691.15	12.2%
3 - 6 months	88,029.72	3,245.25	551.33	33,644.66	7,743.02	133,213.98	11.9%
6 - 12 months	95,549.83	3,598.99	1,001.63	54,336.61	14,911.89	169,398.95	15.1%
12 - 24 months	123,990.65	1,226.72	529.34	62,004.91	15,905.55	203,657.17	18.2%
More than 24 months	15,1095.8	4,367.34	555.15	84,085.07	39,024.44	279,127.80	24.9%
Total	716,490.60	25,770.09	7,677.33	280,877.65	88,347.52	1,119,163.19	100.0%
%	64.0%	2.3%	0.7%	25.1%	7.9%	100.0%	

* Defined as individuals investing ₹ 5 lakh and above.

Source: www.AMFIIndia.com

Chapter 3

Legal Structure of Mutual Funds in India

SEBI regulates the mutual fund sector in India. However, RBI, as regulator of banks, would need to authorize the commencement of mutual fund operations by a banking entity. Further, since it is the regulator of money supply in the economy, it has control over the money market and foreign exchange market. Measures that it announces for the money market and foreign exchange market could impact mutual fund operations. Besides such areas of overlap with other regulators, all regulation of mutual funds is by SEBI.

The guidelines applicable to mutual funds are set out in the SEBI (Mutual Funds) Regulations, 1996 ("the regulations"). SEBI has prescribed a legal structure with inbuilt checks and balances in the form of independent agencies for the various critical roles, namely trusteeship, asset management and custody of investments.

3.1 Sponsor

Every project needs a promoter, a prime mover who has overall responsibility for the project. The promoter of a mutual fund is referred to as "sponsor". As per the regulations, a sponsor means, "any person who, acting alone or in combination with another body corporate, establishes a mutual fund."

A sponsor has to meet the following qualifications prescribed by SEBI:

- Sponsor should have a sound track record and general reputation of fairness and integrity in all business transactions.

  Sound track record means:

  - Carrying on business in financial services for a period of not less than five years.
  - Having a profit, after providing for depreciation, interest and tax, in three out of the immediately preceding five years, including in the latest year.
  - Having a positive net worth in all the immediately preceding five years. (Net worth = paid up capital plus free reserves, minus miscellaneous expenditure

not written off, minus deferred revenue expenditure, minus intangible assets, minus accumulated losses).
  - In the immediately preceding year, having a net worth that is more than the capital contribution of the sponsor in the AMC.
- The sponsor has to contribute at least 40 per cent to the net worth of the AMC. Further, any person who holds 40 per cent or more of the net worth of an AMC is deemed to be a sponsor and should, therefore, meet all the qualifications prescribed for a sponsor.
- Sponsor should be a fit and proper person.
- Sponsor, or any of its directors, or the principal officer to be employed by the mutual fund should not be guilty of fraud or convicted of an offence involving moral turpitude or found guilty of any economic offence.

While meeting the prescribed qualifications makes a person eligible to promote a mutual fund, the venture cannot be promoted unless SEBI permits it.

3.2 Trusteeship

3.2.1 Trust Deed

A mutual fund has to be constituted in the form of a trust, created through a trust deed. The trust deed:

- Has to contain certain clauses prescribed by SEBI;
- Can not contain any clause that:
  - limits or extinguishes the obligations and liabilities of the trust with respect to the mutual fund or its investors; and
  - indemnifies the trustees or the AMC for loss or damage caused to the unit holders on account of negligence or acts of commission or omission;
- Has to be duly registered under the provisions of the Indian Registration Act, 1908; and
- Has to be executed by the sponsor in favour of the trustees named in the deed.

3.2.2 Technicalities

Indian companies are governed by the Companies Act, 2013. Limited Liability Partnerships (LLPs) in India are governed by the LLP Act, 2008. Other Indian partnership firms are governed by the Indian Partnerships Act, 1932. Similarly, mutual fund trusts in India are governed by Indian Trusts Act, 1882.

Companies are real entities that are eligible to contract in their own name. Trusts, on the other hand, are notional entities that are not eligible to contract in their own name. Trusts, therefore, need to enter into contracts in the name of the trustees.

The Indian Trusts Act, 1881 gives two options for the constitution of trustees:

- An individual can be appointed as trustee. When more than one trustee is appointed, they would together constitute the Board of Trustees.
- A company can be appointed as trustee. Such a trustee company, like any company under the Companies Act, 2013, would have a Board of Directors.

Every trust has beneficiaries, namely the persons for whose benefit the trust has been created — and trustees, namely the persons who are responsible for protecting the interest of beneficiaries.

When a trust is created for mutual fund operations, the beneficiaries are the investors who invest in the various schemes promoted by the mutual fund.

3.2.3 Disqualifications for Trustees

Given the critical role of trustees, the regulations provide stringent disqualifications. A person cannot be appointed trustee unless she:

- is a person of ability, integrity and standing;
- has not been found guilty of moral turpitude; and
- has not been convicted for any economic offence or violation of any securities laws.

A person who does not suffer from these disqualifications is eligible to become a trustee in a mutual fund. But she can be appointed as a trustee only after the prior approval of SEBI.

3.2.4 Governance

In order to strengthen the trusteeship and avoid potential conflicts of interest, it is provided that:

- Any mutual fund will have a minimum of four trustees.
- Two-thirds of the trustees need to be independent trustees, namely persons, who are not associates of the sponsors, or associated with them in any manner whatsoever.
- If consequent to an independent trustee vacating office, the number of independent trustees falls below the prescribed minimum, another independent trustee has to be appointed to fill the gap within three months.
- Relatives (as defined in the Companies Act) of the sponsor, directors of the sponsor company, or relatives of associate directors of the AMCs and trustee companies are considered as "associate".
- Similarly, nominees of companies who are stakeholders in the sponsor company or AMC are considered to be "associate".
- Persons providing any type of professional service to the mutual fund, asset management company, trustee company and the sponsors are considered as associate directors.

- Also, persons having any material pecuniary relationship with these entities, which in the judgment of the trustees may affect independence of directors, are treated as associate directors.
- An asset management company, or any of its officers or employees, are not eligible to act as trustee of any mutual fund.
- No person who has been appointed as trustee of a mutual fund can be appointed as a trustee of any other mutual fund unless:
  - the person is an independent trustee; and
  - the mutual fund where she is already a trustee gives prior approval for the proposed appointment in the other mutual fund.

  (If a company is appointed as a trustee, then its directors can act as trustees of any other trust provided that the object of the trust is not in conflict with the object of the mutual fund).
- A person who is an "associate" in accordance with definition in the Regulations cannot be appointed as independent director even after she ceases to be an "associate" unless a cooling off period of three years has elapsed from the date of her disassociation.
- The quorum for any meeting of the trustees shall be deemed not to have been reached, unless at least one independent trustee / director is present.
- The auditor for the mutual fund has to be different from the auditor of the AMC.

3.2.5 Obligations of Trustees

Some key obligations of trustees are as follows:

- The trustees shall enter into an investment management agreement with the AMC.
- Before the launch of any scheme, they shall ensure that the AMC has:
  - Systems in place for its back office, dealing room and accounting;
  - Appointed all key personnel including fund managers;
  - Appointed a compliance officer to comply with regulatory requirements and to redress investor grievances;
  - Appointed auditors and made suitable arrangements to handle the function of registrars;
  - Prepared a compliance manual and designed internal control mechanisms including internal audit; and
  - Specified norms for empanelment of brokers and marketing agents.
- They shall be accountable for, and be custodian of, the funds and property of the respective schemes and shall hold the same in trust for the benefit of the unit holders.

- Trustees shall ensure that all activities of the AMC are in accordance with the provisions of the SEBI regulations.
- If they have reason to believe that the conduct of business of the mutual fund is not in accordance with the regulations or the offer document of the scheme, they shall take appropriate remedial steps and inform SEBI immediately.
- Each trustee shall file the details of her transactions in securities with the mutual fund on a quarterly basis.
- They shall meet at least once every two calendar months, and at least six such meetings shall be held every year.
- The trustees shall obtain the consent of the unit holders:
  - Whenever SEBI asks for it;
  - Whenever three-fourths of the unit holders of any scheme ask for it;
  - When the majority of the trustees decide to wind up or prematurely redeem the units; and
  - When there is a change in the fundamental attributes of any scheme or the trust or fees and expenses payable or any other change that would modify the scheme or affect the interest of the unit holders is proposed.
- They shall call for details of transactions in securities by the key personnel of the AMC.
- They shall review quarterly, all transactions between the mutual fund, AMC and its associates.
- They shall review quarterly, the net worth of the AMC and ensure that any shortfall is made up.
- They shall periodically review the investor complaints received and their redressal by the AMC.
- They shall abide by the prescribed code of conduct.
- While filing a new scheme offer document, the trustees need to confirm that the new scheme is a new product of the mutual fund, and not a minor modification of an existing scheme, fund or product. This is however not applicable to fixed maturity plans and closed-end schemes.
- Every half-year, the trustees shall furnish to SEBI:
  - A report on the activities of the mutual fund;
  - A certificate that they have satisfied themselves that there have been no instances of self-dealing (e.g., selling own securities to the fund or buying securities from the fund) or front running (e.g., buying or selling shares for self, prior to executing similar transaction on behalf of the fund) by any of the trustees, directors and key personnel of the AMC; and
  - A certificate that the AMC has been managing the schemes independent of any other activities.

- The independent trustees shall give their comments on the report received from the AMC regarding investments by the mutual fund in the securities of group companies of the sponsor.
- The trustees shall be discerning in the appointment of directors on the board of the AMC.

3.2.6 Rights of Trustees

- The trustees have the right to obtain from the AMC, such information as they consider necessary to fulfil their obligations.
- A majority of the trustees have the right to terminate the appointment of an AMC. Any change in the appointment of the AMC is, however, subject to prior approval of SEBI and the unit holders.
- The trustees shall not be held liable for acts done in good faith if they have exercised adequate due diligence honestly.

3.3 Asset Management Company (AMC)

3.3.1 Appointment and Termination

It is obligatory for every mutual fund to have an AMC to manage the mutual fund and operate its schemes. The actual appointment could be made either by the sponsor or, if so authorized by the trust deed, the trustees.

The appointment can be terminated by a majority of the trustees or by 75 per cent of the unit holders. Any change in the appointment of the AMC is, however, subject to prior approval of SEBI and the unit holders.

3.3.2 Business Activities for AMC

An AMC shall not:

- Act as a trustee of any mutual fund.
- Undertake any other business activities except portfolio management services and advisory services to offshore funds, pension funds, provident funds, venture capital funds, management of insurance funds, financial consultancy and exchange of research on commercial basis ("other activities"). This would again be subject to:
    - the other activities not conflicting with the activities of the mutual fund;
    - SEBI being satisfied that the key personnel, systems, back office, bank and securities accounts of the other activities are segregated from the mutual fund activities; and
    - the AMC meeting the capital adequacy requirements, if any, of each such activity.

- Invest in any of its schemes unless full disclosure of the intention to invest has been made in the offer documents (The AMC cannot charge management fee on its investment in the scheme).

3.3.3 Qualifications for AMC

AMCs need to fulfil the following conditions:

- Existing AMCs should have a sound track record (net worth and profitability), and general reputation for fairness and integrity in transactions;
- The AMC has to be a fit and proper person;
- Key personnel of the AMC should not have been found guilty of moral turpitude or convicted of economic offence or violation of any securities laws nor should they have worked for any AMC or mutual fund or any intermediary during the period when its registration has been suspended or cancelled at any time by SEBI; and
- The AMC should have a net worth of not less than ₹ 50 crore if it wants to manage mutual fund schemes. The requirement is ₹ 10 crore if the AMC wants to only manage infrastructure debt funds.

3.3.4 Corporate Governance

- The directors of the AMC need to be persons having adequate professional experience in finance and financial services related fields and shall not have been found guilty of moral turpitude or convicted of economic offence or violation of any securities laws.
- At least 50 per cent of the directors on the AMC's board shall not be associate of, or be associated in any manner with, the sponsor or any of its subsidiaries or the trustees (these are referred to as "independent directors"; other directors are "associate directors").
- If, consequent to an independent director vacating office, the number of independent directors falls below the prescribed minimum, another independent director has to be appointed to fill the gap within three months.
- The provisions regarding "associate", mentioned in the section on trustees, are also applicable for associate directors in AMCs.
- The chairman of the AMC shall not be a trustee of any mutual fund.
- No appointment of a director of an AMC shall be made without prior approval of the trustees.
- No person who has been appointed as director of an AMC can be appointed as a director of any other AMC unless:
    - the person is an independent director, and
    - the AMC where she is already a director approves the proposed appointment in the other AMC.

- Broking limits:
  - An AMC cannot, through any broker associated with the sponsor (related broker), purchase or sell securities worth 5% or more of the aggregate purchases and sales of securities made by the mutual fund in all its schemes (the 5% limit is applicable for a block of any three months and excludes the sale and distribution of units issued by the mutual fund).
  - An AMC shall not through any broker (other than a related broker) purchase or sell securities worth 5% or more of the aggregate purchases and sales of securities made by the mutual fund in all its schemes unless it justifies the same in writing and reports all such investments to the trustees on a quarterly basis (the 5% limit is applicable for a block of three months).
- An AMC shall not utilize the services of the sponsor or any of its associates, employees or their relatives for any securities transaction and distribution and sale of securities unless it is disclosed to the unit holders and the brokerage or commission paid is disclosed in the half-yearly and annual accounts of the mutual fund.
- If the AMC enters into any securities transactions with any of its associates, a report to that effect shall be sent to the trustees at its next meeting.
- In case any company has invested more than 5 per cent of the net asset value of a scheme, the investment by that scheme or by another scheme of the same mutual fund in that company or its subsidiaries has to be brought to the notice of the trustees by the AMC and also disclosed in the half-yearly and annual accounts along with justification for such investment. The disclosure is to be made if the latter investment has been made within one year of the date of the former investment calculated on either side.

  For instance, if Company A holds more than 5% of the units of a scheme floated by Mutual Fund XYZ, then investments by all schemes of Mutual Fund XYZ in Company A or its associates are to be disclosed. Such disclosure is to be made if the subsequent investment has been made within 1 year of the first investment.
- The AMC has to give a quarterly report to the trustees giving details and adequate justification about the purchase and sale of the securities of the group companies of the sponsor or the AMC.
- Every quarter, the AMC has to give the trustees, a statement of securities transactions of the directors of the AMC. For this purpose, security transactions below ₹ 100,000 in value may be ignored.
- The mutual fund shall disclose, at the time of declaring half-yearly and yearly results:
  - Underwriting obligations undertaken by the schemes of the mutual fund with respect to issues of securities by associate companies;

- Devolvement;
- Subscription by schemes in issues lead managed by associate companies; and
- Subscription to any issue of equity or debt on private placement basis where the sponsor or its associate companies have acted as arranger or manager.

3.3.5 Other Obligations of an AMC

- The AMC will float schemes for the mutual fund only after the trustees approve them.
- It shall issue or publish offer document of a scheme, key information memorandum, abridged half-yearly results and annual results only after prior written approval of the trustees.
- The AMC shall take all reasonable steps and exercise due diligence to ensure that the investment of funds pertaining to any scheme is not contrary to the provisions of the regulations and the trust deed.
- The sponsor or AMC need to invest at least 1% of the amount raised in NFOs of open-end schemes. The investment, subject to a cap of ₹ 50 lakh, is to be made in the growth option of the scheme, and cannot be redeemed until the scheme is wound up.
- It shall not carry out its operations including trading desk, unit holder servicing and investment operations outside the territory of India.
- It shall exercise due diligence and care in all its investment decisions as would be exercised by other persons engaged in the same business.
- The AMC shall maintain proper books of accounts, records and documents for each scheme. It shall maintain and preserve these for a period of eight years.
- The AMC shall be responsible for the acts of commission or omission of its employees and its other service providers.
- The AMC shall submit to the trustees, quarterly reports on its activities and the compliance with the regulations.
- The AMC shall file with the trustees, details of transactions in securities by key personnel of the AMC.
- The AMC shall appoint RTA who are registered with SEBI, unless the activity is to be handled in-house.
- Any change in the controlling interest of the AMC shall be only with the prior approval of the trustees, SEBI and the unit holders.
- The AMC shall furnish such information and documents to the trustees as and when required by them.

3.4 Maintenance of Investor Records

The AMC can either handle the RTA work in-house, or it can appoint a SEBI-approved RTA.

If handled in-house, the AMC can charge the schemes competitive market rates for the service. If the AMC proposes to charge higher than the competitive market rates, then prior approval of the trustees is to be obtained and reasons for such higher rates has to be disclosed in the annual accounts.

3.5 Unique Client Code

Mutual funds need to obtain a unique client code for each of their schemes and plans. This is to be conveyed only to the member-broker through whom the fund transacts in the market. It may also be shared with unit holders to enable them to claim the tax benefits associated with payment of STT.

3.6 Custody of Investments

The mutual fund shall appoint a custodian to carry out the custodial services for the schemes of the fund and inform SEBI about the appointment within 15 days.

The mutual fund shall enter into a custodian agreement with the custodian. The agreement, the service contract, terms and appointment of the custodian shall be after prior approval of the trustees.

If the sponsor or its associates hold 50% or more of the voting rights of the share capital of the custodian, or where 50% or more of the directors of the custodian represent the interest of the sponsor or its associates, then such custodian will not be appointed for a mutual fund constituted by the same sponsor or any of its associate or subsidiary company. This limitation is not applicable if:

- The sponsor has a net worth of at least ₹ 20,000 crore at all times;
- 50% or more of the directors of the custodian are those who do not represent the interests of the sponsor or its associates;
- The custodian and AMC are not subsidiaries of each other;
- No person is a director of both custodian and AMC; and
- The custodian and AMC give an undertaking to operate independent of each other.

3.7 Setting up a Mutual Fund Operation

First, the sponsor needs to apply to SEBI in Form A prescribed under Schedule I of SEBI (Mutual Funds) Regulations 1996 along with the requisite application fees. While applying, it is to be ensured that the main objects of the memorandum of the sponsor company permit it to carry on mutual fund activities. An applicant should also submit the following documents, and wherever relevant, additional information for the sponsor as well as for the other shareholders in the proposed asset management company:

- Draft Trust Deed.
- Draft Investment Management Agreement.

- Draft Custodian Agreement.
- List of group / associate companies and their registrations with SEBI, RBI or regulatory agencies abroad.
- Details of listing of the sponsor, or its group / associate companies in any stock exchange(s).
- Penalties, details of suspension / cancellation of registrations.

SEBI may conduct an on-site due-diligence of the existing businesses of the sponsor to study the following:

- Existing infrastructure for client servicing, complaints handling;
- Track record of complaint / grievance handling; and
- Compliance philosophy and practice.

SEBI may seek further information, which would need to be provided within 30 days of the request. After examining the application against its eligibility criteria, SEBI conveys its decision on the eligibility status.

If found eligible, the following critical preliminaries would need to be done within 12 months of SEBI's communication:

- The sponsor would set up the trust through the trust deed. If the sponsor has opted for the trustee company route — as distinct from board of trustees — then this company would need to be incorporated.
- Executed trust deed has to be submitted to SEBI.
- If not already in existence, the sponsor would promote the AMC. Two copies of the memorandum and articles are to be submitted to SEBI for forwarding to the Registrar of Companies.
- A chartered accountants' certificate would have to be submitted to SEBI to show that net worth of the AMC is at least ₹ 50 crore, and more than 40% of the equity is held by the Sponsor(s).
- Either the sponsor or (if permitted by the trust deed) the trustees will appoint the AMC for the mutual fund. Investment Management Agreement would be executed between the trustees and the AMC, and submitted to SEBI.
- The mutual fund will enter into a custodial agreement with the custodian for handling the securities in which its schemes would invest.
- If the AMC chooses to perform the RTA activity in-house, then appropriate arrangements would need to be put in place. Alternatively, the AMC can appoint a SEBI-registered RTA for the purpose.
- A note would have to be submitted to SEBI indicating the infrastructural arrangements and other progress made. This would include office premises, organization chart, profile of key personnel (including fund managers and equity research personnel), hardware, software, investor servicing arrangements and internal control systems and procedures.

SEBI will, after a review of the above factors, and receipt of requisite fees, grant a Certificate of Registration for the mutual fund and approve the AMC.

Once the Certificate of Registration is granted:

- The trustees would appoint the statutory auditor for the mutual fund, who would audit the various schemes to be promoted by the mutual fund.
- The AMC would appoint statutory auditors who would audit the accounts of the company, as distinct from the schemes. The auditor of the AMC, as seen earlier, would need to be different from the auditor of the mutual fund.
- The AMC will put in place guidelines for empanelment of brokers for purchase and sale of securities by the mutual fund schemes, and distributors who would distribute the schemes of the mutual fund.
- The AMC will appoint other key personnel and set up systems for investment management, accounting, internal audit, etc.
- The AMC will draft the first schemes of the mutual fund.
- The AMC will prepare the offer document, which has to contain adequate disclosures to enable investors to make an informed investment decision. This needs to be filed with SEBI, which has a period of 21 working days to stipulate modifications.
- SEBI's observations would need to be incorporated in the Offer Document.
- The scheme's offer document, key information memorandum, etc., would need to be approved by the trustees in writing.
- Once all the above are in place, the trustees will authorize the AMC to launch the scheme's New Fund Offer (NFO). The NFO should be open for not more than 15 days (but this limitation is not applicable for Equity Linked Savings Schemes — ELSS).

  In case no mutual fund scheme is launched within 12 months from the date of registration, the registration granted would be treated as cancelled.
- After approval of the trustees, the AMC can market the scheme. Advertisements would have to conform to the advertising code and submitted to SEBI within 7 days from the date of issue.
- Once subscriptions equivalent to the minimum amount specified in the offer document are received, the AMC can allot units to the subscribers on behalf of the mutual fund. There is no statutorily prescribed minimum unit capital, although offer documents mention a nominal minimum amount of ₹ 1 crore.
- The AMC has to allot units / refund money and send confirmation specifying the number of units allotted to the applicant by way of email and/or SMS's to the applicant's registered email address and/or mobile number as soon as possible but not later than five working days from the date of closure of the initial subscription list and/or from the date of receipt of the request from the unit holders. The new units shall be available for ongoing sale / re-purchase / trading within 5 business days of allotment (not applicable for ELSS).

Account statements are computer generated. They provide details of transactions under the schemes during the relevant period, and give the closing balance of units held in the investor's name. An account statement is not construed as proof of title. Unit certificates are proof of title.

The general market practice is that open end schemes issue account statements (and not unit certificates), which are non-transferable. Closed-end schemes need to issue unit certificates (if not demat units), which are transferable. SEBI has stipulated that demat units (open-end as well as close-end schemes) would be freely transferable.

- The AMC can start investing the funds only on or after the closure of the NFO period. Post-allotment, the AMC is to invest in line with the investment objectives set out in the offer document. Pending such investment, the money may be invested in short-term deposits of scheduled commercial banks.

3.8 Change in Fundamental Attributes

Consent of three-fourths of the unit holders is required for making a change in the fundamental attributes of any scheme, or the trust, or fees and expenses payable, or any other change which would modify the scheme or affect the interest of the unit holders.

The following are fundamental attributes:

Types of Scheme

(a) Open end / closed end / interval scheme.
(b) Sectoral fund / equity fund / balance fund / income fund / debt fund / index fund / Any other type of fund.

Investment Objective(s)

(a) Main Objective — growth / income / both.
(b) Investment pattern — The tentative equity / debt / money market portfolio break-up with minimum and maximum asset allocation, while retaining the option to alter the asset allocation for a short term period on defensive considerations.

Terms of Issue

(a) Liquidity provisions, such as listing, re-purchase, redemption.
(b) Aggregate fees and expenses charged to the scheme.
(c) Any safety net or guarantee provided.

Although the regulations refer to consent of "three-fourths of the unit holders", in practice it is not the number of unit holders that is relevant but the unit holding they represent. If the unit holding of person A is twice that of person B, then A would have twice the number of votes that B has.

Apart from this requirement of approval of three-fourths of unit holders, those unit holders who do not give their consent need to be given the option of redeeming their holdings in the scheme.

The approval of unit holders is, however, not required in the case of open-end schemes if:

- The change in fundamental attribute is carried out after one year from allotment of units;
- Individual communication is given to unit holders about the proposed change;
- Advertisement is issued in an English daily newspaper having national circulation and in a newspaper published in the language of the region where the head office of the mutual fund is situated; and
- Unit holders are given an option to exit at the prevailing net asset value, without any exit load ("load" is explained in Chapter 5).

Further, minor changes in the scheme, e.g. change in registrar's address, may be effected with the approval of trustees, without the requirement of unit holder approval.

3.9 Mergers and Acquisitions

The sponsor promotes the AMC which, in turn, manages the mutual fund operation under the supervision of the trustees. A change in control could happen due to a change in any of these instrumentalities of the fund, namely sponsor, AMC, trusteeship or the schemes.

The authorization for such inorganic changes in the structure of a mutual fund or its schemes is determined by the following broad principles:

SEBI Regulations

As per SEBI regulations, any material change would require the consent of unit holders with at least 75 per cent voting rights, subject to the exceptions applicable to open-end schemes mentioned in the earlier section. Investors who do not agree have to be given the option to exit at the NAV applicable on the date of exit.

SEBI Approval

Regulator of mutual fund operations in the country, SEBI has to approve any change before it can be implemented. In the absence of clear provisions in the regulations, approval of such changes is influenced significantly by "precedence." SEBI is, however, not bound by the precedence — it has the authority to set new precedents.

Companies Act, 2013

Apart from SEBI's approval, if the proposed change is with respect to a company (sponsoring company, asset management company, or trustee company) then the provisions of the Companies Act, 2013 would apply.

Under the companies act, approval of merger of two companies entails:

- Special resolution to be passed at a general meeting of each company. Special resolution means that the votes of members, present in person or proxy or voting by postal ballot, supporting the resolution is at least three times the votes of those opposing the resolution.
- Approval is also required from the National Company Law Tribunal. Simplified process is possible for "small" companies.

The Competition Act, 2002

In certain cases of business combinations, permission of the Competition Commission of India is also required.

SEBI Takeover Code

If the proposed change involves a company that is listed, then the provisions of SEBI Takeover Code would also need to be complied with. The takeover code requires that if any one acquires more than 25 per cent of the share capital of a listed company, then an open offer would need to be made to acquire at least a further 26 per cent of the share capital from other shareholders.

In the light of these broad principles, let us evaluate each possible situation.

3.9.1 Consolidation of Two Schemes

There are several such precedents in India, including by UTI Mutual Fund, Kotak Mutual Fund, JP Morgan Mutual Fund, JM Mutual Fund, etc.)

SEBI had stipulated that a consolidation would be viewed as a change in the fundamental attribute of the schemes. Permission of the boards of the AMC and Trustees is to be taken before approaching SEBI with the draft Offer Document of the new scheme.

The letter to the unit holders, giving them the option to exit at prevailing NAV without exit load, shall disclose all relevant information enabling them to take well informed decisions, including information on the following aspects:

- Information on the investment objective, asset allocation and the main features of the new consolidated scheme;
- Basis of allocation of new units by way of a numerical illustration;
- Percentage of total Non-Performing Assets (NPAs) and percentage of total illiquid assets to net assets of the individual schemes as well as in the consolidated scheme;
- Tax impact of the consolidation of schemes on the unit holders;

- Any other disclosures as specified by the trustees; and
- Any other disclosures as directed by SEBI.

SEBI has provided that merger or consolidation shall not be seen as change in fundamental attribute of the surviving scheme if the following conditions are met:

- Fundamental attributes of the surviving scheme do not change. The "surviving scheme" means the scheme which remains in existence after the merger.
- Mutual funds are able to demonstrate that the circumstances merit merger or consolidation of schemes and the interest of the unit holders of surviving scheme is not adversely affected.
- After approval by the boards of AMCs and trustees, the mutual funds file such proposal with SEBI which would communicate its observations on the proposal within 21 working days.
- The letter to unit holders is issued only after the final observations communicated by SEBI have been incorporated and final copies of the same have been filed with SEBI.

3.9.2 Conversion of Closed-end Schemes to Open-end

(Precedent in India — Mastershare of UTI)

Such conversion is possible if the unit holders are provided with an option to redeem their units in full.

Draft of the communication to unit holders that is to be submitted to SEBI for such cases shall include the following:

- The latest portfolio of the scheme in the format prescribed for half yearly disclosures.
- Details of financial performance of the scheme since inception in the manner prescribed under the Standard Offer Document along with comparison with appropriate benchmarks.
- Addendum to the offer document detailing the modifications (if any) made to the scheme.

Since the scheme would re-open for fresh subscriptions, the disclosures contained in the scheme information document of the scheme would have to be revised and updated. A copy of the draft scheme information document would also need to be filed with SEBI.

The letter to unit holders and scheme information document shall be issued only after SEBI's final observations have been incorporated and its final copy filed with SEBI.

Further, unit holders shall be given a time period of at least 30 days for the purpose of exercising the exit option. Unit holders who opt to redeem their holdings in part or full during the prescribed period, shall be allowed to exit at the NAV applicable for the day on which such a request is received.

3.9.3 Takeover of Schemes

(Precedent in India — Schemes of Apple Mutual Fund taken over by Birla AMC; schemes of IL&FS Mutual Fund taken over by UTI Mutual Fund; schemes of GIC Mutual Fund taken over by Canbank; schemes of Alliance Mutual Fund taken over by Birla Mutual Fund; schemes of Morgan Stanley Mutual Fund taken over by HDFC Mutual Fund; schemes of Pine Bridge Mutual Fund taken over by Kotak Mutual Fund).

This is the most popular form of consolidation among AMCs, because the acquirer gains control of the schemes, without having to worry about the divesting AMC's financials, assets, employees and legal traps. Besides, the divesting AMC can continue with its non-mutual fund activities such as Portfolio Management Schemes.

In the Apple-Birla case, apart from 75 per cent unit-holder approval and exit option, SEBI insisted on a synchronization of trusteeship and asset management roles. Therefore, along with Birla AMC taking up the asset management responsibility for the transferred schemes, Birla trusteeship had also to be extended to these transferred schemes. SEBI was not comfortable with an arrangement where Birla AMC would manage two sets of schemes — one under the Birla trusteeship and another under Apple trusteeship.

3.9.4 Merger of Two AMCs

(Precedent in India — HB and Taurus)

The legal requirements are:

- 75 per cent unit holder approval and exit option for dissenting investors in all the schemes managed by the two AMCs;
- Since it is a merger of two companies, special resolution of shareholders and permission of the respective high courts (now National Company Law Tribunal) is also required, unless they are "small companies"; and
- Revised trusteeship arrangements has to be conveyed to SEBI.

3.9.5 Change of AMC

(Precedent in India — None)

Under SEBI's regulations, an AMC can be changed by:

- Majority of trustees, but subject to approval of SEBI and 75 per cent of the unit holders of the scheme; or
- 75 per cent of the unit holders of the scheme, present and voting at a meeting called with the prior approval of SEBI.

3.9.6 Change of Trusteeship

Precedent in India — Change in trustees comprising any Board of Trustees is a normal phenomenon. There is no precedent for a change of Trustee company in India, though the transfer of Apple schemes to Birla Mutual Fund (mentioned earlier) also entailed a change of trusteeship responsibility.

Under the regulations:

- The trust deed cannot be amended without SEBI's approval. If the proposed amendment materially affects the unit holders, then even their permission would be required. Unit holder permission is, however, not required for conversion from a Board of Trustee format into a trustee company format.
- The sponsor may appoint and remove trustees as provided in the trust deed. But such appointment and removal is subject to prior SEBI approval.
- Investors do not have the right to remove the trustees.

3.9.7 Change of Sponsor / Takeover of Mutual Fund Business

Precedent in India: (i) Zurich — 20th Century Finance; (ii) Zurich — ITC Threadneedle; (iii) Sun F&C; (iv) Sahara — First India; (v) Goldman Sachs — Benchmark; and (vi) Dewan Housing Finance Limited's acquisition of 50% stake of Prudential Group (US) in Pramerica's mutual fund business.

The regulations stipulate that SEBI's permission is required in such cases. SEBI did not insist on permission of unit holders in the case of 20th Century Finance; but such permission was called for in the case of ITC Threadneedle.

The case of Sun F&C is significant because there was no change in the share holding within the Indian AMC. Foreign & Colonial (F&C) of Britain continued to hold a stake in the Sun F&C Asset Management India. Only the controlling interest in F&C, Britain changed hands from Germany's Hypovereins Bank to Eureko, the insurer. SEBI took the view that this is a material change, and therefore insisted on an exit option for investors.

It is important to recognize that when a sponsor changes, control over the AMC changes. After seeing several such changes, SEBI has drawn up the following detailed guidelines:

- The mutual fund handing over control would need to submit a draft letter that is to be sent to investors. This would include the following information:
  - The activities of the new sponsor and its financial performance as prescribed in the standard offer document;
  - In case of takeover of the schemes by an existing mutual fund registered with SEBI, the draft letter should also include the condensed financial information of all the schemes in the format prescribed in the standard offer document; and

  - The amount of unclaimed redemption and dividend, and procedure for claiming such amount by the unit holders.

- If the applicant proposing to take control is not an existing mutual fund, then the applicant would need to apply to SEBI for registration as a mutual fund. Thus, the various requirements of sponsor would need to be complied with.
- Also, the party assuming control of the AMC would need to give the following undertakings:
  - Take full responsibility of the management and the administration of the schemes including matters relating to the reconciliation of accounts (as if the schemes had been floated by the new trustees on the date of taking over).
  - Assumption of trusteeship of the assets and liabilities of the schemes including unclaimed dividends and unclaimed redemptions.
  - Assumption of all responsibilities and obligations relating to the investor grievances, if any, in respect of the schemes taken over, in accordance with and pursuant to the SEBI (Mutual Funds) Regulations.
- In cases such as indirect change in control over AMC, change in promoter of sponsor etc, full information is to be given to SEBI. Within 21 working days, SEBI will communicate any procedural requirements.
- SEBI insists on 30-days window for investors to exercise the exit option in such cases of change of control.

SEBI's stipulation of higher net worth for AMCs is likely to lead to a consolidation in the industry. Some of the smaller AMCs may choose to sell their businesses to larger players.

3.10 Categorisation and Rationalisation of Mutual Fund Schemes

SEBI expressed its concern several times over scheme proliferation. It wants the various schemes offered by a single mutual fund to be distinct in terms of asset allocation and investment strategy. Further, similar types of schemes should have uniform characteristics across mutual funds. This is essential to ensure that investors are not confused by the universe of mutual fund schemes.

In October 2017, SEBI took a decisive step in this direction for open-end schemes which comprise 91% of the AUM in the industry. It classified mutual fund schemes into five groups, namely. Equity schemes, debt schemes, hybrid schemes, solution oriented schemes, and other schemes. Scheme categories have been defined under each of these groups. The categories under the first four groups were discussed in Chapter 2. There are two categories under 'Other schemes', namely. Index funds / ETFs and Fund of Funds (Overseas / Domestic). For every category under each of these five groups, SEBI stipulated standard 'metrics'.

SEBI has mandated that all existing schemes needed to revise their offer documents, advertisements, marketing material etc. to fall in line with the SEBI defined categories and type of scheme. This change alone do not make it a change of fundamental attribute. However, consequent to this change, investment objective, investment strategy and benchmark may need to be changed. These would qualify as change of fundamental attribute, calling for unit-holder approval, exit option at NAV, and other procedural requirements.

Any consequential portfolio was to be executed within one month of the change of scheme type.

SEBI allows any mutual fund to have only one open-end scheme in each of these categories. Three exceptions have been provided:

- The AMC can have multiple index / ETFs so long as they replicate or track different indices.
- Similarly, the AMC can have multiple Fund of Funds, each having different underlying schemes.
- The AMC can also have multiple sectoral / thematic funds, each investing in different sectors / themes.

Mutual funds were directed to map their current schemes to these SEBI-mandated categories and develop a plan (winding up / merger / change of fundamental attribute) to ensure that they have only one open-end scheme in each category. They were mandated to implement this plan within three months of SEBI giving its observations on the plan.

Some in the mutual fund industry have viewed this move as a curb on innovation. However, it was a huge step in simplifying mutual fund investment in the country.

Chapter 4

Investments by Mutual Fund Schemes

Investments are the foundation of any mutual fund scheme. The valuation of these investments affects the Net Asset Value of the scheme. This chapter gives a brief overview into debt, equity, gold and real estate, which are the principal asset classes in which investors deploy money. For a more exhaustive understanding of these asset classes, please refer to my book, *Wealth Engine* [Vision Books, 2012].

4.1 Types of Equity

The financial market differentiates equities as follows:

4.1.1 Traditional Classification

Growth Stocks

These are expected to demonstrate earnings growth that is better than the market. From time to time various promising sectors in the economy emerge, such as software during 1998-2000, telecom in the early 2000s and e-commerce companies in the last couple of years. Good companies in such sectors are viewed as growth stocks and attract high level of investment interest.

Income Stocks

Hall puts this category in perspective "In the old days, these shares were often called 'widow and orphan' stocks — a reference to the once 'typical' investors who would buy the stock for its reliability and size of dividend payments."[8]

Income stocks provide attractive dividend return on the amount invested. In accounting terminology, they provide high dividend yield.

If we look at power generation companies for instance, once the plant is set up and it maintains operation, the off take is relatively certain, and so is the price. In such a situation, the profits are steady, thus giving the company the luxury of declaring stable dividends. In India, concerns over the financials of most state electricity boards, which buy the power from the power generating company, raise issues of credit risk. Such risks would be reduced in a situation of direct supply to consumers, coupled with right to disconnect power to consumers who do not pay.

Another example of income stock in the power sector would be power transmission companies — being out of generation and distribution, such companies' throughput is transmitting the power — a business that is expected to steadily increase on account of mismatches between demand and supply of power.

Let us now consider a company whose business model revolves around collecting toll for use of infrastructure. If the infrastructure is a bridge, then during the life of the bridge usage will keep increasing steadily — and so will the toll for the period for which the company is allowed to collect toll. Thus there would be little volatility in earnings, enabling the company to pay steadily increasing dividends.

Cyclical Stocks

These shares move in tandem with the economy. Basic industries such as cement, steel, etc. are examples of industries whose performance is closely linked to that of the economy. Therefore, stocks of companies belonging to such industries are cyclical in nature.

Shipping could be an example of a cyclical industry. As trade activity goes up, shipping rates increase too. However, earnings of shipping companies often do not fully reflect the cyclicality because:

- Shipping companies enter into long term charters for their fleet. So changes in shipping rates affect only the uncommitted capacity.
- Shipping companies also trade ships. Therefore, "other income", frequently a significant contributor to earnings, cushions the cyclicality.
- Profits of shipping companies are also influenced by the nature of long-term arrangements they make for their fuel supplies, a significant cost factor.

Defensive Stocks

These are relatively protected from economic cycles. Pharmaceutical stocks and healthcare stocks are a good example because consumption of medicine does not vary with the ups and downs of the economy. Education sector again offers defensive plays. In India, people prioritise education over other basic necessities. In the US, during weak economic conditions when jobs are lost, the demand for seats in MBA programs goes up.

As the celebrated Peter Lynch noted, "A great patients' drug is one that cures an affliction once and for all, but a great investor's drug is one that the patient has to keep buying."[9] Thus, a drug for treating diabetes, hypertension or AIDS represents a much better investment proposition — until the medical world discovers a permanent cure for these ailments.

Pivotals or Momentum Stocks

These shares move the market. Reliance Industries and Infosys are examples of such stocks in India. Any listing of pivotals would have significant overlaps with growth stocks, since the large companies in the latter category are likely to influence the direction of the market.

Value Stocks

The current valuation of these shares does not reflect some aspect of the company that could be extremely valuable.

For instance, an investor who felt that the last mile connectivity that MTNL had in the two important cities of Mumbai and Delhi was not fully reflected in the price, would be viewing it as a value stock. She would aim to "unlock value" when the market appreciates the value of MTNL's last mile connectivity and pushes up its stock valuation. As it turned out, the advent of wireless communication reduced the importance of MTNL's cables that provided the last mile connectivity.

"Under-valuation" is normally viewed through fundamental analysis measures such as the ratio of share price in the market to the company's earnings per share (P/E Ratio) and the ratio of share price in the market to the company's book value per share (P/BV Ratio).

Typically, value gets hidden in the company in the form of ownership of real estate, license entitlement, etc. Several manufacturing companies that are sitting on prime real estate property can be viewed as value stocks. The land is reflected in their books of accounts at negligible historical cost. When the promoters decide to develop these as part of a real estate business, the value is unlocked.

The challenge in value stocks is the unpredictable time horizon. For instance, it is not clear if and when the promoters will choose to consider the real estate development business. However, the low acquisition cost of these shares minimises the downside risk.

GARP Stocks

These stocks offer "growth at a reasonable price". Alvin Hall explains how this can be achieved: "The GARP manager looks for reasonably priced stocks that promise above-average earnings growth."[10] The PEG ratio (discussed in the section "Value Drivers in the Equity Market") is an important tool in the kit of the GARP investor.

4.1.2 Peter Lynch's Six Stock Categories[11]

Peter Lynch outlines his investment philosophy in these words: "Once I've established the size of the company relative to others in a particular industry, next I place it into one of six general categories."

Slow Growers (Sluggards)

These are erstwhile fast growers that have seen their growth taper off over a period of time. Their stock charts indicate a flat price trend; dividends are generous and regular. This would be akin to income stocks in the traditional classification. The key metric to watch out for in such stocks, is the payout ratio. Lower payout would be indicative of a cushion available to maintain the generous dividend even if the company's performance turns adverse.

Medium Growers (Stalwarts)

These companies stand tall even in the face of market drops and recessions. Such stocks typically are those of big companies that aren't likely to go out of business. Key investment issue is the price and P/E ratio. Their penchant for "diworseification" (making the company worse through diversification) is something to watch out for.

Fast Growers (Super-Stocks)

These are like the growth stocks described earlier. The product that is supposed to enrich the company — the engine of growth — should ideally be a major part of the company's business. They should have established their success in replicating the performance / scaling up, and there should be room to grow in the industry.

In the Indian context, the software sector has several examples to illustrate this thought process. Let us compare TCS and Wipro on this parameter. Until 31 March 2013, software, consumer care products, lighting and infrastructure engineering business were part of a single company, Wipro. An investor desirous of capitalising on the software growth engine would prefer TCS, because Wipro was also engaged in these non-software businesses, which would have stunted the Wipro growth story.

Besides, till the time of writing, software companies like TCS and Cognizant have demonstrated their ability to grow, even on a large existing base; some other software companies faced problems in ramping up — either because of the market, or their inability to recruit and manage ever increasing human resources. The latter stopped being growth stories, and this was reflected in the lower P/E ratios they commanded in the market. With the emergence of newer technologies like artificial intelligence, even TCS and Cognizant have joined the ranks of software companies with stunted growth prospects. This has contributed to a decline in their P/E ratios.

Cyclicals

Timing is critical for an investment in cyclicals. Key would be to figure out the economic cycles, which can help anticipate changing P/E ratios, Inventories and supply-demand relationships in the industry would be factors to watch.

For example, commodity stocks went up for a few years from 2004 as a part of the upturn in the economic cycle seen across the globe. At the time of writing, fears of a trade wars and declining expectations of global growth have caused a downturn in commodity prices.

Asset Plays

These are like value stocks. A raider would particularly help an investor reap the benefits of their under valuation.

Action in the airlines industry in India during 2005-06 serves as a good example. The government stipulated that only domestic airlines with a five-year track record would be permitted to ply on international routes. Sahara was entitled to the license, but for various reasons could not fully leverage on it. Thus, investors in Sahara (had it been a listed company) would not, in the normal course, have benefited from the company's international license. Sahara would be an under-valued stock.

But Sahara's international license had value for other airlines — and hence the asset play possibility for an investor. An airline like Kingfisher, which was otherwise not permitted to fly international, wanted to acquire Sahara, largely on account of this license. Thus, a raider in the form of Kingfisher, would help investors in Sahara encash the value of the international license. Finally, it was Jet Airways that concluded a deal with Sahara (value encashment for investors).

Turnarounds

The critical issue in such cases is whether the company has a strategy to turn itself around — and the finances and the management grit to carry it through — without a raider coming in to short circuit the potential valuation gains from the turnaround story. Thus, a raider is an investor's friend in "asset plays", but villain of the piece when it comes to "turnarounds".

Bajaj Auto is a good example. At the turn of the century, the company was in the doldrums. The scooter industry, where the company had a 70% market share, had turned adverse and motorcycles, which represented a minor portion of Bajaj Auto's product portfolio, had emerged as a major constituent of the two-wheeler industry. Hero Honda emerged as the hero of the two-wheeler industry. The company's "fill it-shut it-forget it" is what the market spoke about. But was Hero Honda able to fill Bajaj Auto, or shut it out of the market or get the market to forget it? No.

Did Bajaj Auto have a strategy to get out of the problem? Yes, the next generation took over the business. The problem was identified — poor R&D capability and inadequate product portfolio. And the new management aggressively moved to rectify the weakness.

Did Bajaj Auto have the money to implement the strategy? Yes, it was sitting on thousands of crores of idle cash invested in the financial market.

Was there a fear of takeover? No, the Bajaj family had firm control over the company.

Thus, Bajaj Auto had all the elements required to make it a turnaround stock. No wonder, investors who invested at that time were able to laugh their way to the bank.

Continuing the interesting story of the group, Bajaj Auto had a subsidiary that was into financing two wheelers. The financing business remained under the shadows of the much larger auto business until in April 2007 it was demerged into a separate company, Bajaj Finserv. The demerger, a consequence of a family arrangement, gave wings to the finance business. Bajaj Finserv built up a reasonably diversified financial services business that made it a darling of the stock market. A great turnaround for investors who reposed their faith in the business.

4.2 Risks in Equity Investing

Legends from the investment world have highlighted the concept of risk in unique ways. These are paraphrased below:

"Stock market is not pure science and not like chess, where the superior position always wins. If seven out of ten of my stocks perform as expected, then I'm delighted. If six out of ten of my stocks perform as expected, then I'm thankful. Six out of ten is all it takes to produce an enviable record on Wall Street." (Peter Lynch)[12]

"Market frenzies are not isolated and not unique episodes in financial history. On the contrary, market bubbles — situations in which prices are way higher than values — happen all too often. There was a technology stock bubble from 1959 to 1960; a bubble in the so-called 'Nifty Fifty' stocks in the late 1960s and early 1970s; a gambling stock bubble in 1978; a bubble in oil and energy stocks in the late 1970s; a home shopping bubble in 1986 and 1987; and a biotechnology bubble in the early 1990s (with a resurrection in the early 2000s), and all of these resemble the Internet or dot-com bubble of the late 1990s and early 2000s." (Lawrence A. Cunningham)[13]

"Intriguingly, the disastrous boom and bust of 1999-2002 also came roughly 35 years after the previous cycle of insanity. Perhaps it takes about 35 years for investors who remember the previous 'New Economy' craze to become less influential than those who do not. If this intuition is correct, the intelligent investor should be particularly vigilant around the year 2030." (Jason Zweig)[14]

"History tells us that corrections (declines of 10 per cent or more) occur every couple of years, and bear markets (declines of 20 per cent or more) occur every six years. Severe bear markets (declines of 30 per cent or more) have materialized five times since the 1929-32 doozie." (Peter Lynch)[15]

"On 7 January 1973, the *New York Times* featured an interview with one of the nation's top financial forecasters, who urged investors to buy stocks without hesitation: 'It's very rare that you can be as unqualifiedly bullish as you can now.' That forecaster was named Alan Greenspan, and it's very rare that anyone has ever been so unqualifiedly wrong as the future Federal Reserve chairman was that day: 1973 and 1974 turned out to be the worst years for economic growth and the stock market since the great depression." (Jason Zweig)[16]

If a person of Alan Greenspan's stature, who went on to be a much-acclaimed chairman of the US Federal Reserve for nearly two decades, under various presidents of diametrically opposite political ideologies, can be so wrong, what about lesser mortals?

"According to Mark Twain, October is one of the peculiarly dangerous months to speculate in stocks. The others are July, January, September, April, November, May, March, June, December, August, etc., " noted Peter Lynch in his book.[17] Twain's tongue-in-cheek comment has many a grain of truth in it.

An investor in equity is taking a risk that she might lose her invested capital. Economics differentiates risk from uncertainty. When the probability of a future event can be assessed, it is risk. When the probability is indefinite or indeterminate, it is uncertainty. There are three key quantitative measures of risk — variance, standard deviation and beta, which are explained in Chapter 10.

Unlike debt, which would be redeemed by the issuer at a pre-determined price, equity needs to be sold in the marketplace. The option of getting money from outside the stock market comes up only in a buyback situation, when the issuer would pay the investor; or if a safety net is provided, in which case the person providing the safety net will pay the investor. This is part of the rationale behind the oft-repeated view that equity is riskier than debt.

The legendary Benjamin Graham gives a more nuanced understanding of the risks in equity investing: "The risk of paying too high a price for good-quality stocks — while a real one — is not the chief hazard confronting the average buyer of securities. Observation over many years has taught us that the chief losses to investors come from the purchase of *low quality* securities at times of favourable business conditions."[18]

While ruminating over risk, it is usual to remember the words of Peter Lynch in the context of the terrible crash of Black Monday: (19 October 1987) "The losses of last October were only losses to people who took the losses. That wasn't the long-term investor. It was the margin player, the risk arbitrageur, the options player, and the portfolio manager whose computer signalled 'sell' who took the losses."[19]

In the words of the psychologist Paul Slovic, "Risk is brewed from an equal dose of two ingredients — probabilities and consequences." Before you invest, you must ensure that you have realistically assessed your probability of being right, and how you will react to the consequences of being wrong. Investment philosopher Peter Bernstein opines that "in making decisions under conditions of uncertainty, the consequences must dominate the probabilities. We never know the future."[20]

4.3 Value Drivers in Equity Market

"There is a fine passage near the beginning of Aristotle's *Ethics* that goes:

> It is the mark of an educated mind to expect that amount of exactness which the nature of the particular subject admits. It is equally unreasonable to accept merely probable conclusions from a mathematician and to demand strict demonstration from an orator.

"The work of a financial analyst falls somewhere in the middle, between that of a mathematician and of an orator. . . ."[21]

Benjamin Greham's views on managing risk are insightful, "The future itself can be approached in two different ways, which may be called the way of prediction (or projection) and the way of protection. All investors labour under a cruel irony: We invest in the present, but we invest for the future. And unfortunately, the future is almost entirely uncertain. Inflation and interest rates are undependable; economic recessions come and go at random; geopolitical upheavals like war, commodity shortages, and terrorism arrive without warning; and the fate of individual companies and their industries often turns out to be the opposite of what most investors expect. Therefore, investing on the basis of projection is a fool's errand; even the forecasts of the so-called experts are less reliable than the flip of a coin. For most people, investing on the basis of protection — from overpaying for a stock, and from overconfidence in the quality of their own judgment — is the best solution. . . ."[22]

"The first, or predictive, approach could also be called the qualitative approach, since it emphasizes prospects, management, and other non-measurable, albeit highly important, factors that go under the heading of quality. The second, or protective, approach may be called the quantitative or statistical approach, since it emphasizes the measurable relationships between selling price and earnings, assets, dividends, and so forth. . . ."[23]

"In our own attitude and professional work, we were always committed to the quantitative approach. From the first, we wanted to make sure that we were getting ample value for our money in concrete, demonstrable terms. We were not willing to accept the prospects and promises of the future as compensation for a lack of sufficient value in hand. This has by no means been the standard view point among investment authorities; in fact, the majority would probably subscribe to the view that prospects, quality of management, other intangibles, and 'the human factor' far outweigh the indications supplied by any study of the past record, the balance sheet, and all the other cold figures."[24]

Thus, quantitative measures of value are important. Some of the measures commonly used are discussed below.

4.3.1 EPS and P/E Ratio

These are easily the most popular tools for determining valuation. For instance, if the aluminium industry has a P/E ratio of 10 times, and if Company Z has an EPS of ₹ 12, then the value of Company Z stock should, theoretically, be:

EPS x P/E Ratio, namely ₹ 120 per share.

A high P/E ratio means either of two things:

- The market views the stock favourably.
- Or, the share is over-valued — perhaps being pushed up by manipulators.

A low P/E ratio could mean the reverse, namely either the market does not view the stock favourably, or that it is undervalued (value stock).

The skill of the analyst is in identifying which of the implications is applicable for any stock. This is a critical judgment call, which determines whether the stock would be bought or sold.

According to Aswath Damodaran, there are various refinements of the P/E Ratio:[25]

- Current P/E — Current price divided by the EPS in the most recent financial year.
- Trailing P/E — EPS is based on the last 4 quarters. Thus, the EPS used is more updated.
- Forward P/E — Expected earnings is used in the denominator. Quality of the earnings estimate thus becomes key in this case.
- Primary P/E — EPS is calculated based on the actual number of shares outstanding.
- Fully Diluted P/E — EPS is calculated based on the number of shares that would be outstanding, if all the outstanding options get exercised.

At times, analysts compare P/E ratios between different countries. This can lead to faulty conclusions, when apart from other dichotomies, the earnings are not comparable on account of differences in accounting standards between countries.

Damodaran rightly mentions that "The revenue recognition principles need to be investigated in detail. Microsoft, for example, has had a history of being conservative in its recording of revenues from its programme updates (Windows 98, Windows 2000, etc.). On the other hand, telecommunication firms, in their zeal to pump up revenue growth, in the late 1990s were often aggressive in recording revenues early."[26]

4.3.2 PEG Ratio

In a loose way, the P/E ratio indicates over how many years an investor buying stock at the current price would be paid back through earnings in the company. This obviously assumes that the earnings stream in the company would be constant. Higher the growth in earnings, the faster the investor would be paid back. It, therefore, stands to reason that P/E needs to be seen in the context of earnings growth.

The PEG ratio follows from this maxim. It is calculated as:

P/E ratio *divided by* Expected Earnings growth rate.

Growth stocks are expected to have high P/E ratios. How to ensure that one does not over-pay for growth? Check the PEG ratio. Some analysts view PEG of 1 or less as a desirable metric for investing in a company's equity shares.

Thus, if a company's earnings are growing at 25% p.a., and it is trading in the market at 20 times, then the PEG ratio of 20 ÷ 25, i.e. 0.8 would be viewed favourably as offering GARP.

4.3.3 CEPS and P/CE Ratio

Earnings are calculated after depreciation, which in turn is a function of accounting policy. Cash earnings (earnings plus depreciation and other non-cash charges) are less affected by accounting policy.

For example, if the CEPS of Company Z is ₹ 15, and the P/CE ratio of the industry is 9 times, then the price of each share of Company Z should theoretically be ₹ 15 x 9, namely ₹ 135.

This measure is particularly useful when a stock has positive cash earnings, but negative earnings after non-cash charges.

4.3.4 Dividend Yield

According to Cunningham, the cash dividend-based approach to valuation was championed by John Burr Williams, who argued, "Earnings are only a means to an end. Therefore we must say that a stock derives its value from its dividends, not its earnings. In short, a stock is worth only *what you can get out of it.*"[27]

4.3.5 Price to Book Value

In industries such as banking and non-banking finance companies, where financial assets are a significant component of the balance sheet, price to book value of the industry, multiplied by the book value of the individual stock could give an indication of the stock's value.

This measure would be meaningful in all situations where the book value is representative of realizable values. The ratio loses meaning if a bank artificially raises the book value of its assets by not providing for loans that are non-performing.

Similarly, the ratio will not be meaningful in cases like Coca Cola, where value comes out of its brand, or Infosys, where value comes out of its people.

4.3.6 Turnover Multiple

This ratio is calculated as sales turnover divided by market capitalization of the company.

Market capitalization is the total number of equity shares issued by the company multiplied by market price of the shares in the market place.

Example 4.1

Suppose Company Z has issued 100,000 equity shares that are valued in the market place at ₹ 15. Assume that the company's sales turnover is ₹ 300 lakh.

The market capitalization of Company Z would be:

100,000 x ₹ 15, namely ₹ 1,500,000.

Turnover multiple of Company Z would be:

₹ 300 lakh ÷ ₹ 15 lakh, namely 20 times.

Sales turnover is a surrogate for market share and significance of the company's role in a sector — particularly in a multi-product set-up.

For instance, if Company X were looking at taking over either of two companies, namely Company Z whose turnover multiple is 20 times or, a Company Y whose turnover multiple is 25 times. If other factors such as fitment in product mix, margins, locational advantages, company culture, merger economics etc. are comparable, then Company X would prefer Company Y, because, for every rupee that it spends on the acquisition, it will gain sales of ₹ 25. Comparatively, it will gain only ₹ 20 of incremental sales for every rupee it invests in acquiring Company Z.

4.3.7 Others

The above are the commonly used tools. But analysts tend to use several additional creative tools. For instance:

- During the height of the dotcom boom, companies were enamoured with market capitalization to eye-balls comparison.
- Lately, e-commerce companies have started harping on Gross Merchandise Value (GMV). If goods worth ₹ 100 are sold for ₹ 30, the company has a turnover of only ₹ 30, and the transaction would have led to a loss of ₹ 70. GMV of ₹ 100 looks so appealing to a company that needs to sell its shares to fund more losses arising out of need to meet GMV growth targets.
- Retailers are valued based on stock keeping units (SKU).

- Billing rates and mix of offshore and onsite revenues are relevant for software development companies.
- Telecom service operators swear by Average Revenue per User (ARPU).
- Value of land bank is considered in real estate companies.

Alert to all shenanigans, Graham actually observed: "Given the three ingredients of:

(a) optimistic assumptions as to the rate of earnings growth,
(b) a sufficiently long projection of this growth into the future, and
(c) the miraculous workings of compound interest.

lo! the security analyst is supplied with a new kind of philosopher's stone which can produce or justify any desired valuation for a really 'good stock' . . . I have never seen dependable calculations made about common-stock values, or related investment policies, that went beyond simple arithmetic or the most elementary algebra. Whenever calculus is brought in, or higher algebra, you could take it as a warning signal that the operator was trying to substitute theory for experience, and usually also to give to speculation the deceptive guise of investment."[28]

Even Graham did not anticipate an era when companies would go beyond earnings to eye-balls and GMV to justify valuations!

4.4 Valuation of Equity Securities in Mutual Fund Schemes

Shares held in the portfolio of any mutual fund scheme need to be assigned a value, in order to determine the NAV of the scheme. The valuation is based on the following principles.

4.4.1 Traded Equity Securities / Equity Related Securities

To start with, the mutual fund determines a stock exchange that would be the "principal" stock exchange for valuation of each such security. The principal stock exchange can even be determined as a policy such as "exchange where the trading volume is maximum on that day"; or "NSE preferred, else BSE". Once a stock exchange has been selected for a security, it can be changed only with a valid justification and with the approval of the trustees.

So long as the security is traded in the principal stock exchange on the valuation date, the closing price in that exchange on that date will be used for valuation.

If a security is not traded in the principal stock exchange on the valuation date, then the closing price in any other stock exchange in the country where it is traded on that date would be used for valuation.

If the security is not traded in any stock exchange on the valuation date, then the last traded price in any stock exchange in the country would be used for valuation, so long as the trade is on a date not more than thirty days prior to the valuation date.

If there is no trade in any exchange during the thirty days period prior to the date of valuation, it will be valued as a non-traded security (valuation norms explained in the next section).

4.4.2 Thinly Traded Equity / Equity Related Securities

An equity share, convertible debenture, equity warrant, etc. is considered as thinly traded if it trades less than ₹ 5 lakh in value and 50,000 shares in volume, during the preceding calendar month. For this purpose, trading in all recognized stock exchanges in India is considered.

Formula for valuation in "good faith" of non-traded / thinly traded equity securities is as follows:

- The above approach is equally applicable to unlisted equity shares. The adjustment for illiquidity would however be 15% (instead of 10% given above). Thus, if the above example related to an unlisted equity share, it would be valued at ₹ 17 less 15%, i.e. at ₹ 14.45 per share.
- Unless the accounting year is changed, the shares shall be valued at zero if audited balance sheet is not available within nine months from close of the year.
- If an individual security accounts for more than 5 per cent of the total assets of the scheme, an independent valuer has to be appointed for valuing the security.

Table 4.1

	Say,
Calculate the net worth per share based on latest audited balance sheet. If the net worth is lower after considering outstanding warrants / options, then the lower number would need to be considered.	₹ 16
Calculate the earnings per share (EPS) based on latest audited balance sheet.	₹ 3
Determine the average capitalization rate (Price-Earnings Ratio) for the industry based on BSE or NSE data (to be consistently followed). Discount this capitalization rate by 75 per cent, i.e. use only 25 per cent of the capitalization rate for further calculations.	24 times less 75% = 6 times
Determine the capital earning value per share, viz. EPS multiplied by the reduced capitalization rate. If EPS is negative, capital earning value is to be taken as zero.	₹ 3 ×6 times = ₹ 18
Calculate the average of net worth per share (₹ 16) and capital earning value per share (₹ 18).	₹ 17
Reduce this average by 10 per cent for illiquidity. The resultant number is to be treated as the price for valuation purposes (fair value).	₹ 17 less 10% = ₹ 15.30

4.5 Equity Investment Restrictions for Mutual Funds

- Illiquid securities: These include non-traded, thinly traded and unlisted equity shares. Value of such securities is treated as zero if it exceeds:
  - 15 per cent of total assets for open-end schemes; and
  - 20 per cent of total assets for closed-end schemes.
- Investment in equity shares or equity related instruments of a single company is restricted to 10 per cent of net assets of the scheme. Exceptions are:
  - Index funds, where the proportion would need to reflect the stock's weight in the index.
  - Sector funds, where a higher proportion in an individual stock may become necessary if it plays a larger role in the sector.
  - The percentage is applicable at the time of investment. Post-investment, if the proportion of a stock's value in the net assets of a scheme goes up on account of changes in share prices in the stock exchange, then the fund manager is not forced to sell.

    (This is a debatable approach. Exposure to an individual stock should be controlled at all times — not only when the investment is made.)
- Investment in unlisted shares by closed-end schemes is subject to a cap of 10 per cent of net assets of the scheme. Such investment may be in a single company, or distributed over several such companies. The cap is 5 per cent for open-end schemes.
- All the schemes of a mutual fund put together cannot hold more than 10 per cent of a company's paid up capital carrying voting rights.

  For instance, if Company W has issued 10 crore equity shares, no AMC (all its schemes put together) can own more than 1 crore shares of Company W.
- Inter-scheme investments within the same mutual fund as well as schemes of other mutual funds may be made subject to management fee not being charged on such investment. There is a limit of 5 per cent of net assets of the mutual fund, for inter-scheme investments.

  For instance, if the net assets of a mutual fund (all schemes put together) is ₹ 1,500 crore, then more than ₹ 75 crore cannot be invested in other schemes. Management fee cannot be charged on such amount invested in other schemes.

  Fund of Funds schemes are an obvious exception of this 5 per cent rule.
- Investment and disinvestment have to be directly in the name of concerned scheme, not in a general account to be distributed across schemes later. So, the broker's contract note would mention the name of the scheme for which the purchase or sale has been made. This is a useful investor-friendly stipulation, which ensures that the AMC cannot manipulate NAVs by buying a block of shares early in the day, and allocating it to schemes later in the day depending on how the market has moved.

- Mutual funds are not permitted to use their money for carry forward transactions. However, they can enter into derivative transactions in a recognised stock exchange.
- Long-term investments would have to be purchased and transferred in the name of the mutual fund for the relevant scheme.
- Lending of securities in accordance with SEBI's Stock Lending Scheme is permitted.
- Investment in unlisted securities or securities issued through private placement by an associate or group company of the sponsor is not permitted.
- Mutual funds cannot invest in unlisted shares at a price higher than that obtained by the method mentioned earlier for valuation of unlisted equity shares. This restriction is, however, not applicable for investment made in the initial public offers (IPOs) of companies or firm allotment in public issues where all the regulatory requirements and formalities pertaining to public issues have been complied with by the companies and where the mutual funds are required to pay just before the date of public issue.
- Investment in listed securities of group companies of the sponsor is subject to a cap of 25 per cent of net assets of any of the schemes.
- Inter-scheme transfers would need to be at market value.
- A specific disclosure is to be made about investment by all schemes of the mutual fund, in companies or their associates, which constitute more than 5 per cent of NAV of any scheme of the mutual fund.
- Restrictions on international investments by Indian mutual fund schemes:

  For the Indian mutual fund industry as a whole, there is a cap of USD 7 bn on overseas investments. The foreign investment limit for each mutual fund is USD 300 mn.

With a view to protect domestic investors, SEBI has specified the kinds of international investments that Indian mutual fund schemes can take exposure to:

- American Depository Receipts (ADRs) and/or Global Depository Receipts (GDRs) issued by Indian or foreign companies.
- Equity of overseas companies listed on recognized stock exchanges overseas.
- Initial and follow on public offerings for listing at recognized stock exchanges overseas.
- Foreign debt securities in the countries with fully convertible currencies, short term as well as long term debt instruments with rating not below investment grade by accredited/ registered credit rating agencies.
- Money market instruments rated not below investment grade.
- Repos in form of investment, where the counter party is rated not below investment grade; repo shall not however involve any borrowing of funds by the mutual funds concerned.

- Government securities where the countries are rated not below investment grade.
- Derivatives traded on recognized stock exchanges overseas only for hedging and portfolio balancing with underlying as securities.
- Short term deposits with banks overseas where the issuer is rated not below investment grade.
- Units / securities issued by overseas mutual funds or unit trusts registered with overseas regulators and investing in:
  - The above securities; or
  - Real estate investment trusts (REITs) listed on recognized stock exchanges overseas; or
  - Unlisted overseas securities, not exceeding 10% of their net assets.

  The mutual fund needs to appoint a Dedicated Fund Manager for overseas investments (not required if international investment is only in units / mutual funds / unit trusts).

The mutual fund industry as a whole is also permitted to invest up to USD 1 bn in overseas ETFs that invest in securities. There is also a sub-limit of USD 50 mn for any single mutual fund.

4.6 Management of Equity Portfolio

4.6.1 Investment Styles

Depending on the approach to investment, the fund management could be either passive — as in the case of index funds — or active. “Buy and hold” is passive in terms of activity, but can be very dangerous in terms of implications.

The fund management could be value oriented (investing primarily in value stocks), growth oriented (investing primarily in growth stocks), or momentum oriented (investing primarily in momentum stocks).

4.6.2 Fundamental and Technical Analysis

Investment and dis-investment decisions are broadly taken based on either of the following two approaches.

Fundamental Analysis

Fundamental analysis is a study of the industry scenario, company’s financials, management, etc. collectively known as a company’s fundamentals, to determine whether the company’s stock is properly valued. If the view is that it is undervalued, then the portfolio manager may choose to buy the security. If it is overvalued, the decision would be to sell the existing stock. Analysis of Price-Earnings Ratio, Price to Book Value Ratio etc. are all examples of fundamental analysis.

Technical Analysis

Technical analysis is a review of the movements of the stock price in the market. A technical analyst would compare these movements with past volume and price trends of the stock, as well as with the market movements, to form a view on whether the market or an individual stock is over-bought or over-sold, whether a stock is near a support level or resistance level and accordingly choose to buy or sell the stock/s.

A parallel can be drawn with the assessment of the two teams' prospects in a limited over cricket match. Like the ratios in the financial world, the channels provide various averages and strike rates. Someone who views the prospects by considering the inherent strength of the batsmen who are not out, and the bowlers who have not completed their quota of overs is taking a fundamental view; someone who merely looks at the required runs per over and past trends in the same is taking a technical view.

In Benjamin Graham's words, "The one principle that applies to nearly all these so-called 'technical approaches' is that one should buy because a stock or the market has gone up, and one should sell because it has declined. This is the exact opposite of sound business sense everywhere else, and it is most unlikely that it can lead to lasting success on Wall Street. . . ."[29]

"Classic studies have shown that someone who tries to time the market and move in and out of it quickly to exploit its gyrations has to be right 70% of the time to profit. Do you know anybody who can perform that well consistently? Even the best hitters in baseball — say, Rod Carew, George Brett, and even Ted Williams — bat at most 400 (the equivalent of 'being right' only 40% of the time)."[30]

While the data for a fundamental analysis comes sporadically, for instance when the financial results are announced or an earnings warning is issued, data for technical analysis gets added with every day of trading.

Generally, fundamental analysis is seen to help decide on the action to take, namely whether to buy or sell a particular share. Having decided to take an action, when to implement the decision — the timing — could be determined by technical analysis.

Another perspective is that fundamental analysis is useful for long term investments — investments made with the view that the share prices will increase manyfold; technical analysis is the main tool of day traders, who get in and out of stocks several times during the day to exploit small movements in the share price.

4.6.3 Quantitative Analysis

Some investors work with investment models which are based on quantitative evaluation of risk, return and other features of securities. In such cases, the investment model decides what securities would be retained in the portfolio in what proportion.

For instance, a model might go as follows:

- The universe of companies considered for investment would be those that have market capitalisation above ₹ 1,000 crore.
- Among these, shares with P/E ratio of less than 15 and dividend yield of above 3% will be selected.
- The portfolio will have stocks of the selected companies in the ratio of their market capitalisation.
- The portfolio will be re-balanced on the 7th of every month, based on information as at the end of the previous month.

This kind of an approach is thus a cross between active and passive management. Unlike passive management, the investment is not based on blindly following an index. However, unlike active management, the fund manager does not have discretion in stock selection. The stocks are self-selected based on the investment model promised.

A lot of these quantitative models look sexy on paper. But as they are based on historical data, there is no guarantee that a similar pattern will be repeated in future.

4.6.4 Margin of Safety

"There is no reliable tool to pinpoint the value of a business. So intelligent investors must observe Benjamin Graham's and Warren Buffett's cardinal rule of prudent investing: getting a margin of safety between the price you pay and the value you are paying for." (Lawrence Cunningham)[31]

Based on fundamental analysis, if the analyst is of the view that a stock is worth ₹ 200, buying it at ₹ 150 would imply a margin of safety of (₹ 200 – ₹ 150) ÷ ₹ 200, i.e. 25%. This means that the analyst can be wrong in his estimate to the extent of 25% and still not lose money.

"Your best approach remains artistic judgment rather than scientific precision. Phil Carret made it one of his investing commandments to 'ignore mechanical formulas for valuing securities' . . . Graham thought you should give yourself a break by making sure the price you pay is way lower than the low end of your valuation estimate . . . Indeed, Graham repudiated a strategy that overemphasizes what the fashion plates of finance call 'growth stocks'. If you can get the same margin of safety by carefully estimating the future of growth stocks, more power to you, but the danger is that growth stocks tend to be favourites and favouritism in stocks is measured by high prices that steal safety margins." (Lawrence Cunningham)[32]

4.7 Types of Debt

Unlike equity, debt instruments have a fixed maturity. During the tenor of the instrument, the investor is entitled to interest, also referred to as "coupon" in financial terminology. The interest may be structured in either of the following formats:

- Fixed rate, where the issuer pays a fixed rate of interest irrespective of the interest rates prevailing in the market from time to time; or
- Floating rate, where the issuer pays interest at a rate that varies with interest rates prevailing in the market at the time of payment. When the instrument is issued, the issuer specifies a *base* on which interest would be calculated periodically, for instance, the bank fixed deposit rate; and the *spread* that would be paid over the base rate.

Thus, if a company proposes to pay 364-day Treasury bill rate plus 3 per cent, then:

- Base is the return that is available on 364-day Treasury bills, and
- Spread is 3 per cent.

The offer document for the issue would also explain the mechanics of how the base would be applied. For instance, would the base be the latest 364-day Treasury bill rate, or average of rates in previous five auctions, or any other method.

The Indian debt market offers the following investment options:

4.7.1 Central Government Securities and Treasury Bills

Rupee-denominated debt securities issued by the central government have the highest safety because there is no risk of default. If pushed to the wall, the government can print currency notes to meet its obligations. Local currency issues of the central government are, therefore, referred to as "sovereign borrowings". These are the most liquid securities of the debt market.

Treasury bills (T-Bills) are short term debt securities (up to 364-days maturity) issued by the Reserve Bank of India to meet the short term borrowing requirements of the government.

4.7.2 State Government Securities

Unlike the central government, the state government has no right to print currency notes. Therefore, technically state government can default. In reality, this does not happen, because the central government can ensure redemption of securities and adjust any financial support against the plan allocation for the concerned state government.

Over the years, many state governments have guaranteed borrowings by companies promoted by them, without giving a thought to either the viability of the borrower or the ability of the government to honour its guarantees, should such a situation arise. Therefore, the Ministry of Finance has stipulated that borrowing by special purpose vehicles (SPVs) promoted by state governments would be subject to approval of the central government.

The yield on state government securities is generally higher than what is available on central government securities. They are also less liquid.

4.7.3 Public Sector Bonds

In order to ensure that capital investment by public sector undertakings does not become a drag on the resources of the national economy, such undertakings have been given the liberty to borrow from the market. These borrowings are in the form of taxable bonds or tax-free bonds.

4.7.4 Bonds Issued by Domestic Financial Institutions

The borrowing of financial institutions is normally in the form of unsecured "bonds in the nature of promissory notes".

4.7.5 Corporate Debentures

Private corporate issuers use the bond market as a means of directly tapping investors for resources, instead of going through banks and financial institutions. The objective is to lower cost of funds in the short term, and to build brand equity in the market in the long term. This strategy, called disintermediation, is a realistic possibility for large and financially strong companies.

4.7.6 Commercial Paper

These are issued by companies to finance their short-term working capital needs. The tenor generally varies from 30 days to 6 months.

4.7.7 Certificate of Deposit

These are issued by banks and financial institutions. Banks issue CDs for a maximum of 1 year, while financial institutions issue CDs for a minimum of 1 year and maximum 3 years.

4.7.8 Repo / Reverse Repo

Repos (and reverse repos) are transactions where a party sells (or buys) a security in spot and buys (or sells) the same security on a forward basis. The difference between spot and forward rates would effectively be the interest cost (or income) on the repo (or reverse repo). Such transactions were earlier referred to as "ready forwards".

Technically, a repo transaction can be done using any security as the basis. Since the lender in a repo transaction is lending against the security, an element of comfort on the security is essential. Therefore, repos are done against debt securities.

Repos are of two types — with RBI and inter-bank. The transactions with RBI affect the liquidity in the economy. Through a repo, liquidity is injected into the economy; a reverse repo sucks out liquidity from the market. Inter-bank repos however do not affect the overall liquidity in the economy.

In the inter-bank market, banks and primary dealers (PDs) can do repo and reverse repo transactions in a range of debt securities, including central government dated securities, state government securities, treasury bills, bonds of financial institutions or public sector undertakings, corporate bonds and private debt securities. These securities need to be in demat form, and the transactions need to be executed in a recognised stock exchange.

Non-bank entities holding Subsidiary General Ledger (SGL) account with RBI can enter into reverse repo transactions in all government securities with banks and PDs (i.e., non-bank entities can lend money to banks and PDs).

4.7.9 Collateralised Borrowing and Lending Obligation (CBLO)

CBLO was conceptualised by Clearing Corporation of India Limited (CCIL) to assist non-bank parties who were phased out of the call money market. It is an RBI approved money market instrument, issued for a maximum tenor of 1 year. The generally traded maturities are for the next 7 business days and three month-end dates. The instrument is backed by gilts as collateral. Trades are guaranteed by CCIL.

4.7.10 Floating Rate Notes

These are bonds / debentures that entitle the holder to a floating rate of interest. They can be issued by government or any other borrower.

4.7.11 Zero Coupon / Deep Discount Instruments

These do not entail any regular interest payment; instead the difference between the redemption value and the investment amount represents interest income for the investor. When the instruments are for very long tenors (e.g., 15 years), these are called deep discount instruments.

4.7.12 Kisan Vikas Patra

This is a popular instrument where the value of the investment doubles in 9 years and 8 months. The return of 7.3% is taxable.

4.7.13 National Savings Certificate (VIII & IX Issue)

This 5-year instrument (NSC VIII issue) earns 7.6% p.a. compounded annually. Thus, ₹ 100 would become ₹ 144.23 on maturity.

The interest is compulsorily re-invested, but is taxable. However, tax is not deducted at source. Initial investment, as well as interest re-invested is entitled to benefits of Section 80C of the Income Tax Act (discussed in Chapter 17).

4.7.14 Post Office Deposits

These can be savings or time or recurring deposits.

Post office savings account yield interest of 4% p.a.

Post Office Monthly Income Scheme is a popular investment option that offers an attractive return (7.3 per cent per annum, payable monthly). However, investment cannot exceed ₹ 4.5 lakh for a single account, or ₹ 9 lakh for joint account. Maturity period is 5 years.

Post Office Time Deposits offer 6.6% (for 1 year) to 7.4% p.a, (for 5 years). The interest is compounded quarterly, but paid annually. The investment in 5-year Time Deposit qualifies for Section 80C Income Tax benefit.

4.7.15 Senior Citizens Savings Scheme

This option of saving with a post office is available for depositors who are above 60 — or are above 55 and retired under a VRS or special voluntary retirement scheme. Minimum age is 50 years for defence personnel. Only one deposit is permitted, not exceeding ₹ 15 lakh. The investment qualifies for Section 80C Income Tax benefit. The deposit earns 8.3% interest per annum, payable quarterly, for a period of 5 years. The tenor can be extended by 3 years on maturity. Tax is deducted at source if the amount is more than ₹ 10,000. There is a provision for premature withdrawal (at a cost) after the end of one year. The prepayment charge is 1.5% of deposit up to 2 years, and 1% beyond 2 years.

4.7.16 GOI 7.75% Savings Bonds

The interest rate is 7.75 per cent p.a., payable semi-annually, for 7 years. The interest is subject to Tax Deducted at Source (TDS). However, it is exempt from wealth tax. There is no maximum limit to the investment.

4.7.17 Public Provident Fund (PPF)

These are offered by State Bank of India, Nationalised Banks and Post Offices. Currently, interest rate is 7.6% p.a., tax-free. Deposits are entitled to deduction under Section 80C. Annual limit for investment are minimum ₹ 500, and maximum ₹ 150,000.

4.7.18 Sukanya Samriddhi Account Scheme

Under this scheme, account can be opened in the name of a girl child up to 10 years of age, in a bank or post office. A guardian can open only one account in the name of one girl child and maximum two accounts in the name of two different girl children. Deposits are entitled to deduction under Section 80C. Deposits can be made until she completes 14 years of age. On attaining the age of 10 years, she herself can operate the account. The account can be closed when she completes 21 years of age. However, after she attains the age of 18 years, 50% of the fund can be withdrawn for her higher education and marriage. Interest rate is currently 8.1% p.a., tax-free. Annual limits for investment are minimum ₹ 1,000, and maximum ₹ 150,000.

4.7.19 Section 80C Fixed Deposits

Banks offer these fixed deposits for minimum 5 years duration, with no option for early redemption. Interest, which depends on market situation, is subject to TDS.

4.7.20 Money Market Securities

This category includes all debt securities that mature within a year. T-Bills and commercial paper are examples of money market securities. Even certificates of deposits, debentures, etc., which are due to mature within a year, are treated as money market securities.

As Bogle says, "Bonds are best used as a source of regular income and as a moderating influence on a stock portfolio, not as an alternative to stocks. Remember, the goal of the long-term investor is not to preserve capital in the short run, but to earn real, inflation-adjusted, long-term returns."[33]

Mutual funds are not permitted to invest in the investments mentioned in 4.7.12 to 4.7.19. These are meant for investors who are individuals. NRIs are not permitted to invest in some of these investments. Retail money in debt is largely invested in these investments, although individuals are permitted to invest in the other debt investment types,

4.8 Risks in Debt Investing

A number of risks are inherent to the debt market and these are described below:

4.8.1 Interest Risk (Price Risk)

This is the risk that the value of a debt security changes when interest rates in the market change.

Suppose a company has issued ₹ 100 face value debt securities of one-year tenor offering coupon (interest) of 12% on 1 January 2001. On 3 January 2001, when the interest rates in the market rise by a percentage, the same company decides to issue securities of the same tenor at 13% coupon.

In the above example, will an investor in the security issued on 1 January, be able to sell her security at ₹ 100? The answer is no.

- In layman's terms, the earlier instrument has become inferior, and therefore deserves to lose value.
- In quantitative terms, people would rather invest the same ₹ 100 in the new security that would give them 13%. The investor who has invested in the 12% security will be able to sell her holding only if she can give a buyer a return of

13%. This can happen only if the 12% security is sold at a price which is lower than its face value, in which case the original investor books a loss.

Therefore, there is an inverse relationship between interest rates and market value of debt securities:

- When interest rates go up, debt securities that promise a fixed interest become relatively inferior, and therefore lose value.
- When interest rates go down, fixed coupon debt securities gain in value.

The extent to which a security changes value when interest rates change in the market is influenced by its modified duration. Modified Duration is not the same as "original tenor" (maturity when the instrument was issued — 1 year, in the above example) or "term to maturity" (revised maturity after some time has elapsed since issue of the instrument — 2 days less than 1 year, in the above example). It is a calculated number that will be lesser than or equal to term to maturity. The concept of modified duration, and its difference from Macaulay duration, which was introduced in Chapter 2, is explained in detail in Chapter 10.

The coupon that investors receive on floating rate instruments keeps changing in line with changes in the market. This ensures that they do not become relatively inferior or superior in the market. Since the return on the instrument adjusts to the market, there is no reason for such instruments to gain or lose value when interest rates change.

But even floating rate instruments can change in value if the base used by the instrument is not fully representative of changes in the market place. Similarly, there could be demand and supply factors arising out of interest rate views in the market.

4.8.2 Credit Risk

This is the risk that the issuer of the security (the borrower) is not able to repay the amount borrowed when the securities mature.

Credit rating agencies assign ratings to securities that reflect the risk of such default. Other things being similar, a lower rated borrower would need to offer higher coupon rates to borrow. Arising out of this is a "credit rating risk".

What happens if a "AAA" rated security is downgraded to "A"? Investors will now expect a higher return from the security, in line with the higher risk of default. Since the security would already have been issued with a certain coupon, the higher return expectations out of the security can be met only if the price of the security is lowered.

Thus, if credit rating of a borrower is downgraded, then the securities issued by the borrower lose value. If, however, the borrower is upgraded, then the securities gain value.

When the government of a country issues debt securities in its local currency, then it cannot default. In the worst-case scenario, as seen earlier, it can print currency notes to redeem the securities. Therefore, there is no credit risk when the government of a country borrows in its local currency (sovereign borrowings). However, there would be a credit risk if the government borrows in a currency other than its local currency.

Since credit risk is zero, sovereign securities offer the lowest returns in the market. The rate at which the government can borrow for various tenors is called "sovereign yield" and is typically depicted in the form of a "sovereign yield curve". Similarly, "AAA" yield curve can be built, which would be higher than the sovereign yield curve for all maturities. "Term structure of interest rates" assesses the borrowing cost of the government for different tenors, using yield on zero coupon securities as the basis.

In 2011, Standard & Poors (S&P) reduced the credit rating of the US from AAA to AA+. This is indicative of a view that even the government can default in its local currency borrowing. It cannot print currency notes indiscriminately, because of the hyper-inflation it can trigger. As explained by S&P, the US downgrade reflected the political reality of the ruling Democtrats and opposition Republicans being unable to work cohesively towards addressing the economic problems of the country.

4.8.3 Re-investment Risk

An investor has invested ₹ 5,000 in a 2-year security that gives 10% interest every year.

At the end of the first year, she would earn ₹ 500 as interest, which, if she deposits in a bank at 10%, would yield ₹ 50 at the end of the second year. This would be in addition to the interest for the second year at 10 per cent on ₹ 5,000, which would be paid by the issuer.

During the second year, the ₹ 500 received as interest from the issuer, together with the ₹ 50 received as interest from the bank on the first year's interest, would mean a return of ₹ 550 on a base of ₹ 5,500, which represents investment plus first year interest — an effective return of 10%.

Thus, at the end of the 2nd year, the investor would be left with ₹ 6,050 as follows:

Table 4.2

	₹
Principal redemption	5,000
Interest for 2nd year on original investment	500
Deposited in the bank in 1st year from interest earned	500
Bank interest on 1st year interest	50
Terminal Value	6,050

Obviously, the terminal value of ₹ 6,050 is subject to her being able to invest the first year's interest at 10%. If she is able to earn an interest of only 8% on the first year interest of ₹ 500, then she will be left with only ₹ 6,040, thus giving an overall return which is lower than 10%. However, if the first year interest of ₹ 500 earns an interest of 12% in the bank, then the closing value of ₹ 6,060 ensures an overall return higher than 10%.

Re-investment risk is the risk arising out of not knowing the interest rate at which moneys received during the tenor of a security can be re-invested. Depending on market conditions at the time of each such re-investment, the effective return on a security can either be lower or higher than what was envisaged when the investment was first made.

Zero coupon securities do not entail any cash flows during the tenor of the security. A typical structure, for instance, would be to invest ₹ 5,000 upfront and get back ₹ 6,050 at the end of 2 years. When there is no cash to re-invest during the two-year period, there is no re-investment risk.

4.8.4 "Call" Risk

"Call" option is an option that the issuer of a security retains to prematurely repay the investor. "Put" option, on the other hand, is an option that the investor in a security has to demand premature repayment from the issuer. Such options, if applicable, are announced at the time of the security's issue.

Suppose an investor has invested in a 12% fixed rate instrument of 5 years, having a call option at the end of 3 years. In such a case, the investor cannot be sure that she will earn the same return of 12% for the entire 5-year period.

If at the end of 3 years, the issuer finds that the instrument can be substituted with a lower interest rate borrowing, then the company may exercise the call option. At the end of 3 years then, the investor will get back her money, which would be subject to a re-investment risk — the possibility of having to re-invest it for the remaining 2 years at a rate lower than 12 per cent.

Thus, debt investors also need to provide for a call risk, which is likely to materialize if interest rates in the market go down.

The reverse of this is the put risk that issuers face. The risk would materialize if interest rates in the market rise, because investors would then prefer to exercise their "put" option and re-invest the proceeds at the then prevailing higher rates.

4.8.5 Foreign Currency Risk

The moneys that would be recovered in local currency from an investment that is denominated in foreign currency would be subject to exchange rates, which change continuously. This was discussed in Chapter 2. If the foreign currency appreciates in value in relation to the local currency, then the investor's redemption proceeds from the international investment would be higher in local currency terms.

Suppose an investor invests in a bond of face value $100, at a time when each US dollar is worth ₹ 40. The investor would then pay ₹ 4,000 for the bond. On maturity, if the US dollar is worth ₹ 50, the redemption proceeds would amount to ₹ 5,000 — a gain of ₹ 1,000 on account of exchange rate — which would be in addition to the interest that the investor earns on the bond.

4.8.6 Inflation Risk

"Americans are getting stronger. Twenty years ago, it took two people to carry ten dollars' worth of groceries. Today, a five-year old can do it: Henry Youngman."[34]

Jokes apart, inflation is a serious risk for the debt investor. If the inflation rate turns out to be higher than the return earned on the debt investment, then in real terms, the investor would lose money.

Equities, on the other hand, are considered a hedge against inflation. While selling prices of companies' products rise with inflation, costs do not increase proportionately. Thus profits increase, and equity share prices go up in moderately inflationary situations. If inflation is severe, then consumers may reduce the consumption. Thus companies' profits may not increase and equity may not protect against the high inflation.

4.9 Yield to Maturity and Price

Transactions in the debt market are effected on the basis of return / yield expectations.

4.9.1 The Mathematics

Suppose an investor expects a return of 10% from an instrument that is to mature to ₹ 1,100 in one year. How much should she pay for such a security today?

If she invests ₹ 1,000 today, and recovers ₹ 1,100 at the end of one year, then she would effectively have a return of 10%.

A simple formula for determining price (P) in such an instrument yielding a single cash flow at the end of 1 year is:

$P = A \div (1 + r)$,

where "P" is the price, "A" is the amount at the end of 1 year and "r" is the expected return.

Thus, P would be:

₹ 1,100 ÷ (1 + 10%)
= ₹ 1,100 ÷ (1 + 0.1)
= ₹ 1,000.

If the same instrument were to mature at ₹ 1,210 at the end of the 2nd year, then its value at the end of the 1st year would be:

₹ 1,210 ÷ (1 + 10%), i.e. ₹ 1,210 ÷ (1 + 0.1) = ₹ 1,100.

From this, we can determine the value of the instrument today as:

₹ 1,100 ÷ (1 + 10%), i.e. ₹ 1,100 ÷ (1 + 0.1) = ₹ 1,000.

Therefore, today's price (P) for any instrument having a single cash flow at the end of any period (n), and where the investor has an expected return (r), can be calculated as:

$P = A \div (1 + r)^n$

In the above 2-year situation, the price today would be:

$P =$ ₹ 1,210 $\div (1 + 0.1)^2$, i.e. ₹ 1,210 ÷ 1.21 = ₹ 1,000.

If an instrument entails multiple cash flows at different points of time, then it can be viewed as multiple securities, each with a single cash flow.

"Today's price" would need to be worked out for each cash flow. The total of "today's price" for each such cash flow would be "today's price" for the security. Thus, given the amount and expected return over a specified time frame, the price of any debt security can be worked out.

Given a price (P) and the amount (A) to which it will grow over a certain number of years (n), the effective return (r) can be worked out using the formula:

$r = (A \div P)^{(1/n)} - 1$

In the above example,

$$\begin{aligned} r &= (1,210 \div 1,000)^{(1/2)} - 1 \\ &= 1.21^{1/2} - 1 \\ &= 1.1 - 1 \\ &= 0.1 \\ &= 10\%. \end{aligned}$$

4.9.2 The Financial Terminology

In the above example, when we said that ₹ 1,000 today is worth ₹ 1,210 in 2 years at 10 per cent, we were effectively adding compound interest to the principal (price or present value) to determine amount (future value). The process of determining a future value from a present value is called "compounding".

The reverse of compounding is "discounting", where the present value of a security is determined from its future value. In financial terminology, we determine price (present value) by calculating the present value of future cash flows, discounted at the yield rate. Thus, ₹ 1,210 two years down the line, discounted at 10 per cent, gives the present value of ₹ 1,000.

Given a present value (price or principal), a future value (amount) and time (the period between the two points of time), it would be possible to determine the yield rate, which when applied to the present value would give us the future value. For instance, 10 per cent, when applied to ₹ 1,000, gives ₹ 1,210 in 2 years

This yield, in financial terminology, is the "internal rate of return" (IRR). If the future cash flows are considered up to maturity, then the calculated yield is called "yield to maturity" (YTM). If the future cash flows are considered only up to the date of any call or put option, then the calculated yield is called "yield to call" (YTC) or "yield to put" (YTP) respectively.

4.9.3 Using MS Excel Spreadsheet

4.9.3.1 Price

It is much easier to determine the price and yield using any of the spreadsheet packages.

To determine price, put down the cash flows on the instrument at various points of time in future and apply the "=present value" function using the yield as the IRR value.

The "=present value" function will give valid results only if the periodicity of future cash flows is constant, say, every 6 months, or every year, or every quarter. If the periodicity of cash flows is not constant, then formulas would need to be fed in to calculate the present value of each future cash flow separately. Thereafter, these present values would need to be totalled to arrive at the price that will give the required yield, given the future cash flows expected on the instrument.

The "=price" function is another useful function to determine the price of a debt security.

4.9.3.2 Yield

If you know the price (present value) and the future cash flows, then the "=IRR" function could be applied on the present and future cash flow stream.

The IRR function would give valid results only if the periodicity of future cash flows is constant. Where the periodicity is not constant, you will need to apply the "=XIRR" function to the same cash flows. Use of the XIRR function is illustrated in Chapter 9.

The "=yield" function is another useful function to determine the yield offered by a debt security.

4.10 Valuation of Debt Securities in Mutual Fund Schemes

4.10.1 Government Securities

Any government security is to be valued at the prevailing market price. Securities that are not traded on the valuation date need to be valued based on yield to maturity implicit in the prevailing market prices of similar securities, unless it has up to 60 days to maturity. For the sake of uniformity in NAV, mutual funds have been advised to use the yields for Government Securities released by an agency suggested by AMFI.

4.10.2 Money Market and Debt Securities with Residual Maturity of up to 60 Days

Such securities (including floating rate securities) are to be valued at the weighted average price at which they are traded on the particular valuation day. When such securities are not traded on a particular valuation day, they are to be valued on amortization basis, i.e. cost plus accrued interest till the beginning of the valuation day plus the difference between the redemption value and the cost, spread uniformly over the remaining maturity period.

Floating rate securities with floor and cap on coupon rate are to be valued taking the floor to be the coupon.

4.10.3 Money Market and Debt Securities with Residual Maturity of Over 60 Days

Such securities (including floating rate securities) are to be valued at the weighted average price at which they are traded on the particular valuation day.

If such securities are not traded on the valuation date, then valuation would be on the basis of yields and spreads for these securities released by an agency suggested by AMFI.

Provisioning for Non-performing Assets (Debt Securities)

- If the principal and / or interest on a security remains outstanding for more than one quarter from due date, it will be classified as non-performing asset (NPA). Thus, if due date was 31 December 2001, it will become NPA on 1 April 2002, if dues are not received by then.
- Interest will be accrued for one quarter after due date. Thus, in the above case, interest will be accrued until 31 March 2002.

  On 1 April 2002, when it is classified as NPA, provision will need to be made for interest accrued on 31 December 2001. Thereafter, no interest will be accrued.

  Provision will be made on 1 July 2002 for interest accrued on 31 March 2002.
- NPAs will have to be fully provided for before the closure of the scheme. Subject to this, provision will need to be made as per the following schedule, irrespective of whether the principal is due for repayment or not:

3 months from classification as NPA	10% of book value
6 months from classification as NPA	20% of book value
9 months from classification as NPA	20% of book value
12 months from classification as NPA	25% of book value
15 months from classification as NPA	25% of book value

If they so wish, mutual funds can choose to make faster provisions.

Provisioning for Deep Discount Bonds

Investment in deep discount bonds will be classified as NPAs if any two of the following conditions are satisfied:

- Rating of the bond comes down to grade "BB" or below;
- If the issuer is defaulting on other commitments; and
- Net worth of the issuer is fully eroded.

On classification as NPA, provisioning would need to be done as per the above schedule. The moment the rating of the bond comes down to D, full provisioning would be required.

Re-classification of NPAs (Debt Securities)

- Interest provision can be written back when all interest arrears are cleared.
- Thereafter, if the debt is regularly serviced for the next 2 quarters, then the asset can be re-classified as a performing asset.
- Provisions for principal can be written back as follows:
  - If the provision for principal was only on account of interest default, then the entire provision can be written back at the end of the 2nd quarter.
  - If the provision for principal was on account of default in interest and principal, then 50 per cent of the provision can be written back at the end of the 2nd quarter; and 25 per cent at the end of each subsequent quarter.
- The asset will be re-classified as "standard asset" when both overdue interest and overdue principal are paid in full and for the subsequent period of 6 months, it is serviced properly.

Valuation of Securities Not Covered in Current Valuation Policy

- In case securities purchased by mutual funds do not fall within the current framework of the valuation of securities then such mutual fund shall report immediately to AMFI regarding the same. Further, at the time of investment AMCs shall ensure that the total exposure in such securities does not exceed 5% of the total AUM of the scheme.
- AMFI has been advised that the valuation agencies should ensure that the valuation of such securities gets covered in the valuation framework within six weeks from the date of receipt of such intimation from mutual fund.
- In the interim period, till AMFI makes provisions to cover such securities in the valuation of securities framework, the mutual funds shall value such securities using their proprietary model which has been approved by their independent trustees and the statutory auditors.

4.11 Debt Investment Restrictions for Mutual Funds

- Investment cap of 10 per cent of net assets of scheme is applicable on debt instruments issued by a single issuer. This can be stretched to 12 per cent with prior approval of Boards of AMCs and Trustees.

  The per issuer investment restrictions are not applicable to money market and government securities issued by the central or state governments, or issued by RBI on their behalf. It is also not applicable for CBLO. The restrictions are however applicable to all debt securities which are issued by public bodies / institutions such as electricity boards, municipal corporations, state transport corporations, etc. guaranteed by either state or central government.
- Investment cap of 25 per cent of net assets of scheme is applicable on all unrated paper and paper below investment grade, subject to prior approval of Boards of AMCs and Trustees.
- Debt-oriented mutual fund schemes cannot invest more than 25 per cent of net assets in a single sector. An additional 5 per cent exposure is permitted for investment in housing finance companies (HFCs) in the financial sector. This relaxation is available only if the HFC is registered with National Housing Bank (NHB) and the security is rated AA or above. Further, the total investment in HFCs cannot go beyond 25 per cent of net assets.

  The sectoral limit is not applicable for investments in bank CDs, CBLO, government securities, T-Bills, short term deposits of scheduled commercial banks and AAA rated securities issued by public financial institutions and public sector banks.
- The total exposure of debt schemes to securities issued by a group (excluding PSUs, public financial institutions and public sector banks) cannot exceed 20 per cent of the net assets of the scheme. This can be extended to 25 per cent of net assets of the scheme with the prior approval of the Board of Trustees. "Group" includes include an entity, its subsidiaries, fellow subsidiaries, its holding company and its associates.
- Cash funds are to be held only in scheduled banks. The following guidelines are applicable for deployment of funds in short term deposits with the banks:
  - "Short term" for parking of funds by mutual funds shall be treated as a period not exceeding 91 days.
  - Such deposits shall be held in the name of the concerned scheme.
  - Mutual funds shall not park more than 15% of their net assets in short term deposits of all scheduled commercial banks put together. This limit however may be raised to 20% with prior approval of the trustees.
  - Also, parking of funds in short term deposits of associate and sponsor scheduled commercial banks together shall not exceed 20% of the total deployment by the mutual fund in short term deposits.

> - Mutual funds shall not park more than 10% of the net assets in short term deposits with any one scheduled commercial bank including its subsidiaries.
> - Trustees shall ensure that funds of a particular scheme are not parked in short term deposit of a bank which has invested in that scheme.
> - In case of liquid and debt oriented schemes, AMC(s) shall not charge any investment management and advisory fees for parking of funds in short term deposits of scheduled commercial banks.

- Liquid funds / plans are permitted to make investment in / purchase debt and money market securities with maturity of up to 91 days only.

> - In case the principal is to be repaid in more than one payout then the maturity of the securities shall be calculated on the basis of weighted average maturity of security.
> - In case of securities with put and call options (daily or otherwise) the residual maturity of the securities shall not be greater than 91 days.

- Mutual funds are not permitted to lend money (though they may invest in debt securities).
- Investment in unlisted securities or securities issued through private placement by an associate or group company of the sponsor is not permitted.
- Investment in listed securities of group companies of the sponsor is subject to a cap of 25 per cent of net assets of any of the schemes.
- Transactions in government securities would have to be settled in dematerialised form only.
- Inter-scheme transfers would need to be at market value.
- As seen earlier, a specific disclosure is to be made about investment in companies or their associates, which constitute more than 5 per cent of NAV of any scheme of a mutual fund. Cut-off for such disclosure is if the subsequent investment has been made within a band of + / – 1 year of the first investment.
- Restrictions on international investments by mutual funds were discussed earlier in this chapter.

4.12 Management of Debt Portfolio

As in the case of equity, the fund management could be either passive (index funds) or active. For equities, as seen earlier, "buy and hold" can be very dangerous. In debt, the same style is less dangerous, because, the investor will at least get her principal back when the instrument is redeemed — though in the interim valuation gains or losses may be seen. A "buy and hold" style becomes a problem if a debt investor does not read the signals that a company is heading towards bankruptcy. In the process, she can end up holding worthless paper, while losing out on the opportunity of realizing some value in the market earlier.

As far as positioning on the yield curve is considered, investment style could be:

- Bullet (aiming for a single point in the yield curve, say 5 years),
- Barbell (aiming for investments in two extreme maturities, say 1 year and 10 years), or
- Ladder (equal spreading of investments across maturities).

A debt portfolio manager has to balance the risks outlined earlier, namely interest (price) risk, credit risk, re-investment risk, inflation risk, foreign currency risk and call risk, and also ensure adequate liquidity for meeting re-purchase obligations. Some of the inherent dynamics that the debt portfolio manager balances are:

- Investment in sovereign securities would be the safest. But the interest income too is low.
- Sovereign securities represent the most liquid segment of the debt market. So it is easier to buy the securities required as well as sell one's investment holding.
- Since sovereign securities have a ready market, valuation at which sovereign securities are reflected in the schemes are representative of their value in the market. Higher the market fluctuations, more volatile would be the valuations in the schemes. On the other hand, if investments are in less liquid private corporate paper, the valuation guidelines give adequate flexibility to temper the volatility.

  The point to remember here is that in a fundamental sense, non-sovereign paper is not less volatile than sovereign paper. It is just that in the absence of a regular market benchmark, the inherent volatility of non-sovereign paper is not adequately captured in its valuation in the schemes. Ignorance (of value) is bliss.
- When the sovereign yield curve is upward sloping, interest income is higher if the investment is made in longer term paper. But then, longer tenor comes with longer modified duration. So if interest rates increase, then the longer term paper will also take a greater hit. Further, if the money is required earlier, and the security is not sufficiently liquid in the market, then there can be a problem in realising money.
- High coupon bonds offer attractive interest income. But then they also have the highest risk of early redemption if the issuer has a "call" option.
- Performance of the issuer as well as the industry to which the issuer belongs affects rating. Is there a likelihood of a change in credit rating of the issuer?
- If the investment is in a debt instrument that is denominated in foreign currency, then what is the view on exchange rates?
- How much money should be retained in low earning money market securities to provide for redemptions and expenses?

4.13 Types of Derivatives

Let us say you gave ₹ 20,000 to a friend who promised to give you an amount equivalent to 10 grams of gold, 1 year down the line. You will receive more value, if gold prices go up. Conversely, you will receive less value, if gold prices go down. You have effectively invested in a derivative whose value depends on the value of gold. In this case, the underlying for the derivative is gold.

Derivatives are instruments whose value is derived from the value of one or more underlying exposures. The underlying could be a stock, exchange rate, interest rate, commodity, precious metal, index, weather, etc. The commonly known derivatives are forwards, futures, options and swaps. Their product structures and implications are discussed in my *Wealth Engine* (Vision Books, 2012).

Fundamentally, derivatives are instruments for hedging exposures. People invest in mutual fund schemes to have an exposure. When they do not want the exposure, they get out of their investment in the scheme. What then is the role of a hedge in a mutual fund scheme?

Two counters to this line of thinking are:

- Most investors are not in a position to actively decide on their exposure to schemes. They would rather let the fund manager decide on the best possible exposure within the scheme on an ongoing basis. The fund manager, depending on the view on the markets as well as the arbitrage options, may choose to have a position in derivatives and / or underlying securities. The SEBI view is that fund managers have an onus to create their preferred positions in the most cost-effective manner, through use of cash markets, derivative markets or both. SEBI has also stipulated certain prudential limits on the derivative exposure that mutual fund schemes can take.
- Derivatives (and short selling, which is not permitted for mutual funds) provide an avenue for schemes to make money even when the market is moving sideways or falling. Without derivatives, returns from schemes are directly correlated to the direction of the markets where the scheme is invested.

The benefit of investing in a derivative, as distinct from investing in the underlying, is that the funds outlay in a derivative contract is lower. Typically, only a percentage is to be paid upfront in the shape of initial margin. If the investment is in an exchange-traded derivative, then depending on movement in prices, each day a variation margin would either be payable or receivable. Thus, for the same fund outlay, a much larger exposure is possible through a derivative contract.

4.14 Investment in Derivatives by Mutual Funds

Mutual funds are permitted to invest in financial derivatives, including interest rate derivatives traded on a stock exchange. Mutual funds are placed on par with registered foreign institutional investors (FIIs) for position limits in index futures, index options, stock options and stock futures contracts. Like the FIIs, mutual funds are treated as "trading members" in the exchange, while mutual fund schemes are treated as clients, as it happens with sub-accounts of FIIs.

Similarly, mutual fund schemes are permitted to undertake transactions in forward rate agreements and interest rate swaps (for hedging) with banks, primary dealers (PDs) and financial institutions (FIs) as per applicable RBI guidelines. Exposure to a single counterparty in such transactions should not exceed 10% of the net assets of the scheme.

Mutual funds can also trade in interest rate derivatives through the stock exchanges subject to requisite disclosures in the scheme information document.

Further, mutual funds can invest in derivatives traded on recognised stock exchanges overseas. Such investment in derivatives is permitted only for hedging and portfolio balancing with the underlying as securities.

SEBI has set the following limits to the exposure:

- The cumulative gross exposure through equity, debt and derivative positions should not exceed 100% of the net assets of the scheme.
- Mutual funds shall not write options or purchase instruments with embedded written options.
- The total exposure related to option premium paid must not exceed 20% of the net assets of the scheme.
- Cash or cash equivalents with residual maturity of less than 91 days may be treated as not creating any exposure.
- Exposure due to hedging positions may be excluded from the limits, subject to the following:
  - Hedging positions are the derivative positions that reduce possible losses on an existing position in securities. These are excluded from the limits till the existing position remains.
  - Hedging positions taken for existing derivative positions are not excluded from the limits.
  - Any derivative instrument used to hedge should have the same underlying security as the existing position being hedged.
  - The quantity of underlying associated with the derivative position taken for hedging purposes should not exceed the quantity of the existing position against which the hedge has been taken.
- The exposure in derivative transactions is calculated as follows:
  - Long Future — Futures Price x Lot Size x Number of Contracts.
  - Short Future — Futures Price x Lot Size x Number of Contracts.
  - Option Bought — Option Premium Paid x Lot Size x Number of Contracts.

The limits to derivative positions need to be set by the board of trustees (within the overall limits prescribed by SEBI).

For this, the Board needs to convince itself that the AMC has instituted adequate risk containment measures.

The following disclosure requirements have been prescribed:

- Each mutual fund has to disclose the limits in the offer documents / addendum of the respective schemes to the investors. The data of actual exposures need to be disclosed in the half yearly portfolio statements.
- When calculating the industry exposure for disclosure on monthly basis, the total exposure per scrip including derivatives exposure needs to be considered.
- Gap reporting / Calendar spread analysis of all derivative positions has to be reported internally on a weekly basis to a committee which should be appointed by the Board of Trustees

All the details have also to be reported to the Board of Trustees in the immediate next meeting after such positions are initiated.

SEBI regulations insist that the offer document of schemes should have a specific provision for such investment in derivatives. If not, the scheme would need to obtain positive consent from a majority of the unit holders. The communication with investors to seek approval would have to provide a one-month window for dissenting investors to exit from the scheme without any exit load.

As per SEBI guidelines, valuation of traded derivatives would be at the market price. Non-traded derivatives would be valued in accordance with the valuation method for non-traded investments.

4.15 Gold

Gold is the only tangible asset that has stood the test of time — 6,000 years of human history. In India, gold has sentimental value too. Marriages are incomplete without gold. The traditionally patriarchal society did not give daughters a share in the wealth left behind by the parents. Gold given away in marriage thus became a mechanism to transfer family wealth to daughters. It is not a wonder that India has a 15% share in the global gold market.[35]

Gold is often proposed as a hedge against inflation. At Advantage-India we evaluated the strength of gold as a hedge against inflation [as measured by Consumer Price Index (CPI) for Industrial Workers] over 45 years since 1970-71. We concluded that the utility of gold as a long-term inflation hedge is debatable. The reasons to hold gold in a portfolio are:

- It behaves differently from other asset classes.
- It is a less volatile asset class as compared to equity.
- It is a hedge against investment in financial markets.
- It offers short term upside in periods of stress in the financial markets.

Vast sections of India are untouched by the financial markets. But gold can be bought and sold, even in small quantities, anywhere in the country. Its power of liquidity too is an attraction in India. Further, unlike equity, gold investment does not call for detailed research. However, purity issues can be a huge hidden cost in physical gold investment.

In India, gold can be held in multiple forms:

- Physical gold — Coins and bars are preferable.
- ETF gold — Good vehicle for holding gold over a long period. Since transactions in the units happen in the stock exchange, investors need to have a demat account.
- Gold fund of funds — Investor invests in a gold fund of funds which, in turn, invests in ETF Gold. This obviates the need for investors to have a demat account. It also makes SIP facility possible.
- Electronic gold (E-Gold) — Gold in demat form is ideal for holding over long period.
- Gold futures — Good for speculating in gold. If margin is 4%, then on an investment of ₹ 1,000 in physical gold, the investor can have an exposure worth ₹ 1,000. Through futures, on the other hand, with the same investment an investor can have an exposure worth ₹ 1,000 ÷ 4%, i.e. ₹ 25,000.
- Gold investment in the form of jewellery is not advisable, because:
  - The process of jewellery making adds impurities to gold.
  - Jewellery is not liquid in the market.

The vast volume of privately held gold in India is a national resource. The country tried to bring this into the formal economy through gold bonds. But this has not succeeded, because of fears of attracting the unwelcome attention of the Income Tax authorities. The government A new gold monetisation scheme too has not met with much success.

Palladium, platinum, silver, radium, iridium, ruthenium, osmium, and rhenium are other precious metals that are traded globally. In recent years, silver has performed even better than gold. Investors have the option of holding silver in demat form (e-Silver). But gold's long record as a store of value is difficult to beat.

4.16 Real Estate

"Like shares, property or real estate, is an investment involving ownership (or equity). This is in contrast to debt-type securities which attract interest and which have contractual obligations for the capital to be repaid at some agreed date."[36]

"The return from property includes income in the form of rent, and capital gains from appreciation of the property over time. This potential for capital gains makes property, like shares, a growth asset. Internationally, investments in property may be made either directly, through the purchase of specific buildings or structures, or indirectly through the purchase of either listed or unlisted property trusts."[37]

Real estate, unlike financial markets, gold and various commodities, is not a standardized product. India has the additional problem of widely prevalent black money (parallel economy) in the industry. As such, no reliable valuation benchmarks exist in India. This, along with the extremely high government levies, are a key deterrent to the emergence of property funds in a big way.

SEBI initially laid down operating guidelines for real estate mutual funds (REMF). Later, it laid down guidelines for Real Estate Investment Trusts (REITs). On account of certain operational and tax issues, no REMF schemes were launched in India. REITs too are yet to gain popularity in the country.

A few property funds, promoted by large groups like HDFC, ICICI and Kotak in the financial services space, and by retail giants like Pantaloon (Future group) have come up. These funds are structured as venture capital funds, rather than real estate mutual funds or real estate investment trusts. As such, the investors in these funds are large banks and institutions. Retail investment in real estate through property funds will hopefully take off soon.

Property in India is typically classified as residential or commercial. The view of experts is that residential offers better capital appreciation, but less attractive rental incomes, as compared to commercial.

Internationally, commercial is further split into office buildings, retail (malls and shopping centres), industrial (factories and warehouses), tourism and infrastructure. Specific funds have interest in select kinds of properties.

Property as an asset class is not that volatile. It tends to move secularly up or down, with the economic cycles, and local neighbourhood development. Since it behaves differently from other financial assets as well as gold, it is a useful asset class for diversification in a portfolio.

There is a view in India that real estate looks up towards the end of a bull-run in the stock markets. People encash their profits in the stock market and invest in real estate. There is, however, no empirical research to support this view.

Retail investors can gain significantly out of direct investment in real estate because of the tax benefits available on principal repayment as well as the interest payments.

As a humorist once said, "Two of the most lucrative businesses in the world are buying whiskey by the bottle and selling it by the shot, and buying land by the acre and selling it by the plot."[38]

Chapter 5

Expenses, Net Asset Value and Loads

5.1 Initial Issue Expense

An NFO entails several initial expenses, such as:

- SEBI filing fees and other regulatory expenses related to bringing the issue to the market.
- Printing expenses for offer document, forms, key information memorandum, etc.
- Scheme advertising (but not general corporate advertising) and conference expenses.
- Marketing expenses, including commission to distributors.
- Bank charges.

Earlier, the schemes could be made to bear such initial expenses within the limit of up to 6% of the resources mobilised in the NFO. This impacted the NAV through the process of deferred load (discussed in the next section).

Such charging of initial expenses to the scheme (effectively, the investors had to bear the cost through lower NAV) was first scrapped for open-end schemes. Subsequently, it has been barred for all schemes.

5.2 Deferred Load

Suppose a new closed-end scheme was launched with unit capital of ₹ 100 crore and the issue expenses were ₹ 6 crore (6% was permitted). How should the expense be accounted?

- One possibility is that the entire expense is borne by the AMC, i.e. it is not charged to the scheme. In that case, there is nothing to account in the scheme.
- A second possibility is to treat the entire ₹ 6 crore as an immediate expense in the scheme. This means that the scheme would start with a loss of ₹ 6 crore — not a very appealing proposition to the AMC as well as to the scheme's investors.
- A third possibility is to charge the initial expense to the scheme, but spread the impact over a period. This can be justified on the ground that the initial issue

expenses were incurred to get subscriptions into the scheme, which could continue for a period of time. Why not, therefore, spread the initial issue expenses over the period of the scheme? This accounting treatment is called "amortisation".

Thus, in the above example, if the scheme were a 6-year closed-end scheme, then each year the AMC could charge ₹ 1 crore to expenses.(More specifically, the charge would be ₹ 1 crore ÷ 365, i.e. ₹ 27,397 per day). The portion of the initial issue expense that was not yet charged to expenses would be shown in the balance sheet as an asset under "issue expenses not written off". It was treated as an asset because the expense was already incurred, but benefit continued to accrue in future.

The table below shows how the issue expenses would be written off during the tenor of the scheme:

Table 5.1

Year	*Deferred Load Charged During Year (₹ Cr)*	*Cumulative Charge Until End of Year (₹ Cr)*	*Balance Sheet Figure of "Issue Expenses not Written Off" (₹ Cr)*
1	1	1	5
2	1	2	4
3	1	3	3
4	1	4	2
5	1	5	1
6	1	6	0

Since the investor was bearing the load of the expense, and it was deferred over a period of time, it was called "deferred load".

As explained earlier, the 6% limit for initial issue expenses, and levy of deferred load is no longer permitted for any scheme of any kind.

5.3 Net Asset Value

5.3.1 How NAV is Determined

In order to calculate the NAV of a scheme, each asset and liability of the scheme needs to be valued:

NAV = Value of all assets *minus* value of liabilities other than to unit holders

It can also be calculated as: Unit capital plus reserves.

There is a significant element of subjectivity in the valuation of assets. SEBI, has been trying to ensure some degree of standardization in the manner in which different AMCs handle this subjectivity. Accordingly, it has stipulated detailed valuation norms for each asset class. These were discussed in Chapter 4.

Example 5.1

Suppose a scheme with 1,000 units has the following items in its balance sheet:
Unit Capital ₹ 10,000; investments at market value ₹ 25,000; other assets (e.g., investments sold, but money not received) ₹ 4,000; other liabilities (e.g., investments purchased, but payment not made) ₹ 2,000; reserves ₹ 17,000.

What would be its NAV?

A good starting point would be to put down the numbers in a tabular form to ensure that all items are treated properly (and the value of total assets matches the value of total liabilities):

Table 5.2

Liabilities (₹)		*Assets (₹)*	
Unit Capital	10,000	Investment (market value)	25,000
Reserves	17,000	Other assets	4,000
Other Liabilities	2,000		
Total liabilities	**29,000**	**Total assets**	**29,000**

NAV = Total assets *minus* Liabilities other than to unit holders, i.e.:

₹ 29,000 *minus* ₹ 2,000
= ₹ 27,000.

Alternatively, NAV = Unit capital plus reserves:

= ₹ 10,000 *plus* ₹ 17,000
= ₹ 27,000.

NAV per unit = NAV *divided by* number of units:

= ₹ 27,000 / 1,000
= ₹ 27.

The NAV is required to be rounded to 4 decimal places in the case of index funds, Gold ETF and all debt funds, and 2 decimal places in the case of equity and balanced funds. Mutual funds can, after suitable disclosure in the Scheme Information Document, choose to round off the NAV to a higher number of decimal places in the case of equity and balanced funds too.

5.3.2 Comparison of NAV between Different Dividend-related Options

Let us assume that the NAV of a scheme, which offers all three dividend-related options, has gone up from ₹ 10 per unit to ₹ 16 per unit. The scheme has now declared a dividend of ₹ 1 per unit.

Let us consider that an investor bought 1,500 units under each option (the results will be the same, whatever the number of units the investor starts with).

Table 5.3

	Dividend Option		*Growth Option*		*Dividend Re-invt. Option*	
	Units	*NAV (₹)*	*Units*	*NAV (₹)*	*Units*	*NAV (₹)*
Opening	1,500	10.00	1,500	10.00	1,500	10.00
NAV before dividend declaration		16.00		16.00		16.00
Dividend Declared (Per unit)		1.00	Not Applicable			1.00
Ex-Dividend NAV		15.00		16.00		15.00
Dividend received by investor on her holding		1,500	Not Applicable			0.00
Dividend re-invested by investor		0.00	Not Applicable			1,500,00
Additional units (assuming re-investment at ex-dividend NAV)	Not Applicable		Not Applicable		100	

Thus, the investor's net position is the same in all the options. However:

- In the case of dividend option, ₹ 1,500 is received in the bank, to which extent the NAV falls. Unit holding remains the same at 1,500 units.
- In the case of growth option, no dividend is received and there is, therefore, no fall in the NAV. Unit holding remains the same at 1,500 units.
- In the case of dividend re-investment option, NAV decreases to the extent of dividend declared. But since the dividend is re-invested, no money is received in the bank, but unit holding increases.

The investor would select the option that meets his cash flow needs and minimizes income tax. The income tax implications of the three options are discussed in Chapter 17. Subject to the impact of tax, the investor's monetary value remains the same between the options, as seen below:

Table 5.4

	Dividend Option		*Growth Option*		*Dividend Re-invt. Option*	
	Units	*NAV (₹)*	*Units*	*NAV (₹)*	*Units*	*NAV (₹)*
Unit Holding	1,500	15.00	1,500	16.00	1,600	15.00
Unit holding value (₹)		22,500.00		24,000.00		24,000.00
Add dividend in bank		1,500.00		0.00		0.00
Total		**24,000.00**		**24,000.00**		**24,000.00**

5.3.3 Perspectives on NAV

5.3.3.1 Conservative and Aggressive NAV

The NAV of an open-end scheme is a key determinant of how much a person has to pay for each unit that she proposes to buy, as well as the amount she would recover if she sells a unit. Therefore, it is imperative to ensure fairness in calculation of NAV.

Accountants are trained to be conservative. Translated into operational terms, they would undervalue investments and over-provide for expenses. What is the impact of this approach?

If the moneys that an investor would recover on selling the units are determined by this "conservative NAV", then an exiting investor will recover lesser than what is really due. Concomitantly, a new investor will pay lesser than what she ought to pay for buying new units. Thus, it would penalize an exiting investor, while benefiting new investors and investors who continue in the scheme.

The reverse is an "aggressive NAV", where investments are over-valued and expenses are under-provided. In this situation, an investor exiting from the scheme would take away more than what is due, thus penalizing the investors who choose to continue in the scheme. Thus, it would penalize new investors and continuing investors, while benefiting exiting investors. This is what happens in a Ponzi scheme.

Normal temptation for funds is towards an aggressive NAV because:

- It helps the scheme show better performance for the period; and
- Management fees are calculated on the basis of net asset value.

An aggressive NAV is like inflating the closing stock figure in the balance sheet of a manufacturing company. This closing stock also becomes the opening stock for the next period. Therefore, to sustain the performance, it will have to inflate the closing stock in the next period also. It becomes difficult to break out of this cycle.

Therefore, funds that use an aggressive NAV to demonstrate superior performance get caught in a trap from which it is tough to get out.

Neither a conservative NAV nor an aggressive NAV is fair. Fairness to unit holders comes out of a fair NAV. This is equally applicable to a closed-end scheme, where the units would be traded in the market place on the basis of the NAV declared by the scheme.

5.3.3.2 Historic and Forward NAV

As seen above, NAV is impacted by changes in both liability and asset sides of schemes. The general practice is to look at both liabilities and assets on day-end basis.

If the sale and re-purchase of units are effected on the basis of the previous day's NAV, then it is called historical NAV basis. The danger in this is that if an investor can sell or re-purchase units after trading has commenced the next day, then she is able to benefit from information that is not factored into the historical NAV. This would be unfair to the other investors in the scheme.

An alternative for the mutual funds is to effect sale and re-purchase of units on the basis of the next succeeding NAV (forward NAV basis). In that case, an investor seeking to offer her units for re-purchase would not know how much she would recover until the end of the day. Similarly, a prospect desirous of investing a certain amount would not, at the time of effecting the transaction, know how many units she would be allotted.

Mutual fund schemes other than liquid schemes mostly transact on the basis of forward NAV (Read discussion on "cut off time" in Chapter 15). Investors are given the choice to define their re-purchase instruction in number of units or the value of units. Thus an investor knows precisely, either the number of units or the value of the units that she would be offering for re-purchase.

5.3.3.3 Real-Time NAV

A few mutual funds have put in place systems whereby the asset side of the scheme can be marked to market on real time basis. This entails capture of information on sales and purchases of securities on an ongoing basis and weighting this with market feeds on current values of the securities. However, the liability information, viz. the number of units is still determined as of the end of the day.

With various forms of instantaneous money transfer coming into vogue, it would be possible to structure a scheme where even the liability side is factored into the NAV on a real time basis. This can facilitate real time NAV calculations.

Currently, only ETFs provide a mechanism for intra-day variations in the price at which investors can sell and re-purchase units. This variability, as seen earlier, comes on account of the market makers changing their bid and ask quotes, though NAV is only determined at the end of each trading day.

5.4 Recurring Expenses

The following recurring expenses can be charged to the fund:

- Investment and advisory fees, which has to be fully disclosed in the Offer Document (i.e. management fees that the AMC charges the scheme);
- Marketing and selling expenses, including agents' commission (distributor commission is not chargeable on 'direct plans' i.e. plans where investor has not availed of the services of a distributor);
- Brokerage and transaction cost;
- Fees and expenses of trustees;
- Registrar's charges for transfer of units sold or redeemed;
- Audit fees;

- Custodian fees;
- Expenses on investor communication, account statements, dividend / redemption cheques and warrants;
- Expenses on fund transfers;
- Insurance premium paid by the fund;
- Winding up costs for terminating a fund or a scheme;
- Costs of statutory advertisements;
- In case of a gold exchange traded fund scheme, recurring expenses incurred towards storage and handling of gold;
- In case of a capital protection oriented scheme, rating fees;
- In case of a real estate mutual fund scheme, insurance premia and costs of maintenance of the real estate assets (excluding costs of development of such assets);
- Listing fees, in case of schemes listed on a recognised stock exchange; and
- Such other costs as may be approved by SEBI.

Expenses charged to a scheme on this basis, divided by its net assets gives the base Total Expense Ratio (TER) of the scheme.

Expenses other than the above cannot be charged to the scheme. For example, the following expenses, if incurred, will have to be borne by the AMC or trustee or sponsors, but cannot be charged to the scheme:

- Penalties and fines for infraction of laws;
- Interest on delayed payment to the unit holders;
- Legal, marketing, publication and other general expenses not attributable to any scheme(s);
- Expenses on investment management / general management (as distinct from "investment and advisory fees" which is a permitted expense, as mentioned earlier);
- Expenses on general administration, corporate advertising and infrastructure costs; and
- Depreciation on fixed assets and software development expenses.

The regulations prescribe the following limit on base TER (excluding the issue expenses and redemption expenses, but including management fees):

Table 5.5

Daily Average Net Assets	*Equity Schemes*	*Debt Schemes*
First ₹ 100 crore	2.50%	2.25%
Next ₹ 300 crore	2.25%	2.00%
Next ₹ 300 crore	2.00%	1.75%
Excess over ₹ 700 crore	1.75%	1.50%

For balanced schemes, the limit would depend on whether the scheme is predominantly invested in equity or debt. Accordingly, either the equity scheme limit or the debt scheme limit would apply.

Fund of funds scheme has a total expense limit of 2.50% of daily average net assets, including the weighted average of charges levied by the underlying schemes.

In the case of index funds and exchange traded funds, the total expense ratio cannot be more than 1.50% of average net assets.

The base TER limits applicable to equity schemes are applicable to Gold ETF scheme(s).

It may be noted that brokerage and transaction charges on purchases and sales of securities (part of scheme's investment portfolio) are capitalised. This means that if securities are bought at ₹ 100 and brokerage and transaction charges are 10 paise, the purchase cost will be taken as ₹ 100 plus 10 paise i.e. ₹ 100.10. In the case of a sale, the sale realisation would have been taken as ₹ 100 minus 10 paise i.e. ₹ 99.90. Such capitalisation is however restricted to 12 paise for cash market transactions, and 5 paise for derivatives transaction. Thus, brokerage and transaction charges upto these limits of 12 paise and 5 paise do not get accounted as recurring expense.

The following three additional heads of expense are permitted to be charged beyond the base TER:

- Goods and Service Tax (GST) on investment and advisory fees charged to the scheme. This is permitted beyond the base TER limit.
- Expenses on mobilisation from B30 cities

The top 30 cities from which mutual funds in India mobilise money are called T30 cities. AMFI publishes this list. Other cities are called B30 cities. If the new inflows from B30 cities are at least (a) 30% of gross new inflows in the scheme or (b) 15% of the average assets under management (year to date) of the scheme, whichever is higher, funds can charge additional expense (i.e. beyond the base TER) of up to 30 basis points on daily net assets of the scheme.

In case inflows from B30 cities is less than the higher of (a) or (b) above, additional total expense on daily net assets of the scheme can be charged on pro rata basis as follows:

$$\frac{\text{Daily net assets} \times 30 \text{ basis points} \times \text{New inflows from B30 cities}}{365^{*} \times \text{Higher of (a) or (b) above}}$$

* 366, where applicable

However, this additional expense that is charged beyond the base TER on account of inflows from B30 cities, needs to be clawed back in case such investment is redeemed within a period of 1 year from the date of investment. Further, the additional expense charged must be utilised only for distribution expenses incurred for bringing inflows from such cities.

- Additional levy in lieu of exit load
  As will be discussed in the next section, exit load charged by schemes need to be written back to the scheme. In lieu of this, schemes are allowed to charge 0.05% beyond the base TER.

Thus, TER has two components — Base TER, and additional TER. GST on management fees, Expenses for mobilisation from B30 cities and Additional levy in lieu of exit load can be charged beyond the base TER limit. Other recurring expenses listed above have to be accommodated within the base TER limit.

Any expense in excess of the above limits would need to be borne by the AMC, trustees or sponsors. A few AMCs do pay high upfront commissions in the range of 6-8% to distributors for their closed-end schemes, hoping to recoup the losses through management fees during the life of the fund.

Noting the risk of mis-selling of mutual fund schemes to investors, arising out of such high upfront commissions, AMFI has set a ceiling of 1% that AMCs can pay distributors as upfront commission. However, unlike a SEBI directive that has to be complied it, AMFI directives are recommendatory. AMFI has limited powers to enforce such directives.

Mutual funds need to disclose in their website, in downloadable spreadsheet format, the TER of all their schemes on a daily basis.

5.5 Load and Its Implications

5.5.1 Types

5.5.1.1 Deferred Load

Seen earlier in this chapter.

5.5.1.2 Entry load

Earlier, open-end schemes could recover from investors an amount higher than NAV for their investment in each unit of the scheme. This incremental amount paid by new investors was called "entry load", or "front end load". Thus, if a scheme had NAV of ₹ 11 and entry load of 2%, the investor would pay ₹ 11.22 for each unit:

Sale Price = NAV *plus* Entry Load

The entry load (₹ 0.22 in the above case) would be retained in a separate account from which the AMC would meet part of its selling and distribution expenses.

Like deferred load, this too is no longer permitted.

5.5.1.3 Exit Load

An open-end scheme may pay investors an amount less than NAV for the open-end units that they offer for re-purchase. This shortfall, borne by exiting investors, is called the "exit load" or "back end load". Thus, if a scheme has NAV of ₹ 11 and exit load of 3%, the investor receives only ₹ 10.67 for each unit redeemed.

Re-purchase Price = NAV *minus* Exit Load

Exit load is still permitted. However, earlier the exit load (₹ 0.33 in this case) would go into a separate account from which the AMC would meet part of its selling and distribution expenses. Under current regulations, the entire exit load amount needs to be ploughed back into the scheme immediately. Thus, it benefits the unit holders who continue in the scheme.

While charging the load, the scheme cannot differentiate between unit holders on the basis of amount of subscription.

Load cannot be charged on bonus units, and units allotted on re-investment of dividend.

5.5.1.4 Contingent Deferred Sales Charge (CDSC)

Schemes may choose to reward investors who stay with them longer. This is achieved through a Contingent Deferred Sales Charge — CDSC (also called Contingent Deferred Sales Load — CDSL), where the longer an investor holds on to her units, the lower the CDSC she bears.

For instance, there could be a load of 2% if the investor exits within 1 year; the load could go down to 1% if the investor exits after 1 year but within 2 years; and no load if the investor stays on for 2 years.

This too is permitted, but needs to be ploughed back into the scheme for the benefit of unit holders who continue in the scheme.

5.6 Profitability Metric

I introduced this simple concept to understand profitability of a scheme in the NISM MFD Certification Workbook.[39]

A scheme can be said to have handled investments profitably, if the following profitability metric is positive:

Interest income
+ Dividend income
+ Realized capital gains
+ Valuation gains
– Realized capital losses
– Valuation losses
– Scheme expenses.

When the investment activity is profitable, the true worth of a unit goes up; when there are losses, the true worth of a unit goes down. The true worth of a unit of the scheme is nothing but its net asset value (NAV). Thus, the profitability metric for any period is the bridge that connects the opening NAV and closing NAV of the growth option of the scheme for that period.

As will be seen in Chapter 9, if you assess the scheme profitability through its NAV, then dividend payments would need to be adjusted for if you are doing the calculations based on dividend option of the scheme.

A scheme may be profitable — but did the investor make money? To reckon that, you need to adjust for the load she has incurred. This again is discussed in Chapter 9.

Chapter 6

Liability of Schemes

6.1 Unit Capital Accounting

6.1.1 Units and Unit Capital

As seen in Chapter 1, units are to a mutual fund scheme, what shares are to a company. Similarly, unit capital of a mutual fund scheme is akin to share capital in a company. The number of units of a scheme outstanding at any point of time multiplied by their par value (face value) is the unit capital of the scheme. Generally, units have par value of ₹ 10, though some schemes do have a different par value.

6.1.2 NAV and Load

As seen in the previous chapter, the difference between NAV and the sale price on account of the entry load (no longer permitted) and exit load would earlier go into a separate account from which the AMC would meet part of its selling and distribution expenses. Therefore, sale and re-purchase transactions were reflected in the scheme at NAV. The working is explained in an example that follows.

6.1.3 NAV and Par Value

When investors buy new units or offer their existing units for re-purchase, the unit capital is increased or reduced by the number of units multiplied by the par value.

The difference between the par value and NAV, multiplied by the number of units is adjusted:

- In the Equalisation Reserve, to the extent it is represented by realized gains (Distributable reserves).
- The balance is adjusted in the Unit Premium Reserve. The adjustment is as explained in the following table:

Table 6.1

	If transaction is at higher than par value	*If transaction is at lower than par value*
Sale	Added to reserve	Reduced from reserve
Re-purchase	Reduced from reserve	Added to reserve

Such an accounting treatment ensures that sale and redemption of units does not change the NAV, as will be clear from the example that follows. The equalisation account captures the full value of realised income earned during the year. At the end of the year, the balance in the equalization account is transferred to the revenue account. The following examples will clarify the working.

Example 6.1

Day 1: Suppose a scheme is launched where 500 units are sold at par. The moneys are invested in securities.

Day 2: The securities appreciate 20 per cent.

Day 3: The securities appreciate a further 25 per cent. The fund manager sells 10 per cent of her portfolio.

Day 4: The fund sells 100 new units and re-purchases 20 existing units at the previous day's NAV.

What would be the movement in the balance sheet of the scheme?

Liabilities	₹	*Assets*	₹
Day 1 :			
Unit Capital	5,000	Investments	5,000
Total Liabilities	**5,000**	**Total Assets**	**5,000**
Par Value = ₹ 10.00 / unit		No. of units = 500 NAV = ₹ 10.00 / unit	
Day 2 :			
Unit Capital	5,000	Investments	6,000
Unrealised gain (Reserve)	1,000		
Total Liabilities	**6,000**	**Total Assets**	**6,000**
Par Value = ₹ 10.00 / unit Unrealised gain = ₹ 2.00 / unit		No. of units = 500 NAV = ₹ 12.00 / unit	
Day 3 :			
Unit Capital	5,000	Investments	
Unrealised gain (Reserve) — Investment (contra) 6,750 Less Cost 4,500 (5,000 x 90%)		Original 6,000 + Gain (25%) 1,500 S. Total 7,500 – Sold (10%) 750	
Revised value of unrealised gain	2, 250	Revised value of Investments	6,750
Realised gain (Reserve) - Sold (contra) 750 Less Cost 500 (5,000 x 10%)		Bank (Sale proceeds)	750
Revised	250		
Total Liabilities	**7,500**	**Total Assets**	**7,500**

(Contd . . .)

Example 6.1 *(contd.)*

Liabilities	₹	*Assets*	₹
Par Value = ₹ 10.00 / unit Unrealised gain = ₹ 4.50 / unit Realised gain = ₹ 0.50 / unit		No. of units = 500 NAV = ₹ 15.00 / unit	
Day 4:			
Unit Capital		Bank -	
Original 5,000 + Sales 1,000 (100 x ₹ 10) – Re-purchase 200 (20 x ₹ 10)		Original 750 + Sales 1,500 (100 x ₹ 15.00) – Re-purchase 300 (20 x ₹ 15.00)	
Revised	5,800	Revised	1,950
Unrealised Gain	2, 250	Investments	6,750
Realised Gain	250		
Equalisation Reserve			
On sale of units 50 (100 x ₹ 0.50) Less: On re-purchase of units 10 (20 x ₹ 0.50)			
Revised	40		
Unit Premium Reserve			
On sale of units 450 (100 x ₹ 4.50) Less: On re-purchase 90 (20 x ₹ 4.50)			
Revised	360		
Total Liabilities	**8,700**	**Total Assets**	**8,700**
Par Value = ₹ 10.00 / unit Unrealised gain = ₹ 4.50 / unit (unrealised + unit premium) Realised gain = ₹ 0.50 / unit (realized + equalization)		No. of units = 580 NAV = ₹ 15.00 / unit	

Apart from highlighting the movement of NAV and different balance sheet items, the above example also shows that sale and re-purchase transactions, in the normal course, do not have any impact on NAV per unit, realized gains per unit and unrealised gains per unit. As per SEBI regulations discussed in Chapter 5, exit load is now required to be added back to the scheme. This will raise the NAV of the scheme. Thus, re-purchase does affect the NAV of the scheme if exit load is involved.

6.1.4 Distributable Reserves

The net balance in the equalization reserve (which is created from the sale and re-purchase transactions) is periodically transferred to the profit and loss account. This will not, however, affect the net income for the period (which comes out of investment transactions). It will be a direct adjustment "below the line". (*See* Revenue Account in Chapter 8 for detail.)

SEBI regulations stipulate that dividends cannot be distributed out of unrealised gains. Distributable Reserves are those that are available for distribution as dividend.

As seen above, there are basically four different types of reserves that get created in the books of the scheme through investment activities and sale and re-purchase of units. The position of each reserve *vis-a-vis* dividend distribution is as follows:

Table 6.2

Realised gains	Available for dividend distribution
Unrealised gains	Not available for dividend distribution
Equalisation reserve	Written back to revenue account and available for distribution
Unit premium reserve	Not available for dividend distribution

6.2 Management of Liquidity

6.2.1 Bank Balances

The first avenue for schemes to manage their liquidity is the bank balance. SEBI regulations provide that cash funds and other short-term deposits are to be held only in scheduled banks.

6.2.2 Repos

A scheme can generate liquidity against its holding of government securities by doing a repo transaction with RBI. The structure of a repo transaction was discussed in Chapter 4.

6.2.3 Special Facilities for Gilt Schemes

With a view to promoting the market for government securities, the Reserve Bank of India provides liquidity support to dedicated gilt schemes. This is available up to 20 per cent of the outstanding stock of government securities at the close of the previous working day.

In 2008 when mutual funds found it difficult to sell debt securities at fair prices, RBI had to step in to help them meet their re-purchase obligations to investors.

Thereafter, SEBI introduced several restrictions on investments to ensure that schemes do not get caught in extreme asset-liability mismatches.

6.2.4 Loans

Mutual fund regulations give flexibility to schemes to borrow moneys. Since the interest cost would impact the returns to investors, various limitations have been imposed:

- A scheme will borrow only for the purpose of investor servicing, namely paying a dividend or re-purchasing units;
- The borrowing would not be for more than 20 per cent of net assets; and
- The borrowing would be for a maximum of 6 months at a time.

Further, the interest cost too would need to be accommodated within the overall expense limits explained in Chapter 5.

The limitation on borrowings by mutual fund schemes means that there can be no "hedge funds" or "leveraged funds" in India (whose structure was explained in Chapter 2).

Chapter 7

Offer Document, Key Information Memorandum and Advertising

The traditional Hindu match-making goes through several stages, such as:

- Stage 1: Horoscope stage, when an astrologer assesses the match.
- Stage 2: Sight stage, when the boy and girl see each other for the first time. (These days, there is a Stage 1A, when photographs and social networking contacts are exchanged, before they meet).
- Stage 3: Discussion stage, when the parents finalise the terms for the association.

In the above sequence, the horoscope becomes a document that captures history — mainly the place and time of birth of the boy and girl, and resultant star position for each. Based on the two horoscopes, the astrologer gives his views about their future together if the boy and girl were to marry. But the affected parties, namely the boy, girl and their respective parents take independent views on the marriage.

In the investment world, the offer document is like the horoscope. It gives historical information. The offer document also mentions the AMC's views on the investment prospects, and its suitability to investors. The financial adviser, like the astrologer, is expected to assess the match — in this case, between the proposed investor and the investment product. But neither the AMC nor the financial adviser is permitted to promise a return. The proposed investor needs to take an independent view on the investment.

An astrologer, in the normal course, has nothing to gain by giving a biased view on the match. Yet, an unethical astrologer can be influenced into suggesting that the horoscopes match, even when they do not. This is perhaps the reason why some families do not go blindly by the views of an unknown astrologer, especially if the astrologer is introduced by the other party to the proposed marriage.

Cut back to the financial world. The investor needs to be cautious, especially when dealing with a party with whom she is not adequately experienced. The party trying to convince her to invest could be operating with a significant conflict of interest. A sale based on mis-statement can give monetary gain to the party, while the investor would be at a loss. Investors who do not have the requisite knowledge should therefore seek the advice of someone they trust. SEBI has prescribed detailed guidelines to protect the investor.

The Offer Document is a key document that provides essential information about the scheme to help investors make informed decisions about whether to purchase the units being offered.

The Offer Document has two parts:

- Scheme Information Document (SID)
  This has all the information relating to the scheme/s of the mutual fund.
- Statement of Additional Information (SAI)
  This has all the statutory information about the mutual fund, and other information that is common across schemes. Legally, it is a part of SID, although physically it is a different document.

Keeping in mind the profile of prospective investors, the regulations provide that information in the Offer Document has to be presented in "simple language and in a clear, concise and easily understandable manner".

SID and SAI are to be prepared as per the prescribed format. The contents need to follow the same sequence as prescribed.

Besides, SEBI has also laid down certain "standard observations" that need to be incorporated in the Offer Document. While filing the Scheme Information Document (SID) for launching a new scheme / revising and filing existing SAI and SID with SEBI, the mutual funds should highlight and clearly mention the page numbers of the SAI and SID on which each observation has been incorporated.

Mutual funds also need to label their mutual fund scheme as follows:

- Nature of the scheme: Whether to create wealth or provide regular income in an indicative time horizon (short / medium / long term).
- A brief about the investment objective (in a single line sentence) followed by kind of product in which investor is investing (equity / debt).
- Level of risk, depicted by a risk-o-meter. On next page the box that is applicable for liquid schemes is illustrative.
- Similarly, depending on the nature of risk in the scheme, the position of the arrow inside the meter, and the description below the meter varies.
- A disclaimer that investors should consult their financial advisers if they are not clear about the suitability of the product.

Risk-O-Meter

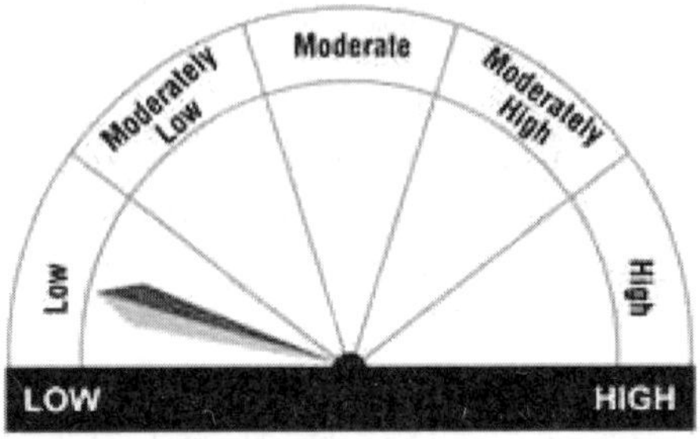

Investors understand that their principal will be at Low risk

This product is suitable for investors who are seeking*:

- Regular Fixed Income for Short Term
- Investment in Debt / Money Market Instruments / Government Securities.

***Investors should consult their financial advisors if in doubt about whether the product is suitable for them**

The product label is to be disclosed in —

- Front page of application forms, Key Information Memorandum (KIM) and Scheme Information Documents (SIDs).
- Common application form — along with the information about the scheme.
- Scheme advertisements placed in manner so as to be prominently visible to investors.

A mutual fund is free to add in the Offer Documents, any other disclosure, which in the opinion of the trustees of the mutual fund (Trustees) or the Asset Management Company (AMC) is material for the investor. However, the information should not be presented in an "incomplete, inaccurate or misleading manner". Further, inclusion of such information should not, by virtue of its nature, or manner of presentation, obscure or impede understanding of any information that is required to be included.

Application forms for schemes of mutual funds have to be accompanied by the Key Information Memorandum (KIM), the format for which is outlined by SEBI. This memorandum has to be "printed at least in 7 point font size with proper spacing for easy readability".

KIM is a concise version of the SID that is more easily available at the offices of various intermediaries who sell the units. The investor, however, has the right to insist on the detailed SID.

Draft SID, filed with SEBI, is made available on SEBI's website at http://www.sebi.gov.in for 21 working days to enable the public to comment on the adequacy of disclosures.

A point to be noted is that SEBI does not approve or disapprove offer documents. The mutual fund has to file the SID and KIM for the proposed scheme with SEBI. A 21-working day window is provided for SEBI to give its comments.

The AMC has to file its replies to the modifications suggested by SEBI within 6 months of the letter. The scheme has to be launched within 6 months from the date of issuance of final observations by SEBI. If either of these periods lapses, then the AMC will need to re-file the SID and pay the relevant filing fees, in order to proceed with the issue.

Final SID (after incorporating SEBI's comments) must reach SEBI before it is issued for circulation. Soft copy of the final SID in pdf format along with a printed copy should be filed with SEBI two working days prior to the launch of the scheme.

The AMC also needs to submit an undertaking to SEBI while filing the soft copy that information contained in the soft copy of SID to be uploaded on SEBI website is current and relevant, and matches exactly with the contents of the hard copy, and that the AMC is fully responsible for the contents of the soft copy of SID. The soft copy of SID should also be uploaded on AMFI website two working days prior to launch of the scheme.

In the certificate submitted by trustees with regard to a new scheme proposed to be offered by the AMC, the trustees are required to certify as follows:

> "The Trustees have ensured that the (name of the scheme / Fund) approved by them is a new product offered by (name of the Mutual Fund) and is not a minor modification of any existing scheme / fund / product."

This certification has to be disclosed in the SID along with the date of approval of the scheme by the trustees.

This certification is not applicable to close ended schemes except for those close ended schemes which have the option of conversion into open ended schemes on maturity.

All information in the offer document has to be updated 30 days before the launch of a scheme.

Extracts from select Offer Documents are featured later in this Chapter. "Investment Objective" is an important section that is part of the SID and KIM. According to Alvin Hall "In reality, the distinction among objectives of some of the equity funds is not clear-cut. The actual stocks that constitute a specific mutual fund portfolio depend on the analysis and perspective of the fund's manager. Hence, a generic investment objective (e.g., growth, income) can be interpreted and executed differently by different managers. One company's aggressive growth fund may look like another company's specialty fund, which may look like another company's world fund. It is important to read the fund's prospectus and review the list of its top holdings before making an investment decision".[40]

7.1 Scheme Information Document (SID)

The SID needs to be updated regularly:

- For schemes launched in the first half of a financial year (say, May 2018), the SID is to be updated within 3 months from the end of the financial year, i.e. by June 2018.
- For the schemes launched in the second half of a financial year (say, October 2018), SID is to be updated within 3 months of the end of the subsequent financial year, i.e. by June 2019.

Thereafter, the SID is to be updated every year. A soft copy of updated SID has to be filed with SEBI in pdf format along with a printed copy of the same.

In case of change in fundamental attributes, the SID has to be revised and updated immediately after completion of the exit option duration for investors. For other changes:

- The AMC is required to issue an addendum and display it on its website.
- The addendum has to be circulated to all the distributors / brokers / investor service centres (ISC) so that it can be attached to copies of SID already in stock, till the SID is updated.
- In case any information in SID is amended more than once, the latest applicable addendum shall be a part of SID. For example, in case of changes in load structure the addendum carrying the latest applicable load structure has to be attached to all KIM and SID already in stock till these are updated.

  The account statements issued to investors too will have to indicate the applicable load structure.
- A public notice has to be given in respect of such changes in one English daily newspaper having nationwide circulation as well as in a newspaper published in the language of region where the head office of the mutual fund is situated.
- A copy of the change has to be filed with SEBI within 7 days of the change.

  Some of the key contents of the SID are given in Annexure 7.1.

7.2 Statement of Additional Information

SAI is common for all schemes of a mutual fund. First, the draft SAI needs to be filed with SEBI. After incorporating the comments / observations, if any, from SEBI, the AMC has to file a soft copy of the final SAI with SEBI in pdf format along with printed copy of the same. Final SAI is also to be uploaded on the AMC's website and on the AMFI website.

A printed copy of SAI has to be made available to the investor(s) on request. SAI is to be updated within 3 months from the end of financial year and filed with SEBI.

Any material changes in the SAI have to be made on an ongoing basis by way of update on the mutual fund and AMFI websites. SEBI has to be intimated of the changes made in the SAI within 7 days. The effective date for such changes has to be mentioned in the updated SAI.

Some of the key contents of the SAI are given in Annexure 7.2.

7.3 Standard Observations

The offer document has to include certain standard observations set out by SEBI. A few such key disclosures in SID are:

- The AMC shall not invest in any of the schemes unless full disclosure of its intention to invest has been made in the Scheme Information Document and that the AMC shall not be entitled to charge any fees on such investments.
- In case the mutual fund intends to invest in ADRs / GDRs and foreign securities, the risk factors associated with such investments including currency risk.
- If the scheme proposes to invest in securitised debt, the table on investment pattern should disclose the maximum limit up to which such investment in securitised debt would be made.
- In case the mutual fund intends to trade in derivatives, the strategies and risks associated with such activities should be disclosed at relevant places in the Scheme Information Document. Following risk factor pertaining to investments in derivatives may also be given (except in case where the scheme is investing in derivatives only for the purpose of hedging and portfolio rebalancing):
    - "Derivative products are leveraged instruments and can provide disproportionate gains as well as disproportionate losses to the investor. Execution of such strategies depends upon the ability of the fund manager to identify such opportunities. Identification and execution of the strategies to be pursued by the fund manager involve uncertainty and decision of fund manager may not always be profitable. No assurance can be given that the fund manager will be able to identify or execute such strategies".
    - "The risks associated with the use of derivatives are different from or possibly greater than, the risks associated with investing directly in securities and other traditional investments".
    - Specific risk factors pertaining to the derivative strategies too need to be mentioned.

A few such key disclosures in SAI are:

- If the AMC is undertaking other business activities, brief details of such activities, giving SEBI registration particulars, if applicable, and certification that there is no conflict of interest.

- The detailed procedures followed for investment decisions has to be set out — whether an individual or committee takes decisions, role of chief executive of AMC in investment decisions, recording of each investment decision, how these decisions and performance are monitored by the AMC Board and the trustees.
- Disclosure to the effect that it is mandatory for investors of mutual fund schemes to mention their bank account numbers in their applications / request for redemptions.
- Suspension or restriction of re-purchase / redemption facility under any scheme of the mutual fund shall be made applicable only after the approval from the board of directors of the asset management company and the trustees. The approval from the AMC Board and the Trustees giving details of circumstances and justification for the proposed action shall also be informed to SEBI in advance.

7.4 Key Information Memorandum

SEBI has also prescribed the contents of the KIM, which is essentially a summary of the Scheme Information Document. The contents of KIM need to follow the same sequence as prescribed in the format.

KIM is to be updated at least once a year.

SEBI's standard format of KIM is given in Annexure 7.3.

7.5 Extracts from Select Offer Documents

7.5.1 Debt Scheme

7.5.1.1 Type of Scheme

Open-end dedicated gilts scheme

7.5.1.2 Investment Objectives

The objective of the scheme is to generate risk-free returns through investments in sovereign securities issued by the Central Government and / or a State Government and / or any security unconditionally guaranteed by the Government of India, and / or reverse repos in such securities as and when permitted by RBI.

A small portion of the fund may be invested in the inter-bank money market in order to meet the day-to-day liquidity requirements of the scheme. To ensure total safety of unit holders' funds, the scheme does not invest in any other securities such as shares, debentures or bonds issued by any other entity. The fund will seek to underwrite issuance of government securities if and to the extent permitted by SEBI / RBI and subject to the prevailing rules and regulations specified in this respect and may also participate in their auction from time to time.

The fund will apply to SEBI and RBI for permission to invest in securities abroad in conformity with the guidelines, rules and regulations in this respect. The fund will seek permission to invest in government securities issued by G-7 nations, provided that such securities are considered as investment grade and provided RBI permits such investments under the guidelines for a dedicated gilts fund.

There is no assurance that the investment objective of the scheme / plans will be realized. It is, however, emphasized, that investments under all plans of this scheme are made in government securities, where there is no risk of default of payment of principal or interest amount.

7.5.1.3 Investment Strategy

The scheme has two plans where investments are segregated. The two plans have distinct portfolios. The Savings Plan predominantly invests in such government securities that the weighted average maturity of the portfolio is up to two years whereas the Investment Plan invests in such government securities that there is no restriction on maturity of the securities. The two plans have different interest rate risks, and therefore, separate NAVs.

7.5.1.4 The Risk Profile and Investment Pattern

The following table indicates, by maturity and category, the risks associated with government securities:

Table 7.1

Balance Maturity	*Risk Profile*	
	Price Risk	*Credit Risk*
Less than 1 year	Lowest	Zero
Between 1 to 5 years	Lower	Zero
More than 5 years	Low	Zero
Securities held under Reverse Repos	Zero	Very low

The risk profile described above indicates that the risks of a portfolio of government securities are invariably lower than those of a portfolio of investments of other types of securities. Since government securities do not pose any credit risk, they are usually referred to as risk-free securities.

Investment patterns of the Savings Plan and Investment Plan respectively are:

Table 7.2

Plan	*Investment Pattern*
Savings Plan	Portfolio of securities with Weighted Average Maturity of up to 2 years
Investment Plan	No restriction on maturity of securities

The Savings Plan and Investment Plan have segregated portfolios, consistent with the above investment patterns.

(*Note*: The asset allocation shown above is indicative and may change for a short term on defensive considerations. Should the weighted average maturity of the portfolio under the Savings Plan exceed 2 years, the portfolio will be reviewed and rebalanced.)

7.5.2 Equity Scheme

7.5.2.1 Type of Scheme

Open-end equity growth scheme.

7.5.2.2 Investment Objectives

The objective of the scheme is to generate capital appreciation from a portfolio of predominantly equity and equity related securities. The portfolio generally comprises equity of not more than 30 companies at any point of time and these 30 companies may or may not be the same that constitute the BSE Sensitive Index (S&P BSE Sensex — Sensex) or the NSE Nifty Index (CNX Nifty — Nifty). It is the investment manager's belief that having a portfolio constituting a greater number of investments does not necessarily result in either superior returns or a significant reduction in risk.

The performance of the scheme is benchmarked against the Sensex and the Nifty.

To reduce the risk of the portfolio, the scheme may also use various derivative and hedging products from time to time, if and when and in the manner permitted by SEBI.

7.5.2.3 Portfolio Turnover

The portfolio turnover will not normally exceed 150%. Portfolio turnover will exclude:

- The turnover caused on account of investing the initial corpus.
- The turnover caused on account of investing in debt and money market securities; and
- The turnover caused on account of fresh purchases and redemptions by unit holders.

Turnover means the simple average of the aggregate of purchases and sales net of the above exclusions. These purchases and sales invite transaction costs, viz. brokerage, stamp duty and custodian transaction charges. The portfolio turnover limit of 150% is essential to enable portfolio restructuring when warranted.

There is no assurance that the investment objective of the scheme will be realized.

7.5.2.4 Investment Strategy

The investment strategy of the AMC is directed to investing in stocks, which, in the opinion of the Investment Manager, are priced at a material discount to their intrinsic value. Such intrinsic value is a function of both past performance and future growth prospects. The process of discovering the intrinsic value is through in-house research supplemented by research available from other sources.

For selecting particular stocks as well as determining the potential value of such stocks, the AMC is guided, *inter alia*, by one or more of the following considerations:

- The financial strength of the companies, as indicated by well-recognized financial parameters;
- Reputation of the management and track record;
- Companies that are relatively less prone to recession or cycles, either because of the nature of their business or superior strategies followed by their management;
- Companies which pursue a strategy to build strong brands for their products or services and those which are capable of building strong franchises; and
- Market liquidity of the stock.

Risk is managed by adequate diversification by spreading investments over a range of industries.

The scheme is not restrained from investing in listed / unlisted and / or rated / unrated debt or money market securities, provided the investments are within the limits indicated in the investment pattern table. Investment in unrated debt securities is made with the prior approval of the Board of the AMC, provided the investment is in terms of the parameters approved by the Board of the Trustee. Where the proposed investment is not within the parameters as mentioned above, approval of the Boards of both the AMC and the Trustee is taken before making the investment.

The scheme may invest in GDRs / ADRs, if and in the manner permitted by SEBI / RBI. Such investments will be in conformity with the investment objectives of the scheme and the prevailing guidelines and regulations. The scheme may also use various derivative and hedging products from time to time, if and when and in a manner permitted by SEBI to reduce the risk of the portfolio.

7.5.2.5 The Risk Profile and Investment Pattern

The Investment Manager generally invests up to 90% of the funds in equity and equity linked instruments and the balance in debt and money market instruments.

The asset allocation under the scheme, under normal circumstances, is as follows:

Table 7.3

Investments	*Indicative Allocation*	*Risk Profile*
Equity and Equity Related Securities	90%	Medium to High
* Debt & Money Market Securities	10%	Low to Medium

* Debt securities / instruments are deemed to include securitised debt.

(*Note*: The asset allocation shown above is indicative and may change for a short term on defensive considerations. The allocation of equity and equity related securities in the portfolio can fall up to 70% before a review and rebalancing is called for. Likewise, should this proportion reach 98%, review and rebalancing will be conducted.)

7.5.3 Balanced Scheme

7.5.3.1 Type of Scheme

Open-end Balanced (Equity and Debt) scheme.

7.5.3.2 Investment Objectives

The investment objective of the scheme is to achieve growth by investing in equity and equity-related instruments, balanced with income generation by investing in debt and money market instruments.

7.5.3.3 Benchmark

The scheme's performance is measured against the simple average of the percentage movement of two benchmarks, viz. BSE 30 (Sensex) and Crisil AAA Bond Index. Though (a) the proportion of equity and debt may not always be equal, and (b) the scheme may invest in debt instruments, which are rated below AAA giving yields higher than AAA instruments, the benchmark selected is a broad indicator of the market trends.

7.5.3.4 Investment Strategy

Balancing Equity and Debt Risk

The investment strategy is aimed at exploiting the potential for capital appreciation of equity and the stable returns of debt while balancing the risks of equity with the comparative safety of debt. Emphasis is given to choosing securities, which, in the opinion of the fund manager, are less prone to market risk and default risk, while bearing in mind the liquidity needs arising out of the open-end nature of the scheme.

7.5.3.5 The Risk Profile and Investment Pattern

The asset allocation under the scheme, under normal circumstances, is as follows:

Table 7.4

Investments	*Indicative Allocation*	*Risk Profile*
Equity and Equity Related Securities	65%	Medium to High
* Debt & Money Market Securities	35%	Low to Medium

* Debt securities / instruments are deemed to include securitised debt.

(*Note*: The asset allocation shown above is indicative and may change for a short term on defensive considerations. The above allocation may change to maintain the ratio required for the scheme to qualify as an equity oriented scheme under Section 115R and 115T of Income Tax Act, 1961. Under the said provision, dividend distributed by equity oriented schemes is liable to dividend distribution tax at 10%. However, the equity exposure can vary between 40% and 80% of the net assets of the scheme. If the exposure falls below the said lower limit or exceeds the upper limit the same will be restored within three working days.)

7.5.4 Right to Limit Redemption

The Board of Directors of the Trustee and the AMC may, in the general interest of the unit holders of all or any of the schemes / plans under this Offer Document and keeping in view the unforeseen circumstances / unusual market conditions, limit the total number of units which may be redeemed on any working day to 5% of the total number of units then issued and outstanding under the scheme / plan or to such other percentage as the said boards may determine. In such a case, the approval of both the Boards, giving details of circumstances and justification for the proposed action shall be informed to SEBI in advance.

Any units, which, by virtue of these limitations, are not redeemed on a particular day, are carried forward for redemption to the next day for which NAV is declared, in the order in which the requests for redemption were received. Redemptions so carried forward are priced on the basis of the redemption price of the day on which redemption is made. Under such circumstances, to the extent multiple redemption requests are received at the same time on a single working day, redemptions are made on pro-rata basis, based on the size of each redemption request, the balance amount being carried forward for redemption to the next day(s) for which NAV is declared.

7.5.5 Suspension of Purchase and Redemption of Units

The purchase and / or redemption of units may be suspended temporarily or indefinitely when any of the following conditions exist:

- The stock markets stop functioning or trading is restricted;
- Extreme volatility occurs in the stock markets / money market / debenture / bond market / foreign exchange market, which, in the opinion of the Investment Manager, is prejudicial or to the disadvantage to the interests of the investors;
- There is a natural calamity, civil strife, complete breakdown of law and order, war, act of God or *force majeur*; and or
- SEBI, by order, so directs.

In case of suspension of redemption, the approval of the Boards of Directors of the Trustee company and the AMC, giving the details of circumstances and justification for the proposed action shall be informed to SEBI in advance.

The mutual fund also reserves the right to withdraw sale of units in a scheme temporarily or indefinitely, if the Trustee and the AMC view that increasing the scheme's size further may prove detrimental to the existing unit holders of the scheme.

An order to purchase units is not binding on and may be rejected by the Trustee, the AMC or their respective agents, until it has been confirmed in writing by the AMC or its agents and payment has been received.

7.6 Advertising

With a view to ensuring investor protection, SEBI imposes several restrictions on advertising by mutual funds.

7.6.1 Advertising Code

Some of the key limitations mentioned in the advertising code are as follows:

(a) Advertisements shall be accurate, true, fair, clear, complete, unambiguous and concise.

(b) Advertisements shall not contain statements which are false, misleading, biased or deceptive, based on assumption/projections and shall not contain any testimonials or any ranking based on any criteria.

(c) Advertisements shall not be so designed as likely to be misunderstood or likely to disguise the significance of any statement. Advertisements shall not contain statements which directly or by implication or by omission may mislead the investor.

(d) Advertisements shall not carry any slogan that is exaggerated or unwarranted or slogan that is inconsistent with or unrelated to the nature and risk and return profile of the product.

(e) No celebrities shall form part of the advertisement.

(f) Advertisements shall not be so framed as to exploit the lack of experience or knowledge of the investors. Extensive use of technical or legal terminology or complex language and the inclusion of excessive details which may detract the investors should be avoided.

(g) Advertisements shall contain information which is timely and consistent with the disclosures made in the Scheme Information Document, Statement of Additional Information and the Key Information Memorandum.

(h) No advertisement shall directly or indirectly discredit other advertisements or make unfair comparisons.

(i) Advertisements shall be accompanied by a standard warning in legible fonts which states "Mutual Fund investments are subject to market risks, read all scheme related documents carefully." No addition or deletion of words shall be made to the standard warning.

(j) In audio-visual media based advertisements, the standard warning in visual and accompanying voice over reiteration shall be audible in a clear and understandable manner. For example, in standard warning both the visual and the voice over reiteration containing 14 words running for at least 5 seconds may be considered as clear and understandable.

7.6.2 Dividend Advertisements

While advertising pay out of dividends, all advertisements shall disclose the dividends declared or paid in rupees per unit along with the face value of each unit of that scheme and the prevailing NAV at the time of declaration of the dividend.

While advertising returns by assuming reinvestment of dividends, if distribution taxes (a topic that is discussed in Chapter 17) are excluded while calculating the returns, this fact shall also be disclosed.

While advertising pay outs, all advertisements shall disclose, immediately below the pay out figure (in percentage or in absolute terms) that the NAV of the scheme, pursuant to pay out would fall to the extent of payout and statutory levy (if applicable).

7.6.3 Performance Advertisements

When the scheme has been in existence for more than three years:

- Point-to-point returns on a standard investment of ₹ 10,000 shall also be shown in addition to CAGR for a scheme in order to provide ease of understanding to retail investors.
- Performance advertisement shall be provided since inception and for as many twelve month periods as possible for the last 3 years, such periods being counted from the last day of the calendar quarter preceding the date of advertisement, along with benchmark index performance for the same periods.

Where scheme has been in existence for more than one year but less than three years, performance advertisement of scheme(s) shall be provided for as many as twelve month periods as possible, such periods being counted from the last day of the calendar quarter preceding the date of advertisement, along with benchmark index performance for the same periods.

Where the scheme has been in existence for less than one year, past performance shall not be provided.

In case of Money Market schemes or cash and liquid schemes, wherein investors have very short investment horizon, the performance can be advertised by simple annualisation of yields if a performance figure is available for at least 7 days, 15 days and 30 days provided it does not reflect an unrealistic or misleading picture of the performance or future performance of the scheme.

For the sake of standardization, a similar return in INR and by way of CAGR must be shown for the following apart from the scheme benchmarks:

Scheme Type	**Benchmark**
Equity Scheme	Sensex or Nifty
Long term debt scheme	10 year dated GOI security
Short term debt fund	1 year T-bill

These disclosures shall form a part of the SAI and all advertisements of mutual funds.

Any disclosure regarding quarterly / half yearly / yearly performance shall pertain to respective calendar quarterly / half yearly / yearly only.

When the performance of a particular mutual fund scheme is advertised, the advertisement shall also include the performance data of all the other schemes managed by the fund manager of that particular scheme.

In case the number of schemes managed by a fund manager is more than six, then the AMC may disclose the total number of schemes managed by that fund manager along with the performance data of top 3 and bottom 3 schemes (in addition to the performance data of the scheme for which the advertisement is being made) managed by that fund manager in all performance related advertisement. However, in such cases AMCs shall ensure that true and fair view of the performance of the fund manager is communicated by providing additional disclosures, if required.

7.6.4 Indicative Portfolios and Yields

Mutual funds cannot offer any indicative portfolio and indicative yield. No communication regarding the same in any manner whatsoever can be issued by any mutual fund or distributor of its products. The compliance of this point has to be monitored by the AMC and the trustees and reported in their respective reports to SEBI.

Annexure 7.1: Key Contents of SID

7.1.1 Cover Page

- This includes basic information such as name of the Scheme, type of Scheme (equity, balanced, income, debt, liquid, ETF, etc.; open-end / closed-end / interval), name of the AMC, classes of units offered for sale, price of the units, opening date, closing date and scheme re-opening date (if applicable).
- Names of mutual fund, AMC and trustee company, along with address and website details.
- Name of the scheme cannot be deceptive or misleading, and has to be consistent with investment policy. For instance, we cannot call a scheme that will invest 20% in debt as a debt scheme or income scheme.
- If the scheme is an assured returns scheme, then the name of the guarantor is to be disclosed.

  A few specific disclosures are required to the effect that:

  - The scheme particulars have been prepared in accordance with the Securities and Exchange Board of India (Mutual Funds) Regulations, 1996, as amended till date, and filed with SEBI, along with Due Diligence Certificate from the AMC. The units being offered for public subscription have not been approved or recommended by the Securities and Exchange Board of India nor has Securities and Exchange Board of India certified the accuracy or adequacy of the Scheme Information Document.
  - The Scheme Information Document sets out concisely the information about the scheme that a prospective investor ought to know before investing. Investors should also ascertain about any further changes to the Scheme Information Document after the date of this document from the mutual fund / investor service centres / website / distributors or brokers before investing in the scheme.
  - The investors are advised to refer to the Statement of Additional Information (SAI) for details of the mutual fund, tax and legal issues and general information on the website of the mutual fund.
  - SAI is incorporated by reference (is legally a part of the Scheme Information Document). For a free copy of the current SAI, please contact your nearest Investor Service Centre or log on to the mutual fund website.
  - The Scheme Information Document should be read in conjunction with the SAI and not in isolation.
  - This Scheme Information Document is dated ________.

- This would be followed by the Table of Contents and the Highlights / Summary.

- The Highlights / Summary section should include the following:
  - Investment objective.
  - Liquidity.
  - Benchmark.
  - Transparency / NAV Disclosure.
  - Loads.
  - Minimum Application Amount.

7.1.2 Requirement of minimum investors in the scheme

The Scheme/Plan shall have a minimum of 20 investors and no single investor shall account for more than 25% of the corpus of the Scheme/Plan(s).
Consequences of breach of this condition

7.1.3 Definitions

The language and terminology used in the Offer Document has to be as provided in the Regulations. Any new term, if used, needs to be clearly defined.

7.1.4 Risk Factors

Some risk factors may be peculiar to mutual funds in general, while some may be specific to the investment policies and objectives of the scheme. These need to be disclosed "in legible fonts".

Standard Risk Factors

- Investment in mutual fund units involves investment risks such as trading volumes, settlement risk, liquidity risk, default risk including the possible loss of principal.
- As the price / value / interest rates of the securities in which the scheme invests fluctuates, the value of your investment in the scheme may go up or down (Mutual funds may also provide factors affecting capital market in general and not limited to the aforesaid).
- Past performance of the sponsor / AMC / mutual fund does not guarantee future performance of the scheme.
- The name of the scheme does not in any manner indicate either the quality of the scheme or its future prospects and returns.
- The sponsor is not responsible or liable for any loss resulting from the operation of the scheme beyond the initial contribution of _____ made by it towards setting up the fund.
- The present scheme is the first scheme being launched under its management. (Applicable, if the AMC has no previous experience in managing a Mutual Fund).

The present scheme is not a guaranteed or assured return scheme (applicable to all schemes except assured return schemes)

Scheme Specific Risk Factors

- Arising from the investment objective, the investment strategy and the asset allocation of the scheme, e.g. risks arising out of investing in equity, debt, foreign securities, derivatives, securitised debt, short-selling and securities lending, as may be applicable to the scheme
- Arising from non-diversification, if any.
- Arising out of closed-end schemes, namely infrequent trading, discount to NAV, etc.
- In the case of assured returns schemes, the net worth and liquidity position of the guarantor and the source of the guarantee has to be disclosed. If the return is assured only for a specific period, then a statement to the effect that there is no guarantee that such return may be generated for the remaining duration of the scheme.

7.1.5 Due Diligence by AMC

The due diligence certificate is to be signed by the compliance officer, chief executive officer, managing director, whole time director, or executive director of the Asset Management Company and is to be incorporated in the Scheme Information Document.

The due diligence certificate incorporates a confirmation that:

- The draft Scheme Information Document forwarded to SEBI is in accordance with the SEBI (Mutual Funds) Regulations, 1996 and the guidelines and directives issued by SEBI from time to time.
- All legal requirements connected with the launch of the scheme as also the guidelines, instructions, etc. issued by the government and any other competent authority in this behalf, have been duly complied with.
- The disclosures made in the Scheme Information Document are true, fair and adequate to enable the investors to make a well-informed decision regarding investment in the proposed scheme.
- The intermediaries named in the Scheme Information Document and Statement of Additional Information are registered with SEBI and such registration is valid, as on date.

7.1.6 Information about the Scheme

- Type of scheme, i.e. open / close / interval, equity / debt / income / liquid / balanced / ETF, etc.
- What is the investment objective of the scheme?

Scheme's investment objective and policies (including the types of securities in which it will invest) is to be clearly and concisely stated

- How will the scheme allocate its assets?

  This includes asset allocation table giving the broad classification of assets and indicative exposure level in percentage terms specifying the risk profile.

If the scheme's name implies that it will invest primarily in a particular type of security, or in a certain industry or industries, the scheme shall have an investment policy which requires that, under normal circumstances, at least 65 per cent of the value of its total assets be invested in the indicated type of security or industry.

The asset allocation should be consistent with the investment objective of the scheme:

Instrument	*Indicative Allocation (% of total assets)*		*Risk Profile*
	Maximum	Minimum	High / Medium / Low

Percentage of investment in foreign securities, derivatives, stock lending, securitized debt, etc. is to be indicated:

- Where will the scheme invest?

  Brief narration on the types of instruments in which the scheme will invest and the concerned regulations and limits applicable.

Brief narration on the various derivative products specifying (i) the instruments to be used and (ii) the applicable limits:

- What are the investment strategies?

Information about investment approach and risk control should be included in simple terms.

In case the scheme proposes to invest in derivatives, disclosures on the various strategies to be adopted by the fund manager are to be made.

In case of assured return schemes, the Scheme Information Document needs to disclose:

- How many schemes have assured returns, their number and corpus size.
- The justification as to how the net worth and liquidity position of the guarantor would be adequate to meet the shortfall in these schemes.
- Details of the schemes which did not pay assured returns in the past and how the shortfall was met.
- SEBI has proposed that the mutual fund disclose the floors and ceilings within a range of 5% of the intended allocation (in %) against each sub asset class /

credit rating. It may be disclosed that x-y % would be in AAA rated bank CD as per the sample matrix below:

Credit Rating ->	AAA	AA	A	BBB
Instruments:				
CDs				
CPs				
NCDs				
Securitized debt				
Any Other				

Portfolio turnover policy, particularly for equity oriented schemes, has to be disclosed.

In discussing its investment strategies, the scheme shall briefly discuss the probable effect of such strategies on the rate of the total portfolio turnover of the scheme, if such effects are significant; and also other consequences which will result from the higher portfolio turnover rate, e.g. higher brokerage and transaction cost.

- Fundamental Attributes
  Type of Scheme
  Investment Objective:
    Main objective
    Investment pattern
  Terms of the issue:
    Provision for liquidity (Listing, Re-purchase, Redemption)
    Aggregate fees and expenses
    Any safety net or guarantee.
- How will the scheme benchmark its performance?
  The name and the justification (specific to the scheme objective) for the use of benchmark index with which the performance of the scheme can be compared with.
- Who manages the schemes?
  Name, age, qualification and experience of the fund manager to the scheme to be disclosed. The experience of the fund manager should include last 10 years experience and also the name of any other schemes under his / her management.
- What are the investment restrictions?

All the investment restrictions as contained in the Seventh Schedule to SEBI (Mutual Funds) Regulations, 1996 and applicable to the scheme should be incorporated.

Further, in case the fund follows any internal norms *vis-à-vis* limiting exposure to a particular scrip or sector, etc. apart from the aforementioned investment restrictions, the same need to be disclosed.

In case of equity schemes only equity related investment restrictions need to be disclosed, though the scheme would be investing a portion of the assets in bonds for liquidity or for other purposes.

In the case of a fixed income / debt schemes, only the investment restriction applicable to bonds is to be disclosed.

In the case of balanced schemes, all investment restrictions are to be disclosed:

- How has the scheme performed?

<table>
<tr><td rowspan="6">[In case of a new scheme, this is not applicable. Hence give the statement-"This scheme is a new scheme and does not have any performance track record"]
Or
[In case of a scheme in existence, the return figures shall be given for that scheme only. For a scheme which is in existence for more than 1 year, the returns given will be Compounded Annualised Returns and for scheme which is in existence for less than 1 year, the returns would be absolute returns since inception. Absolute returns for each financial year for the last 5 years shall be represented by means of a bar diagram as per the adjacent format.]</td><td>Compounded Annualised Returns</td><td>Scheme Returns %</td><td>Benchmark Returns %</td></tr>
<tr><td>Returns for the last 1 year</td><td></td><td></td></tr>
<tr><td>Returns for the last 3 years</td><td></td><td></td></tr>
<tr><td>Returns for the last 5 years</td><td></td><td></td></tr>
<tr><td>Returns since inception</td><td></td><td></td></tr>
<tr><td colspan="3">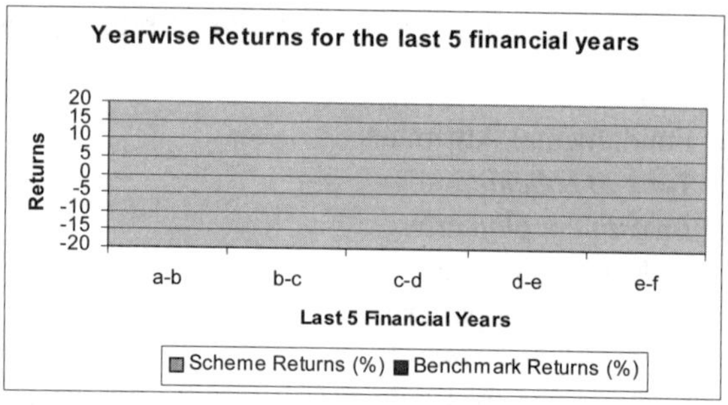</td></tr>
</table>

7.1.7 Units and Offer

- New Fund Offer (NFO).

  Opening date, Closing Date, Offering Price, Minimum Application Amount, Minimum Target Amount, Maximum Amount to be raised (if any), Plans / Options offered, Dividend policy, Allotment procedure, Refund procedure, Who can invest, Where to submit applications, How to apply, Listing, Special facilities (e.g., SIP, SWP, STP), Restrictions on Transfer

- Ongoing Offer.

  Re-opening date, How sale and re-purchase price will be determined, Cut-off timing, Where applications are to be submitted, Minimum amount for transactions, Minimum balance to be maintained, Consequences of non-maintenance of minimum balance, Special facilities, Procedures regarding account statement, dividend, redemption and consequences of delay

- Periodic disclosures.
  NAV
  Half-Yearly Portfolio Disclosure
  Half-Yearly Results
  Annual Report
  Associate Transactions
  Taxation (implications for resident investors and the mutual fund)
  Investor Services (Name, address and telephone number and e-mail of the contact person / grievances officer who would take care of investor queries and complaints)
- Computation of NAV.
  Brief policies of the mutual fund with regard computation of NAV of the scheme in accordance with SEBI (Mutual Funds) Regulations, 1996.
  Rounding off policy for NAV as per the applicable guidelines.
  Policy on computation of NAV in case of investment in foreign securities.

7.1.8 Fees and Expenses

Initial Issue Expenses

For the scheme proposed to be issued, the nature of the issue expenses to be incurred, such as advertising expenses, commission to agents or brokers, registrar's expenses, printing and marketing expenses and postage and miscellaneous expenses need to be described. The source for meeting these expenses may be disclosed.

Annual Scheme Recurring Expenses (as a per cent of Average Net Assets)

Expenses chargeable to the scheme need to be quantified. This would include investment management and advisory fee, trustee fee, custodian fee, registrar and transfer agent fee, marketing and selling expenses, brokerage and transaction cost on distribution of units, audit fee, investor communications cost, investor servicing cost, fund transfer cost, insurance premium, winding up costs for termination, cost of statutory advertisement, etc. Some of these expenses can be clubbed together.

If there is more than one plan, then the expense is to be given separately for each plan.

The mutual fund has to update the current expense ratios on the website within three working days, mentioning the effective date of the change.

The maximum limit for annual scheme running expense as per SEBI regulations too are to be disclosed.

Load Structure

Details of Exit Load, CDSC

7.1.9 Rights of Unit Holders

Refer to SAI.

7.1.10 Penalties, Pending Litigation or Proceedings, Findings of Inspections or Investigations for which action may have been taken or is in the process of being taken by any regulatory authority

This section contains the details of penalties, pending litigation, and action taken by SEBI and other regulatory and Govt. Agencies.

Annexure 7.2: Key Contents of SAI

7.2.1 Information about Sponsor, AMC and Trustee Companies

Constitution of the Mutual Fund

ABC (the "Mutual Fund") has been constituted as a trust on _______ in accordance with the provisions of the Indian Trusts Act, 1882 (2 of 1882) with XYZ, as the Sponsor and DEF as the Trustee. The Trust Deed has been registered under the Indian Registration Act, 1908. The Mutual Fund was registered with SEBI on ___________under Registration Code MF

Sponsor

ABC Mutual Fund is sponsored by XYZ. The Sponsor is the Settler of the Mutual Fund Trust. The Sponsor has entrusted a sum of ₹ _______ to the Trustee as the initial contribution towards the corpus of the Mutual Fund.

Financial Performance of the Sponsor (past three years) is as follows:

- Net Worth.
- Total Income.
- Profit after Tax.
- Assets Under Management (if applicable).

Trustees

DEF (the "Trustee"), through its Board of Directors, shall discharge its obligations as trustee of the ABC Mutual Fund. The Trustee ensures that the transactions entered into by the AMC are in accordance with the SEBI Regulations and will also review the activities carried on by the AMC.

Details of Trustee Directors are as follows:

Name, Age, Qualifications, Brief Experience
Responsibilities and duties of the Trustee as well as the specific and general due diligence.

Asset Management Company

STP Ltd. is a private limited company incorporated under the Companies Act, 1956 on ________, having its Registered Office at ____________________. STP Ltd. has been appointed as the Asset Management Company of the ________ Mutual Fund by the Trustee vide Investment Management Agreement (IMA) dated ___________, and executed between DEF and STP.

Details of AMC Directors are as follows:

Name, Age, Qualifications, Brief Experience
State the Duties and obligation of the AMC as specified in the SEBI Mutual Fund Regulations.

Information on Key Personnel is as follows:

Name, Age, Qualifications, Brief Experience of CEO, CIO, Operations Head, Compliance Officer, Sales Head, Risk Manager, Investor Relations Officer.

The AMC may decide on the key personnel it wants to mention in the SAI in addition to the persons mentioned above.

Service Providers
Details of Custodian, Transfer Agent, Statutory Auditor, Legal Counsel, Fund Accountant, Collecting Bankers.

7.2.2 Condensed Financial Information
Details to be given for all schemes launched by the mutual fund in last 3 fiscal years (excluding redeemed schemes):

NAV at beginning of year, Dividend, NAV at end of year, Annualised Return, Net Assets at end of period, Ratio of Recurring Expenses to Net Assets.

Dividend details do not need to be provided for liquid schemes.

Details may be given only for the growth option, and justification can be given for not providing details of the other options

7.2.3 How to Apply?
Procedures and KYC Requirements

7.2.4 Rights of Unit Holders in Scheme
The rights are to be listed here. These are discussed in Chapter 16.

7.2.5 Investment Valuation Norms for Securities and Other Assets

7.2.6 Tax, Legal and General Information
Applicable tax provisions for Mutual Fund and for investments in Mutual Fund scheme.

Information on Nomination Facility, KYC Requirements, Requirements of Prevention of Money Laundering Act, Transfer and transmission of units, Duration of the scheme/Winding up, Procedure and manner of winding up, etc.

Information on Underwriting, Securities Lending and Borrowing by the Mutual Funds, Inter-scheme transfers, Associate Transactions, etc.

Documents available for inspection

The following documents will be available for inspection at the office of the Mutual Fund at ______________________________ during business hours on any day (excluding Saturdays, Sundays and public holidays):

- Memorandum and Articles of Association of the AMC.
- Investment Management Agreement.
- Trust Deed and amendments thereto, if any.
- Mutual Fund Registration Certificate.
- Agreement between the Mutual Fund and the Custodian.
- Agreement with Registrar and Share Transfer Agents.
- Consent of Auditors to act in the said capacity.
- Consent of Legal Advisors to act in the said capacity.
- Securities and Exchange Board of India (Mutual Funds) Regulations, 1996 and amendments from time to time thereto.
- Indian Trusts Act, 1882.

Investor Grievances Redressal Mechanism

Brief description of the investors' complaints history for the last three fiscal years for existing schemes, and the redressal mechanism thereof. The SAI should include data updated every two months on the number of complaints received, redressed and pending with the Mutual Fund.

Annexure 7.3

Name of AMC & MF________________

(Type of Scheme)

KEY INFORMATION MEMORANDUM
Scheme
(_____________________________)
Offer for Units of ₹ 10 Per Unit for cash during the
Initial Offer Period and at NAV based prices upon re-opening

Initial Offer Opens on: Initial Offer Closes on: Scheme Re-opens for continuous sale and re-purchase on:

This Key Information Memorandum (KIM) sets forth the information, which a prospective investor ought to know before investing. For further details of the scheme/Mutual Fund, due diligence certificate by the AMC, Key Personnel, investors' rights & services, risk factors, penalties & pending litigations, associate transactions etc. investors should, before investment, refer to the Scheme Information Document and Statement of Additional Information available free of cost at any of the Investor Service Centres or distributors or from the website www. -----.

The Scheme particulars have been prepared in accordance with Securities and Exchange Board of India (Mutual Funds) Regulations 1996, as amended till date, and filed with Securities and Exchange Board of India (SEBI). The units being offered for public subscription have not been approved or disapproved by SEBI, nor has SEBI certified the accuracy or adequacy of this KIM.

Investment Objective			
Asset Allocation Pattern of the scheme	Types of Instruments		Normal Allocation (% of Net Assets)
	Equity and Equity Linked Instruments		
	Debt securities		
	Money market instruments		
	Gold and Gold Linked Instruments		
Risk Profile of the Scheme	Mutual Fund Units involve investment risks including the possible loss of principal. Please read the SID carefully for details on risk factors before investment. Scheme specific Risk Factors are summarized below:		
Plans and Options			
Applicable NAV (after the scheme opens for re-purchase and sale)			
Minimum Application Amount/ Number of Units	Purchase	Additional Purchase	Re-purchase
Despatch of Re-purchase (Redemption) Request	Within 10 working days of the receipt of the redemption request at the authorised centre of the ------- Fund.		
Benchmark Index			
Dividend Policy			
Name of the Fund Manager			

(Contd. . .)

Annexure 7.3 *(contd.)*

<table>
<tr><td>Name of the Trustee Company</td><td colspan="3"></td></tr>
<tr><td rowspan="6">[In case of a new scheme, the statement should be given "This scheme does not have any performance track record"]
Or
[In case of a scheme in existence, the return figures shall be given for that scheme only, as per the following:
▪ For a scheme which is in existence for more than 1 year, the returns given will be Compounded Annualised Returns and
▪ For a scheme which is in existence for less than 1 year, the returns would be absolute returns since inception.
Absolute returns for each financial year for the last 5 years shall be represented by means of a bar diagram as per the adjacent format.]</td><td>Compounded Annualised Returns</td><td>Scheme Returns %</td><td>Benchmark Returns %</td></tr>
<tr><td>Returns for the last 1 year</td><td></td><td></td></tr>
<tr><td>Returns for the last 3 years</td><td></td><td></td></tr>
<tr><td>Returns for the last 5 years</td><td></td><td></td></tr>
<tr><td>Returns since inception</td><td></td><td></td></tr>
<tr><td colspan="3">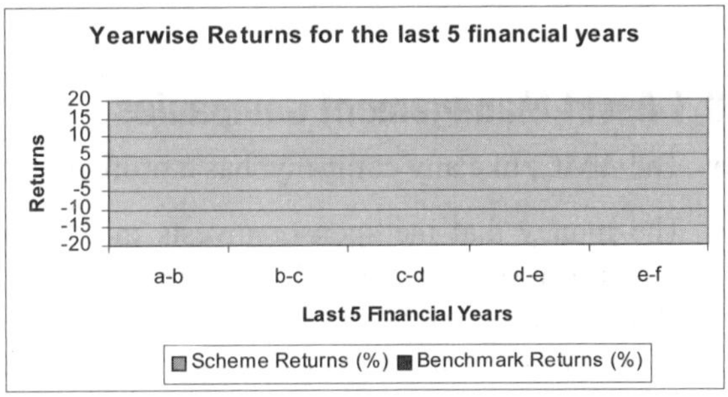
</td></tr>
</table>

<table>
<tr><td rowspan="2">Expenses of the Scheme
(i) Load Structure</td><td>New Fund Offer Period</td><td>Continuous Offer</td></tr>
<tr><td>Entry load : ----
Exit load : ----
CDSC (if any) :</td><td>Entry load : ----
Exit load : ----
CDSC (if any) : __</td></tr>
<tr><td>(ii) Recurring expenses (% of average net assets)</td><td>First ₹ 100 crores :
Next ₹ 300 crores :
Next ₹ 300 crores :
Balance :</td><td>Actual expenses for the previous financial year: ----
(Not Applicable in case of a new scheme)</td></tr>
<tr><td>Tax treatment for the Investors (Unit holders)</td><td colspan="2">Investor is advised to refer to the details in the Statement of Additional Information and also independently refer to his tax advisor.</td></tr>
<tr><td>Daily Net Asset Value (NAV) Publication</td><td colspan="2">The NAV will be declared on all ------- days and will be published in 2 newspapers. NAV can also be viewed on www.___ and http://www.amfiindia.com/ [You can also telephone us at ------ (optional)].</td></tr>
<tr><td>For Investor Grievances please contact</td><td>Name and Address of Registrar</td><td>Name, address, telephone number, fax number, e-mail id of ------Mutual Fund</td></tr>
<tr><td>Unit holders' Information</td><td colspan="2">Give frequency and the policy of the fund house for providing the Accounts Statement, Annual Financial results and Half yearly portfolio to the investors.</td></tr>
</table>

Date: N. B. Data and information shall be up-to-date but in no case older than 30 days from the date of KIM.

Chapter 8

Financial Statements

8.1 Asset Management Companies

- The AMC, like any company, has a profit and loss account and a balance sheet.
- The money that the sponsor invests in the AMC would go towards its share capital (or share premium). The prescribed minimum net worth (share capital plus reserves) is ₹ 50 crore. This helps in meeting the infrastructure costs such as premises, furniture, software etc. relating to asset management and also various expenses until the operation breaks even.
- Income for the AMC would be in the form of management fees earned from the schemes.
- Expense would be in rent, infrastructure, systems development, salary cost of staff, corporate advertisements, issue expenses, etc. Further, to make a scheme attractive, the AMC may choose to bear certain expenses that it is otherwise permitted to charge to the scheme.

  Recently, some AMCs adopted a practice of paying a high upfront commission to distributors of closed-end schemes. This meant an initial cash outgo for the AMC that would be recovered from the scheme during the tenor of the scheme through management fees.
- When the recurring expenses of a scheme are more than the prescribed ceilings, the excess has to be borne by the AMC (or trustees or the sponsor).
- If expenses are more than income, then the capital of the AMC gets eaten up. SEBI prescribes that the ₹ 50 crore minimum net worth is to be maintained at all times. The Trustees are obliged to review the net worth of the AMC quarterly, and ensure that any shortfall is made up.
- It is mandatory for AMCs to make their financial statements available on their website. Unit holders may, if they so desire, request for the annual report of the AMC.

- The balance sheet of AMCs, like that of any company, comprises the following heads of accounts:

Table 8.1

Sources of Funds	
a. Share Capital	
b. Reserves & Surplus	
c. Net Worth (a + b)	
d. Non-current Liabilities such as Long-term Loans	
Total Sources of Funds (c+d)	
Application of Funds	
a. Non-current assets such as Net Fixed Assets (Gross Block less Depreciation)	
b. Investments	
c. Net Current Assets (Current Assets plus Loans & Advances minus Current Liabilities)	
d. Miscellaneous Expenses (to the extent not written off or adjusted)	
e. Profit & Loss account (if negative)	
Total Application of Funds (a+b+c+d+e)	

- The profit and loss account of AMCs generally includes:

Table 8.2

Income	
a. Revenue from Operations e.g. Investment Management & Advisory Fee	
b. Other Income, e.g. interest on deposits	
c. Total Income (a+b)	
Expenses	
d. Personnel Cost	
e. Operating & Administration (rent, electricity, transport, communication etc.)	
f. Depreciation	
g. Finance costs such as interest	
h. Total Expenses (d+e+f+g)	
i. Profit before Tax (c – h)	
j. Tax expenses	
k. Profit / (Loss) for the year (I – j)	
Add: Balance brought forward from previous year	
Less: Dividend (paid to sponsor and other investors in the AMC)	
Balance carried to balance sheet	

8.2 Schemes

- The revenue account and balance sheet of the schemes are independent of the profit and loss account and balance sheet of the AMC. Each scheme would have its own revenue account and balance sheet.
- During the NFO, when units are issued at face value, the money brought in by investors would become part of the scheme's unit capital (on the liability side of the balance sheet) and bank account (on the asset side of the balance sheet).
- Post-NFO, the money invested by investors in the schemes would go into the balance sheet of the scheme, split into unit capital, unit premium reserve and equalization reserve, to the extent of the NAV, as explained in Chapter 6.
- The load collected from investors would be shown in the scheme accounts, and accrue to the benefit of unit holders.
- Income for the scheme would be in the form of interest, dividend and any capital gains realized.
- Expenses for the scheme would be in the nature of trusteeship fees, agent's commission, audit fees, registrar and transfer agent fees, management fees, etc. apart from any capital losses incurred.
- The income, net of expenses and losses on investments sold, would be the profit or loss for the period.
- The net appreciation or depreciation in investments held as at the end of the period would be added to the profit or loss for the period. This is a "below the line" adjustment. The balance would be carried to the balance sheet as reserves, subject to any dividend payout and additional tax thereon.
- The appreciation or depreciation, as the case may be, in investments is calculated on the basis of valuation policies mandated by SEBI.
- Often there are multiple options under a scheme, say, dividend option and growth option. The investment, income and expenses may be maintained for the entire scheme, and the profits or losses may then be apportioned between the options based on net assets to determine the NAV of each option.
- The balance sheet of schemes comprises the following heads of accounts:

Table 8.3

Sources of Funds	
a. Unit Capital	
b. Reserves & Surplus (Unit Premium Reserve, Unrealised Appreciation, Retained Earnings)	
c. Current Liabilities	
Total Sources of Funds (a+b+c)	

(Contd . . .)

Application of Funds	
a. Investments	
b. Deposits	
c. Other Current Assets	
d. Net Deficit (if Unrealised appreciation and retained earnings is negative)	
e. Accumulated Unit Discount (if Unit Premium Reserve is negative)	
Total Application of Funds (a+b+c+d+e)	

- The revenue account of schemes comprises the following heads of accounts:

Table 8.4

Income	
a. Dividend	
b. Interest	
c. Profit on sale / redemption of investments and derivatives	
d. Other income	
e. Total (a+b+c+d)	
Expenses and Losses	
f. Loss on sale / redemption of investments and derivatives	
g. Management Fee	
h. Trusteeship Fee	
i. Custodial Service Fee	
j. Registrar Service Fee	
k. Commission to Distributors	
l. Audit Fee	
m. Advertising & Publicity	
n. Other Operating Expenses	
o. Total Expenses and Losses (f + g + h +.......+n)	
p. Net Realised Gains / Loss for the period (e – o)	
q. Change in Net Unrealised Appreciation / (Depreciation) in Value of Investments and Derivatives	
r. Net Gains / Loss for the period (p + q)	
Add Income Equalisation Reserve	
Less Dividend to unit holders	
Less Income Tax on Dividend Distributed	
Retained Surplus, transferred to balance sheet	

(*Note:* The reserve would be calculated separately for each option / plan.)

8.3 Disclosures and Other Commitments

8.3.1 Daily Disclosures

- Mutual funds are required to update the NAV and sale / re-purchase prices (other than for fund of funds) on the AMFI website (www.amfiindia.com) by 9 p.m every day.
- Fund of fund schemes have time till 10 am on the following business day to upload the NAV and sale / re-purchase prices on the AMFI website.
- NAVs have to be published daily in at least two daily newspapers. Fund of funds need to mention with an asterisk that the NAV information has a lag of one day / actual number of days of lag.
- Total Expense Ratio of each scheme needs to be disclosed daily in downloadable spreadsheet format.

8.3.2 Monthly Disclosures

Scheme portfolio [including International Securities Identification Number (ISIN)] needs to be disclosed every month on the mutual fund website, in a user-friendly and downloadable format (preferably in a spreadsheet). The portfolio, as on the last day of each month, has to be disclosed on or before the 10th working day of the succeeding month. For example, portfolio as of 31 August 2018 has to be disclosed by 10 September 2018.

8.3.4 Half-yearly Disclosures

- Within one month of the close of each half-year, i.e. 31st March and 30th September, mutual funds (i.e. the schemes) are required to publish their unaudited financial results as per the prescribed format along with other mandated disclosures, such as:
    - Effect of changes in any accounting policies;
    - Investments made in associate companies, payments to associate companies, etc.;
    - Investments made in companies that have invested more than 5 per cent of the NAV;
    - Large holdings (over 25 per cent of the corpus of the scheme), including information about the number of investors and total holdings by them in percentage terms. This also needs to be disclosed in allotment letters after initial public offerings, and in the annual results;
    - Any bonus declared during the half-year in respect of the scheme;
    - Borrowings above 10 per cent of the NAV;
    - Exposure to derivatives above 10 per cent of the NAV;
    - Deferred revenue expenditure; and
    - Brokerage and commission paid to associates / related parties / group companies of sponsor / asset management company.

The half-yearly unaudited financial results have to be published in one national English daily newspaper and in a newspaper in the language of the region where the head office of the fund is situated.

Within 7 days of their publication, copies of the advertisement need to be filed with SEBI.

- Similarly, within one month from the close of each half-year, namely 31st March and 30th September, mutual funds are required to publish their scheme portfolio in the prescribed format in one national English daily newspaper and in a newspaper in the language of the region where the head office of the fund is situated. The portfolio disclosure shall include:
  - Equity-oriented schemes — Portfolio turnover, name of industry against each security.
  - Debt-oriented schemes — Average maturity of portfolio.
  - Prescribed details of derivatives. Margin amounts paid are to be separately disclosed under cash and bank balances.

Instead of publishing the portfolio, the mutual fund can send the portfolio statement to unit holders within one month of the close of each half-year.

Besides, the portfolio statement is to be put up on the mutual fund web site in a user-friendly and downloadable format (preferably in a spreadsheet), and also filed with SEBI.

8.3.5 Annual Disclosures

Abridged scheme-wise annual report has to be mailed to all unit holders not later than six months from the date of closure of the relevant accounting year. Also, the full and unabridged annual report has to be available for inspection at the head office of the fund and a copy made available to the unit holders on request on payment of nominal fees, if any.

In order to bring cost effectiveness in printing and despatch, and as part of a green initiative, mutual funds are now allowed to send the annual reports or abridged summary by e-mail instead of in a physical format, wherever the address is available. Mutual funds need to continue sending physical copy if they do not have a unit holder's e-mail ID. They can however write to the investors asking for their e-mail ID. Investors have the right to ask for the physical copy.

The number of investors holding over 25 % of the NAV in a scheme and their total holdings in percentage terms need to be disclosed along with the annual results.

Brokerage and commission paid to associates / related parties / group companies of sponsor / asset management company need to be disclosed in the abridged scheme-wise annual report and the Statement of Additional Information.

The requirement of publishing the scheme-wise annual report or abridged annual report has been scrapped. However, it has to be featured in the AMC's website. The AMC's website has also, in turn, to be linked to AMFI's website.

Mutual funds have to disclose on their websites, on the AMFI website, as well as in their annual reports, details of investor complaints received by them from all sources. The said details should be vetted and signed off by the trustees of the concerned mutual fund. The report is to be uploaded within 2 months of the end of the financial year.

The annual report of the AMC should be displayed on the website of the mutual funds. It should also be mentioned in the annual report of the mutual fund schemes that the unit holders, if they so desire, may request for a copy of the annual report of the AMC.

Chapter 9

Scheme Comparison — Returns

Just as bananas can be bought by number or weight; oil can be purchased by weight or volume, so too scheme returns can be viewed through different frames. Absolute Returns and Relative Returns are two forms of return that get discussed in mutual fund schemes.

9.1 Absolute Returns

The following sections discuss various facets of absolute returns, and the associated statistical techniques.

9.1.1 Simple Returns& Annualisation

If the NAV of a scheme has gone up from ₹ 10 to ₹ 12 during a year, and no dividend has been declared during this period, then we know that the return on the scheme is:

(₹ 12 – ₹ 10) ÷ ₹ 10, i.e. 0.2

namely, 20 per cent (simple return).

If the NAV of a scheme has gone up from ₹ 10 to ₹ 30 during a 2-year period, then the return is effectively:

(₹ 30 – ₹ 10) ÷ ₹ 10, i.e. 2.0

namely, 200 per cent over a 2-year period (cumulative aggregate return).

Lay investors would crudely argue that the annual return is 200% ÷ 2 namely, 100 per cent (average annualised return).

The counter to the above crude argument is that the return would be 100 per cent only if ₹ 10 doubled to ₹ 20 during the first year, and then, the ₹ 20 doubled to ₹ 40 during the second year. Thus, if ₹ 10 grows to anything less than ₹ 40 during two years, the annual return is less than 100 per cent.

The difference between the two arguments is essentially the impact of compounding. The longer the time period for which we are calculating the return, more would be the absurdity in results if compounding is ignored and returns are calculated based on simple interest. For instance, an IDBI 25-year Deep Discount Bond, where ₹ 2,700 was to grow to ₹ 1 lakh in 25 years, had an average annualised return of 144 per cent!

[{(₹ 1,00,000 – ₹ 2,700) ÷ ₹ 2,700} ÷ 25 years]

As we will discuss later in this chapter, the return from the IDBI Deep Discount Bond, on a compounded basis, was 15.54% p.a.

According to the SEBI regulations on disclosure of information in offer documents, advertisements, etc. simple return is to be used only for periods less than a year. Return for periods exceeding a year is to be calculated on a compounded basis. When the period is exactly a year, the simple return and compounded return would yield the same result.

Suppose the simple return for a scheme that has been in existence for 4 months is 5%. The equivalent annual return would be:

5% × (12 ÷ 4) = 15%.

This adjustment, to determine annual return based on the simple return for a period that is not equal to a year, is called "annualisation".

9.1.2 Arithmetic Mean of Periodic Returns

The investor at times, prefers to evaluate a scheme based on returns over several periods. For instance, she might like to look at monthly returns over a period of 2 years. Thus, she would be working with 24 (2 × 12) such periodic returns. Averaging these periodic returns gives the mean periodic return.

A common method of averaging is arithmetic average (also called "arithmetic mean").

Suppose an investment has yielded a return over the year as follows:

Table 9.1

Month	*1*	*2*	*3*	*4*	*5*	*6*	*7*	*8*	*9*	*10*	*11*	*12*
%	0.1	3.0	0.5	0.3	0.1	– 4.0	– 2.0	– 0.1	4.5	2.0	0.4	1.2

The total of the monthly returns above (i.e., 0.1 + 3.0 + ... + 0.4 + 1.2) is 6%. The number of observations is 12. So arithmetic mean is 6% ÷ 12 = 0.5%.

9.1.3 Time-weighted Mean

In the above arithmetic mean each month's return was given equal importance. An alternative is to give different weights to different periods.

Suppose we decide to give weights as follows:

Quarter	*Weight*
Quarter 1	2
Quarter 2	4
Quarter 3	6
Quarter 4	8

With these weights, you can see that the more recent quarters have got higher weightage. You will also note that since each quarter has 3 months, the total of the weights for a full year is:

(2 × 3) + (4 × 3) + (6 × 3) + (8 × 3), i.e. 60

Let us apply the weights on the numbers we used for calculating arithmetic mean:

Table 9.2

Month	1	2	3	4	5	6	7	8	9	10	11	12
%	0.1	3.0	0.5	0.3	0.1	– 4.0	– 2.0	– 0.1	4.5	2.0	0.4	1.2
Weight	2	2	2	4	4	4	6	6	6	8	8	8
Weight x %	0.2	6.0	1.0	1.2	0.4	– 16.0	– 1.2	– 0.6	27.0	16.0	3.2	9.6

The total of the (weight × %) row is 46.80%.
Time-weighted return is given by the formula:
Total (weight × %) ÷ Total (weights)

i.e., 46.80% ÷ 60 = 0.78%

Thus, by giving higher importance to the recent good performances, the time weighted return is higher at 0.78%, as compared to the simple arithmetic mean of 0.50%.

9.1.4 Mode

Suppose we have a sequence of returns like the following:

1%, 2%, – 1%, 3%, 2%, – 3%, 2%, 5%, – 3%, 2%, 2%

The most common occurrence among these 11 values is 2%, which occurs 5 times in the above sequence. The most frequently occurring data point is called the mode.

While deciding on the Unique Selling Proposition to offer on a mutual fund scheme, the issuing company would look at the most frequently liked feature, i.e. the mode, where the data points would be the single most liked feature in a scheme, ascertained from a sample of investors. If more investors prefer a 51:49 mix of debt and equity in a balanced scheme, then the scheme would be offered with 51:49 as the target asset allocation.

9.1.5 Median

Median is the mid-point of the series, determined after the observations are ordered sequentially. The same sequence of returns used for the mode could be re-ordered as follows:

– 3%, – 3%, – 1%, 1%, 2%, 2%, 2%, 2%, 2%, 3%, 5%

The midpoint of the series of 11 observations would be the 6th observation, i.e. 2%.

Suppose we want to determine out-performers of mutual fund schemes, we could use an average performer as a standard. There would then be some schemes which would have performed better, while others would have performed worse. If the arithmetic mean were to be used as the average, it could get highly influenced by a few schemes that show extremely good, or poor, performance. Instead, if the median is used, then an equal number of schemes would be better or worse than the average.

On account of the cumbersome process of having to re-order the observations so that they fall into a sequence, median is less commonly used.

9.1.6 Frequency Distribution

While working with large volumes of data, it becomes cumbersome to do calculations using every data point. A shortcut that could be used is frequency distribution, which considers the frequency with which data points fall in different ranges of values. In the example used earlier for calculating the mean, for instance:

Table 9.3

Range	*– 4.0 to – 2.1*	*– 2.0 to – 0.1*	*0 to 2.0*	*2.1 to 4.0*	*4.1 to 6.0*
Mid point	– 3.05	– 1.05	1	3.05	5.05
Frequency	1	2	7	1	1

The 12 observations are distributed as per the frequencies given above. When a frequency distribution is used, all the observations within the range are deemed to be equal to the mid-point of the range. This assumption simplifies all further data analysis. The validity of the assumption however depends on the data ranges, statistically referred to as "class intervals", used.

Setting the data ranges is a very subjective and specialised exercise. If we set the ranges too narrowly (e.g., – 4.0 to – 3.8, – 3.8 to – 3.6, – 3.6 to – 3.4, and so on), then the number of ranges would end up being too many to give any benefit of using the frequency distribution. On the other hand, if the ranges are set too broadly (e.g., – 10.0 to – 0.1,0 to 10.0 and so on), then the mid-point may not be truly representative of the underlying data.

9.1.7 Expected Value / Volume Weighted Mean

In a world of uncertainty, it is difficult to make predictions; yet there is no shortage of "views". At times, the number of views is more than the number of people from whom you seek the view!

Let us consider an example.

Television channels often seek the views of research analysts on the profits they expect companies to declare. Suppose the table on next page gives the views of different analysts on the expected profits of a company:

Table 9.4

Profit Estimate (₹ Cr)	– 25 to 0	0 to 25	25 - 50	50 -75	75-100	Total
Mid point	– 12.50	12.50	37.5	62.5	87.5	
Number of Analysts	5	10	20	10	5	50
% of analysts	10%	20%	40%	20%	10%	100%
Mid point multiplied by *% of analysts*	– 1.25	2.50	15.00	12.50	8.75	37.50

Expected value of profits based on the volume weighted mean of analyst estimates is ₹ 37.50 crore. Similarly, expected value of returns from the market or a scheme can be determined.

9.1.8 The Role of Dividend

Whenever a dividend is declared, the NAV of a mutual fund goes down because the dividend amount no longer belongs to the scheme, it belongs to the investors. The reduced NAV, immediately after a dividend distribution is referred to as "Ex-Dividend NAV". If we calculate returns based only on the movement in NAV, it can lead to an understatement of return, whenever a dividend is paid or re-invested.

However, if a scheme has a growth option, i.e. where no dividends are declared, then the earnings would be fully reflected in the NAV. In such cases, the simple return can be calculated based on change in NAV, subject to the issues related to compounding.

9.1.9 Total Return

Total return is calculated like simple return, but the dividend distribution is added to the closing NAV. Suppose the NAV of a scheme has grown from ₹ 10 to ₹ 12 during a period of a year, where dividend of ₹ 1 per unit was paid.

Simple return, we saw earlier, is:

(₹ 12 – ₹ 10) ÷ ₹ 10, i.e. 20 per cent.

Total return is:

(₹ 12 + ₹ 1 – ₹ 10) ÷ ₹ 10, i.e. 30 per cent.

Thus, unlike simple return, total return includes the dividends paid. So it is a superior measure of return. However, the other weakness of simple return, namely no compounding, is a problem with total return too.

Further, we know that receiving a dividend towards the beginning of any period is more valuable (since it can earn interest if that dividend is deposited in a bank) than the same dividend received towards the end of the period. This time value of the dividend needs to be considered while calculating returns. In the above example, total return would be 30 per cent, irrespective of whether the dividend of ₹ 1 was received at the beginning of the period or the end of the period. This is a serious weakness of the total return calculations.

9.1.10 Compounded Annual Growth Rate (CAGR)

If the NAV of the growth option of a scheme (which does not declare a dividend) grows from ₹ 10 to ₹ 12 over a 2-year time period, the CAGR can be calculated using the compound interest formula

$(A \div P)^{(1 \div t)} - 1$,

where:
"A" is the closing wealth,
"P" is the opening wealth, and
"t" is the time period in years.

Thus, in the above example, CAGR would amount to:

$(12 \div 10)^{(1 \div 2)} - 1$
$= 9.54\%$.

In the earlier IDBI Deep Discount Bond example, where ₹ 2,700 was to grow into ₹ 1 lakh over 25 years, the CAGR amounts to 15.54% — a far cry from the simple return of 144% when inappropriately based on simple interest.

9.1.11 CAGR with Re-investment of Dividend

In a situation where dividend is distributed, the CAGR is worked out on the following basis:

- Assume that any dividend declared by a scheme is re-invested in the same scheme at the ex-dividend NAV.
- On the above basis, calculate growth in number of units during the period for which returns are being calculated.
- Opening number of units multiplied by opening NAV would give opening wealth.
- Closing number of units multiplied by closing NAV would give closing wealth.
- Use compound interest formula to determine the CAGR between the opening and closing wealth.

The calculations are shown in the example that follows. CAGR is a superior measure because it considers the dividend distribution (unlike simple return), and is also sensitive to the timing of such distribution (unlike total return). It also assumes that the dividend is re-invested in the same scheme. This is a more appropriate assumption for understanding the scheme's return than an assumption that money is deployed somewhere else.

As discussed earlier, it is mandatory to use compounded return (CAGR) to disclose information in advertisements and offer documents if the period under consideration is more than a year.

Example 9.1

On 1 January 1998, the NAV of an equity scheme of the BCCI Mutual Fund was ₹ 10. It rose to ₹ 30 by 1 January 2000. The scheme paid a dividend of ₹ 1 per unit on 1 January 1999, and a further dividend of ₹ 1 per unit on 1st January 2000. The ex-dividend NAV was ₹ 20 on 1 January 1999. What is the return during the period 1998-99, 1999-2000 and 1998-2000?

For easy calculations, let us assume that the investor started with 18,000 units in the scheme. (Whatever the initial number of units we assume, the calculated returns would be the same.)

The movement in the value of the scheme is as follows:

Date	*No. of Existing Units*	*Dividend (₹)*	*NAV (₹)*	*No. of New Units*	*Wealth (₹)*
1/1/1998	18,000		10.00		1,80,000
1/1/1999		18,000	20.00	900	
1/1/1999	18,900		20.00		3,78,000
1/1/2000		18,900	30.00	630	
1/1/2000	19,530		30.00		5,85,900

The period 1998-99 being exactly 1 year, we can calculate simple returns as follows:

(₹ 3,78,000 – ₹ 1,80,000) ÷ ₹ 1,80,000
= 1.1, i.e. 110 per cent.

Similarly, the period 1999-2000 being exactly 1 year, we can calculate simple returns as follows:

(₹ 5,85,900 – ₹ 3,78,000) ÷ ₹ 3,78,000
= 0.55, i.e. 55 per cent.

The period 1998-2000 is more than 1 year.
Simple return (cumulative aggregate) during the period:

= (₹ 5,85,900 – ₹ 1,80,000) ÷ ₹ 1,80,000
= 2.255
= 225.5 per cent.

Simple return (average annualised) for the 2 years is:

225.5% ÷ 2, i.e. 112.75 per cent.

The CAGR can be worked out using the formula:

(₹ 5,85,900 ÷ ₹ 1,80,000)$^{(1 \div 2)}$ – 1
= 0.8042
= 80.42 per cent.

(Contd . . .)

Example 9.1 *(contd.)*

Interestingly, the same formula applied for 1998-99 would be:

$(₹\ 3,78,000 \div ₹\ 1,80,000)^{(1/1)} - 1$

= 1.1

= 110 per cent.

Similarly, the same formula applied for 1999-2000 would be:

$(₹\ 5,85,900 \div ₹\ 3,78,000)^{(1/1)} - 1$

= 0.55

= 55 per cent.

This confirms that when the period is exactly a year, the simple return is exactly equal to CAGR.

9.1.12 XIRR

CAGR calculations for investors can be cumbersome, particularly when they have done multiple transactions of sale and re-purchase during a period. If the investor wants to know what return she earned from a scheme during such a period of multiple transactions, CAGR can become a nightmare. Further, for every dividend distribution, the analyst would also require the ex-dividend NAV. XIRR comes in handy here.

XIRR, a financial function available in MS Excel software, was discussed in Chapter 4. The formula is "XIRR(cell range of cash flows, cell range of timing of these cash flows)". Thus, the formula captures information on the timing of various cash flows during the holding period of the investment. (Please note that the formula varies from the "IRR" function in MS Excel, where information on the cash flow is captured, but not the timing of these flows).

As seen earlier, CAGR is calculated assuming re-investment at ex-dividend NAV. On the other hand, the XIRR function in MS Excel presumes re-investment at the internal rate of return itself. The cash flows used for the XIRR calculations should therefore not consider increase in the number of units on account of re-investment of dividend. The cash flows for the earlier example were:

Date	₹	
1 / 1 / 1998	– 180,000	Opening NAV = 18,000 × ₹ 10
1 / 1 / 1999	18,000	Dividend = 18,000 × ₹ 1
1 / 1 / 2000	18,000	Dividend = 18,000 × ₹ 1
1 / 1 / 2000	540,000	Closing NAV = 18,000 × ₹ 30

The XIRR would give an annualised return of 81.14 per cent, which is marginally different from the CAGR of 80.42 per cent. This difference is on account of the different principles underlying CAGR and XIRR, namely re-investment at ex-dividend NAV (in the case of CAGR) versus re-investment at the internal rate of return (in the case of XIRR). How does this difference in principles affect us?

- It is not always possible to re-invest moneys at the internal rate of return. Therefore, investors need to be cautious whenever the value of XIRR turns out to be too high. They need to ask themselves, "Will I be able to re-invest the moneys I receive on the investment, at the XIRR rate?" If the answer is no, then it would be better to avoid using the XIRR.
- In some situations, MS Excel will not give a valid answer for XIRR. This happens when there are too many investment and disinvestment transactions, on account of which the pattern of cash flows keeps changing from positive to negative and back. In such situations, one has to use CAGR only.
- The assumption, which XIRR makes, that the re-investment rate would remain constant throughout the period of review, is obviously mistaken. On the other hand, CAGR provides for differential performance during the period of review. For instance, our earlier calculations were based on the first dividend being re-invested at ₹ 20, and the second dividend being re-invested at ₹ 30.

On account of these reasons, the CAGR is a fundamentally stronger method of measuring return. SEBI insists that statutory information from the AMC be disclosed on the basis of CAGR. However, specific calculations for investors are made by both fund houses and distributors on the basis of XIRR.

9.1.13 Rolling Returns

Investors often like to know the returns for various periods of 7 days or 1 month or some such period. These are called "rolling returns".

For example, the return from 1 October 2005 to 8 October 2005 represents a 7-day return. Similar calculation of returns from 2 October 2005 to 9 October 2005, 3 October 2005 to 10 October 2005, and so on, are called *7-day rolling returns*.

Equity returns are highly volatile, when we view them as daily returns. But, when we look at equity returns over longer time periods, the rolling return charts look much more stable. Chapter 3 of *Wealth Engine* [Vision Books, 2012] features some interesting charts of rolling returns on equity for different periods from one year to 20 years.

Debt investments earn interest each day. The longer the period that a person holds on to a debt investment or debt fund, greater would be the interest income available for setting off losses arising out of change in value of securities. On account of this influence of interest income (called "accrued income"), if the rolling returns for a debt scheme are plotted in a graph, the 1-day rolling returns would vary far more significantly (i.e., be more volatile) than 7-day rolling returns, which, again, would vary more significantly than rolling returns for periods longer than 7 days.

It is often easier to convince an investor to invest in a mutual fund scheme by demonstrating the low volatility of 30-day rolling returns (for debt schemes) or 3-year rolling returns (for equity schemes). Of course, this pre-supposes that the investor is prepared to hold the investment for at least 30 days or 3 years, as the case may be.

9.1.14 Load Adjusted Returns

The calculations given above were at the scheme level. NAV was used as a determinant of the scheme's performance.

If an investor has paid an entry load (invested at more than NAV — no longer permitted) or incurred an exit load / contingent deferred sales load (recovered less than NAV on exit), then the investor's actual returns would be less than the scheme's performance calculated based on NAV.

Thus, in the above example if an exit load of ₹ 1.50 was applicable on 1 January 2000, then the investor would recover only ₹ 28.50 per unit — not ₹ 30.00 per unit. In that case, her closing wealth is only ₹ 556,605, giving a CAGR of 75.85 per cent for the two-year period.

All AMCs would have different investors with different applicable load structures. For reasons of convenience, AMCs calculate CAGR on the basis of NAV. Distributors interacting with investors would need to consider the impact of loads while working out the returns for investors. This is easily done by using the sale and re-purchase prices, instead of the NAV, while calculating opening wealth and closing wealth.

9.2 Relative Returns

We have so far calculated the returns of a scheme in various situations. But we have not compared the scheme's returns with the performance of the market. Mutual funds ultimately invest in the financial market. Therefore, returns in schemes need to be viewed in the context of how the market has performed. Such a comparative view on returns is called "relative returns". The comparison could be with respect to the following.

9.2.1 Benchmark Market Indices

In school, my parents would be upset if I scored 90 marks out of 100 in mathematics. I would plead eloquently about outperforming many friends. My parents would highlight the top ranker who scored a perfect 100. The difference between me and my parents was obviously in the benchmark selected! A benchmark should ideally be a standard worth emulating — and outperforming.

In the equity market several indices are available as benchmark. Some are representative of the market in general, such as S&P BSE Sensex, S&P BSE100, S&P BSE200, NSE CNX Nifty, etc. Sector specific indices such as ET Brandex, ET Mindex, BS ICE, etc. are also available.

I-Sec's I-Bex index is available as a benchmark for schemes that invest in government securities. Li-Bex is for longer maturities (over 7 years), Mi-Bex is for medium maturities (3-7 years) and Si-Bex is for shorter maturities (1-3 years). I-Sec's Composite Gilt Index is the average of Li-Bex, Mi-Bex and Si-Bex.

CRISIL maintains 7 standard indices for debt and hybrid products:

- Liquid Fund Index: ["Liquifex" — benchmark for a liquid fund debt portfolio that includes CBLO, certificate of deposit and commercial paper];
- Balanced Fund Index: ["Balance Ex" — benchmark for equity oriented hybrid portfolios that is a blend of the CNX Nifty Index (65%) and the CRISIL Composite Bond Fund Index (35%)];
- Composite Bond Fund Index: ["Compbex" — benchmark for a composite debt portfolio that includes CBLO, certificate of deposit, commercial paper, government securities and AAA and AA rated instrument];
- MIP Index: ["Mipex" — benchmark for debt oriented hybrid portfolios and is a blend of the CNX Nifty Index (15%) and the CRISIL Composite Bond Fund Index (85%)];
- Short Term Bond Fund Index: [CBLO, commercial paper, certificate of deposit, government securities as also AAA and AA rated instruments. The index maturity corresponds to short-term debt funds)];
- CRISIL Debt Hybrid 75+25 Index: [Benchmark for hybrid portfolios comprising predominantly of short-term debt and equity securities and is a blend of the CNX Nifty Index (25%) and the CRISIL Short Term Bond Fund Index (75%)]; and
- CRISIL Debt Hybrid 60+40 Index: [Benchmark for hybrid funds comprising of short-term debt and equity securities and is calculated using the returns of the CNX Nifty Index (40%) and the CRISIL Short Term Bond Fund Index (60%)]

JP Morgan too has indices for the debt markets — Treasury Bills [JP Morgan Treasury Bill Index] and GOI Securities.[JP Morgan India Government Bond Index (IGBI)].

These benchmark indices can be used for reviewing the relative performance of various schemes. Thus, for instance, if an equity scheme demonstrated a return of 12 per cent during a period when the benchmark index grew by 5 per cent, then the scheme has outperformed the index.

In a relative comparison, selection of the most appropriate benchmark is critical. Selection of the benchmark, in turn, depends on the investment philosophy of the scheme. Thus, if a scheme is to invest in only 20 to 50 select stocks, then the benchmark has to be a narrow-based index like BSE CNX Sensex (calculated from price quotes of 30 stocks) or NSE Nifty (calculated from 50 stocks). A broad based index like BSE200 (calculated from 200 stocks) would not be representative of the investment philosophy of the scheme.

In order to ensure a valid comparison, even a "synthetic benchmark" can be considered. For instance, a scheme that proposes to invest 40 per cent in broad based equity and the balance 60 per cent in bonds, can consider a synthetic index which would be constructed as the weighted average of 40 per cent on BSE200 and 60 per cent on I-Bex Index.

The proposed construction of a synthetic index is to be disclosed in the offer document. The same can then be used as a benchmark for evaluation of relative performance of the scheme.

The appropriate benchmark index for an index scheme would be the index on which the scheme portfolio is constructed.

In the published half-yearly results which disclose the performance during the last 6 months, 1 year, 3 years, 5 years and since inception, the performance of benchmark indices too needs to be disclosed.

9.2.2 Similar Competing Schemes

Fund houses make internal comparisons of how their scheme has performed against schemes of their competitors that have a similar investment objective and investment style.

As in the case of benchmark index, it is important to select a competing scheme that is representative of the scheme under consideration. For instance, it would be wrong to compare a liquid scheme with a gilt scheme, since the two represent entirely different investment objectives. Similarly, comparing the performance of a large cap fund with that of a mid cap fund would be fallacious.

CRISIL publishes CRISIL AMFI MF Performance Indices every day, based on performance of mutual fund schemes of each type. Unlike the benchmark market indices discussed in the previous section, which are based on security prices in the market, the MF Performance Indices are based on scheme returns (after fund management and other costs charged to the scheme). These indices are available separately for debt, equity and hybrid funds including sub-categories of each of these funds, e.g. equity fund, large cap fund, diversified equity fund, small and mid-cap fund, ELSS fund, debt fund, income fund, gilt fund, short-term debt fund, money market fund, liquid fund, ultra short-term fund, hybrid fund, mip fund and balanced fund. These categories will need to change in line with the new categories mandated by SEBI, as discussed in Chapter 2.

Investors prefer absolute returns with certainty while mutual funds keep referring to relative returns. Thus when the market goes down, mutual fund NAVs too would go down. To the extent the decline in its NAV is lower, in percentage terms, the scheme is claimed to have outperformed the market.

Internationally, there is a category of funds called absolute returns funds. These seek to earn positive returns in all kinds of market situations. Thus, when their market view is bearish, they indulge in aggressive short-selling. Derivatives, too, can help schemes earn positive returns in weak markets. Some of these approaches to earn absolute returns can be extremely dangerous if the bearish view of the market does not come to pass.

Similarly, there are unconstrained funds that operate with flexibility in their asset allocation. They can switch between extreme positions in debt or equity, depending on the view on the asset class. Here, again, wrong calls on the asset class can ruin the scheme's performance.

It is therefore important for investors to consider not only the returns, but also the inherent risks in the management style or the portfolio. The topic of risk is covered in the next chapter.

Chapter 10

Scheme Comparison — Risk

Investors and intermediaries need to get out of their tendency to swing on a single quantitative factor — return. They have to appreciate that return and risk go hand in hand. Contrary to popular perception, even risk can be quantified. Besides, several other qualitative factors go into scheme comparison and selection. This chapter focuses on the statistical tools that form the basis for measurement of risk. Application of the tools in scheme evaluation ratios is discussed in the next chapter.

10.1 Quantitative Factors

According to Hall (2000), "It is probably wise to avoid managers whose year-to-year performance records look like a cardiogram of a person developing a heart attack. Unless you can handle this volatility well, what eventually happens with the money you've invested may cause you to have a heart attack".[41]

Risk in financial securities can be assessed using measures such as variance, standard deviation, and beta.

10.1.1 Variance

Variance is a measure of fluctuation in returns. It is calculated by putting down a single series of values that represents the returns on a security, or fund, for different evenly distributed time periods and then calculating the statistical variance. A simple example given in Table 10.1 would illustrate the concept.

It is clear from the NAV information that Scheme B fluctuates much more than Scheme A. This is also seen from the variance. While the variance of scheme A is 0.0094, i.e. 0.94%, that of scheme B is much higher at 0.1595, i.e. 15.95%.

It is easier to calculate variance using the "VAR" function in MS Excel. The formula would be "VAR (cell range)", where the cell range in the aforesaid example would be the cells from Month 2 to Month 13 under the column "% change". The syntax is "= var (c4:c15)".

Table 10.1

	A	B	C	D	E	F	G	H	I
1		**Scheme A**				**Scheme B**			
2	*Month*	*NAV*	*% change*	*Diff. from avg.*	*Square of diff.*	*NAV*	*% change*	*Diff. from avg.*	*Square of diff.*
3	1	10.00				10.00			
4	2	12.00	20.0%	19.6%	3.8%	14.00	40.0%	32.9%	10.8%
5	3	11.50	– 4.2%	– 4.6%	0.2%	16.00	14.3%	7.2%	0.5%
6	4	13.00	13.0%	12.6%	1.6%	8.00	– 50.0%	– 57.1%	32.6%
7	5	12.00	– 7.7%	– 8.1%	0.7%	13.00	62.5%	55.4%	30.7%
8	6	11.00	– 8.3%	– 8.8%	0.8%	10.00	– 23.1%	– 30.2%	9.1%
9	7	9.50	– 13.6%	– 14.1%	2.0%	7.00	– 30.0%	– 37.1%	13.8%
10	8	9.00	– 5.3%	– 5.7%	0.3%	12.00	71.4%	64.3%	41.3%
11	9	8.50	– 5.6%	– 6.0%	0.4%	9.00	– 25.0%	– 32.1%	10.3%
12	10	9.00	5.9%	5.5%	0.3%	12.00	33.3%	26.2%	6.9%
13	11	9.50	5.6%	5.1%	0.3%	14.00	16.7%	9.5%	0.9%
14	12	9.75	2.6%	2.2%	0.0%	9.00	– 35.7%	– 42.8%	18.4%
15	13	10.00	2.6%	2.1%	0.0%	10.00	11.1%	4.0%	0.2%
No. of observations		13	12	12	12	13	12	12	12
Total			5.0%		10.4%		85.5%		175.5%
Variance {Total square ÷ (n-1)}, where "n" is number of observations.					0.0094				0.1595

10.1.2 Standard Deviation

Standard deviation is the square root of variance. In the example given earlier:

-	*Scheme A*	*Scheme B*
Variance	0.0094	0.1595
Standard Deviation	0.0971	0.3994

Standard deviation can also be calculated using the "STDEV" function in MS Excel. The formula would be "STDEV(cell range)", where the cell range, as in the earlier example, would be the cells from Month 2 to Month 13 under the column "% change". The syntax is "= stdev (c4::c15)".

10.1.3 Annualised Standard Deviation

Measures such as Sharpe Ratio (discussed in the next chapter), use annualised standard deviation. This is calculated by multiplying the standard deviation calculated above, by the square root of the number of observations that would represent a year. Thus, if we were working with weekly NAV, then 52 observations would constitute a year. But if we were working with daily NAV, then, net of Saturdays, Sundays and public holidays, the number of observations in a year would be around 250.

In the above example, the standard deviation was calculated on the basis of monthly observations, which would be 12 in a year. Therefore, annualised standard deviation would be:

Scheme A = 0.0971 × square root of 12 = 0.3364
Scheme B = 0.3994 × square root of 12 = 1.3836

"SQRT" function in MS Excel is used to calculate square root. Square root of 12 is calculated by entering "=SQRT(12)" in MS Excel.

Higher Value of Standard Deviation Means Higher Risk

Ferri (2003) gives an insightful perspective on the concept. "Standard deviation is a mathematical formula that expresses the average amount of price volatility in the market. Standard deviation does not express the limits of market risk; it simply tells us the "average miss", how far the market return in any given year was from its historical average annual returns".[42]

10.1.4 Covariance

Variance and standard deviation are calculated for an individual security or scheme. But there may be two securities which are related such that when the returns in one go up, the returns in the other tend to go down. Therefore, if the two are combined in a portfolio, then the risk (volatility of returns) of the portfolio will reduce.

Markowitz, the father of Modern Portfolio Theory introduced to the financial world, Covariance as a measure of such joint movement of securities. It can be easily calculated using the "COVAR" function in MS Excel. The formula "Covar (Cell Range for returns in Security A, Cell Range for returns in Security B)" would yield an answer 0.001327. The syntax is "= covar (c4::c15, g4::g15)".

Covariance is not a standardized measure that can be used across situations. Given a covariance number, it cannot be said whether the number is too high, too low, or just adequate. Therefore, it is used more as input for certain portfolio risk calculations, rather than as a standalone measure.

10.1.5 Correlation Coefficient (R)

Covariance can be standardised by dividing it by the standard deviation of the returns of the two schemes. The resulting measure is called "Correlation Coefficient".

In the above example:

Correlation = 0.001327 ÷ (0.0930 x 0.3824), i.e. 0.037312.

This means that the returns in the two schemes are correlated to the extent of 3.7312%, an extremely low level of association.

Correlation can also be calculated using the MS Excel Function "Correl (Cell Range for returns in Security A, Cell Range for returns in Security B)". The syntax is "= correl (c4::c15, g4::g15)". The answer, 0.037312, would not change even if you enter the range of Security B returns first, followed by return from Security A.

Correlation co-efficient can have a number between – 100% (perfectly negative correlation) and +100% (perfectly positive correlation).

Perfectly negative correlation between two variables, as seen in Figure 10.1, means that every time one of the variables goes up, the other would go down proportionately, and *vice versa.* For example, when the value of the Indian rupee goes down, the share prices of export-oriented companies go up.

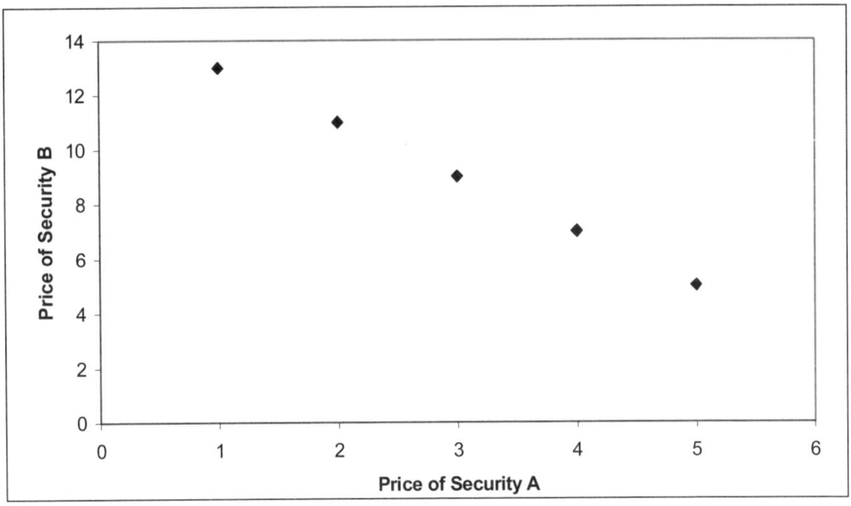

Figure 10.1: **Perfectly Negative Correlation**

Perfectly positive correlation between two variables means that every time one of the variables goes up, the other too would go up proportionately and *vice versa*, as shown in Figure 10.2. For example, when the value of the Indian rupee goes up, the share prices of import-intensive companies will go up.

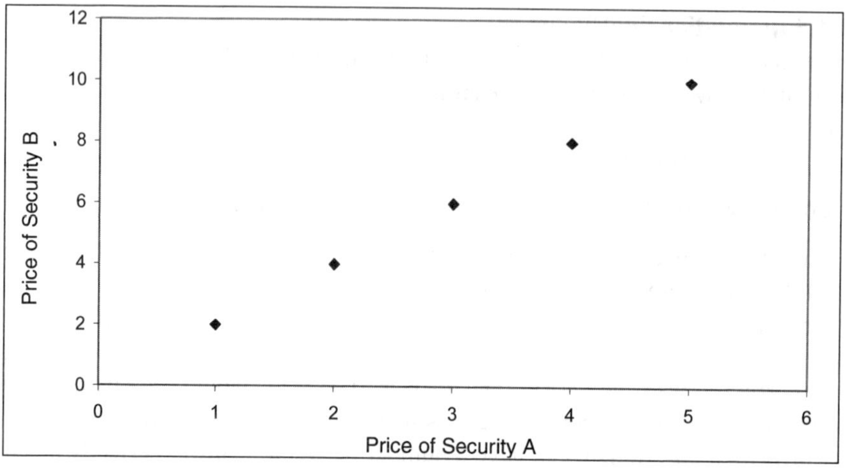

Figure 10.2: **Perfectly Positive Correlation**

We rarely see perfect correlations in the real world. Generally, the relation between variables range between:

- High negative correlation (for instance, the relation between rupee and share prices of export-oriented companies, or interest rates and debt security prices); and
- High positive correlation (for instance, the relation between NAV of index funds and the value of the index on which the fund has been constructed).

10.1.6 Coefficient of Determination / R-squared (R^2)

R^2 is nothing but the square of R. In the above example, the value would be 0.037312^2, i.e. 0.001392. The syntax in MS Excel is "= rsq (c4::c15, g4::g15)"

To understand the implication of R-squared, let us apply it in the following simple example of returns in two schemes (Table 10.2).

Table 10.2

Year	*Scheme C*	*Scheme D*
1	3.0%	3.8%
2	5.0%	5.5%
3	7.0%	7.8%
4	9.0%	9.5%
5	11.0%	11.5%

You can pictorially see the impact of the association between the two schemes, by drawing a scatter graph in MS Excel. First select the range of values of "Scheme C" and "Scheme D" (2 columns) and draw a "XY (scatter)" through the chart menu in MS Excel. Once the scatter graph is ready, take the curser to any of the data points and right click. In the series of options given, select "Add trend line". You need to select trend line type as "linear". Further, under options, you need to tick on two boxes:

- Display equation on chart.
- Display R-square value on chart.

Figure 10.3 would appear as follows:

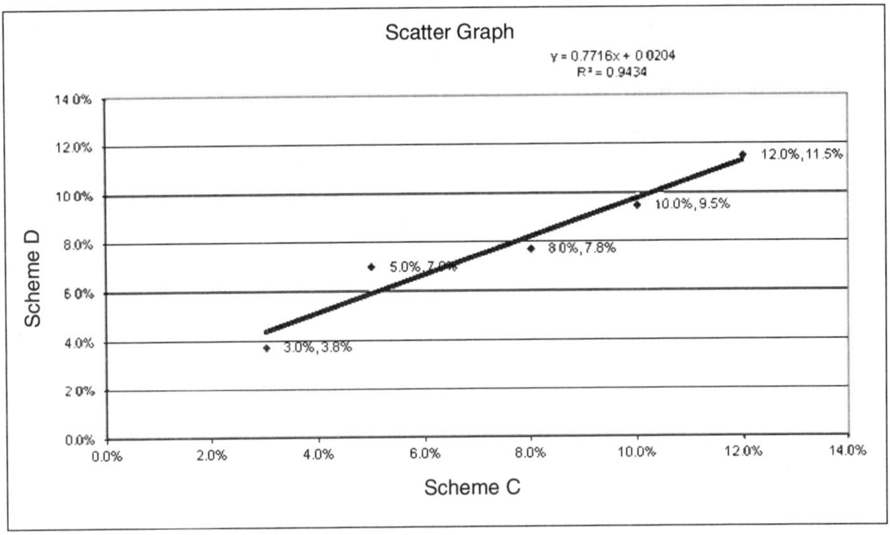

Figure 10.3

You can see all the 5 years returns for the two schemes in the graph. The line tries to describe the relationship between the two. This line can be described by the equation:

Y = 0.7716X + 0.0204.

This means that the association between values in the Y-axis (Scheme D Returns) and values in the X-axis (Scheme C Returns) are defined by that equation. Therefore, given any value of returns on Scheme C, the corresponding predicted value of returns on Scheme D can be determined, and *vice versa.*

For example, if the Scheme C return was 1%, then Scheme D return can be predicted to be:

(0.7716 x 1) + 0.0204, i.e. 0.792%,

as per the equation.

You can see that all our data points are not on the line. Some points are above the line and some are below. So, the equation does not capture entirely the association between returns of Scheme D and returns of Scheme C. There are some other factors affecting Scheme D returns, which have not been captured by the above equation. These factors push the points away from the line. The R^2 value tells us the extent of such deviation from the line.

This line is technically called "the regression line", the equation is called "the regression equation", and the analysis is called "regression analysis". An alternative and more detailed approach to regression analysis is covered (later in this chapter.)

The chart tells us that the R^2 value is 0.9434. This means that 94.34% of the association between the returns in Scheme D and Scheme C can be explained by the equation. The remaining part of the returns (100% minus 94.34%, i.e. 5.66%) is on account of factors unexplained by the equation — maybe factors other than Scheme C, or aspects of Scheme C that are not captured in the equation.

The correlation can be calculated for any two series of data. An extremely illogical comparison, for instance, would be between the rate of growth of the market and the hemline of mini skirts! Economist George Taylor[43] developed this hemline theory in 1926. According to this theory, better market conditions generally are associated with short mini skirts; the short mini skirts give way to long flowing gowns during poor market conditions. Having made the discovery, a justification was found — in good market conditions, women buy expensive stockings. Short mini skirts are in line with their desire to display the expensive stockings. In poor market conditions, long gowns are required to cover the shabby and torn stockings that become the order of the day! This led to the concept of hemline index. The theory received academic validation in the 21st century.

Mui, Ylan Q[44] brought gender-parity in economic understanding with the men's underwear index! It detects the beginning of a recovery during an economic slump. The theory is that purchase of men's underwear may be postponed during a downturn; the "discretionary" spending will re-start when the economy starts recovering.

10.1.7 Beta

According to one of the fundamental principles underlying modern portfolio theory, the Capital Assets Pricing Model, risk can be:

- Systematic (market-related), e.g. interest rates, political disturbance, etc.; or
- Non-systematic (specific to company), e.g. lock out, change of management, etc.

Non-systematic risk can be eliminated through diversification. But systematic risk is non-diversifiable. Investor needs to be compensated for systematic risk only, since she can always diversify away the non-systematic risk.

Beta is a measure of systematic risk, unlike variance and standard deviation which measure the total risk, namely, systematic plus non-systematic risk. It compares the sensitivity of value of a security with the movements in the market.

Beta calculation entails putting down two series of values for a reasonably long period of time — at least 5 years. One series of values would be the market price of the security. The second series would be the market index on all the dates for which the price of the security has been considered.

Given the information, as in Table 10.1 we can work out:

- Periodic returns, both for the market index and the security;
- Co-variance of the returns on the market index and returns on the stock; and
- Variance in returns of the market index.

Beta = [Covariance (Index Returns, Stock Returns) / Variance (Index Returns)].

The unit of measurement of Beta is "times". Thus, a beta of 1.25 means beta is 1.25 times.

Beta equal to 1 is an indication that the security would move precisely in line with the market. An index fund would have beta close to 1.

Beta less than 1 is an indication of a conservative stock or fund, one that moves lesser than the market. Beta more than 1 signifies a security (or fund) that is more aggressive than the market.

Negative beta means an inverse relationship between the security and the market. When the market goes up, the security goes down, and *vice versa*. Investors dream of stocks that enjoy positive beta whenever the market goes up, and negative beta whenever the market goes down. But dreams have no place in the financial markets!

Beta can also be calculated using the "slope" function in MS Excel. The syntax is:

= slope (range of values of security returns, range of values of index returns).

Both covariance and slope functions take the market index returns and security returns as the basis.

Beta can be calculated for a scheme through a principally different approach, i.e. as the weighted average beta of the individual securities in the portfolio. Thus, if 40% of the portfolio is in a stock that has beta of 1.5, and the balance 60% is in a stock that has beta of 1, beta of the portfolio would be:

(40% x 1.5) + (60% x 1.0) = 1.2 times.

The portfolio approach requires details of securities in the portfolio, and their individual betas. SEBI mandates disclosure of complete portfolio only once a month. Further, the requirement of finding beta for each investment makes it cumbersome to calculate scheme beta through this approach. Therefore, beta is usually calculated based on returns on the market index and scheme, through the covariance / slope method. There is some academic research to back this simpler approach to beta measurement.

Cunningham reasons that "What beta really measures is the price volatility of a stock. For a market analyst, that measurement may be of some interest. But for a business analyst, price gyrations are useless analytic tools and so, therefore, is beta. What matters in business analysis might be called "business volatility", the gyrations in earnings or cash flows a business has experienced, as grounds for gauging its future business performance . . . . Beta is therefore of no interest to a business analyst."[45]

Beta should always be used in conjunction with R-square. An R-square value of below 50% means that even half of the association between return in the scheme and return in the index is captured by the regression equation. This could mean that the bench mark index with which the scheme is being compared might be inappropriate. In such situations, the Beta is not representative. Even if the benchmark is appropriate, it is possible that the linear regression model discussed in this text does not capture the relationship effectively. Alternates, such as non-linear regression models can be explored for a better fit.

R-square of index funds would be close to 100 per cent. On the other hand, widely diversified equity funds are likely to show low R-square when compared with a narrow index.

The same beta calculation can also be done for debt securities and debt funds through a comparison with a debt index. This is however considered to be theoretically unsound, because beta is based on the capital assets pricing model, which is empirically tested for equities.

10.1.8 Normal Distribution

Advanced financial modelling operates with certain assumptions regarding how the data points are distributed. A commonly used distribution is called "normal distribution". In a normal distribution, the data is symmetrically distributed. The pattern formed by such distribution is called "normal curve", as shown in Figure 10.4.

The normal curve is also called "bell curve" on account of its bell-like shape. Needless to say, the more the number of observations, more reliable the results. As a thumb-rule, the number of observations would need to be more than 30 to draw reliable conclusions from a normal distribution.

The area under the normal curve is distributed as follows:

- Either side of the mean covers 50% of the area.
- Mean ± 1 standard deviation covers 68.27% area.
- Mean ± 2 standard deviation covers 95.45% area.
- Mean ± 3 standard deviation covers 99.73% area.

Based on this, a number of conclusions can be drawn.

Suppose an investor wants to find the probability of return being less than 5%, from a portfolio whose returns and standard deviation in the past are 8% and 3% respectively:

Mean Return	8%
Standard Deviation	3%
Mean + 1 Standard Deviation =	8% + 3%, i.e. 11%
Mean – 1 Standard Deviation =	8% – 3%, i.e. 5%.

We know that in a normal distribution, mean ± 1 standard deviation (i.e., more than 5% and less than 11%) would cover 68.27% of the area under the curve. This means that there is a 68.27% probability of returns in the scheme being between 5% and 11%.

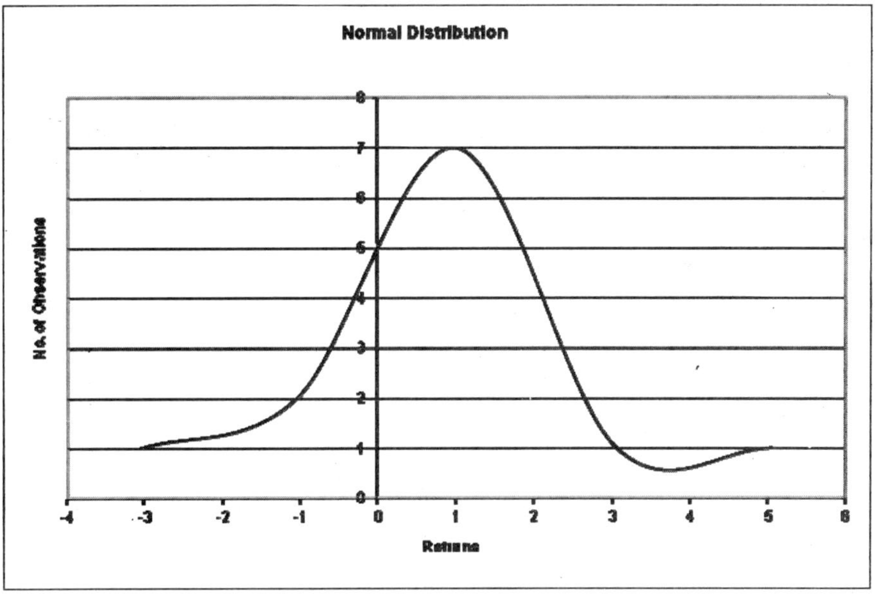

Figure 10.4

The area outside this range would be 1 minus 0.6827, i.e. 31.73% of the total area. This would include the tails on both sides, i.e. returns less than 5% and returns more than 11%. So if we only want to find the area that is less than 5%, the percentage would be 31.73% ÷ 2, i.e. 15.865%.

The range of values (5% to 11%) is referred to as "confidence interval". The probability of the numbers being within a specified range is called as "level of confidence."

The normal distribution tables (Tables 1 to 5 given at the end of this chapter) help in ascertaining the probability, assuming the averages and standard deviation are calculated on the basis of more than 30 observations (as a thumb rule).

Suppose we want to check the probability of return exceeding 12%. The difference of 4% (12% minus 8%) is 4% ÷ 3%, i.e. 1.33 times the standard deviation.

Now refer to the normal distribution table. Look under the Z column for 1.3 and then proceed along that row to the column 0.03. The value is 0.4082.

This means that the probability of the return being between 8% (the mean) and 12% (the return corresponding to 1.33 times standard deviation) is 40.82%.

We also know that each side of the mean covers 50% of the normal distribution curve, i.e. the probability of return being more than 8% is 50%.

Therefore, probability of return being more than 12% is 50% minus 40.82%, i.e. 9.18%.

Similarly, probability of return being below 4% (mean — 1.33 times standard deviation) is 9.18%.

Thus, both investors and fund professional can use this as a tool to assess whether they are comfortable with the odds.

10.1.9 Black Swan[46] (Nassim Nicholas Taleb)

According to Taleb, normal distribution is more relevant for natural phenomena, like height, weight, etc. where the underlying data has a credible natural distribution that approaches normality. For instance, most adults are between 5 feet and 6 feet. You do not have a 100-foot tall human being. One can thus realistically assign a probability for a person being of a particular height or weight.

But when it comes to the financial markets, one cannot assign such probabilities — and the impact of some highly improbable events can be stupendous. Statistically speaking, the distribution has "fat tails". Taleb referred to such improbable events as "black swans".

You may not have seen a black swan, but that does not mean that black swans do not exist. Similarly, you may not have seen certain events but that does not mean that these do not happen — and some of these events, when they do occur, can lead to catastrophe. Investment approaches and risk management practices that do not provide for such black swans can be dangerous. This was evident during the Global Financial Crisis of 2007.

10.1.10 Shortfall Measures

Risk can be given another practical dimension with an additional parameter — a threshold level. This threshold may be zero, a riskless rate of return, or any other level below which if the return falls, the investor is going to feel a sense of shock. For instance, you will get a shock if you score less than 35% marks in a paper, because you will have to repeat the paper. 35% is the threshold.

The probability of going beyond the threshold can be easily read from a cumulative probability distribution, as captured in Figure 10.5. This too is based on the normal distribution.

Suppose the threshold was 0%. In Figure 10.5, find 0% on the horizontal axis. Go up to the curve, then over to the vertical axis. The result is about 0.25. Thus, there is a 25% probability that the return will fall below the selected threshold of 0%. Similarly, there is a 90% probability that the return would fall below 30%.

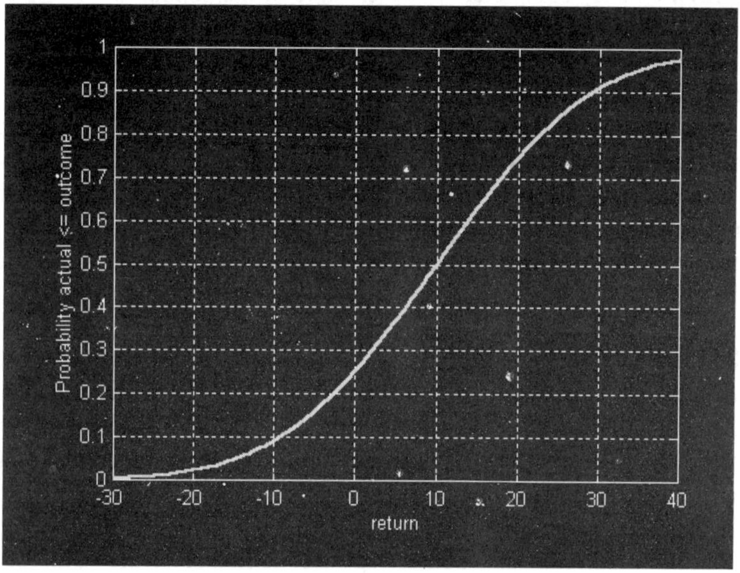

Figure 10.5

10.1.11 Value at Risk (VAR)

This again is a measure of downside risk. Suppose an investor (who has invested, say, ₹ 50,000) wants to know a threshold value of loss, such that there is only a 10% probability of actual loss being more than the threshold loss. This means that the investor is looking for 90% confidence that his position would be better than that threshold.

In Figure 10.5, the 0.1 value (corresponding with the 10% probability targeted) on the vertical axis, corresponds to a value of – 10 on the horizontal axis. This means, there is a 10% probability that loss will be more than 10%, i.e. ₹ 5,000 on a portfolio of ₹ 50,000. Thus, in 90% of the cases, value at risk is below ₹ 5,000. VAR at 90% confidence level is ₹ 5,000. As the confidence level is increased, VAR would keep increasing.

Stock exchanges use sophisticated value at risk models to determine the margin requirements for holding positions.

10.1.12 Standard Error of Mean

In most situations it is not possible to calculate the mean from the entire universe of information (statistically referred to as "population"). Therefore, the mean is calculated based on a few observations extracted from the population (statistically referred to as "sample"). Statisticians operate on the hypothesis that the mean calculated from the sample is representative of the population mean subject to meeting certain conditions.

Samples are rarely completely representative of the population. If the extracted observations are added back to the population and a fresh sample of observations is studied, chances are that the new mean would be different. Thus, the mean would vary from sample to sample.

The inherent error in operating based on sample means can be measured by the standard error of the mean, which is equal to (s ÷ square root of n), where "s" is the standard deviation of the sample and "n" is the number of observations in the sample. Thus, lower the variability (standard deviation) of observations in the sample and more the number of observations considered, lower would be the standard error of the mean.

10.1.13 Standard Error of Estimate

A related concept is the standard error of estimate (S_e). It assesses the inherent error in the estimation by the regression equation — and thus helps in assessing the range of possible results. S_e measures the variability (or scatter) of the observed values around the regression line.

If all the observations lie on the regression line, then S_e would be zero. This means that the regression equation is a perfect estimator of the value of the dependent variable.

Assuming that the observations are normally distributed (a necessary but not sufficient condition is that there are at least 30 observations) around the regression line, it can also be inferred that the area bounded by the:

- Regression Line ± 1 S_e would cover 68.27% of the observations.
- Regression Line ± 2 S_e would cover 95.45% of the observations.
- Regression Line ± 3 S_e would cover 99.73% of the observations.

Calculation of Standard Error of Estimate, and Analysis of Variances (referred to as "ANOVA") are facilitated when we perform the regression analysis through an alternative data analysis approach discussed in the next section. The alternate approach is however meant for readers who are comfortable with advanced statistics. Others can skip the next section.

10.1.14 Regression Analysis (Data Analysis Approach)

This approach requires a few MS Excel "Add-Ins" to be loaded in your computer. For this, take the following sequence of steps:

- Open a MS Excel file.
- Select "Tools — Add-Ins" and ensure that you have ticked "Analysis Toolpak" and "Analysis Toolpak VBA".

(Depending on how the MS Excel application was originally loaded by your software service provider, you may be asked for the relevant MS Excel programme CDs / Serial No. and Password).

Let us consider the Net Asset Value (NAV) of an equity fund and the corresponding Nifty index values spread over a year (Table 10.3).

Table 10.3

Date	*Nifty*	*NAV*	*Returns on Nifty*	*Returns on NAV*
01-Aug-01	1063.15	11.278		
15-Aug-01	1078.95	11.491	1.4861%	1.8886%
02-Sep-01	1048.05	11.195	– 2.8639%	– 2.5759%
16-Sep-01	872.25	9.322	– 16.7740%	– 16.7307%
01-Oct-01	910.10	9.726	4.3394%	4.3338%
15-Oct-01	963.40	10.192	5.8565%	4.7913%
01-Nov-01	994.00	10.564	3.1763%	3.6499%
15-Nov-01	1035.70	11.071	4.1952%	4.7993%
02-Dec-01	1065.40	11.542	2.8676%	4.2544%
14-Dec-01	1087.85	11.713	2.1072%	1.4815%
17-Dec-01	1082.30	11.585	– 0.5102%	– 1.0928%
01-Jan-02	1055.30	10.294	– 2.4947%	– 11.1437%
15-Jan-02	1094.15	10.778	3.6814%	4.7018%
01-Feb-02	1081.65	10.729	– 1.1424%	– 0.4546%
15-Feb-02	1159.95	11.690	7.2389%	8.9570%
28-Feb-02	1142.05	11.854	– 1.5432%	1.4029%
03-Mar-02	1177.35	11.925	3.0909%	0.5990%
15-Mar-02	1169.75	12.000	– 0.6455%	0.6289%
01-Apr-02	1138.95	11.740	– 2.6330%	– 2.1667%
15-Apr-02	1134.15	11.645	– 0.4214%	– 0.8092%
01-May-02	1093.30	11.603	– 3.6018%	– 0.3607%
15-May-02	1107.80	11.580	1.3263%	– 0.1982%
02-Jun-02	1039.75	11.120	– 6.1428%	– 3.9724%
16-Jun-02	1088.90	11.663	4.7271%	4.8831%
01-Jul-02	1068.95	11.539	– 1.8321%	– 1.0632%
15-Jul-02	1048.00	11.568	– 1.9599%	0.2513%
01-Aug-02	957.70	10.785	– 8.6164%	– 6.7687%

The periodic returns can be calculated by taking each value of Nifty and NAV and subtracting it from the previous value of Nifty and NAV and dividing it by the previous value of Nifty and NAV. Thus, periodic return on Nifty between 1 August 2001 and 15 August 2001 would be:

$$(1078.95 - 1063.15) \div 1063.15, \text{ i.e. } 1.4861\%.$$

Once the Toolpak is loaded, you can perform the following sequence of steps:

- Select "Tools — Data Analysis — Regression"
- For the value of "Input Y range" select the range of cells where the returns on NAV are stored
- For the value of "Input X range" select the range of cells where the returns on Sensex are stored
- Select Residuals
- Press "OK".

The Summary Output would appear as shown in Table 10.4 (the boxes and arrows are manual additions to enhance understanding). This can be interpreted as follows:

- Alpha (α) (to be discussed in next chapter) is 0.00235, i.e. 0.235%.
- Beta (β) is 0.96272.
- The regression equation is:

  $Y = \alpha + \beta X$,

  Where,

  Y is the return on NAV, and
  X is the return on Sensex.

  Thus, the regression equation based on our observations is:

  Y (predicted value) = 0.00235 + 0.96272X.

Table 10.4

SUMMARY OUTPUT

Co-efficient of correlation

Co-efficient of Determination

Standard Error of Estimate

Regression Statistics	
Multiple R	0.90804679
R Square	0.82454896
Adjusted R Square	**0.8172385**
Standard Error	**0.02280302**
Observations	26

Regression sum of squares

Error sum of squares

Total sum of squares

Mean square

Degrees of freedom

Sum of squares

ANOVA

	df	*SS*	*MS*	*F*	*Significance F*
Regression	**1**	0.058648454	0.058648454	**112.7903009**	1.49825E-10
Residual	**24**	0.012479468	0.000519978		
Total	25	0.071127922			

Alpha

Standard error of regression co-efficients

	Coefficients	*Standard Error*	*t Stat*	*P-value*	*Lower 95%*	*Upper 95%*
Intercept	**0.00235016**	0.004478864	0.524722103	0.604589967	-0.006893761	0.01159408
X Variable 1	**0.96272137**	0.090649359	**10.62027782**	1.49825E-10	0.775630329	1.14981241

Beta

RESIDUAL OUTPUT

Observation	*Predicted Y*	*Residuals*
1	0.0166576	0.0022287
2	-0.0252212	-0.0005381
3	-0.1591368	-0.0081700
4	0.0441260	-0.0007877
5	0.0587319	-0.0108191
6	0.0329286	0.0035706
7	0.0427380	0.0052552
8	0.0299574	0.0125862
9	0.0226365	-0.0078211
10	-0.0025615	-0.0083666
11	-0.0216667	-0.0897705
12	0.0377920	0.0092257
13	-0.0086483	0.0041021
14	0.0720410	0.0175293
15	-0.0125063	0.0265354
16	0.0321072	-0.0261177
17	-0.0038644	0.0101537
18	-0.0229987	0.0013320
19	-0.0017071	-0.0063849
20	-0.0323253	0.0287186
21	0.0151183	-0.0171006
22	-0.0567879	0.0170643
23	0.0478589	0.0009720
24	-0.0152881	0.0046562
25	-0.0165179	0.0190311
26	-0.0806019	0.0129152

As can be seen from the equation, NAV of the scheme moves closely with the Sensex. 1% change in the Sensex is likely to be associated with a change of 0.96272% in the NAV of the scheme:

- Coefficient of correlation is positive. There is high positive correlation, i.e. both returns on Sensex and returns on NAV are associated, and move in the same direction.
- Coefficient of Determination (R^2) is high. 81.72% of the returns on NAV can be explained by returns on Sensex as captured in the regression equation.
- Standard error of the estimate is 0.0228. This is used to determine the confidence intervals, as follows:
    - Suppose we want to know with 95% confidence level, what is likely to be the range of Returns (Confidence Interval) on the NAV, if the Returns on the Sensex were 1%.

From the regression equation, we know that:

$$\grave{Y} \text{ (predicted value of Y)} = 0.00235 + (0.96272 \times 1\%)$$
$$= 1.19772\%$$

Thus 1% returns on Sensex, are likely to be associated with 1.19772% returns on NAV.

Since the number of observations is less than 30, we cannot use the normal distribution to determine the confidence interval (*see also* Tables 1 to 5 given at the end of this chapter). The t-distribution would be more appropriate. Table 2, which gives the t-distribution requires two inputs:

The confidence level, which we know is 95%. Therefore we need to look for values under the 100% minus 95%, i.e. 5%, i.e. 0.05 column.

Degrees of freedom is 24, as per the Summary Output of the regression analysis. Therefore we need to look along the 24 row.

The intersection of 0.05 column and 24 row gives us a t-value of 2.064.

With 95% confidence, we can say that if the return on the Sensex is 1, return on the NAV would be:

Minimum: $\grave{Y} - (t \times S_e)$, i.e. 1.19772% – (2.064 × 0.0228) = – 3.5%
Maximum: $\grave{Y} + (t \times S_e)$, i.e. 1.19772% + (2.064 × 0.0228) = 5.9%

Thus, the Confidence Interval at 95% confidence level is
– 3.5% to +5.9%.

This means that 95% times, the true value of NAV return for 1% Sensex return would lie between – 3.5% and +5.9%.

A less rigorous corresponding statement could be: "There is only a 5% chance that the true value of NAV return for 1% Sensex return would lie outside the – 3.5% to +5.9% range."

- ➢ Suppose you want a 99% confidence level, then the Confidence Interval will widen as follows:

T-Value (0.01%, 24 degrees of freedom) = 2.797
Minimum: Ỳ – (t × Se), i.e. 1.19772% – (2.797 × 0.0228) = – 5.2%
Maximum: Ỳ + (t × Se), i.e. 1.19772% + (2.797 × 0.0228) = 7.6%

Thus, the Confidence Interval at 99% confidence level is

– 5.2% to +7.6%

- The computed t-stat value for X-Variable 1 is 10.62. This should be greater than the standard t-value as per Table 2, for us to conclude that the Returns on Sensex is a significant explanatory variable for the NAV. We saw earlier that the standard t-value at 99% confidence level and 24 degrees of freedom is 2.797, as per Table 2. Since the computed t-stat value is higher than the standard t-value, we can conclude that the Return on Sensex is a significant explanatory variable for Return on NAV.
- The computed p value for X-variable 1 is an extremely low number. This means that even at very high confidence levels, the Return on Sensex would be a significant explanatory variable.
- Is the regression as a whole significant in explaining the association? This is what the F-test conveys.

The computed F-value for our observations is 112.79. This needs to be greater than the standard value derived from the F-Distribution table (Tables 4 and 5). The difference between Table 4 and 5 is only in the Confidence Level used. Let us say that we want to operate with 95% confidence level. Then Table 4 would be relevant.

In the F-distribution table, "degrees of freedom for numerator" refers to "degrees of freedom for regression", i.e. 1 in our Summary Output table. Similarly, "degrees of freedom for denominator" refers to "degrees of freedom for residual", i.e. 24 in our Summary Output table. The standard F value for 1 degree of freedom in numerator and 24 degrees of freedom in denominator is 4.26 (from Table 4).

Since the computed F-value of 112.79 is much higher than the standard F-value of 4.26, we can conclude that the regression as a whole is statistically significant.

- Lastly, we should also check the Residual Output, which lists for each observation, "Predicted Y" and "Residuals":
  - "Predicted Y" is the value calculated for each observation based on the regression equation. For example, we know that the first observation of Sensex return in our data is 1.4861% for the period between 1 August 2001 and 15 August 2001. Applying this in our regression equation, we get the predicted value as 0.002235 + (0.9627 × 1.4861%), i.e. 1.66576%.
  - "Residual" is the difference between the predicted value (1.66576%) for the first observation in the residual table) and the actual value (1.88863% for the first observation in the data), i.e. 0.22287%

The residual column is to be checked for any observable pattern in it. There is no discernible pattern in our data. But there could be situations of a pattern. For example, if over a range of values or time periods the residuals are consistently positive or negative, then that is indicative that the regression equation fit can be improved. For example, seasonality has to be factored in, or a curvilinear model might be a better fit than the linear model.

Regression is a rich topic. Depending on the visible patterns, data can be transformed (for example, log-normal or exponential transformation) and regression applied on the transformed data. Those complexities are beyond the scope of this book.

10.2 Quantitative Factors Applicable Only to Debt

10.2.1 Weighted Average Maturity / Macaulay Duration

This is the average time it will take to recover moneys from a bond. In the example below, the actual tenor of the bond is 4 years. But the average time in which the amount invested will be paid back is 3.4869 years. Macaulay Duration is typically used by portfolio managers when they seek to mitigate risk through immunisation of their debt portfolio.

Macaulay Duration can be calculated using '=duration' function in MS Excel.

A few key features of duration are:

- Longer the balance tenor, higher the duration.
- Higher the coupon, lower the duration.
- Higher the yield, lower the duration.
- Duration of a zero coupon security would be equal to its balance tenor.

Example 10.1

What is the duration of a 10% debenture of 4 years being issued at par? Interest is payable annually.

Year	*Cash flow*	*Disc. Factor*	*Present Value*	*Proportion*	*Weighted Proportion*
(1)	(2)	(3)	(4) = (2)*(3)	(5) = (4) / 10000	(6) = (1)*(5)
0	– 10,000	1.0000	– 10,000.0		
1	1,000	0.9091	909.1	0.0909	.0909
2	1,000	0.8264	826.4	0.0827	.1653
3	1,000	0.7513	751.3	0.0751	.2254
4	11,000	0.6830	7,513.2	0.7513	3.0053
Total			0	1.0000	3.4869

IRR = 10%
Duration = 3.4869 years
Discount factor is calculated using the formula:
$1 \div (1 + i)^t$,
where "i" is the IRR and "t" is the time period in years.

10.2.2 Modified Duration

Modified Duration is a measure of the price sensitivity of a coupon paying debt security. Arithmetically, it is the Macaulay Duration ÷ (1 + IRR÷n), where 'n' is the number of coupon payments during the year.

In the above example, Modified Duration = 3.4869 ÷ (1 + 10%÷1) i.e. 3.17. This means that a 0.5% change in yields in the market is likely to cause a 0.5% × 3.17, i.e. 1.585% change in the value of the debt security.

Modified Duration can also be calculated using '=mduration' function in MS Excel.

10.2.3 Convexity

We know that price and yield on a security are negatively related. Thus, as price falls, yield increases and *vice versa*. As shown below in Figure 10.6, this relation can be linear (Security A) or curvi-linear (Security B):

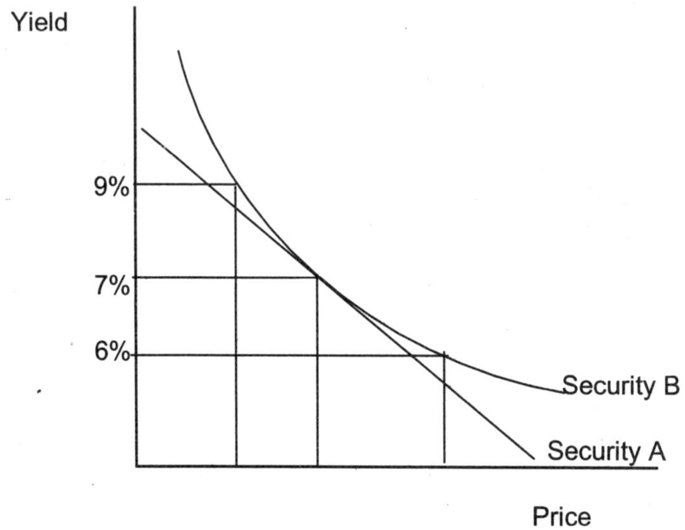

Figure 10.6

At 7%, both securities have the same price. As yield falls from 7% to 6%, both securities gain value — but Security B gains more. However, as yield rises from 7% to 9%, Security B loses less value than Security A. Thus, Security B is superior to Security A.

Since the price-yield line of Security A is straight, it is said to have zero convexity. Security B "however" has positive convexity. More convex the security, better it is as an investment proposition.

Like securities, even portfolios have convexity. A debt index fund manager would, for instance, construct a portfolio of securities that would have the same weighted average duration as the securities in the index portfolio, but greater convexity. Such portfolio construction will help her out-perform the index that her fund is tracking.

10.3 Qualitative Factors

10.3.1 Portfolio Concentration / Diversity

Diversification reduces unsystematic risk. Therefore, generally more the number of securities, lesser would be the unsystematic risk. But beyond a point, diversification only increases the time and effort involved in monitoring the portfolio.

Portfolio concentration can be compared across schemes by studying, for instance, how much of the portfolio is represented by the top 10 stocks, or how many stocks constitute the top 40 per cent of the portfolio.

10.3.2 Portfolio composition

The risk in a fund originates from the risk inherent in the securities in its portfolio. A diversified bond fund for instance would be less risky (credit risk) than a junk bond fund. Among bond funds, schemes that invest only in gilt and "AAA" rated paper would be less risky (credit risk) than a more diversified bond fund. As will be seen in the next chapter, credit rating agencies provide a rating even for bond funds.

10.3.3 Borrowings

In Chapter 2 in the context of hedge funds, we saw that leveraging increases the risk profile of the fund. For any fund, greater the percentage of borrowings in the net assets, more will be the volatility in its returns for the investors. As discussed in Chapter 2, SEBI has imposed restrictions on borrowings by mutual fund schemes.

10.3.4 Investor Concentration

An open-end scheme with few investors contributing the bulk of the net assets is susceptible to volatility on account of investors' actions. The size of such schemes will fluctuate significantly, depending on sale and re-purchase transactions of these investors. This can put pressure on the fund manager in managing the scheme. Schemes that have a widely distributed investor profile are less susceptible to such volatile flows.

Table 1: **Normal Distribution**

Area under the Standard Normal Probability Distribution between the Mean & Positive Values of Z

Z	*0.00*	*0.01*	*0.02*	*0.03*	*0.04*	*0.05*	*0.06*	*0.07*	*0.08*	*0.09*
0.0	0.0000	0.0040	0.0080	0.0120	0.0160	0.0199	0.0239	0.0279	0.0319	0.0359
0.1	0.0398	0.0438	0.0478	0.0517	0.0557	0.0596	0.0636	0.0675	0.0714	0.0753
0.2	0.0793	0.0832	0.0871	0.0910	0.0948	0.0987	0.1026	0.1064	0.1103	0.1141
0.3	0.1179	0.1217	0.1255	0.1293	0.1331	0.1368	0.1406	0.1443	0.1480	0.1517
0.4	0.1554	0.1591	0.1628	0.1664	0.1700	0.1736	0.1772	0.1808	0.1844	0.1879
0.5	0.1915	0.1950	0.1985	0.2019	0.2054	0.2088	0.2123	0.2157	0.2190	0.2224
0.6	0.2257	0.2291	0.2324	0.2357	0.2389	0.2422	0.2454	0.2486	0.2517	0.2549
0.7	0.2580	0.2611	0.2642	0.2673	0.2704	0.2734	0.2764	0.2794	0.2823	0.2852
0.8	0.2881	0.2910	0.2939	0.2967	0.2995	0.3023	0.3051	0.3078	0.3106	0.3133
0.9	0.3159	0.3186	0.3212	0.3238	0.3264	0.3289	0.3315	0.3340	0.3365	0.3389
1.0	0.3413	0.3438	0.3461	0.3485	0.3508	0.3531	0.3554	0.3577	0.3599	0.3621
1.1	0.3643	0.3665	0.3686	0.3708	0.3729	0.3749	0.3770	0.3790	0.3810	0.3830
1.2	0.3849	0.3869	0.3888	0.3907	0.3925	0.3944	0.3962	0.3980	0.3997	0.4015
1.3	0.4032	0.4049	0.4066	0.4082	0.4099	0.4115	0.4131	0.4147	0.4162	0.4177
1.4	0.4192	0.4207	0.4222	0.4236	0.4251	0.4265	0.4279	0.4292	0.4306	0.4319
1.5	0.4332	0.4345	0.4357	0.4370	0.4382	0.4394	0.4406	0.4418	0.4429	0.4441
1.6	0.4452	0.4463	0.4474	0.4484	0.4495	0.4505	0.4515	0.4525	0.4535	0.4545
1.7	0.4554	0.4564	0.4573	0.4582	0.4591	0.4599	0.4608	0.4616	0.4625	0.4633
1.8	0.4641	0.4649	0.4656	0.4664	0.4671	0.4678	0.4686	0.4693	0.4699	0.4706

(Contd . . .)

Table 1: **Normal Distribution**

Area under the Standard Normal Probability Distribution between the Mean & Positive Values of Z *(contd.)*

Z	*0.00*	*0.01*	*0.02*	*0.03*	*0.04*	*0.05*	*0.06*	*0.07*	*0.08*	*0.09*
1.9	0.4713	0.4719	0.4726	0.4732	0.4738	0.4744	0.4750	0.4756	0.4761	0.4767
2.0	0.4772	0.4778	0.4783	0.4788	0.4793	0.4798	0.4803	0.4808	0.4812	0.4817
2.1	0.4821	0.4826	0.4830	0.4834	0.4838	0.4842	0.4846	0.4850	0.4854	0.4857
2.2	0.4861	0.4864	0.4868	0.4871	0.4875	0.4878	0.4881	0.4884	0.4887	0.4890
2.3	0.4893	0.4896	0.4898	0.4901	0.4904	0.4906	0.4909	0.4911	0.4913	0.4916
2.4	0.4918	0.4920	0.4922	0.4925	0.4927	0.4929	0.4931	0.4932	0.4934	0.4936
2.5	0.4938	0.4940	0.4941	0.4943	0.4945	0.4946	0.4948	0.4949	0.4951	0.4952
2.6	0.4953	0.4955	0.4956	0.4957	0.4959	0.4960	0.4961	0.4962	0.4963	0.4964
2.7	0.4965	0.4966	0.4967	0.4968	0.4969	0.4970	0.4971	0.4972	0.4973	0.4974
2.8	0.4974	0.4975	0.4976	0.4977	0.4977	0.4978	0.4979	0.4979	0.4980	0.4981
2.9	0.4981	0.4982	0.4982	0.4983	0.4984	0.4984	0.4985	0.4985	0.4986	0.4986
3.0	0.4987	0.4987	0.4987	0.4988	0.4988	0.4989	0.4989	0.4989	0.4990	0.4990

The selected value 0.2291 is the area under the normal distribution curve between the mean and a point 0.61 standard deviations to the *right of the mean*. The area under the curve, that is 0.61 standard deviations on *both* sides of the mean is therefore 0.2291 X 2 = 0.4582 i.e. 45.82%

Mean + / -	1	SD =	68.27%
Mean + / -	2	SD =	95.45%
Mean + / -	3	SD =	99.73%

Table 2: **t-Distribution (2 tailed)**

Area in both tails combined for Student's t distribution

Degrees of freedom	***Area in both tails combined***									
	0.10	***0.09***	***0.08***	***0.07***	***0.06***	***0.05***	***0.04***	***0.03***	***0.02***	***0.01***
1	6.314	7.026	7.916	9.058	10.579	12.706	15.894	21.205	31.821	63.656
2	2.920	3.104	3.320	3.578	3.896	4.303	4.849	5.643	6.965	9.925
3	2.353	2.471	2.605	2.763	2.951	3.182	3.482	3.896	4.541	5.841
4	2.132	2.226	2.333	2.456	2.601	2.776	2.999	3.298	3.747	4.604
5	2.015	2.098	2.191	2.297	2.422	2.571	2.757	3.003	3.365	4.032
6	1.943	2.019	2.104	2.201	2.313	2.447	2.612	2.829	3.143	3.707
7	1.895	1.966	2.046	2.136	2.241	2.365	2.517	2.715	2.998	3.499
8	1.860	1.928	2.004	2.090	2.189	2.306	2.449	2.634	2.896	3.355
9	1.833	1.899	1.973	2.055	2.150	2.262	2.398	2.574	2.821	3.250
10	1.812	1.877	1.948	2.028	2.120	2.228	2.359	2.527	2.764	3.169
11	1.796	1.859	1.928	2.007	2.096	2.201	2.328	2.491	2.718	3.106
12	1.782	1.844	1.912	1.989	2.076	2.179	2.303	2.461	2.681	3.055
13	1.771	1.832	1.899	1.974	2.060	2.160	2.282	2.436	2.650	3.012
14	1.761	1.821	1.887	1.962	2.046	2.145	2.264	2.415	2.624	2.977
15	1.753	1.812	1.878	1.951	2.034	2.131	2.249	2.397	2.602	2.947
16	1.746	1.805	1.869	1.942	2.024	2.120	2.235	2.382	2.583	2.921
17	1.740	1.798	1.862	1.934	2.015	2.110	2.224	2.368	2.567	2.898

(Contd . . .)

Table 2: **t-Distribution (2 tailed)**

Area in both tails combined for Student's t distribution *(contd.)*

Degrees of freedom	***Area in both tails combined***									
	0.10	***0.09***	***0.08***	***0.07***	***0.06***	***0.05***	***0.04***	***0.03***	***0.02***	***0.01***
18	1.734	1.792	1.855	1.926	2.007	2.101	2.214	2.356	2.552	2.878
19	1.729	1.786	1.850	1.920	2.000	2.093	2.205	2.346	2.539	2.861
20	1.725	1.782	1.844	1.914	1.994	2.086	2.197	2.336	2.528	2.845
21	1.721	1.777	1.840	1.909	1.988	2.080	2.189	2.328	2.518	2.831
22	1.717	1.773	1.835	1.905	1.983	2.074	2.183	2.320	2.508	2.819
23	1.714	1.770	1.832	1.900	1.978	2.069	2.177	2.313	2.500	2.807
24	1.711	1.767	1.828	1.896	1.974	2.064	2.172	2.307	2.492	2.797
25	1.708	1.764	1.825	1.893	1.970	2.060	2.167	2.301	2.485	2.787
26	1.706	1.761	1.822	1.890	1.967	2.056	2.162	2.296	2.479	2.779
27	1.703	1.758	1.819	1.887	1.963	2.052	2.158	2.291	2.473	2.771
28	1.701	1.756	1.817	1.884	1.960	2.048	2.154	2.286	2.467	2.763
29	1.699	1.754	1.814	1.881	1.957	2.045	2.150	2.282	2.462	2.756
30	1.697	1.752	1.812	1.879	1.955	2.042	2.147	2.278	2.457	2.750
40	1.684	1.737	1.796	1.862	1.936	2.021	2.123	2.250	2.423	2.704
60	1.671	1.723	1.781	1.845	1.917	2.000	2.099	2.223	2.390	2.660
120	1.658	1.709	1.766	1.828	1.899	1.980	2.076	2.196	2.358	2.617

To find the value of t that corresponds to an area of 0.08 in both tails (combined) of the distribution, when there are 8 degrees of freedom, look under the 0.08 column, and proceed down to the 8 degrees of freedom row; the appropriate value is 2.004.

Table 3: **Chi-Square Distribution (Right tail)**

Area in the Right Tail of a Chi-square Distribution

Degrees of freedom	*Area in Right Tail*														
	0.990	*0.975*	*0.950*	*0.900*	*0.800*	*0.700*	*0.600*	*0.500*	*0.400*	*0.300*	*0.200*	*0.100*	*0.050*	*0.025*	*0.010*
1	0.00016	0.00098	0.00393	0.01579	0.06418	0.14847	0.27500	0.45494	0.70833	1.07420	1.64238	2.70554	3.84146	5.02390	6.63489
2	0.02010	0.05064	0.10259	0.21072	0.44629	0.71335	1.02165	1.38629	1.83258	2.40794	3.21888	4.60518	5.99148	7.37778	9.21035
3	0.11483	0.21579	0.35185	0.58438	1.00517	1.42365	1.86917	2.36597	2.94617	3.66487	4.64163	6.25139	7.81472	9.34840	11.34488
4	0.29711	0.48442	0.71072	1.06362	1.64878	2.19470	2.75284	3.35669	4.04463	4.87843	5.98862	7.77943	9.48773	11.14326	13.27670
5	0.55430	0.83121	1.14548	1.61031	2.34253	2.99991	3.65550	4.35146	5.13187	6.06443	7.28927	9.23635	11.07048	12.83249	15.08632
6	0.87208	1.23734	1.63538	2.20413	3.07009	3.82755	4.57015	5.34812	6.21076	7.23113	8.55806	10.64464	12.59158	14.44935	16.81187
7	1.23903	1.68986	2.16735	2.83311	3.82232	4.67133	5.49324	6.34581	7.28321	8.38343	9.80325	12.01703	14.06713	16.01277	18.47532
8	1.64651	2.17972	2.73263	3.48954	4.59357	5.52742	6.42264	7.34412	8.35053	9.52446	11.03009	13.36156	15.50731	17.53454	20.09016
9	2.08789	2.70039	3.32512	4.16816	5.38006	6.39330	7.35703	8.34283	9.41364	10.65637	12.24214	14.68366	16.91896	19.02278	21.66605
10	2.55820	3.24696	3.94030	4.86518	6.17908	7.26722	8.29547	9.34182	10.47323	11.78072	13.44196	15.98717	18.30703	20.48320	23.20929
11	3.05350	3.81574	4.57481	5.57779	6.98867	8.14787	9.23729	10.34100	11.52983	12.89867	14.63142	17.27501	19.67515	21.92002	24.72502
12	3.57055	4.40378	5.22603	6.30380	7.80733	9.03428	10.18197	11.34032	12.58384	14.01110	15.81199	18.54934	21.02606	23.33666	26.21696
13	4.10690	5.00874	5.89186	7.04150	8.63386	9.92568	11.12914	12.33975	13.63557	15.11872	16.98479	19.81193	22.36203	24.73558	27.68818
14	4.66042	5.62872	6.57063	7.78954	9.46733	10.82148	12.07848	13.33927	14.68529	16.22209	18.15077	21.06414	23.68478	26.11893	29.14116
15	5.22936	6.26212	7.26093	8.54675	10.30696	11.72117	13.02975	14.33886	15.73322	17.32169	19.31065	22.30712	24.99580	27.48836	30.57795
16	5.81220	6.90766	7.96164	9.31224	11.15212	12.62435	13.98273	15.33850	16.77954	18.41789	20.46507	23.54182	26.29622	28.84532	31.99986

(Contd . . .)

Table 3: **Chi-Square Distribution (Right tail)**

Area in the Right Tail of a Chi-square Distribution *(contd.)*

Degrees of freedom	***Area in Right Tail***														
	0.990	*0.975*	*0.950*	*0.900*	*0.800*	*0.700*	*0.600*	*0.500*	*0.400*	*0.300*	*0.200*	*0.100*	*0.050*	*0.025*	*0.010*
17	6.40774	7.56418	8.67175	10.08518	12.00226	13.53068	14.93727	16.33818	17.82439	19.51102	21.61456	24.76903	27.58710	30.19098	33.40872
18	7.01490	8.23074	9.39045	10.86494	12.85695	14.43986	15.89321	17.33790	18.86790	20.60135	22.75955	25.98942	28.86932	31.52641	34.80524
19	7.63270	8.90651	10.11701	11.65091	13.71579	15.35166	16.85044	18.33765	19.91019	21.68913	23.90042	27.20356	30.14351	32.85234	36.19077
20	8.26037	9.59077	10.85080	12.44260	14.57844	16.26585	17.80883	19.33743	20.95137	22.77454	25.03750	28.41197	31.41042	34.16958	37.56627
21	8.89717	10.28291	11.59132	13.23960	15.44461	17.18227	18.76831	20.33723	21.99150	23.85779	26.17109	29.61509	32.67056	35.47886	38.93223
22	9.54249	10.98233	12.33801	14.04149	16.31404	18.10072	19.72880	21.33704	23.03066	24.93901	27.30145	30.81329	33.92446	36.78068	40.28945
23	10.19569	11.68853	13.09051	14.84795	17.18650	19.02109	20.69020	22.33688	24.06892	26.01837	28.42879	32.00689	35.17246	38.07561	41.63833
24	10.85635	12.40115	13.84842	15.65868	18.06180	19.94323	21.65249	23.33673	25.10635	27.09596	29.55332	33.19624	36.41503	39.36406	42.97978
25	11.52395	13.11971	14.61140	16.47341	18.93975	20.86704	22.61558	24.33658	26.14298	28.17191	30.67520	34.38158	37.65249	40.64650	44.31401
26	12.19818	13.84388	15.37916	17.29188	19.82019	21.79240	23.57943	25.33646	27.17888	29.24632	31.79461	35.56316	38.88513	41.92314	45.64164
27	12.87847	14.57337	16.15139	18.11389	20.70298	22.71923	24.54400	26.33634	28.21408	30.31929	32.91168	36.74123	40.11327	43.19452	46.96284
28	13.56467	15.30785	16.92788	18.93924	21.58797	23.64746	25.50925	27.33623	29.24861	31.39087	34.02657	37.91591	41.33715	44.46079	48.27817
29	14.25641	16.04705	17.70838	19.76774	22.47505	24.57698	26.47514	28.33613	30.28254	32.46116	35.13937	39.08748	42.55695	45.72228	49.58783
30	14.95346	16.79076	18.49267	20.59924	23.36411	25.50776	27.44162	29.33603	31.31586	33.53024	36.25018	40.25602	43.77295	46.97922	50.89218

In a chi-square distribution with 15 degrees of freedom, to find the chi-square value of 0.99 of the area under the curve, look under 0.99 column in the table and the 15 degrees of freedom row; the appropriate chi-square value is 5.22936

Table 4: **F Distribution**

F Distribution with 0.05 of area in the Right Tail

Deg. of fr. for denominater	*Degrees of Freedom for Numerater*																				
	1	*2*	*3*	*4*	*5*	*6*	*7*	*8*	*9*	*10*	*11*	*12*	*13*	*14*	*15*	*20*	*24*	*30*	*40*	*60*	*120*
1	161.45	199.50	215.71	224.58	230.16	233.99	236.77	238.88	240.54	241.88	242.98	243.90	244.69	245.36	245.95	248.02	249.05	250.10	251.14	252.20	253.25
2	18.51	19.00	19.16	19.25	19.30	19.33	19.35	19.37	19.38	19.40	19.40	19.41	19.42	19.42	19.43	19.45	19.45	19.46	19.47	19.48	19.49
3	10.13	9.55	9.28	9.12	9.01	8.94	8.89	8.85	8.81	8.79	8.76	8.74	8.73	8.71	8.70	8.66	8.64	8.62	8.59	8.57	8.55
4	7.71	6.94	6.59	6.39	6.26	6.16	6.09	6.04	6.00	5.96	5.94	5.91	5.89	5.87	5.86	5.80	5.77	5.75	5.72	5.69	5.66
5	6.61	5.79	5.41	5.19	5.05	4.95	4.88	4.82	4.77	4.74	4.70	4.68	4.66	4.64	4.62	4.56	4.53	4.50	4.46	4.43	4.40
6	5.99	5.14	4.76	4.53	4.39	4.28	4.21	4.15	4.10	4.06	4.03	4.00	3.98	3.96	3.94	3.87	3.84	3.81	3.77	3.74	3.70
7	5.59	4.74	4.35	4.12	3.97	3.87	3.79	3.73	3.68	3.64	3.60	3.57	3.55	3.53	3.51	3.44	3.41	3.38	3.34	3.30	3.27
8	5.32	4.46	4.07	3.84	3.69	3.58	3.50	3.44	3.39	3.35	3.31	3.28	3.26	3.24	3.22	3.15	3.12	3.08	3.04	3.01	2.97
9	5.12	4.26	3.86	3.63	3.48	3.37	3.29	3.23	3.18	3.14	3.10	3.07	3.05	3.03	3.01	2.94	2.90	2.86	2.83	2.79	2.75
10	4.96	4.10	3.71	3.48	3.33	3.22	3.14	3.07	3.02	2.98	2.94	2.91	2.89	2.86	2.85	2.77	2.74	2.70	2.66	2.62	2.58
11	4.84	3.98	3.59	3.36	3.20	3.09	3.01	2.95	2.90	2.85	2.82	2.79	2.76	2.74	2.72	2.65	2.61	2.57	2.53	2.49	2.45
12	4.75	3.89	3.49	3.26	3.11	3.00	2.91	2.85	2.80	2.75	2.72	2.69	2.66	2.64	2.62	2.54	2.51	2.47	2.43	2.38	2.34
13	4.67	3.81	3.41	3.18	3.03	2.92	2.83	2.77	2.71	2.67	2.63	2.60	2.58	2.55	2.53	2.46	2.42	2.38	2.34	2.30	2.25
14	4.60	3.74	3.34	3.11	2.96	2.85	2.76	2.70	2.65	2.60	2.57	2.53	2.51	2.48	2.46	2.39	2.35	2.31	2.27	2.22	2.18
15	4.54	3.68	3.29	3.06	2.90	2.79	2.71	2.64	2.59	2.54	2.51	2.48	2.45	2.42	2.40	2.33	2.29	2.25	2.20	2.16	2.11
16	4.49	3.63	3.24	3.01	2.85	2.74	2.66	2.59	2.54	2.49	2.46	2.42	2.40	2.37	2.35	2.28	2.24	2.19	2.15	2.11	2.06
17	4.45	3.59	3.20	2.96	2.81	2.70	2.61	2.55	2.49	2.45	2.41	2.38	2.35	2.33	2.31	2.23	2.19	2.15	2.10	2.06	2.01
18	4.41	3.55	3.16	2.93	2.77	2.66	2.58	2.51	2.46	2.41	2.37	2.34	2.31	2.29	2.27	2.19	2.15	2.11	2.06	2.02	1.97

(Contd . . .)

Table 4: **F Distribution**

F Distribution with 0.05 of area in the Right Tail *(contd.)*

Deg. of fr. for denominater	*Degrees of Freedom for Numerater*																			
	1	*2*	*3*	*4*	*5*	*6*	*7*	*8*	*9*	*10*	*11*	*12*	*13*	*14*	*15*	*20*	*24*	*30*	*40*	*60*	*120*
19	4.38	3.52	3.13	2.90	2.74	2.63	2.54	2.48	2.42	2.38	2.34	2.31	2.28	2.26	2.23	2.16	2.11	2.07	2.03	1.98	1.93
20	4.35	3.49	3.10	2.87	2.71	2.60	2.51	2.45	2.39	2.35	2.31	2.28	2.25	2.22	2.20	2.12	2.08	2.04	1.99	1.95	1.90
21	4.32	3.47	3.07	2.84	2.68	2.57	2.49	2.42	2.37	2.32	2.28	2.25	2.22	2.20	2.18	2.10	2.05	2.01	1.96	1.92	1.87
22	4.30	3.44	3.05	2.82	2.66	2.55	2.46	2.40	2.34	2.30	2.26	2.23	2.20	2.17	2.15	2.07	2.03	1.98	1.94	1.89	1.84
23	4.28	3.42	3.03	2.80	2.64	2.53	2.44	2.37	2.32	2.27	2.24	2.20	2.18	2.15	2.13	2.05	2.01	1.96	1.91	1.86	1.81
24	4.26	3.40	3.01	2.78	2.62	2.51	2.42	2.36	2.30	2.25	2.22	2.18	2.15	2.13	2.11	2.03	1.98	1.94	1.89	1.84	1.79
25	4.24	3.39	2.99	2.76	2.60	2.49	2.40	2.34	2.28	2.24	2.20	2.16	2.14	2.11	2.09	2.01	1.96	1.92	1.87	1.82	1.77
26	4.23	3.37	2.98	2.74	2.59	2.47	2.39	2.32	2.27	2.22	2.18	2.15	2.12	2.09	2.07	1.99	1.95	1.90	1.85	1.80	1.75
27	4.21	3.35	2.96	2.73	2.57	2.46	2.37	2.31	2.25	2.20	2.17	2.13	2.10	2.08	2.06	1.97	1.93	1.88	1.84	1.79	1.73
28	4.20	3.34	2.95	2.71	2.56	2.45	2.36	2.29	2.24	2.19	2.15	2.12	2.09	2.06	2.04	1.96	1.91	1.87	1.82	1.77	1.71
29	4.18	3.33	2.93	2.70	2.55	2.43	2.35	2.28	2.22	2.18	2.14	2.10	2.08	2.05	2.03	1.94	1.90	1.85	1.81	1.75	1.70
30	4.17	3.32	2.92	2.69	2.53	2.42	2.33	2.27	2.21	2.16	2.13	2.09	2.06	2.04	2.01	1.93	1.89	1.84	1.79	1.74	1.68
40	4.08	3.23	2.84	2.61	2.45	2.34	2.25	2.18	2.12	2.08	2.04	2.00	1.97	1.95	1.92	1.84	1.79	1.74	1.69	1.64	1.58
60	4.00	3.15	2.76	2.53	2.37	2.25	2.17	2.10	2.04	1.99	1.95	1.92	1.89	1.86	1.84	1.75	1.70	1.65	1.59	1.53	1.47
120	3.92	3.07	2.68	2.45	2.29	2.18	2.09	2.02	1.96	1.91	1.87	1.83	1.80	1.78	1.75	1.66	1.61	1.55	1.50	1.43	1.35

In an F distribution with 2 degrees of freedom for the numerator and 24 degrees of freedom for the denominator, to find the F value for 0.05 of the area under the curve, look under the 2 degrees of freedom column and across the 24 degrees of freedom; the appropriate F value is 3.4

Table 5: **F Distribution**

F Distribution with 0.01 of area in the Right Tail

Deg. of fr. for denominater	*Degrees of Freedom for Numerater*																				
	1	*2*	*3*	*4*	*5*	*6*	*7*	*8*	*9*	*10*	*11*	*12*	*13*	*14*	*15*	*20*	*24*	*30*	*40*	*60*	*120*
1	4052.18	4999.34	5403.53	5624.26	5763.96	5858.95	5928.33	5980.95	6022.40	6055.93	6083.40	6106.68	6125.77	6143.00	6156.97	6208.66	6234.27	6260.35	6286.43	6312.97	6339.51
2	98.50	99.00	99.16	99.25	99.30	99.33	99.36	99.38	99.39	99.40	99.41	99.42	99.42	99.43	99.43	99.45	99.46	99.47	99.48	99.48	99.49
3	34.12	30.82	29.46	28.71	28.24	27.91	27.67	27.49	27.34	27.23	27.13	27.05	26.98	26.92	26.87	26.69	26.60	26.50	26.41	26.32	26.22
4	21.20	18.00	16.69	15.98	15.52	15.21	14.98	14.80	14.66	14.55	14.45	14.37	14.31	14.25	14.20	14.02	13.93	13.84	13.75	13.65	13.56
5	16.26	13.27	12.06	11.39	10.97	10.67	10.46	10.29	10.16	10.05	9.96	9.89	9.82	9.77	9.72	9.55	9.47	9.38	9.29	9.20	9.11
6	13.75	10.92	9.78	9.15	8.75	8.47	8.26	8.10	7.98	7.87	7.79	7.72	7.66	7.60	7.56	7.40	7.31	7.23	7.14	7.06	6.97
7	12.25	9.55	8.45	7.85	7.46	7.19	6.99	6.84	6.72	6.62	6.54	6.47	6.41	6.36	6.31	6.16	6.07	5.99	5.91	5.82	5.74
8	11.26	8.65	7.59	7.01	6.63	6.37	6.18	6.03	5.91	5.81	5.73	5.67	5.61	5.56	5.52	5.36	5.28	5.20	5.12	5.03	4.95
9	10.56	8.02	6.99	6.42	6.06	5.80	5.61	5.47	5.35	5.26	5.18	5.11	5.05	5.01	4.96	4.81	4.73	4.65	4.57	4.48	4.40
10	10.04	7.56	6.55	5.99	5.64	5.39	5.20	5.06	4.94	4.85	4.77	4.71	4.65	4.60	4.56	4.41	4.33	4.25	4.17	4.08	4.00
11	9.65	7.21	6.22	5.67	5.32	5.07	4.89	4.74	4.63	4.54	4.46	4.40	4.34	4.29	4.25	4.10	4.02	3.94	3.86	3.78	3.69
12	9.33	6.93	5.95	5.41	5.06	4.82	4.64	4.50	4.39	4.30	4.22	4.16	4.10	4.05	4.01	3.86	3.78	3.70	3.62	3.54	3.45
13	9.07	6.70	5.74	5.21	4.86	4.62	4.44	4.30	4.19	4.10	4.02	3.96	3.91	3.86	3.82	3.66	3.59	3.51	3.43	3.34	3.25
14	8.86	6.51	5.56	5.04	4.69	4.46	4.28	4.14	4.03	3.94	3.86	3.80	3.75	3.70	3.66	3.51	3.43	3.35	3.27	3.18	3.09
15	8.68	6.36	5.42	4.89	4.56	4.32	4.14	4.00	3.89	3.80	3.73	3.67	3.61	3.56	3.52	3.37	3.29	3.21	3.13	3.05	2.96
16	8.53	6.23	5.29	4.77	4.44	4.20	4.03	3.89	3.78	3.69	3.62	3.55	3.50	3.45	3.41	3.26	3.18	3.10	3.02	2.93	2.84
17	8.40	6.11	5.19	4.67	4.34	4.10	3.93	3.79	3.68	3.59	3.52	3.46	3.40	3.35	3.31	3.16	3.08	3.00	2.92	2.83	2.75
18	8.29	6.01	5.09	4.58	4.25	4.01	3.84	3.71	3.60	3.51	3.43	3.37	3.32	3.27	3.23	3.08	3.00	2.92	2.84	2.75	2.66
19	8.18	5.93	5.01	4.50	4.17	3.94	3.77	3.63	3.52	3.43	3.36	3.30	3.24	3.19	3.15	3.00	2.92	2.84	2.76	2.67	2.58

(Contd . . .)

Table 5: **F Distribution**

F Distribution with 0.01 of area in the Right Tail *(contd.)*

Deg. of fr. for denominater	*Degrees of Freedom for Numerater*																			
	1	*2*	*3*	*4*	*5*	*6*	*7*	*8*	*9*	*10*	*11*	*12*	*13*	*14*	*15*	*20*	*24*	*30*	*40*	*60*	*120*
20	8.10	5.85	4.94	4.43	4.10	3.87	3.70	3.56	3.46	3.37	3.29	3.23	3.18	3.13	3.09	2.94	2.86	2.78	2.69	2.61	2.52
21	8.02	5.78	4.87	4.37	4.04	3.81	3.64	3.51	3.40	3.31	3.24	3.17	3.12	3.07	3.03	2.88	2.80	2.72	2.64	2.55	2.46
22	7.95	5.72	4.82	4.31	3.99	3.76	3.59	3.45	3.35	3.26	3.18	3.12	3.07	3.02	2.98	2.83	2.75	2.67	2.58	2.50	2.40
23	7.88	5.66	4.76	4.26	3.94	3.71	3.54	3.41	3.30	3.21	3.14	3.07	3.02	2.97	2.93	2.78	2.70	2.62	2.54	2.45	2.35
24	7.82	5.61	4.72	4.22	3.90	3.67	3.50	3.36	3.26	3.17	3.09	3.03	2.98	2.93	2.89	2.74	2.66	2.58	2.49	2.40	2.31
25	7.77	5.57	4.68	4.18	3.85	3.63	3.46	3.32	3.22	3.13	3.06	2.99	2.94	2.89	2.85	2.70	2.62	2.54	2.45	2.36	2.27
26	7.72	5.53	4.64	4.14	3.82	3.59	3.42	3.29	3.18	3.09	3.02	2.96	2.90	2.86	2.81	2.66	2.58	2.50	2.42	2.33	2.23
27	7.68	5.49	4.60	4.11	3.78	3.56	3.39	3.26	3.15	3.06	2.99	2.93	2.87	2.82	2.78	2.63	2.55	2.47	2.38	2.29	2.20
28	7.64	5.45	4.57	4.07	3.75	3.53	3.36	3.23	3.12	3.03	2.96	2.90	2.84	2.79	2.75	2.60	2.52	2.44	2.35	2.26	2.17
29	7.60	5.42	4.54	4.04	3.73	3.50	3.33	3.20	3.09	3.00	2.93	2.87	2.81	2.77	2.73	2.57	2.49	2.41	2.33	2.23	2.14
30	7.56	5.39	4.51	4.02	3.70	3.47	3.30	3.17	3.07	2.98	2.91	2.84	2.79	2.74	2.70	2.55	2.47	2.39	2.30	2.21	2.11
40	7.31	5.18	4.31	3.83	3.51	3.29	3.12	2.99	2.89	2.80	2.73	2.66	2.61	2.56	2.52	2.37	2.29	2.20	2.11	2.02	1.92
60	7.08	4.98	4.13	3.65	3.34	3.12	2.95	2.82	2.72	2.63	2.56	2.50	2.44	2.39	2.35	2.20	2.12	2.03	1.94	1.84	1.73
120	6.85	4.79	3.95	3.48	3.17	2.96	2.79	2.66	2.56	2.47	2.40	2.34	2.28	2.23	2.19	2.03	1.95	1.86	1.76	1.66	1.53

In an F distribution with 2 degrees of freedom for the numerator and 24 degrees of freedom for the denominator, to find the F value for 0.01 of the area under the curve, look under the 2 degrees of freedom column and across the 24 degrees of freedom; the appropriate F value is 5.61

Chapter 11

Scheme Comparison — Risk Adjusted Returns

As a person moves along the risk spectrum from a risk-free investment, say, government securities which have zero credit risk, to a risky investment like equity, the returns need to be higher to justify the higher risk. Risk adjusted returns enable comparison between schemes based on both risk and return.

Risk adjusted returns typically use a "risk free return" as a benchmark. Risk free return is one where the investor does not assume a risk. Academics prefer the return on T-Bills as a measure of risk-free return. Richard A Ferri however proposes rate of inflation as an alternative because: "I do not believe T-Bills are a good indicator for the risk-free rate. T-bill rates are artificial. They are very close to being directed by the dealings of the Federal Reserve Board. A better risk-free rate is to just use inflation itself. That takes all the biases out."[47]

A very simple way to combine risk and return is the Z-scale. Suppose an agency wishes to select the best fund house, based on the performance of the best debt and equity schemes of each mutual fund. The agency has collected the performance of different mutual funds during a period which are given in Table 11.1.

One option would be to rank each fund house for its performance in each scheme category, and then total the ranks across scheme categories. Thus, if Mutual Fund A ranks 5th among equity schemes and 1st among debt schemes, its composite score (total of both ranks) would be 6 (5 + 1). This being the lowest composite score among all the funds, Mutual Fund A would have a composite rank of 1. Mutual Fund A would share the first rank with Mutual Fund I, which again has a composite score of 6 (2 + 4). With two first ranks (A and I), the next rank would be 3.

Mutual Fund B, which ranks 4th both among equity and debt schemes would have a composite score of 8, which would give it a composite rank of 3, and so on.

(The scheme with the lowest composite rank would be the best fund house).

But in such an approach the extent of a funds superior performance within a category does not get captured. Thus, Mutual Fund C would have been ranked 1st on equity, irrespective of whether its next ranking competitor earned a return that was only 0.05% lower, or a significant 5% lower.

Table 11.1

Mutual fund	*Best Equity Scheme*	*Equity Rank*	*Best Debt Scheme*	*Debt Rank*	*Total of both ranks*	*Composite Rank*
A	1.000%	5	1.000%	1	6	1
B	2.000%	4	0.300%	4	8	3
C	5.000%	1	0.100%	9	10	5
D	– 2.000%	7	0.400%	3	10	5
E	– 3.000%	8	0.300%	4	12	7
F	3.000%	3	– 0.500%	10	13	10
G	1.000%	5	0.300%	4	9	4
H	– 5.000%	10	0.500%	2	12	7
I	4.000%	2	0.300%	4	6	1
J	– 3.000%	8	0.300%	4	12	7
Average	**0.300%**		**0.300%**			
Standard Deviation	**3.368%**		**0.368%**			

Suppose we find outperformance for both categories of schemes, then the above criticism is addressed. The average return among various equity schemes is 0.3%. Similarly, the average debt return too is 0.3%.

Thus Mutual Fund C, with its return of 5% has out-performed the average equity performance by:

5.0% – 0.3% = 4.7%,

while Mutual Fund A has out-performed the average debt fund by:

1.0% – 0.3% = 0.7%.

The outperformance of each mutual fund for both schemes can be totalled. The fund with the highest number (Fund C) can be declared winner as given in Table 11.2.

Table 11.2

Mutual fund	*Best Equity Scheme*	*Outperformance*	*Best Debt Scheme*	*Outperformance*	*Total Outperformance*	*Composite Rank*
A	1.000%	0.7%	1.000%	0.7%	**1.4%**	**5**
B	2.000%	1.7%	0.300%	0.0%	**1.7%**	**4**
C	5.000%	4.7%	0.100%	– 0.2%	**4.5%**	**1**
D	– 2.000%	– 2.3%	0.400%	0.1%	**– 2.2%**	**7**
E	– 3.000%	– 3.3%	0.300%	0.0%	**– 3.3%**	**8**
F	3.000%	2.7%	– 0.500%	– 0.8%	**1.9%**	**3**
G	1.000%	0.7%	0.300%	0.0%	**0.7%**	**6**
H	– 5.000%	– 5.3%	0.500%	0.2%	**– 5.1%**	**10**
I	4.000%	3.7%	0.300%	0.0%	**3.7%**	**2**
J	–3.000%	–3.3%	0.300%	0.0%	**– 3.3%**	**8**
Average	**0.300%**		**0.300%**			
Standard Deviation	**3.368%**		**0.368%**			

In such a comparison, the debt fund manager in Mutual Fund A would, however, feel hard done by. She would argue that though her equity counterpart too had an outperformance number of 0.7%, it was more difficult to secure outperformance in the debt scheme, as is evident from the lower standard deviation of 0.368%, as compared to the standard deviation of 3.368% in the equity schemes. So she would question the whole logic of totalling the numbers of the two types of schemes, irrespective of whether the ranks, or the outperformance numbers are totalled.

An alternative that addresses such concerns is the Z score, which is given by the formula:

$Z = X \div \sigma$

where, X is the outperformance with respect to the mean,
σ is the standard deviation of returns.

The working can be seen in Table 11.3.

Table 11.3

Mutual fund	Best Equity Scheme	Out-performance	Z score	Best Debt Scheme	Out-performance	Z score	Total of both Z scores	Rank
A	1.000%	0.700%	0.2078	1.000%	0.700%	1.9013	2.1091	1
B	2.000%	1.700%	0.5047	0.300%	0.000%	0.0000	0.5047	4
C	5.000%	4.700%	1.3954	0.100%	– 0.200%	– 0.5432	0.8522	3
D	– 2.000%	– 2.300%	– 0.6829	0.400%	0.100%	0.2716	– 0.4113	6
E	– 3.000%	– 3.300%	– 0.9798	0.300%	0.000%	0.0000	– 0.9798	7
F	3.000%	2.700%	0.8016	– 0.500%	– 0.800%	– 2.1729	– 1.3712	10
G	1.000%	0.700%	0.2078	0.300%	0.000%	0.0000	0.2078	5
H	– 5.000%	– 5.300%	– 1.5736	0.500%	0.200%	0.5432	– 1.0303	9
I	4.000%	3.700%	1.0985	0.300%	0.000%	0.0000	1.0985	2
J	– 3.000%	– 3.300%	– 0.9798	0.300%	0.000%	0.0000	– 0.9798	7
Mean	0.300%			0.300%				
Std Dev	3.368%			0.368%				

As can be seen from Table 11.3, the 4.7% outperformance of Mutual Fund C in equity schemes gave it a Z score of only 1.3954, while a mere 0.7% outperformance by Mutual Fund A in debt schemes gave it a Z score of 1.9013. The debt manager of Mutual Fund A has been rewarded for the difficulty she would have encountered in securing the outperformance.

Since the Z score considers both risk and return, it is a standardized measure. Z scores can be totalled between debt and equity schemes. Mutual Fund A, with the highest total Z score (equity plus debt) would be declared as the best fund house.

With this overview into the utility of combining risk and return in various analyses, let us understand the measures of risk-adjusted returns, with the help of the example shown in Table 11.4.

Table 11.4: **Scheme and Index Values**

Date	*Scheme NAV*	*Sensex*	*T-Bill Index (JP Morgan 30 day)*
15-Aug-04	24.184	5102.92	189.25
01-Sep-04	25.018	5210.85	189.75
15-Sep-04	25.530	5420.09	190.05
01-Oct-04	26.290	5675.54	190.49
15-Oct-04	26.318	5686.73	190.77
01-Nov-04	26.221	5704.10	191.23
15-Nov-04	26.957	5964.01	191.43
01-Dec-04	28.439	6227.83	192.07
15-Dec-04	30.184	6402.29	192.44
01-Jan-05	31.860	6602.69	192.99
15-Jan-05	30.105	6173.82	193.32
01-Feb-05	31.885	6552.47	193.85
15-Feb-05	33.111	6670.06	194.16
01-Mar-05	33.242	6651.08	194.57
15-Mar-05	33.480	6752.45	194.90
01-Apr-05	32.617	6605.04	195.43
15-Apr-05	31.404	6248.34	195.78
01-May-05	30.673	6154.44	196.15
15-May-05	31.871	6451.54	196.54
01-Jun-05	32.890	6729.90	197.06
15-Jun-05	33.540	6906.98	197.44
01-Jul-05	33.993	7210.77	197.89
15-Jul-05	35.969	7271.54	198.28
01-Aug-05	37.683	7669.45	198.84
15-Aug-05	40.768	7767.49	199.16

The array of returns can be easily derived as given in Table 11.5.

Table 11.5: **Periodic Returns**

Date	*Scheme Return*	*Sensex Return*	*T-Bill Return*	*Differential Return*		
				Sensex minus T-Bill	*Scheme minus Sensex*	*Scheme minus T-Bill*
01-Sep-04	3.4%	2.1%	0.26%	1.9%	1.3%	3.2%
15-Sep-04	2.0%	4.0%	0.16%	3.9%	−2.0%	1.9%
01-Oct-04	3.0%	4.7%	0.23%	4.5%	−1.7%	2.7%
15-Oct-04	0.1%	0.2%	0.15%	0.0%	−0.1%	0.0%
01-Nov-04	−0.4%	0.3%	0.24%	0.1%	−0.7%	−0.6%
15-Nov-04	2.8%	4.6%	0.10%	4.5%	−1.7%	2.7%
01-Dec-04	5.5%	4.4%	0.33%	4.1%	1.1%	5.2%
15-Dec-04	6.1%	2.8%	0.19%	2.6%	3.3%	5.9%
01-Jan-05	5.6%	3.1%	0.28%	2.8%	2.4%	5.3%
15-Jan-05	−5.5%	−6.5%	0.17%	−6.7%	1.0%	−5.7%
01-Feb-05	5.9%	6.1%	0.28%	5.9%	−0.2%	5.6%
15-Feb-05	3.8%	1.8%	0.16%	1.6%	2.1%	3.7%
01-Mar-05	0.4%	−0.3%	0.21%	−0.5%	0.7%	0.2%
15-Mar-05	0.7%	1.5%	0.17%	1.4%	−0.8%	0.5%
01-Apr-05	−2.6%	−2.2%	0.27%	−2.5%	−0.4%	−2.8%
15-Apr-05	−3.7%	−5.4%	0.18%	−5.6%	1.7%	−3.9%
01-May-05	−2.3%	−1.5%	0.19%	−1.7%	−0.8%	−2.5%
15-May-05	3.9%	4.8%	0.20%	4.6%	−0.9%	3.7%
01-Jun-05	3.2%	4.3%	0.26%	4.1%	−1.1%	2.9%
15-Jun-05	2.0%	2.6%	0.19%	2.4%	−0.7%	1.8%
01-Jul-05	1.4%	4.4%	0.23%	4.2%	−3.0%	1.1%
15-Jul-05	5.8%	0.8%	0.20%	0.6%	5.0%	5.6%
01-Aug-05	4.8%	5.5%	0.28%	5.2%	−0.7%	4.5%
15-Aug-05	8.2%	1.3%	0.16%	1.1%	6.9%	8.0%

The mean and standard deviation of the periodic returns is as follows:

	Scheme Return	*Sensex Return*	*T-Bill Return*	*Sensex minus T-Bill*	*Scheme minus Sensex*	*Scheme minus T-Bill*
Mean Periodic Return	2.26%	1.82%	0.21%	1.60%	0.44%	2.04%
Annualised Mean	70.80%	54.06%	5.23%	46.51%	11.07%	62.47%
Standard Deviation of Periodic Returns	3.43%	3.26%	0.06%	3.24%	2.29%	3.42%
Annualised Std. Dev.	16.81%	15.95%	0.27%	15.87%	11.21%	16.75%

Annualised mean has been calculated using the formula $(1 + i)^n - 1$, where, "i" is the mean periodic return; "n" is the number of data points which would be equivalent to a year. Since we have 2 observations per month, $2 \times 12 = 24$ data points would equate a year. Thus, n = 24.

Annualised standard deviation has been calculated as:

Standard Deviation of Periodic Returns x square root of n (which is 24).

Square root can be calculated using the "SQRT(n)" function in MS Excel.

Regression analysis [As detailed in Chapter 10], with range of scheme returns as "Y Value", and range of Sensex returns as "X Value" yields the results shown in Table 11.6.

Table 11.6

SUMMARY OUTPUT

Regression Statistics	
Multiple R	0.76702
R Square	0.58832
Adjusted R Square	0.56961
Standard Error	0.02252
Observations	24

ANOVA

	Df	*SS*	*MS*	*F*	*Significance F*
Regression	1	0.01594	0.01594	31.44020	0.00001
Residual	22	0.01115	0.00051		
Total	23	0.02709			

	Coefficients	*Standard Error*	*t Stat*	*P-value*	*Lower 95%*	*Upper 95%*	*Lower 99.0%*	*Upper 99.0%*
Intercept	0.00786	0.00529	1.48619	0.15142	– 0.00311	0.01884	– 0.00705	0.02278
Sensex Return	0.80864	0.14422	5.60716	0.00001	0.50955	1.10772	0.40213	1.21514

RESIDUAL OUTPUT

Observation	*Predicted Scheme Return*	*Residuals*
1	0.02497	0.00952
2	0.04033	– 0.01987
3	0.04597	– 0.01621
4	0.00946	– 0.00839
5	0.01033	– 0.01402
6	0.04471	– 0.01664

PROBABILITY OUTPUT

Percentile	*Scheme Return*
2.08333	– 0.05508
6.25000	– 0.03719
10.41667	– 0.02578
14.58333	– 0.02328
18.75000	– 0.00369
22.91667	0.00107

(Contd . . .)

Table 11.6 (contd.)

RESIDUALOUTPUT

Observation	*Predicted Scheme Return*	*Residuals*
7	0.04363	0.01134
8	0.03052	0.03084
9	0.03317	0.02235
10	– 0.04466	– 0.01042
11	0.05746	0.00167
12	0.02237	0.01608
13	0.00556	– 0.00161
14	0.02019	– 0.01303
15	– 0.00979	– 0.01599
16	– 0.03581	– 0.00138
17	– 0.00429	– 0.01899
18	0.04690	– 0.00784
19	0.04275	– 0.01078
20	0.02914	– 0.00938
21	0.04343	– 0.02992
22	0.01468	0.04345
23	0.05211	– 0.00446
24	0.01820	0.06367

PROBABILITY OUTPUT

Percentile	*Scheme Return*
27.08333	0.00396
31.25000	0.00716
35.41667	0.01351
39.58333	0.01976
43.75000	0.02047
47.91667	0.02807
52.08333	0.02977
56.25000	0.03197
60.41667	0.03449
64.58333	0.03845
68.75000	0.03906
72.91667	0.04765
77.08333	0.05498
81.25000	0.05553
85.41667	0.05813
89.58333	0.05913
93.75000	0.06136
97.91667	0.08187

Now we can calculate the measures of risk adjusted returns.

11.1 Sharpe Ratio

Sharpe Ratio measures the return earned per unit of risk, with risk being measured by standard deviation. A higher Sharpe Ratio implies better reward for the risk taken. Therefore, between two schemes of the same type, the one with the higher Sharpe Ratio offers superior payoff to the investor.

This ratio, named after William Sharpe, thus measures *reward to variability*. The widely prevalent approach to Sharpe Ratio is to use the T-bill index as the benchmark. But in practice, the benchmark can also be a market index like the Sensex. Ultimately, Sharpe Ratio measures excess return and divides it by the excess risk. Therefore, in some circles, it is also referred to as Excess Returns Sharpe Ratio.

When Sharpe Ratio is calculated for historic data, it is called Ex-post Sharpe Ratio; when it is estimated for the future, it is called Ex-Ante Sharpe Ratio.

11.1.1 Ex-Post Sharpe Ratio

As compared to Benchmark: T-Bill a ÷ b		**3.73**
a Annualised Mean of Differential Return (Scheme minus T-Bill)	62.47%	
b Annualised Standard Deviation of Differential Return	16.75%	
As compared to Benchmark: Sensex c ÷ d		**0.99**
c Annualised Mean of Differential Return (Scheme minus Sensex)	11.07%	
d Annualised Standard Deviation of Differential Return	11.21%	

11.1.2 Ex-Ante Sharpe Ratio

(e – f)÷g			**1.67**
e Expected Return on the Scheme	(say)	30.00%	
f Expected Return on the T-Bill	(say)	5.00%	
g Expected Standard of Deviation of Scheme	(say)	15.00%	

Since Sharpe ratio uses standard deviation as a measure of risk, it evaluates returns with respect to total risk, not just systematic risk. Therefore, it can be used even for non-diversified portfolios, which have both systematic as well as non-systematic risks.

Bogle (1999) had his reservations on the ratio. He wrote: "The Sharpe Ratio is a somewhat blunt instrument measuring risk-adjusted returns. Past returns don't predict future returns. And although relative risks among funds have a good deal of consistency over time, standard deviation is only a rough proxy for a concept as elusive as risk. Further, weighting risk as equal to return in importance in the formula is completely arbitrary. Here is the reality of investing, as I see it: An extra percentage point of standard deviation is meaningless, but an extra percentage point of return is priceless."[48]

11.2 Treynor Ratio

The Treynor Ratio, named after Jack Treynor, is similar to the Sharpe Ratio, except that the risk measure used is Beta instead of standard deviation. The ratio thus measures *reward to volatility*. The scheme with the higher Treynor ratio offers a superior risk-reward equation for the investor.

(a – b)÷c		**81.1%**
a Annualised Scheme Return	70.80%	
b Risk Free Return	5.23%	
c Beta	0.81%	

Since Treynor ratio uses beta as a risk measure, it evaluates excess returns with respect to systematic risk only. It is therefore more appropriate for diversified equity schemes, where the non-systematic risks have been eliminated. Generally, large institutional investors have the requisite funds to maintain such highly diversified portfolios. For smaller investors, Sharpe ratio would be better.

Also since beta is based on capital asset pricing model, which is empirically tested for equity, Treynor Ratio would be inappropriate for debt schemes.

11.3 Jensen Alpha

When the market goes up, high beta funds will show better returns than the low beta funds. When the market turns adverse, the losses would be lower in low beta funds. If the performance of funds depends on market returns and beta, then how do we evaluate the role of the fund manager in generating excess returns? The answer lies in the Jensen Alpha for the scheme.

This ratio, named after Michael Jensen, is the gap between the fund's expected return (based on its beta, i.e. systematic risk) and its actual returns. Higher the alpha, better the fund manager has performed. If the benchmark return is zero, and the scheme has still generated a return, then that scheme return — the alpha — is the contribution of the fund manager. Alpha can be positive or negative. It can be easily calculated using the "intercept" function in MS Excel. The syntax is = intercept (range of cells showing scheme returns, range of cells showing benchmark returns). The answer, in the above case would be 0.79%. A framework for Alpha with more incremental information is available through the regression analysis approach.

In the Data Analysis — Regression screen, if you select "line-fit plot", then you get the following chart. The small diamonds are the **actual** data points representing various combinations of scheme and Sensex returns. The large diamonds, which are along a straight line, represent **estimates** of scheme returns, for various levels of Sensex returns. The estimates are based on the regression line equation. To find details of this equation, you can right click on any of the small diamonds, then click "Add Trend Line". Thereafter, under options, select "Display Equation on Chart" and "Display R-square value on Chart". The resulting chart is shown in Figure 11.1 &11.2 that has a line connecting the big diamonds.

We now know that the regression line is defined by the equation,

$$Y = 0.8086X + 0.0079$$

This means that if the Sensex return were 1%, the scheme return is likely to be:

(0.8086 x 1%) + 0.0079, i.e. 1.59%.

If the Sensex returns were 0%, the scheme return is still likely to earn a return of 0.79%. In the absence of a Sensex return, this return on the scheme would be attributable entirely to the fund manager's performance. Thus, the fund manager's outperformance, also called Alpha, is 0.79%. This corresponds with the Coefficient of the Intercept in the Summary Output table generated by the Regression Analysis

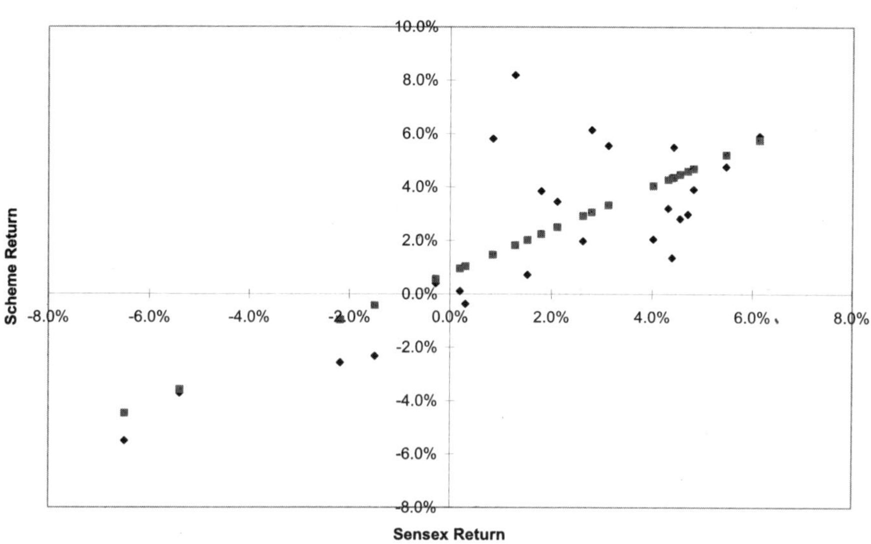

Figure 11.1: **Sensex Return Line Fit Plot**

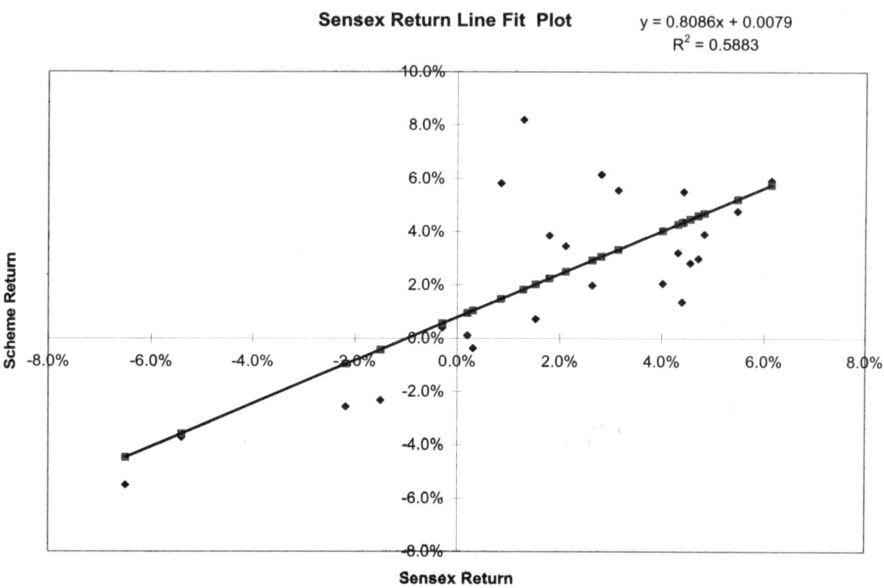

Figure 11.2: **Sensex Return Line Fit Plot**

It may be noted that Jensen Alpha helps in assessing the excess returns generated by the fund manager, given the beta. It however does not help assess her prescience in shuffling her portfolio (changing beta) in line with market movements.

As in the case of Treynor ratio, Jensen Alpha can be used for diversified equity portfolios, where the non-systematic risk would be closer to zero.

While the above explains the concept of Alpha and its computation, an important statistical red flag is to be noted in this example. Assuming one operates with a 95% confidence level, the P-value of the intercept should be less than 0.05. In this case, the P-value is much higher at 0.15142. Thus, at the 95% confidence level it cannot be said that the Alpha is significantly different from 0.

P-value given against the Sensex return row essentially is the P-value of the Alpha. At 0.0001 it is much lower than 0.05. It is even lower than 0.01. Thus, even at 99% confidence level the slope is significant.

It can be concluded that while Sensex return is significant in determining the returns from the scheme, the computed Alpha cannot be said to be significant.

11.4 Eugene Fama

The ratio has elements of conceptual similarity to Jensen Alpha. However, it uses standard deviation instead of beta. Since standard deviation is a measure of total risk, the ratio can be used even for non-diversified portfolios.

Eugene Fama		
h – g		**14.09%**
a Risk Free Return	5.23%	
b Market Return	54.03%	
c Risk Premium (b – a)	48.82%	
d Annualised Standard Deviation of Market	15.95%	
e Risk Premium per unit of Standard Deviation of Market (c ÷ d)	306.13%	
f Annualised Standard Deviation of Scheme	16.81%	
g Expected Return based on Scheme SD a + (e x f)	56.71%	
h Annualised Scheme Return	70.80%	

A positive Eugene Fama number means the fund manager's performance is better than what is expected based on the scheme's total risk, as measured by standard deviation.

11.5 Appraisal Ratio

Jensen Alpha, we saw earlier, considers only systematic risk. Appraisal Ratio considers the unsystematic risk too, by dividing the Jensen Alpha by the scheme's unsystematic risk.

Schemes that are poorly diversified would have a high element of unsystematic risk — and hence show a low appraisal ratio. Higher the appraisal ratio, better the scheme for the investor.

The unsystematic risk in our example is 0.00529, which corresponds with the Standard Error of the Intercept, in the Regression Results table.

	a ÷ b		**1.49**
a Alpha		0.79%	
B Non-systematic Risk		0.53%	

This explains the computation. However, since Alpha is not statistically significant, the Appraisal Ratio too is not meaningful in this example.

11.6 Modigliani and Modigliani (M^2)

This is a measure that is named after Franco Modigliani and his grand daughter, Lea Modigliani. It is closely related to Sharpe Ratio, but more recently conceptualised. It operates on the concept that a scheme's portfolio can be levered or delevered to reflect a standard deviation that is identical with that of the market. The return that this adjusted portfolio earns is called M^2. Since the standard deviations have been equalized, M^2 can be directly compared with the return in the market.

	a + (c x e ÷ d)		**67.43%**
a Risk Free Return		5.23%	
b Annualised Scheme Return		70.80%	
c Excess Returns		65.57%	
d Annualised Standard Deviation of Scheme		16.81%	
e Annualised Standard Deviation of Market		15.95%	

The M^2 value of the scheme at 67.43% compares favourably with the market return of 54.06% during the same period. The scheme has outperformed the market on a risk adjusted basis.

11.7 Sortino Ratio

Unlike Sharpe Ratio, which uses standard deviation (effectively both upside and downside risk) as a measure of risk, Sortino Ratio uses only downside risk. The underlying principle is that if returns are better than standard, then it is not a risk. Investors are concerned about losses, not gains.

Thus, Sortino Ratio is a modification of the Sharpe Ratio. The numerator is the same as the Sharpe Ratio. The denominator is the downside risk, the standard deviation of the negative returns (which is also called "semi standard deviation").

In the above example, standard deviation of only the negative values in the Scheme minus T-Bill column gives a value of 1.505791%. Multiplying by sqrt (24), the annualised standard deviation of the negative returns comes to 7.37684%. Accordingly, Sortino ratio can be calculated as follows:

As compared to Benchmark: T-Bill a ÷ b		**8.47**
a Annualised Mean of Differential Returns (Scheme minus T-Bill)	62.47%	
b Annualised Standard Deviation of Differential Returns which are negative	7.38%	

11.8 Which is the Best Measure?

Human beings cannot be evaluated based on any one measure. In selection interviews, an accountant will score based on her knowledge of accountancy; but the security guard will score based on his height, muscles and moustache!

Similarly, the relevance of measures is context specific:

- For diversified equity portfolios, Treynor and Jensen Alpha can be used.
- Sharpe, Sortino, Eugene Fama and Modigliani & Modigliani can be used for non-diversified portfolios and debt portfolios.

If a scheme were not adequately diversified, then Treynor Ratio (which ignores the unsystematic risk) would show a high number. A lay investor may accordingly invest in the scheme on the basis of the Treynor Ratio when, in fact, the impact of the unsystematic risk would be captured in the Sharpe Ratio or Appraisal Ratio, which would be more appropriate in the context.

Using performance measures is more of an art, than a science. This increases subjectivity. Even for calculations, there are so many different approaches. In practice, different AMCs use different sources of data, or different approaches to calculations, thus rendering the results non-comparable. Therefore, it would be useful for investors to draw conclusions based on analysis of independent agencies (such as CRISIL, Value Research, etc.) rather than the numbers generated by the AMCs themselves.

11.9 CRISIL's Rating and Ranking[1]

11.9.1 Superior Returns Score

CRISIL in its Composite Performance Ranking — CPR (detail on next page), uses the superior returns score. Superior returns score is calculated based on average daily / weekly return as given in Table 11.7 on next page:

- Equity, Balanced and Gilt Schemes — over a 2-year period — split into 4 half-years with weights of 32.5%, 27.5%, 22.5% and 17.5% (higher weightage for more recent half-years).
- Liquid schemes — over a 1-year period — split into 4 quarters with weights of 32.5%. 27.5%, 22.5% and 17.5% (higher weightage for more recent quarters).

This weighted average return for the peer group (all similar schemes) is used as a benchmark against which each scheme's differential return and standard deviation of such differential return is worked out. The ratio of the scheme's differential return to the standard deviation of such differential return gives the superior returns score.

Thus, unlike the Sharpe ratio where excess return over the risk-free return was considered, the CRISIL superior returns score is calculated on the basis of excess return over the peer group's return.

The top performer gets a score of 1 and others get relative performance scores in relation to the category top performer.

11.9.2 Rating of Schemes

Credit rating agencies rate the credit risk in debt schemes. Greater the proportion of the portfolio in high quality assets, higher would be the credit rating of the scheme. Top rating of "AAAmfs" , for instance, means that the long term mutual fund's portfolio holdings provide very **strong protection** against losses from credit defaults. A poor rating of "Cmfs" means the fund's portfolio holdings have factors present, which make them **vulnerable** to credit defaults. The corresponding symbols for short term mutual fund schemes are "A1mfs" for top rating and "A4mfs" for poor rating.

11.9.3 CRISIL Risk Adjusted Return Ranking (RRR)

CRISIL comes out with risk-adjusted return ranking of mutual fund schemes on a monthly basis. This is calculated on a moving one-year time period for the different categories of funds.

The schemes are ranked under each category.

---

[1] This section demonstrates how the various measurement concepts are applied in the real world. The details are illustrative of the underlying thought process.

11.10.4 CRISIL Composite Performance Ranking (CPR)

CRISIL calculates the CPR every quarter on the basis of factors such as superior returns score, concentration of the scheme portfolio, liquidity of the scheme portfolio, asset quality and asset size of the scheme. The performance period considered is 2 years for equity funds (other than index funds), long term income funds, gilt funds and hybrid funds; 1 year for index, liquid, ultra short term debt, and short term debt funds.

The weights of various factors CRISIL uses in assigning the CPR ranking for some categories of funds are given in Table 11.7.

Table 11.7

	Large Cap Equity	*Long Term Income*	*Balanced*	*Long Term Gilt*
Superior Return Score	75%	60%	75%	75%
Industry Concentration	10%	%	10%	
Company Concentration	5%	5%	5%	
Equity liquidity	10%		10% × K	
Debt — asset quality	17.5%	5% × (100-K)		7.5%
Debt — liquidity	7.5%	5% × (100-K)		
Gilt — liquidity				12.5%
Average maturity / Modified duration	5%			5%

* K is the percentage of equity holding in the balanced portfolio.

Based on Table 11.7, schemes are categorized as:

CPR1	Top 10% of universe	Very good performance
CPR2	Next 20%	Good performance
CPR3	Next 40%	Average performance
CPR4	Next 20%	Below average performance
CPR5	Last 10%	Poor performance

Some of these weightages are refined from time to time. Also measures are dropped and new measures introduced. Readers are advised to check CRISIL's website for the latest measures and their underlying methodology.

Chapter 12

Scheme Comparison — Investment Objective, Style Analysis and Other Factors

12.1 Investment Objective

The Indian mutual fund industry has been maturing, with fund houses launching several different types of schemes. At times, however, AMCs confuse investors with different names for similar schemes – precisely the reason SEBI decided to bring in standardisation of scheme categories and uniformity in their nomenclature. Despite this investor protection initiative, the section in a scheme's offer document which explains its investment objective, investment strategy and benchmark index are important. An investor acquiring units of a scheme is essentially buying into its investment philosophy.

Table 12.1 illustrates the point with the help of extracts from offer documents of some Indian mutual fund schemes.

Table 12.1

Diversified Equity Funds

Scheme Type	*Investment Objective*	*Investment Strategy*	*Benchmark Index*
Open-end equity growth scheme.	The investment objective of the scheme is to generate long-term capital growth from a diversified portfolio of pre-dominantly equity and equity-related securities	The investment approach is bottom up stock picking. The Scheme seeks to add the best opportunities that the market presents, without any sector / cap bias	BSE 200 Index
Aggressive Growth, Open-end diversified equity schemes	To provide medium to long term capital appreciation as primary objective and income as secondary objective	To achieve capital appreciation through investments in relatively smaller, faster growing companies.	CNX 500
Growth, Open-end diversified equity schemes.	To provide growth of capital plus regular dividend through a diversified portfolio of equities, fixed income securities and money market instruments	The scheme looks to identify such companies through research by giving due focus to the qualitative aspects such as management capabilities, business strengths and unique business models which given	CNX 500

(Contd . . .)

Table 12.1 (contd.)

Scheme Type	*Investment Objective*	*Investment Strategy*	*Benchmark Index*
		them a sustainable competitive advantage	
Steady Growth, Open-end diversified equity scheme	To provide medium to long term capital appreciation	Aims to achieve steady and consistent capital appreciation through investment in well – established, large size blue-chip companies	BSE Sensex
Open-end Equity Growth Scheme	To achieve long term growth of capital	Investing in equity and equity related securities through a research based investment approach	BSE 100
Open-end equity growth Scheme	To generate capital appreciation	To have a portfolio of predominantly equity and equity related securities with investment in, generally, not more than 30 stocks	BSE Sensex, CNX Nifty
Open-end equity growth scheme	To achieve capital appreciation	Investing predominantly in growth companies. Companies selected under this portfolio would as far as practicable consist of medium to large sized companies which: (a) are likely to achieve above average growth than the industry; (b) enjoy distinct competitive advantages, and (c) have superior financial strengths	BSE Sensex, NSE Nifty
Open-end equity growth scheme	To achieve capital appreciation in the long-term	Investing in blue-chip companies at prices which are below fair value in the opinion of the fund managers	BSE Sensex, NSE Nifty
Open-end equity scheme	To generate long-term capital appreciation	Investing predominantly in equity and equity related instruments	CNX Nifty
Open-end scheme	To generate long term capital appreciation	Have a judicious mix of investment in quality debt and equity instruments at relatively low risk levels through research based investments	Crisil's MIPex
Open end pure Growth Scheme	To provide capital growth	Investing mainly in mix of equity instruments	BSE Sensex
Open end Equity Scheme	To achieve capital appreciation	To invest in select stocks of companies which meet criteria of 'Leaders' in their respective sectors/sub sectors. The leaders are identified as the top two/three companies in any sector/sub sector in terms of net revenue or total income	NSE Nifty

(Contd . . .)

Table 12.1 (contd.)

Scheme Type	*Investment Objective*	*Investment Strategy*	*Benchmark Index*
Open Ended Balanced Fund	To provide an enabler to adult female persons in pooling their own savings and/or gifts into an investments vehicle so as to get periodic cash flow near the time of any chosen festival/occasion or to allow income/gains redeployed in the scheme and re-purchase units partially or fully as and when desired.		CRSIL MIP Blended Index
Open End Equity Fund	To provide capital growth as well as to make periodically distribution of income from investment in stocks of respective sectors of the Indian economy.		BSE 100
Open End Equity Fund	To provide capital growth over a period of time as well as to make income distribution from investment in stocks of select growth oriented sectors of the Indian economy	Investing in companies sensitive to economic cycles and commodity pricing cycles. The investment will be in companies which are often referred as cyclical companies.	BSE 200
Open-end growth scheme	To provide long-term growth of capital. The secondary objective is income generation and distribution of dividend	Having a portfolio with a target allocation of 100% equity, focusing on investing in businesses that are driven by India's large population and inherent consumption patterns. The focus of the scheme will be in the consumer and healthcare sectors.	BSE 200

Sector Funds

Scheme Type	*Investment Objective*	*Investment Strategy*	*Benchmark Index*
Sectoral Growth, Open-end Fund	To provide long term capital appreciation	Provide long term capital appreciation by investing primarily in FMCG industry	ET Brandex
Open-End Banking Sector Scheme	To generate continuous returns.	Investing in equity / equity related or fixed income securities of banks	CNX Banks Index
Open-end Pharma Sector Scheme	To generate continuous returns.	Investing in equity / equity related or fixed income securities of Pharma and other associated companies	BSE-Health Care Index

(Contd . . .)

Table 12.1 (contd.)

Scheme Type	*Investment Objective*	*Investment Strategy*	*Benchmark Index*
Open-end FMCG Sectoral Fund	To generate long-term capital appreciation	Investing predominantly in equity and equity related securities of FMCG Companies	CNX FMCG Index
Open-end Equity	To provide capital growth as well as to make periodical distribution of income from investment in stocks of respective sectors of the Indian economy.		BSE Bankex
Open End Equity Fund	To provide capital growth over a period of time as well as to make income distribution from investment in stocks of select growth oriented sectors of the Indian economy.		Petro Index maintained by India Index Services & Products Ltd.

Balanced Funds

Scheme Type	*Investment Objective*	*Investment Strategy*	*Benchmark Index*
Open-end balanced scheme	To provide periodic returns and capital appreciation over a long period of time, from a judicious mix of equity and debt investments, with the aim to prevent / minimise any capital erosion	Investing in debt instruments such as Government securities, money market instruments, securitised debts, corporate debentures and bonds, preference shares, quasi Government bonds, and in equity shares	BSE Sensex, NSE Nifty
Open-end balanced fund	To provide a good investment opportunity to investors who do not wish to be completely exposed to equity markets, but is looking for higher returns than those provided by debt funds		CRISIL Balanced Fund Index
Open-end Income and Growth scheme	To provide regular returns and capital appreciation	Investing in equities and debt	C BalanceEx

(Contd . . .)

Table 12.1(contd.)

Debt Funds

Scheme Type	*Investment Objective*	*Investment Strategy*	*Benchmark Index*
Open-end Income and Liquid (gilt) scheme	To generate credit risk-free return	Investing in sovereign securities issued by the central government and/or state govt. and/or any security unconditionally guaranteed by the central govt. and/or state govt. for repayment of principal and interest	I-Sec Si-BEX
Open-end Gilt Fund (Investment — PF)	To generate income	Investing in Gilts of various maturities.	I Sec Li-Bex
Open-end debt scheme	To generate reasonable returns with low risk and high liquidity	Have a judicious mix of investment in money market instruments and quality debt instruments	C Fund — LX
Open-end Gilt Fund	To provide risk free returns to investors even for a shorter duration	Investing in securities issued by Central or State Government or any security unconditionally guaranteed by the GOI.	

12.2 Investment Styles

Information providers have found several interesting ways of pictorially representing the investment objective. The US fund rating outfit Morningstar pioneered a visual style box for capturing a fund's investment style. In India, some fund research agencies have tried to emulate this and picturise equity schemes in a 3x3 matrix along two parameters — investment style and capitalisation.

Investment Style				
Growth	Blend	Value		
			Large	**Capitalisation**
			Medium	
			Small	

The classification between large, medium and small capitalisations was quite subjective until SEBI defined them. These definitions were discussed in Chapter 2.

Debt schemes are similarly picturised along two parameters — credit quality and interest rate sensitivity.

Credit Quality				
High	Medium	Low		
■			High	**Interest Rate Sensitivity**
			Medium	
			Low	

Every company can be strait-jacketed into a single investment style (growth, blended or value) and a single capitalization category (large, medium or small). However, some returns in a growth stock fund are also associated with returns in a value-investment index. Similarly, some returns in a mid-cap stock are also associated with returns in a large-cap index. In an investment style analysis, how does one factor such correlation of returns between asset classes?

Advanced investment style analysis comes in handy to address such problems. Style analyses go beyond the portfolio statement to the underlying asset return sensitivities. The following details of such an asset class factor model are extracted from William Sharpe's paper on the subject, published in *Journal of Portfolio Management.*[49]

Sharpe used 12 asset classes for his analysis:

- Bills:
  - Cash equivalents with less than 3 months to maturity.
  - Index: Salomon Brothers' 90-day Treasury bill index.
- Intermediate-term government bonds:
  - Government bonds with less than 10 years to maturity.
  - Index: Lehman Brothers' Intermediate-term Government Bond Index.
- Long-term government bonds:
  - Government bonds with more than 10 years to maturity.
  - Index: Lehman Brothers' Long-term Government Bond Index.
- Corporate bonds:
  - Corporate bonds with ratings of at least Baa by Moody's or BBB by Standard & Poor.
  - Index: Lehman Brothers' Corporate Bond Index.
- Mortgage-related securities:
  - Mortgage-backed and related securities.
  - Index: Lehman Brothers' Mortgage-Backed Securities Index.

- Large-capitalization value stocks:
  - Stocks in Standard and Poor's 500-stock index with high book-to-price ratios.
  - Index: Sharpe / BARRA Value Stock Index.
- Large-capitalization growth stocks:
  - Stocks in Standard and Poor's 500-stock index with low book-to-price ratios.
  - Index: Sharpe / BARRA Growth Stock Index.
- Medium-capitalization stocks:
  - Stocks in the top 80% of capitalization in the US equity universe after the exclusion of stocks in Standard and Poor's 500 stock index.
  - Index: Sharpe / BARRA Medium Capitalization Stock Index.
- Small-capitalization stocks:
  - Stocks in the bottom 20% of capitalization in the US equity universe after the exclusion of stocks in Standard and Poor's 500 stock index.
  - Index: Sharpe / BARRA Small Capitalization Stock Index.
- Non-US bonds:
  - Bonds outside the US and Canada.
  - Index: Salomon Brothers' Non-US Government Bond Index.
- European stocks:
  - European and non-Japanese Pacific Basin stocks.
  - Index: FTA Euro-Pacific Ex Japan Index.
- Japanese stocks:
  - Japanese stocks.
  - Index: FTA Japan Index.

A quadratic programming exercise was carried out, for the returns in various schemes and the underlying asset classes, based on monthly returns for the time period January 1985 to December 1989. The following are the results of the analysis, as applied to a leading US fund.

During the period ended December 1989, only 2.7% of the monthly variation in XYZ Fund returns could be attributed to selection of securities within asset classes. Over 97.3% of the monthly variation in XYZ Fund returns could be attributed to the concurrent return on a passive portfolio with the style shown in Figure 12.1.

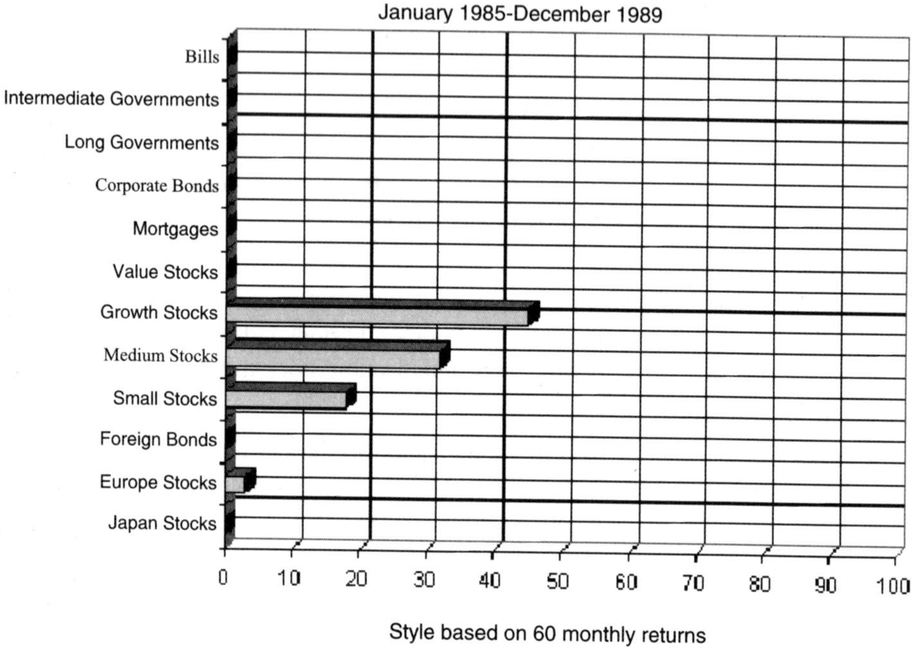

Figure 12.1

This 97.3% was basically the R-squared value that came out of the quadratic programming exercise. Sharpe used R-squared as an indicator of returns that came out of Style (asset class); the balance, namely 1 minus R-squared, was taken as an indicator of returns that came out of selection of securities within the asset class.

By doing a series of such style analyses for different months, it was found that XYZ Fund progressively increased its emphasis on large growth stocks and reduced its exposure to small capitalization stocks during the 1980s. This is not surprising, as the fund grew to approximately $14 billion by the end of the period, making substantial investment in very small stocks increasingly difficult. The change in style over time is evident from Figure 12.2.

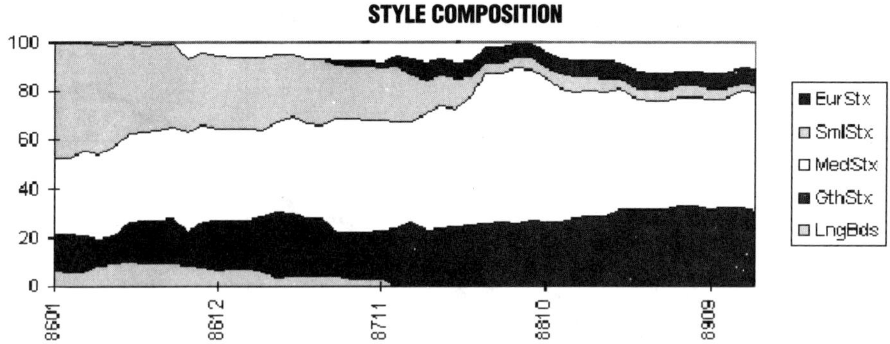

Figure 12.2

The difference in returns between the scheme and the benchmark (S&P 500) was cumulated each month from January 1986 through December 1989. This comparison is shown in Figure 12.3.

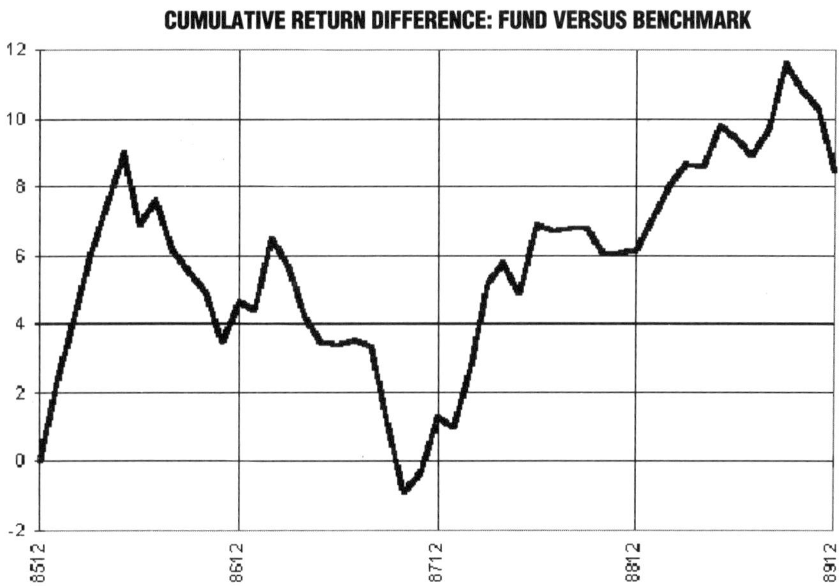

Figure 12.3

XYZ Fund provided a positive but statistically insignificant outperformance when compared with the S&P500 over the period. Such a comparison masked XYZ's truly outstanding selection performance.

In order to capture the selection performance, William Sharpe tweaked the calculations a bit. He found that the fund outperformed its style benchmarks by a cumulative amount of over 25%, as seen in Figure 12.4.

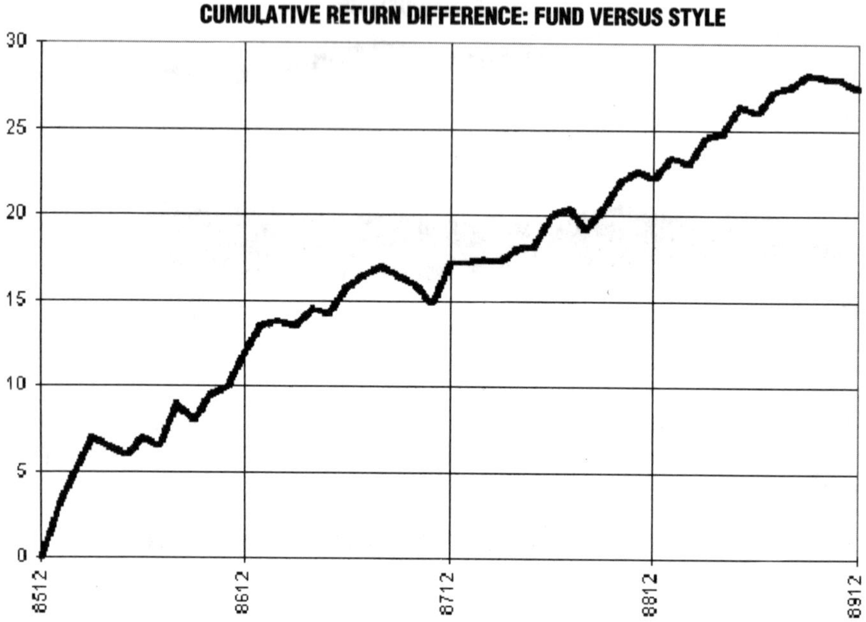

Figure 12.4

Thus, by separating the style and selection returns, style analysis provides excellent insights into a fund's performance. 'Performance Attribution' in the next Chapter gets into some alternate approaches to disaggregating returns into their underlying strategies.

12.3 Qualitative Factors

12.3.1 Management

Every investor who has tasted lasting success in the financial markets gives importance to the management of the investee companies. Good managements try to improve the business, while unethical managements try to improve the business numbers.

According to Faber (2004) "Aggressive or irregular accounting is not a sign of business promise. The trouble is, it is often hard to detect. Buffett quipped: 'It has been far safer to steal large sums with a pen than small sums with a gun.' Steering clear of such robbery requires attention to managers, who shape corporate culture. Some corporate cultures encourage laudable accounting practices, while others — as these chicaneries illustrate — encourage what Ben Graham called 'prestidigitation' or magical numbers"[50].

Warren Buffett emphasizes that while management quality can dramatically affect returns on equity, it is never a substitute for a good business within one's circle of competence, saying that "a good managerial record (measured by economic returns) is far more a function of what business boat you get into than it is of how effective you row (though intelligence and effort help considerably, of course, in any business, good or bad)."[51]

Integrity is an additional independent factor in investment selection. Is there a sensible way to think about managerial integrity? Buffett says the key is to invest with managers you "like, trust, and admire." His test for whether an investment meets this requirement is whether the managers are "men you would be pleased to see your daughters marry"[52].

Further:

"You can put all the governance bells and whistles you want on a board, but if its CEO or other strong leaders lack integrity, you can be sure they will neither ring nor blow."[53]

"When he was pursuing his due diligence on the deal, Silverman asked Walter Forbes for references. I'm told that Forbes furnished five of them. One from Bill Gates. One from Jack Welch. One from Henry Kravis. One from Warren Buffet, and another from Louis Gerstner. I don't think it would be possible to put together a better set of business references. And yet, while all those men were attesting to Walter Forbes's reputation, the company he ran was fabricating hundreds of millions in sales."[54]

Thus, quality of management is a key variable whose assessment places significant demand on investors' time and skills. Further, despite best efforts, even a professional can make mistakes.

12.3.2 Expenses

Expenses are a critical factor, which eat into the returns available to investors. Internationally, therefore, expense ratio is an important parameter when funds are compared.

Several years ago, one scheme in India came out with two different plans — one for wholesale investors with a lower expense ratio, and the other for retail investors. Wholesale investors, initially, did not seem to notice the lower expense ratio as compared to other schemes in the market. Subsequently, investors began to appreciate the significance of expense ratios. Many schemes thereafter offered separate institutional plans for larger investors.

Commenting on the US experience, an observer noted: "I recommend Vanguard mutual funds to many people. The fees are very low and The Vanguard Group is the only non-profit investment company that is owned by investors in the funds. The Vanguard Group is owned by people who invest in its mutual funds, not a separate group of stockholders. If Vanguard has a profit at the end of the year, the management fees in the mutual funds are lowered. In this way, the more money that gets invested with Vanguard, the greater the economy of scale and the lower the fee. Over the years, Vanguard's mutual fund fees have fallen to the lowest in the industry"[55].

12.3.3 Portfolio Turnover

Portfolio turnover is measured as value of purchase and sale transactions in a scheme divided by the average value of its portfolio. More the number of times the portfolio is turned over, more actively the fund manager is managing the scheme. The flip side to this is that more the number of turnovers, greater would be the brokerage and other transaction costs.

In India, the brokerage paid on purchase and sale of securities are reflected in the Total Expense Ratio of the scheme only to the extent they exceed SEBI's brokerage limit of 12 paise for transactions in the cash market, and 5 paise for transactions in the derivative market. Even this is subject to the overall Total Expense Ratio limit. For brokerage upto these limits, purchase of securities is accounted in the books at prices inclusive of brokerage on purchase. Similarly, on sale of securities, the net realization is accounted. Thus, the impact of high portfolio turnover does not get properly reflected in the expense ratio. However, that does not take away from the fact that a higher turnover ratio comes with the cost of higher brokerage, which gets reflected in the capital gains or losses.

A portfolio turnover ratio of 2 times means, that on an average, investments are held in the portfolio for 6 months. Schemes that aim to capitalize on shorter-term fluctuations in the market would need to aim for higher portfolio turnover ratios. Thus, a portfolio turnover ratio of 10 times implies that on average, investments are held for 25 working days (assuming 250 working days in a year).

Investors who aim for a long-term low risk exposure may prefer to invest in low portfolio turnover schemes. Investors desirous of capitalizing on short-term movements in the market may prefer schemes that have high portfolio turnover ratios. On account of issues of market size, it is difficult for funds to operate with high portfolio turnover in the mid-cap and small-cap space.

12.3.4 Fund Size

Funds need to have a certain critical mass to justify the expenses of administering the scheme. Further, the fund should also not be too large in the context of the markets where they are invested.

"Schemes that are too big, too, cause management problems. Just what constitutes 'too big' is a complex issue. It relates to fund style, management philosophy, and portfolio strategy," says John Bogle.[56]

Depth of the markets where the fund would invest and the fund management style significantly determine the optimum size. A value investment style that buys significant stocks of equity directly from the issuer, holds on to them for years, and then sells through an IPO (like a venture capital investor), does not need to be constrained by the market size. On the other hand, an aggressive investment style fund manager who turns over the portfolio fast would need to view the fund size in the context of the market size and liquidity.

12.3.5 Investor Concentration

A situation where one or more investors are significant contributories to the net assets of a mutual fund scheme can be extremely risky. The actions of the large investor(s) could have a significant bearing on the experience and benefits that other investors get from the scheme.

For instance, if a large investor who holds 20 per cent of the units of a scheme offers them for re-purchase, 20 per cent of the portfolio may have to be sold to generate the money needed. The sudden sale could have a bearing on the price realized in the market. There is also a concern that the scheme may favour the big investor to the detriment of other investors, for instance by accepting applications for sale or re-purchase of units beyond the specified cut-off time; or by offering the large investor a re-purchase facility just before closing down the re-purchase option for other investors.

This is the reason SEBI mandated that more than 25% of the corpus of any scheme cannot be owned by a single investor. This is to be calculated on a daily basis and averaged each quarter.

Similarly, funds have to make half-yearly disclosure of investments made in companies that have, in turn, invested more than 5 per cent of the NAV. Thus, if a company's investment in the net assets of a ₹ 100 crore scheme amounts to ₹ 10 crore (more than 5 per cent), then the scheme's investment in that company and its affiliates needs to be disclosed. This acts as a check against "back to back" deals between investors and the fund.

Such disclosures help investors take a view on the investor concentration and objectivity of the scheme, and accordingly decide about investing or disinvesting from schemes.

12.3.6 Investor Servicing

Finally, investors also need to ensure that they will receive proper service from the mutual fund. Servicing aspects in a mutual fund scheme would include regularity of disclosures of NAV and portfolio; ensuring dividend payments and redemptions as per committed time frame; speed of response on queries, and such like.

As explained in Chapter 7, the offer document of any scheme contains a section on investor servicing performance during the previous 3 years for all existing schemes. Based on this information, updated up to 30 days before the date of the offer document, the investor can take a call on the level of servicing to expect.

Chapter 13

Performance Attribution, Drivers and Smart Beta

13.1 Performance Attribution

This section draws on my incisive research in the field. The discussions on the technical subject are kept here, at a level that is accessible to most readers. However, you are free to skip this section without affecting your understanding of the rest of this book.

Performance Attribution seeks to attribute reasons for the performance of a portfolio or scheme. For instance, how much of the performance of an equity portfolio is on account of superior sector selection and how much can be attributed to stock selection. Or in the case of a debt portfolio, how much of the performance can be attributed to duration management and how much to credit risks taken by the fund manager.

The risk-adjusted measures discussed in Chapter 11 serve the purpose of a "composite measure" — namely a single number that explains the performance of a portfolio. However, these do not help in understanding how the performance came about.

Sharpe's style analysis, discussed in the previous chapter provides one frame for understanding the performance better. However, the quadratic programming approach involved is rather complex.

Gary Brinson and Nimrod Fachler proposed a simple approach to performance attribution in the *Journal of Portfolio Management*[57]. Performance attribution models seek to analyse the excess returns, namely the difference between portfolio return and benchmark return. The Brinson-Fachler approach, which focused on equity portfolios, has been revised in Brinson's subsequent papers. Each has its limitations. Further, some of the terminology can be confusing. I have refined the model to make it, hopefully, more meaningful and insightful. The discussion that follows is based on this refined model.

13.1.1 Equity (Refined Model)[58]

Broadly, it can be said that out-performance in an equity portfolio is caused by prudent selection of sectors, or prudent selection of stocks within each sector. Accordingly, equity performance attribution can be determined as follows:

$$\Sigma\text{Excess Return i.e., } (R_p - R_i) = \Sigma(W_{y,p} - W_{y,i})\underset{\downarrow}{(R_{y,i} - R_I)} + \Sigma(R_{y,p} - R_{y,i})\underset{\downarrow}{(W_{y,p})}^{*}$$

i.e., Excess Return = Sector Selection+ Stock Selection

Where,

R_p is the overall return in the portfolio (across sectors);

R_i is the overall return in the index (across sectors);

$W_{y,p}$ is proportion of sector y in the portfolio ($\Sigma W_{y,p} = 1$);

$W_{y,i}$ is proportion of sector y in the index ($\Sigma W_{y,i} = 1$);

$R_{y,i}$ is return on sector y in the index; and

$R_{y,p}$ is return on sector y in the portfolio.

Results from application of this model to a scheme for a period are shown in Table 13.1.

Automobile sector yielded a benchmark return of 0.916% which is higher than the overall benchmark return of 0.819%. So, logically, the scheme (portfolio) should have taken higher exposure to automobile sector. However, the scheme had a lower weight of 7.367%, for the automobile sector, as compared to the benchmark weight of 8.653%. So, the scheme deserves to have a negative score on sector selection for automobiles.

The scheme however managed to earn 1% from the automobile sector, which is higher than the 0.916% return of the automobile sector in the benchmark. This indicates better stock selection by the scheme. So, the scheme deserves to have a positive score on stock selection for automobiles.

Thus, as far as automobiles is concerned, the fund is negative for sector selection (-0.001%) and positive for stock selection (+0.006%). Both effects together, give a positive of 0.005% for automobiles.

---

* The Brinson formulae provide for a cross-product term in the equation. I have rolled that into the other two terms for reasons explained in my detailed report.

Table 13.1

Performance Attribution for Equity Portfolio

	Data				Refined Model		
Sector	**Portfolio ROR (1)**	**Benchmark ROR (2)**	**Portfolio Weight (3)**	**Benchmark Weight (4)**	**Stock Selection (3) X {(1)-(2)}**	**Sector Selection (Relative Sector Return) X {(3)-(4)}**	**Total**
Automobile	1.000%	0.916%	7.367%	8.653%	0.006%	-0.001%	0.005%
Communication	0.750%	1.267%	2.955%	2.030%	-0.015%	0.004%	-0.011%
Construction	0.000%	0.769%	0.000%	2.819%	0.000%	0.001%	0.001%
Diversified	1.000%	1.659%	7.460%	4.336%	-0.049%	0.026%	-0.023%
Energy	0.500%	0.611%	19.374%	16.091%	-0.021%	-0.007%	-0.028%
Engineering	0.000%	0.224%	0.000%	0.581%	0.000%	0.003%	0.003%
Financial	0.443%	1.438%	27.041%	25.262%	-0.269%	0.011%	-0.258%
FMCG	0.500%	-0.152%	8.049%	12.400%	0.052%	0.042%	0.095%
Healthcare	0.500%	0.194%	5.239%	6.545%	0.016%	0.008%	0.024%
Metals	0.500%	1.011%	5.662%	3.928%	-0.029%	0.003%	-0.026%
Paints	0.000%	1.455%	0.000%	1.114%	0.000%	-0.007%	-0.007%
Services	0.200%	0.000%	2.635%	0.000%	0.005%	-0.022%	-0.016%
Technology	0.500%	0.666%	14.218%	16.239%	-0.024%	0.003%	-0.020%
All Sectors	**0.558%**	**0.819%**	**100.000%**	**100.000%**	**-0.327%**	**0.066%**	**-0.261%**

(Source: Sectoral Portfolio ROR is assumed; other mutual fund-related data is from website of Value Research; CNX Nifty-related data is from www.nseindia.com)

Applying the same logic for "Energy", the stock selection and sector selection are correctly negative. Since the energy sector earned a lower return in the benchmark, exposure to the sector should have been lower. However, the scheme decided to take a higher exposure to the energy sector, as compared to the weightage for the sector in the index. The scheme compounded the problem by earning lower from the energy sector in the scheme, as compared to the energy return in the index.

The decision to avoid the under-performing construction sector is appropriately reflected as a positive under sector selection and nil under stock selection.

Paints, which earned 1.455% in the index, is an out-performer as compared to the index return of 0.819%. The scheme however, chose not to have an exposure to the sector. This is captured in the negative sector selection and zero on stock selection.

Thus the refined model captures a sensible picture of the decomposition of excess returns into sector allocation and stock selection.

Across sectors, the scheme under-performed to the extent of -0.261% (0.558% *minus* 0.819%). However, the scheme has done well on sector selection (+0.066%). If there was a strategist deciding on sector exposures, then she brought positive value to the scheme. The problem was with the stock selection (-0.327%). Within this, financial (-0.269%) is the prime culprit.

Thus, performance attribution helps in x-raying the performance of schemes.

13.1.2 Debt[59]

Debt, as an asset class, has unique features that are not suitably captured by the Brinson models. Some performance attribution models have been developed for debt portfolios as well. Many of these are proprietary. Stephen Campisi proposes an interesting fixed income attribution model in *The Journal of Performance Measurement*[60]. Figure 13.1 presents an overall perspective of the model.

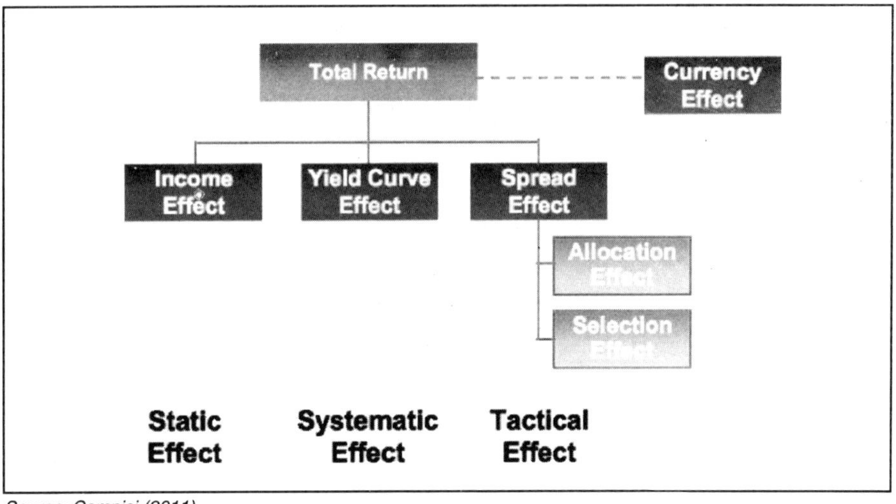

Source: Campisi (2011)

Figure 13.1: **Campisi's Fixed Income Attribution Model**

The income effect is just the daily accrual of interest, arising out of holding the position. Hence it is considered a "static effect".

Yield-curve effect captures the effect of change in sovereign yields in the market. A debt portfolio manager cannot wish this away. This is inherent to investing in the debt market. Hence it is treated as "systematic effect".

The change in market yields for non-sovereign securities does not mirror the change in sovereign yields. There are differences in spreads. Hence the "spread effect".

Performance differences may be on account of mix between different types of non-sovereign securities (e.g., investment grade and non-investment grade) or better selection of securities within each type. Accordingly, the spread effect can be decomposed into "allocation effect" and "selection effect". These are tactical in nature.

Campisi's return decomposition model is summarised in Figure 13.2 (decomposition of spread into allocation and selection is not shown).

Despite some limitations, the Campisi model has the benefit of simplicity and elegance of attribution as compared to earlier fixed income performance attribution models. The summary results from the performance attribution of a debt portfolio using this model are given in Table 13.2.

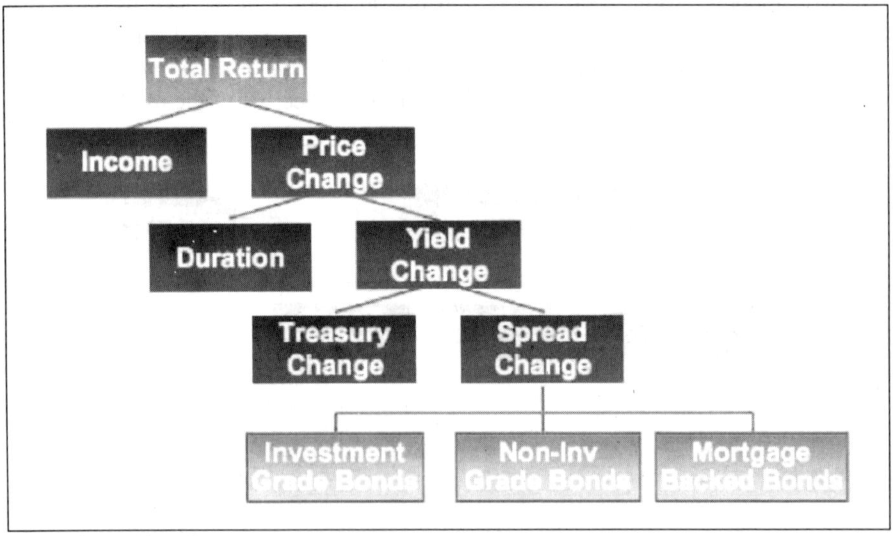

Source: Campisi (2011)

Figure 13.2: **Campisi's Fixed Income Attribution Return Decomposition**

Table 13.2

Summary Results of Fixed Income Performance Attribution

	Income Effect	Treasury Effect	Spread Effect	Section Effect	Toral Return
Benchmark	9.554%	1.135%	-1.414%	0.000%	9.275%
Portfolio	9.241%	1.226%	-1.375%	0.412%	9.505%
Alpha	**-0.312%**	**0.091%**	**0.039%**	**0.412%**	**0.230%**

The portfolio generated a return of 9.505%, as compared to benchmark return of 9.275%. Thus the alpha (out-performance) is 0.230% for the period. This is comprised of:

(i) Income effect (impact of coupon) is adverse to the extent of 0.312%.
(ii) Treasury effect (management of yield curve) showed out-performance of 0.091%.
(iii) Spread effect again showed out-performance of 0.039%.
(iv) The major out-performance has been in selection of securities. It is favourable to the extent of 0.412%.

The alpha can be split sector-wise as shown in Table 13.3.

Table 13.3

Alpha Sectorwise(with market weighting of sectors)

	Income Effect	Treasury Effect	Spread Effect	Selection Effect	Total
Central Govt	-0.886%	-0.173%	0.099%	0.295%	-0.665%
State Govt	0.222%	0.204%	-0.134%	0.020%	0.312%
Bonds	0.540%	0.048%	-0.006%	-0.056%	0.525%
Debentures	0.240%	0.015%	0.056%	0.159%	0.470%
Commercial Paper	-0.429%	-0.002%	0.024%	-0.006%	-0.413%
Alpha	-0.312%	0.091%	0.039%	0.412%	0.230%

Thus, performance attribution facilitates deeper understanding of performance of debt portfolios.

13.2 Alpha Drivers and Beta Drivers

An article by Mark Anson, Chief Investment Officer of CalPERS in the *Journal of Portfolio Management*[61] provides a unique view on institutional portfolio management. According to Mark:

- **Strategic asset allocation** is designed to meet any fund's long-term goals. As such, the objective of strategic asset allocation is not to beat the market, but to achieve the fund's goal in as efficient and cost-effective a manner as possible. Mark refers to such portfolios as "beta drivers".

- **Tactical asset allocation** is designed to facilitate the fund's long-term goals by seeking extra returns. Mark refers to such portfolios as "alpha drivers".

Mark is of the opinion that pursuing both strategic and tactical asset allocation through the same portfolio can lead to inefficient results. As such, institutions should split their portfolios into two — beta drivers and alpha drivers. Figure 13.3 shows the different types of schemes viewed through this prism of different drivers.

Martin Leibowitz has pointed out:

"A handful of investors has produced extraordinary performance over a span of many years — often together with equally extraordinary cross-sectional success in their choices of disparate investments. The approaches of these great investors — Warren Buffett, Bill Miller, Leon Levy, Dave Swensen, Jack Meyer — differ in numerous aspects, but as pointed out by Peter Bernstein (2005), these investors share the common feature of not being in the mainstream, i.e. they are all contrarians in one way or another. The great ones share a number of positive characteristics — focus, patience, a clear-cut philosophy, a willingness to go beyond the diversification mantra and accept high concentration risks, an innovation-prone attitude, the organizational sponsorship and personal fortitude to endure significant periods of underperformance, and a disciplined process for pursuing their goals — in various ways and at various points".[62]

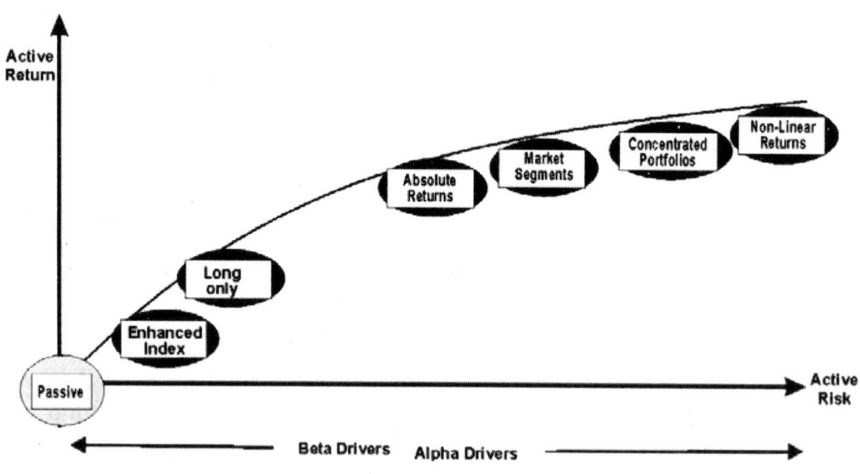

Figure 13.3: **Separating Alpha Drivers from Beta Drivers**

In the words of another commentator:

"The great investors are like great sailors: They have the courage to set forth, they know where they want to go, they have a strong gyroscope to keep them on course, they have appropriate respect for the dangers of the sea and its potential for radical shifts in weather and currents, and they are not afraid to be alone for long stretches."[63]

13.3 Smart Beta

Beta was discussed in Chapter 10. It has its foundations in market indices that are typically weighted by market capitalisation. Smart beta covers rules-based investment strategies that are not based on market-capitalisation weighted indices. Most smart beta strategies are based on some fundamental driver such as dividend yield, book value to market value etc. Hence the term "fundamentally weighted" index. Smart beta can also be based on market factors like momentum and volatility.

If active and passive investment strategies represent opposite ends of a continuum, smart beta is a point that lies in between. Instead of a passive investment strategy of investing as per a market index, the investment institution actively determines rules for investing. For example, it may choose to invest in a low volatility and high dividend yield portfolio. Accordingly, rules are conceptualised that will determine the stocks that would go into the portfolio. Since the rules determine the portfolio composition, the investment institution does not have the same extent of stock selection flexibility that active investment strategies offer. The objective of smart beta strategies is to achieve superior risk-return investment positions.

Smart beta strategies continue to evolve. It is not inconceivable that an Indian investor will have the option of deciding the rules for her portfolio composition on the lines that she wants 20% growth stocks, 10% momentum, 15% gold, 30% value and 25% dividend-yield.

Chapter 14

Managing a Portfolio of Mutual Fund Schemes

In the Introduction, I mentioned about my stained shirt. No Promises Laundry returned my shirt with the stain. This was no ordinary shirt. It was a gift from someone special. A lot of sentiment was attached. I was disheartened until I met someone from Stainless Laundry.

Hearing my tale of woe, she asked to see the shirt. Examining it, she checked with me how the shirt got stained. How could I forget that betel-nut chewing "gentleman" who spat on my shirt that nice Monday morning? Eureka, she said. There is a chemical that eliminates betel stains.

The shirt was back with me in three days — without the stain.

How was Stainless Laundry different from No Promises Laundry? No Promises Laundry did not try to understand my situation. It had a standard prescription — tough stains call for dry cleaning; but dry cleaning itself may not clean the stain. There was no attempt to customise a solution for my problem.

How was Opportunistic Mutual Fund like No Promises Laundry? They too had a standard prescription — if you are investing for the long term, invest in equity; else invest in debt. There was no attempt to customise a solution for my need.

According to Louis Engel, "The cheapest commodity in the world is investment advice from people not qualified to give it."[64]

How can a mutual fund intermediary become the Stainless Laundry of the mutual fund sector? Financial planning holds the key. The subject is discussed in detail in *Wealth Engine* (Vision Books, 2012). Here the focus is on managing a portfolio of mutual fund schemes — a key role that a financial planner needs to perform. This calls for a background understanding of risk profiling and asset allocation.

14.1 Risk Profiling

A participant in one of my seminars shared a joke. A heart patient won a lottery worth ₹ 100 crore. The family wanted to break the good news as softly as possible.

The job was delegated to the family doctor. The conversation went along the following lines:

- Doctor: What will you do if you win a lottery of ₹ 1,000?
- Heart Patient: I will take my family out for dinner.
- Doctor: What will you do if you win a lottery of ₹ 1,000,000?
- Heart Patient: I will repay my housing and car loans.
- Doctor: What will you do if you win a lottery of ₹ 100 crore?
- Heart Patient: I will give you 50 per cent of it.

The doctor immediately suffered a heart attack!

Depending on the health risk a doctor is in the best position to advise a patient on whether she should climb the Himalayas, or whether she should satisfy herself climbing up Malabar Hill in Mumbai. Similarly, a financial planner has to advise investors on their finances depending on their risk profile. She has to look for verbal and non-verbal cues to assess the investor's risk appetite. At one end of the spectrum would be an aggressive risk taker — and at the other, an impulsive risk avoider.

"The most striking thing about Graham's discussion of how to allocate your assets between stocks and bonds is that he never mentions the word "age". That sets his advice firmly against the winds of conventional wisdom — which holds that how much investing risk you ought to take depends mainly on how old you are. A traditional rule of thumb was to subtract your age from 100 and invest that percentage of your assets in stocks, with the rest in bonds or cash."[65]

While risk profiling is a highly subjective exercise, it can safely be said that appetite for risk reduces with:

- Age;
- Increase in dependents;
- Reduction in earning members;
- Any serious health related issues in the family; and
- Job insecurity.

On the other hand, a person would be inclined to take more risks when:

- Major expenses are taken care of. For instance, when the investor owns a house and loans are repaid;
- Other major aspirations are met or provided for;
- The investor is a professional whose income streams are on the upswing; and
- The investor has hit a jackpot.

It would be possible to generate a standard list of questions, the answers to which would be pointers to an investor's risk profile. Some websites do have such risk profilers. However, no ready reckoner of questions can substitute the need for a financial planner to keenly observe the investor and her behaviour. For instance:

A person who jumps the red signal in a traffic crossing is clearly a person who is inclined to take risks.

A person who complains for half an hour about the extra one-rupee wrongly charged by a bus conductor is a difficult equity investor.

If discussions indicate certain submissiveness on an investor's part to the views of her superior at work, and an obsessive concern about job security, then the person is likely to be risk averse.

Even the type of dreams mentioned would be an indication of an investor's risk profile. A Richard Branson who wants to circumnavigate the earth in a hot air balloon would top the chart in terms of risk preference!

Also, in phases of economic uncertainty (layoffs), it would be better for an investor to tone down the risks taken.

"For early savers, the ship is at the dock. Navigational aids help guide the ship out of the harbour and into open water. Early savers need to follow navigational aids to get their ship on its way, even though they do not know yet where it is heading . . . There is a safe harbour out there waiting for the Early Saver, but it is much too early to pick a specific retirement date or to set a specific dollar amount for a retirement nest egg. Later in the journey, after 15 or 20 years of experience, it will be time to think about a retirement time clock and establish a specific dollar and goal to complete the voyage . . . The beacon that should guide investment decisions for Early Savers is known in financial industry as risk tolerance. Risk tolerance is a measure of how rough the financial markets can get before you get seasick and abandon ship. The ideal portfolio has only enough risk in it to make you queasy during stormy market conditions, but not so much up-and-down movement that you make a wild decision to abandon your investment strategy."[66]

A risk profiling exercise would result in suggestions on how an investor should distribute her portfolio between different asset classes.

14.2 Asset Classes and Generic Risk

Debt, Equity, Gold and Real Estate are the commonly held asset classes. Each was introduced in Chapter 4. The details are in *Wealth Engine* (Vision Books, 2012).

Debt is generally viewed as a very safe asset class. Yet, investing the entire portfolio in debt is not necessarily a prudent option. Inflation and re-investment risks can wreak havoc to the lives of such investors. Prudence, therefore, lies in investing in a mix of asset classes.

The performance of different asset classes hinges on how the economy performs. Economies tend to move in cycles — often referred to as business cycles. From a trough, the economy expands, then reaches a peak, and then contracts back into a trough.

returns. But in a contractionary phase in the business cycle, debt investments may be more prudent.

Financial planners need to be able to anticipate the cycles. To draw an analogy, it is difficult to predict the day-to-day temperature and rainfall — but the seasonal cycle can be reasonably predicted. So also financial planners may not be able to read the short-term fluctuations, but the long-term business cycles need to be factored in the financial plans they make. Chapter 11 of *Wealth Engine* [Vision Books, 2012] highlights the role of an "EconoView" in the financial planner's recommendations.

Every asset class and mutual fund type implies a risk-return trade off. Generally, one has to take a greater risk for a chance to earn a higher return. *The AMFI Mutual Fund Testing Programme Workbook*[67] provides a useful comparison of investment alternatives:

	Return	*Safety*	*Volatility*	*Liquidity*	*Convenience*
Equity	High	Low	High	High or low	Moderate
FI Bonds	Moderate	High	Moderate	Moderate	High
Co. Debentures	Moderate	Moderate	Moderate	Low	Low
Co. FDs	Moderate	Low	Low	Low	Moderate
Bank Deposits	Low	High	Low	High	High
PPF	Moderate	High	Low	Moderate	High
Life Insurance	Low	High	Low	Low	Moderate
Gold	Moderate	High	Moderate	Moderate	Low
Real Estate	High	Moderate	High	Low	Low
Mutual Funds	High	High	Moderate	High	High

Note: Table reproduced with permission of the Association of Mutual Funds of India.

An asset categorization relevant for a mutual fund distributor is liquid schemes, gilt schemes, bond schemes, balanced schemes, index schemes, diversified equity schemes, sectoral or focussed schemes, etc.

In the NISM *Workbook*[68], I have put down the generic risk in different kinds of mutual fund Schemes, as shown in the table on next page.

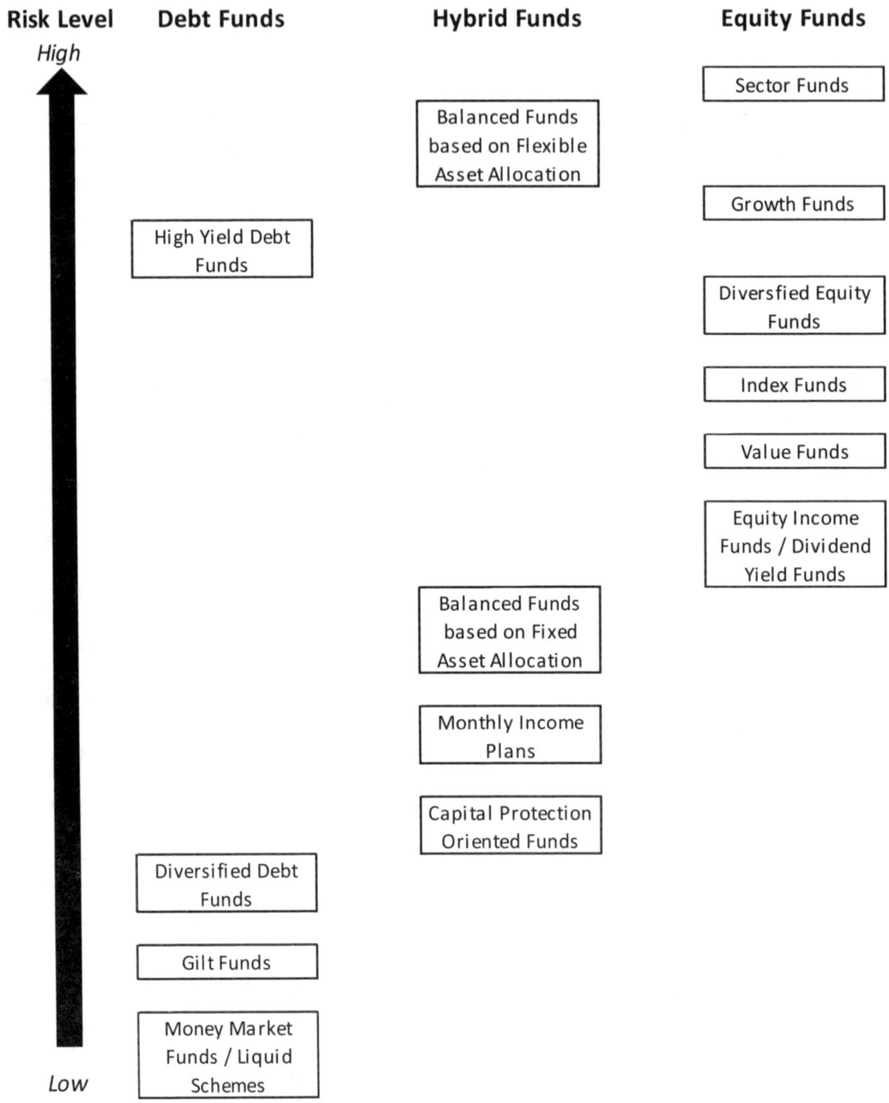

Generic Risk in Different Kinds of Mutual Fund Schemes

(*Source:Workbook for NISM Series V-A: Mutual Fund Distributors Certification Examination,* May 2010, p. 300.)

A financial planner has to obtain information about the investor's current distribution of investment between asset classes and investment types. These would determine what is already available to finance the client's goals, and the risk underlying her investment portfolio. They may also offer clues to possible needs of re-balancing the portfolio (discussed in the following sections).

14.3 Asset Allocation

Credit card issuers use a decision support model to decide whether or not to issue a credit card to the applicant and the exposure limit in case they decide to issue one. It is the same with loan companies. In all these cases, the back-end of the model synthesizes the information given by the applicant and throws up a decision. The parameters of this decision support model are based on statistics of past experiences.

Similarly, it would be possible to have a model that would suggest the mix of asset categories for a client. However, judgement plays a key role — hence the role of financial planner, as distinct from standard tools. The optimum asset allocation for a client would depend on her wealth cycle and life cycle.

14.3.1 The Wealth Cycle

People typically go through three wealth cycle phases:

ACCUMULATION / SOWING

Where the person's saving is much more than current needs. So she is in a position to set apart something for the future.

DISTRIBUTION / REAPING / HARVESTING

Where the person's needs cannot be fully met by current savings. The gap would need to be met out of savings or loans.

TRANSITION

This is a phase between the accumulation and distribution phases, when the distribution needs are very clearly in the person's radar, although the harvesting may not have commenced.

WINDFALL

This is a phase that touches people's lives occasionally. It could be winning from a lottery, super-normal profits booked on investments, inheritance etc.

The risk-based asset allocation would be different for each phase. The *AMFI Mutual Fund Testing Programme Workbook*[69] proposes the following mix:

Accumulation

Asset	*Allocation*
Diversified equity, sector and balanced funds	65 — 80%
Income and gilt funds	15 — 30%
Liquid funds and bank deposits	5%

Distribution

Asset	*Allocation*
Diversified equity and balanced funds	15 — 30%
Income funds	65 — 80%
Cash funds	5%

(*Note:*- Tables reproduced with permission of the Association of Mutual Funds of India)

People often work with a thumb rule to set the debt portfolio percentage at the same level as the age of the person in years. The thumb rule should not be stretched too much — else a person who lives beyond 100 would end up short-selling equity — hardly an age for such portfolio management style! The approach of determining the asset allocation based on client's situation is referred to as "strategic asset allocation".

During the transition stage, the investor would be well advised to park increasing proportions of money in liquid assets. Once the expected goals have been achieved, the investor can go back to the distribution suggested by strategic asset allocation.

The windfall situation is interesting. When the client wins a lottery, she realises there are so many so-called friends or relatives — including many who have not bothered to maintain contact for several years. Money in the bank is always a temptation for a splurge (a person happily accustomed to train travel, overnight deciding to buy a Mercedes Benz!) or altruism.

It would be prudent not to blow up the money, nor invest all of it at the same time. The money could first be invested in a safe and liquid avenue — liquid schemes, for instance. Progressively, the money can be invested in equity or other investments, as per the preferred asset allocation. Through progressive investments, the investor can avail of the benefits of SIP described earlier.

Thus, during the transition and windfall stages, the investor's asset allocation would be temporarily at variance from that suggested by the strategic asset allocation approach.

14.3.2 The Life Cycle

Birth, childhood, graduation, early employment, marriage, children, education / marriage of children and retirement — these are the life phases that people normally go through. The asset allocation and investment choices that are made would need to keep the life cycle in mind.

Thus, in the early stages of one's professional career, the investment mix would be more like that set out above for the "Accumulation" phase in the wealth cycle. Towards retirement, it would be more like the "Distribution" phase in the wealth cycle. The investment mix would need to specifically provide for expected spikes in expenses in between ("Transition" phase), such as for buying house, marriage of children, etc.

An aggressive growth fund would find a place in the portfolio of younger investors with a propensity to take risk. Older investors would find the equity portion of their portfolio dominated by equity income funds. As seen earlier, closer to a large and sure fund outflow for people who are in the transition phase (some requirement of funds in the radar), moneys would be transferred to money market or other debt funds. Thus, scheme selection becomes a function of both risk profile and cash flow needs of an investor.

The choice of funds for an investor would depend on her investment philosophy and portfolio. According to Benjamin Graham, the kind of investment portfolio that is appropriate for different types of investors is as follows:

- Defensive investor:[70]
  - There should be adequate, though not excessive, diversification (10 – 30 stocks);
  - Each company should be large, prominent, and conservatively financed;
  - Each company should have a long record of dividend payments; and
  - The investor should impose some limit on the price he will pay for an issue in relation to its average earnings over, say, the past seven years. (25 times average; 20 times last 12-month period).
- Enterprising investor:[71]
  - Buying in low markets and selling in high markets;
  - Buying carefully chosen "growth stocks";
  - Buying bargain issues of various types; and
  - Buying into "special situations".

Some experts believe that there is nothing like a moderately aggressive investor, mildly conservative investor, and such other shades of differences. Investors are either aggressive or conservative. Benjamin Graham states this emphatically: "The aggressive (enterprising) investor must have a considerable knowledge of security values — enough, in fact, to warrant viewing his security operations as equivalent to a business enterprise. There is no room in this philosophy for a middle ground, or a series of gradations, between the passive and aggressive status. Many, perhaps most, investors seek to place themselves in such an intermediate category; in our opinion that is a compromise that is more likely to produce disappointment than achievement. As an investor you cannot become "half a business-man", expecting thereby to achieve half the normal rate of business profits on your funds."[72]

14.3.3 Re-Balancing the Portfolio

As an old Turkish proverb says, "After you burn your mouth on hot milk, you blow on your yogurt. Hurt badly by the crash of 2000-2002, many investors now view stocks as scaldingly risky; but, paradoxically, the very act of crashing has taken much of the risk out of the stock market. It was hot milk before, but it is room-temperature yogurt now."[73]

The risk profiling and asset allocation process would indicate what ought to be the distribution of an investor's assets. The financial planner would also have obtained the details of what the current distribution is. Based on this, she can decide on the need to re-balance the client's portfolio.

Based on risk-profile, if asset allocation between debt and equity is recommended at 30:70 and the current mix is 35:65, then re-balancing may not be recommended, given the transaction costs involved in selling and buying investments. Only new investments may be directed towards the asset category where the client is short. However, if instead of 30:70, the client is at 70:30, then the difference is significant enough to recommend re-balancing even the current portfolio.

At a seminar many years ago, a participant mentioned about his 88-year old father whose entire portfolio was in equity — blue chips invested at ridiculously low prices. Such an investor (the father) had, perhaps unknowingly, built a high-risk portfolio. Just to re-balance the portfolio by selling some equity, there would have been a heavy incidence of capital gains tax (now withdrawn for most equities). In retrospect, a few thoughts on human behaviour came to my mind. If the old investor was being cared for by the son at his age of 88, then chances of the son abdicating his responsibility are remote. Add to that the tax on capital gains. This may well have been that odd case one encounters in life — where a financial planner may be comfortable recommending 100% equity portfolio for an 88-year old investor!

As Richard Ferri puts it: "Bear markets should only be a minor nuisance in your life and should have no effect on your retirement savings plan or your ability to sleep at night. They occur as a normal part of the economic cycle in every free-market economy and are a natural part of economic growth. If you live to be in your 80s or older, there is a good chance you will be involved in at least two lengthy bear markets during your life and many more short-term market corrections."[74]

"A market decline of 10% to 20% is known as a correction. A bear market is a correction of 20% or more. It is widely believed that bear markets coincide with economic recessions. The truth is, sometimes a bear market forecasts a recession and sometimes it does not. It did not in 1987, but it did in 2000. Economic data is always behind actual economic conditions, so we never know if the market is telling the truth. A standing joke on Wall Street is that the stock market forecast eight out of the last three recessions."[75]

"The people looking for a crystal ball are no dummies. The list of Nobel Laureates who lost money trying to find a mathematical solution is quite long. John Nash, Robert Merton, and Myron Scholes are three who come to mind. Nash tried to develop market-timing systems using mathematical models based on game theory, for which he won the Nobel Prize. He did not succeed. Merton and Scholes were the architects of intrinsic formulas that mathematically predicted the risk and return in hundreds of markets. Those models eventually led to the 1998 collapse of Long-Term Capital Management (LTCM). The failure of LTCM was so potentially devastating to the global economy that the Federal Reserve had to orchestrate a bailout by several Wall Street firms. So, is there a crystal ball that can predict the market? If Nobel Laureates cannot find one that works, then there is no point for us to try."[76]

14.4 Scheme Selection

Most Indians would have played the game of "saaklee" in their childhood. It starts as a one versus the rest. The rest try their best to run away from the one. Whoever, the one person is able to touch from the rest joins the person. Thereafter, it is two versus the rest. The two need to hold hands and run after the rest. The next person who is touched by the other two has to join them. Then, it becomes three versus the rest, with the three holding hands and running after the rest. The game is over when the last person is touched by the others holding hands as a team.

Initially, when one person, say A, is running after the rest, it is tempting to touch the person who is easiest to catch up with, say Z. Thereafter, when A and Z have to run together after the rest, A will be hampered by the speed of Z. Thus, A will take a long time to complete the game of catching all the others. Logically, A should not be tempted into catching the slowest person, who is a ready prey. Instead, she should try to catch the fastest person among the rest. Thereafter, at each stage, if the fastest person among the rest is targeted, the objective of catching all the others will be achieved much faster.

On the same lines, investors should target the better schemes, in order to achieve their goals faster. This calls for comparing between schemes. The parameters to compare schemes were set out in Chapters 9 to 13. Risk profile, asset allocation and relative risk levels in different investments were discussed earlier in this chapter. Based on these, a financial planner would advise the investor on distribution of investment across different schemes. In effect, the financial planner would recommend a model portfolio most appropriate for the investor.

"The key to selection of mutual funds is not to focus on future return which an investor cannot control — but on risk, cost and time, all of which the investor can control," points out Bogle perceptively.[77]

Bogle again: "Don't select funds as if they were simply individual common stocks, to be discarded and replaced as they face the inevitable ebb and flow of performance. Select a fund with the same thoughtful consideration you would give to appointing a trustee for your assets and establish a lifetime relationship."[78]

14.5 Exit from Schemes

Hall hit the nail on the head: "The old idea that you could just invest your money in mutual fund, do a Sleeping Beauty imitation, and then wake up rich is more myth than reality . . . . And when a change needs to be made, do so decisively. After all, selling a mutual fund is not like getting a divorce."[79]

Exit from a mutual fund scheme is warranted in the following situations:

- You need to re-balance your portfolio: In such a case, exit the scheme that is the worst performing in the asset category where you are over-weight.
- You have exceeded your targeted return: Don't get greedy about your return from the scheme. Exit gradually, instead of selling all the investments at the same time.
- The scheme has been consistently under-performing the market or its peer group of schemes.
- There are strong and reliable indications that the operations of the mutual fund are being handled unethically or imprudently or unprofessionally.
- Changes in the scheme structure or the people behind the operation make you uncomfortable.

Let's listen to the experts on this:

"As the investment consultant Charles Ellis puts it, 'If you're not prepared to stay married, you shouldn't get married.' Fund investing is no different. If you're not prepared to stick with a fund through at least three lean years, you shouldn't buy it in the first place. Patience is the fund investor's single most powerful ally"[80].

Cunningham has this to say: "Peter Lynch regards the prevalent practice of rebalancing as backward, saying it is like gardening by watering the weeds and pulling the flowers. The beneficiaries of this backward gardening are not the investors or traders who do the rebalancing, but their advisers — who generate fees from trading — and the US federal and local treasuries — which get tax payments. Buffett put it best in asking whether it would have made sense for the Chicago Bulls to trade Michael Jordan on the grounds that he had become too important and valuable to the team."[81]

14.6 Tips and Tricks

14.6.1. The Role of Savings

Benjamin Graham has highlighted the varying role of savings for investors of different age groups.

"To a young adult, consistent savings is more important than the rate of return on those savings. . . . The person who saves 10% per year and earns 5% on those savings accumulates about $13,600 more than the person who saves 5% and earns 10%. Clearly, it is the savings rate that is more important early in life. . . . From the early 40s on, a high rate of return becomes much more influential than the savings rate. . . . By age 60, the person who saved 5% and earned 10% has accumulated nearly $324,000 more than the person who saved 10% and earned 5%."[82]

14.6.2 Selecting Schemes for Investment

It is humanly impossible to keep track of all the various schemes and options of different mutual funds. Mutual fund distributors are well advised to develop a deeper understanding of around five schemes in each asset category. These schemes should be selected based on performance and investor interest. The list needs to be reviewed from time to time.

Distribution organizations need to have a centralized system of gathering information on all schemes and sharing this information with all sales offices and employees, along with specific tips on the five schemes mentioned above. Such an approach would maximize the time that sales people spend in generating business, as well as ensure some consistency in advice across different sales people / sales offices of the same organisation. A good knowledge management set up is a must.

14.6.3 Role of Taxation

This is discussed in the last chapter. The financial planner has to consider the tax position of the investor and the prevailing policy on taxation of dividend and capital gains, before developing a financial plan.

Investors should, however, avoid the trap of over-emphasising the role of income tax in their investment and disinvestment decisions. Their goal is return maximization — not tax minimization. They should take money out of schemes from time to time, when they feel that they have attained their targeted returns — even if there is an incidence of taxation. Plenty of investors have lost money because they waited for a few additional weeks so that their holding would become long term and exempt from tax. But during the period, the market tanked to an extent where their capital gain position was converted into a capital loss position. The objective of minimising tax was achieved!

14.6.4 Systematic Plans

It is not possible to time the market successfully at all times. Systematic plans of investment, withdrawal and transfer are good options to reduce the impact of bad timing. SIP, SWP and STP are discussed in the next chapter. With such approaches, the investor may not have the best possible upside, but the worst possible downside too is avoided.

14.6.5 Trusts

"There are three big mistakes people make with trusts. First, many trust documents are poorly written and, as a result, it is hard to discern what the owner of the assets really wanted. Second, trust and family situations change frequently, but trust documents are not kept up to date. Third, many people spend thousands of dollars getting trust documents written, but they never title assets in the name of the trust, or direct assets to the trust upon death. This renders a trust document useless. You have to title assets in the name of the trust for it to be an effective estate-planning tool."[83]

Chapter 15

Mechanics of Investing in Mutual Funds: KYC, KYD and Investor Empowerment

Having understood various aspects of mutual funds, let us now consider the mechanics of investing in mutual fund schemes.

15.1 Who Can Invest in Mutual Fund Schemes?

The following categories of investors are eligible to invest in Indian mutual funds:

- Resident Indian adult individuals, either singly or jointly (not exceeding three);
- Parents and lawful guardians on behalf of minors;
- Companies, corporate bodies registered in India;
- Registered societies and co-operative societies authorized to invest in such units;
- Religious and charitable trusts under the provisions of 11(5) of the Income Tax Act, 1961 read with Rule 17C of the Income Tax Rules, 1962;
- Wakf Boards and Endowments and Trustees of private trusts authorized to invest in mutual fund schemes under their trust deeds;
- Partners of partnership firms;
- Association of persons or body of individuals, whether incorporated or not;
- Hindu Undivided Families (HUFs), in the sole name of the Karta;
- Banks, financial institutions and investment institutions;
- Non-resident Indians / persons of Indian origin resident abroad (NRIs / PIOs) on full repatriation or non-repatriation basis;
- Other mutual funds registered with SEBI;
- Foreign institutional investors (FIIs) registered with SEBI;
- International multilateral agencies approved by the Government of India;
- Army / Navy / Air Force, para-military units and other eligible institutions;
- Scientific and industrial research organisations; and
- Provident funds, superannuation funds, gratuity funds, NPS funds, as well as regional rural banks and co-operative banks are permitted to invest in specific

mutual fund schemes. They need to confirm the eligibility with the offer documents of the scheme concerned.

- Qualified Foreign Investors fulfilling KYC requirements (See para 15.2).
- Foreign Portfolio Investors registered under the SEBI (Foreign Portfolio Investors) Regulations, 2014 (see para 15.3).

15.2 Investment by Qualified Foreign Investors (QFIs)

Earlier, foreign nationals who wished to have an exposure to Indian mutual funds had to route their investment through an FII.QFIs, who meet Know-Your-Customer requirements are now permitted to invest directly in debt and equity mutual fund schemes in India. Two routes are available for them:

- Direct route, i.e. they hold their units in a demat account through a SEBI registered Depository Participant.
- Indirect route, i.e. they hold Unit Confirmation Receipt (UCR). The mutual fund will appoint one or more UCR issuing agents overseas and one SEBI registered custodian in India. The agents overseas will issue UCR against the demat units held by the custodian in India.

SIP / SWP / STP facility is not permitted for QFIs. Their unit-holdings are non-tradeable and non-transferable. However, they can sell the units back to the scheme and repatriate the proceeds. Withholding tax at the applicable rates will be collected by the scheme and only the balance will be paid to the QFI.

QFIs are expected to migrate to the FPI regime in due course.

15.3 Investment by Foreign Portfolio Investors (FPIs)

The FPI regulations envisage three categories of foreign investors:

- "Category I foreign portfolio investor" which includes Government and Government related investors such as central banks, Governmental agencies, sovereign wealth funds and international or multilateral organizations or agencies.
- "Category II foreign portfolio investor" which includes:
  (i) appropriately regulated broad based funds such as mutual funds, investment trusts, insurance/reinsurance companies;

  'Broad-based fund means a fund, established or incorporated outside India, which has at least twenty investors, with no investor holding more than forty-nine per cent of the shares or units of the fund. Further, if the broad-based fund has an institutional investor who holds more than forty nine per cent of the shares or units in the fund, then such institutional investor must itself be a broad based fund.

  For ascertaining the number of investors in a fund, direct investors as well as underlying investors are considered.

(ii) appropriately regulated persons such as banks, asset management companies, investment managers/ advisors, portfolio managers;

(iii) broad based funds that are not appropriately regulated but whose investment manager is appropriately regulated:

The investment manager of such broad-based fund has to be registered as Category II foreign portfolio investor, and needs to undertake that it shall be responsible and liable for all acts of commission and omission of all its underlying broad-based funds and other deeds and things done by such broad-based funds under these regulations.

(iv) university funds and pension funds; and

(v) university related endowments already registered with SEBI as foreign institutional investors or sub-accounts.

- "Category III foreign portfolio investor" which includes all others not eligible under Category I and II foreign portfolio investors such as endowments, charitable societies, charitable trusts, foundations, corporate bodies, trusts, individuals and family offices.

Resident Indians, Non-Resident Indians (NRI) and Overseas Citizens of India (OCI) cannot be beneficial owners of FPIs.

15.4 Who cannot Invest in Mutual Fund Schemes?

The following are not permitted to invest in Indian mutual funds:

- Persons residing in countries which require licensing or registration of Indian mutual fund products before selling the same in its jurisdiction, if the fund has not obtained such license or registration.
- Persons residing in any Financial Action Task Force (FATF) declared non-compliant country or territory.
- Overseas Corporate Bodies as specified by RBI in its A.P. (DIR Series) Circular No. 14 dated September 16, 2003.

15.5 Minimum Number of Investors

Every new scheme, and individual plan(s) under any scheme, needs to fulfil both of the following conditions:

- Have a minimum of 20 investors; and
- No single investor should account for more than 25% of the corpus of such scheme / plan(s).

New open-end schemes can fulfil the above requirements within three months or the end of the succeeding calendar quarter, whichever is earlier, from the close of the new fund offer (NFO), failing which the scheme would have to be compulsorily wound up.

In each subsequent calendar quarter thereafter, the schemes (plans) should fulfil both the above conditions on an average basis.

The average is to be calculated at the end of each quarter on the basis of the number of investors as at the end of business hours of the scheme on a daily basis.

If, a scheme has to be compulsorily wound up on account of a failure to fulfil these conditions, redemption has to be made within 10 days of winding up.

Exceptions

- The three-month balancing period is not applicable to fixed maturity plans and closed end schemes. Such schemes, therefore, need to comply with both requirements at the very time of allotment.
- The guideline regarding the number of investors is not applicable to exchange traded funds.

15.6 Know Your Customer (KYC)

KYC formalities are required to be completed by all investors, including guardians and power of attorney holders, for any investment in mutual funds, irrespective of the amount.

Without KYC, transactions such as new/ additional purchase, switch transactions, new SIP / STP/ Dividend Transfer Plan (DTP) registrations cannot be carried out. However, KYC is not applicable for redemption/ re-purchase.

SEBI has made it convenient for investors, by making a single KYC applicable across the capital markets; i.e. mutual funds, brokers, registrars & depositories. Therefore, an investor who has completed her KYC through one capital market intermediary (including mutual fund distributor who has complied with all Know-Your-Distributor requirements) can use that KYC for transactions through other capital market intermediaries.

The five KRAs currently registered with SEBI are:

- NSDL Database Management Ltd (NDML), a subsidiary of National Securities Depository Ltd;
- CDSL Ventures Ltd (CVL), a division of Central Depository Services (India) Ltd;
- DotEx International Ltd, a unit of the National Stock Exchange of India Ltd (NSE);
- Karvy Data Management Services Ltd; and
- CAMS Investor Services Private Ltd.

The process includes submission of application form along with documents to a capital market intermediary. The form can be downloaded from the website of any of the KRAs. In Person Verification of the investor by the capital market intermediary is mandatory.

The following are the typical documentation requirements for investors who are individuals:

- Proof of Identity
- Proof of Address
- PAN Card
  PAN Card is compulsory for all investors except:
  - Micro-SIPs, i.e. SIPs where annual investment (on 12 month rolling basis or for April-March financial year) does not exceed ₹ 50,000
  - Small investors investing in cash, upto ₹ 50,000 per mutual fund per financial year.
- Photograph.

In the case of non-individual investors (e.g. companies or trusts) the following additional documents are required:

- Memorandum of Association and Articles of Association, or Trust Deed to demonstrate the non-individual investor's eligibility to invest.
- Board Resolution authorising the non-individual investor to invest, and authorisation to officials to sign the requisite forms on behalf of the investor.

The originals of these documents along with a copy each have to be presented to the capital market intermediary and the original will be returned after verification. Alternatively, investors can also provide an attested true copy of the relevant documents. Attestation could be done by a notary public / gazetted officer/ manager of a scheduled commercial bank. The intermediary will upload the details of the investor to the server of a KRA.

Any subsequent changes in address or other details needs to be intimated only once to an intermediary with the relevant documentary proof. On completion of the process, the change will reflect in the records of all KRAs.

It is also mandatory for investors to mention their bank account numbers in their applications / request for redemption.

The government had issued a notification under the Prevention of Money Laundering Act, 2002 making it mandatory for every mutual fund folio to be linked to Aadhaar. However, the Supreme Court, through its ruling on 13 March 2018, has held this in abeyance. So, Aadhaar linking is not mandatory as of the date on which this text is being finalised. Investors can, however, choose to do the Aadhaar linking voluntarily. This can be conveniently done through e-verification facility offered by the RTAs. The unit-holder has to enter her e-mail ID, PAN, Aadhaar number and registered mobile number in the relevant screen in the RTA website.

All the AMCs for which the RTA has been appointed, and where the unit holder has a folio will be shown on screen, based on PAN and e-mail ID. The unit holder can select one or more or all the AMCs that are listed. On submitting, the unit holder will receive an OTP on her mobile number that is registered with Aadhaar. This OTP is to be entered on the screen displayed by the RTA website. Once the authentication is done, the unit holder will receive a confirmatory message on her mobile number.

Investor will need to repeat the process with other RTAs, if the first RTA does not service all the mutual funds where the unit holder has a folio. In the case of Sundaram BNP Paribas Mutual Fund and Franklin Templeton Mutual fund, unit holder needs to do the linking directly with the AMC.

15.7 Systematic Investment Plan (SIP), Systematic Withdrawal Plan (SWP) and Systematic Transfer Plan (STP)

The benefits of spreading one's exposure — namely, diversification across asset classes, sectors, countries, etc. — in any investment activity are well chronicled. This was discussed in Chapter 14. What is increasingly recognised is the benefit arising out of spreading the timing of one's actions.

Rather than investing, disinvesting or switching the entire portfolio at a single point of time, it is prudent to spread these actions systematically over a period of time. This also curbs the investor's tendency to time the market, an investment style that several researchers have statistically proved as having a poor chance of success.

This principle of time diversification has given rise to the concepts of:

- Systematic Investment Plan (SIP);
- Systematic Withdrawal Plan (SWP); and
- Systematic Transfer Plan (STP).

15.7.1 Systematic Investment Plan (SIP)

SIP refers to the practice of investing a constant amount regularly, generally every month. When the market goes up, then the money invested in that period gets translated into a fewer number of units for the investor. If the market goes down, then the same money invested gets translated into more units.

Annexures 15.1, 15.2 and 15.3 have illustrations of SIP in three market scenarios, when the investor invests ₹ 1,000 per month over a 12-month period. The results are summarised in Table 15.1.

Table 15.1

Market Scenario (change each month)	*Gain / Loss (₹)*	*Gain / Loss (% to current NAV)*	*Point to Point NAV Change*	*Acquisition Cost (% to average NAV)*
Up 1%	+ 681	+ 5.4%	+ 11.6%	99.99%
Down 1%	– 637	– 5.6%	– 10.5%	99.99%
Random	+ 200	+ 1.6%	0.0%	98.40%

Thus, it is clear that:

- When the market gained 11.6% during the year, the gain for the investor was only 5.4%. On the other hand, when the market fell 10.5% during the year, the investor's loss was only 5.6%. SIP, therefore, tempers the gain or loss from investment.
- SIP does not offer protection from losses. If the market turns adverse, then you can lose money even in an SIP.
- SIP ensures that your acquisition cost approximates the average NAV. Therefore, this investment style is also called "rupee cost averaging".

Investors can do their SIP transactions either by issuing post-dated cheques or giving appropriate standing instructions to the bank.

Value averaging is another approach to investment. Here, the investor operates with a certain target value for her investment. If the investment appreciates beyond the target value, she encashes part of the investment. If the investment depreciates below the target value, the investor brings in fresh funds to bridge the gap. Value averaging ensures that the investor books profits in a rising market and invests in a falling market.

15.7.2 Systematic Withdrawal Plan (SWP)

SWP is a mirror image of SIP. Under SWP, the investor would withdraw constant amounts periodically. The benefits are the same, namely that through SWP the investor can temper gains and losses, though it does not prevent losses. It is also a tool for investors who need a recurring income to meet their monthly outflows.

The withdrawal is done by the AMC through a re-purchase of the requisite number of units on pre-specified dates. The number of units re-purchased would vary depending on the NAV.

Investors need to note the difference between dividend and SWP. In the case of both dividend payout and SWP, investor receives cheque or credit into her bank account from the scheme. So, some intermediaries incorrectly inform investors that they will receive interest every month. This is completely wrong.

- A mutual fund never pays interest; what it pays is income distribution i.e. dividend.
- In a bank fixed deposit, the investor receives regular interest while the capital is protected. In a SWP investor receives a regular cash flow. However, if investment in the scheme has not earned that much of income, capital is eroded.
- Unlike dividend, where investor does not need to pay a tax (the scheme pays instead), SWP has income tax implications, arising out it being a re-purchase transaction. This is discussed in Chapter 17.

15.7.3 Systematic Transfer Plan (STP)

An investor who has won a lottery or received a year-end bonus can invest the receipts in a debt scheme and do a STP into an equity scheme. The regular investment in the equity scheme would operate like a SIP. The money going out of the debt scheme would be like a SWP. Thus, STP is a combination of SIP and SWP.

Mutual funds make it convenient, and sometimes free of cost, to systematically transfer investments between schemes of the same mutual fund.

15.8 Switches, Triggers and Dividend Transfer Plan (DTP)

Investors may switch their money between two schemes of the same mutual fund (inter scheme switch), or between two options under the same scheme (intra-scheme switch).

In the earlier STP example, the investor moving his money out of the debt fund is said to have switched out of that fund. The transfer into the equity fund is a switch into that fund.

Similarly, an investor may switch between the dividend and growth options of the same scheme. This may be necessitated by permanent changes in the tax position of the investor. Since dividend and growth options would have different NAVs, the switch would operate as a re-purchase from one option and investment into the other option, with the resulting tax implications.

Within the dividend option, dividend pay-out and dividend re-investment are sub-options where the NAV is the same. Therefore, a switch between these two sub-options does not entail a re-purchase and fresh investment. Such a switch transaction between payout and re-investment would be tax-neutral.

Investors can also define triggers for certain transactions. For instance, the investor can set a trigger that if the index goes beyond 30,000 or NAV goes above 15, her units are to be automatically re-purchased, entirely or partly. There are two benefits of such triggers:

- The investor does not need to follow the market closely and give the re-purchase transaction at the right time. Since re-purchase is automatic, the investor does not miss any opportunity on account of paucity of time, travel, etc.
- The investor does not fall into the trap of holding on to an investment out of greed, after she has earned her targeted return.

Another facility is the dividend transfer plan. An investor who has opted for the dividend option can issue standing instructions that the money should be invested in a specified scheme of the same mutual fund.

While SIP is offered by all schemes, other facilities are scheme specific. The Scheme Information Document would provide details of the facilities available in any specific scheme.

15.9 Steps to Invest / Dis-invest Mutual Fund Units (Other than through Stock Exchange)

- A first-time investor in mutual funds needs to visit a capital market intermediary to complete the KYC formalities and obtain the KYC acknowledgement.
- An investor who is investing in any mutual fund for the first time has to fill the complete application form that is available along with the KIM. Based on that, the mutual fund will allot a folio number to the investor. Subsequent transactions with the same mutual fund can be effected by merely filling a transaction slip (full application form is not required). This enhances the convenience in investing with that mutual fund. Only while investing with another mutual fund where the investor does not have a folio, the second mutual fund's application form will need to be filled.
- The investor needs to decide the scheme to invest, depending on her asset allocation needs (discussed in the previous chapter) and the risk-return evaluation of the schemes (discussed in earlier chapters of this book).
- Besides the scheme, she also needs to decide on the option and sub-option viz. growth, dividend payout or dividend re-investment.
- In case she wants to opt for SIP, SWP or STP, the date for the systematic transaction needs to be specified. For instance, if the salary is normally received on the 7th of the month, the investor can add a margin and specify 10th of the month as the SIP date. Similarly, the SWP date can be set to match the cash flow needs of the investor.
- If the investor wishes to benefit from the triggers, DTP or any other facility, then the appropriate instruction has to be registered with the mutual fund.
- Re-purchase of open-end schemes would be effected based on transaction slip executed by the investor. The slip would specify either the number of units to re-purchase or the amount for which re-purchase is to be effected.

The investor needs to hand over the duly filled form / transaction slip along with the payment (if new units are being purchased) to the distributor or office of the AMC or investor service center of the RTA. Based on this, the investor would be allotted units. However, the number of units allotted would depend on the NAV that is used. Cut-Off time for determining the applicable NAV is explained later in this Chapter.

15.10 Steps to Invest / Dis-invest Mutual Fund Units (Through Stock Exchange)

Close-end schemes and exchange traded funds (ETFs) are listed in the stock exchange. They get traded, like any share, through the stock exchange trading system.

SEBI was keen to leverage on the reach and cost-efficiency of the stock exchange system. Therefore, National Stock Exchange (NSE) and Bombay Stock Exchange (BSE) extended their trading platform to help the stock exchange brokers become a channel for investors to transact in Mutual Fund Units.

BSE's platform is BSE STAR Mutual Funds Platform. NSE's platform is called NEAT MFSS. These are essentially order routing systems. Both platforms operate from 9 am to 3 pm on every working day. Through these platforms, fresh subscriptions in a mutual fund, as well as additional purchases can be made. Redemptions too are possible. The transactions may be in physical form or demat form.

In the normal course, transactions are entered in the system at their proposed value. Redemption requests can however, be given in number of units. The transaction slip generated by the broking system, which also includes the time stamp, is the acknowledgement for the investor:

- If the transaction is in physical form, then the stock exchange broker would need to send the documents to the nearest RTA. Thereafter, the normal process for handling physical applications would be applicable.
- In other cases, the stock exchanges, together with their clearing corporation, handle the first leg of the transaction, viz. investor's subscription or re-purchase request. The second leg of the transaction, namely sending units against investors' subscription, or sending money against the re-purchase request, is the responsibility of the RTA.

  In the stock exchange, the investor may give a cheque to the stock exchange broker, who in turn transfers money to the clearing corporation. To protect the stock exchange broker from bounced investor cheques, the demat units are made available in the broker's pool account initially. He can then transfer the units to the investor, after confirming receipt of investor's funds.

Unlike transactions in shares and listed close ended schemes done through the stock exchange's normal trading system, mutual fund transactions through the exchanges' order routing system are not backed by the exchange's Settlement Guarantee Fund. Responsibility for settlement is that of the AMC. However, the normal stock exchange redressal mechanism would be available to address any investor complaints.

15.11 Mutual Fund Utilities — The Aggregater

Investors who have invested in schemes of multiple mutual funds know the inconvenience of having to visit the offices or websites of multiple AMCs or RTAs. Similarly, distributors have to visit multiple offices to submit the transactions of their customers in different mutual funds. MF Utilities India Pvt Ltd. (MFU) is the mutual fund industry's "Shared Services" initiative to solve such problems.

The MFU initiative seeks to solve these problems and to remove many duplication of activities and thus save cost. The prime objective of MFU is to "aggregate the transactions" and act as an order routing system.

MFU is formed by AMCs of SEBI registered mutual funds under the aegis of AMFI. Objectives include investor empowerment, distributor convenience, consolidation of information to various agencies, operational efficiency for RTAs and benefits to AMCs, thereby benefiting all stakeholders in the industry. It also provides for a centralised complaints management and tracking system.

Under MFU, investors can use a Common Account Number (CAN) to transact across various AMCs. KYC-compliant investors can obtain CAN by submitting the CAN Registration Form at any POS of MFU or a distributor signed with MFU or at a participating AMC branch.

With the CAN, investors can invest with multiple mutual funds using a common application form and a single cheque. The system also maps existing folios across mutual funds based on PAN, holding pattern and other parameters.

MFU offers 24×7 information access including Online Common Account Statement, Composite Portfolio information, Portfolio holding and scheme related information. It also offers industry level value added services like alerts, triggers, reminders etc. Thus, investors can monitor and manage their investments more effectively.

Further details including form downloads are available at www.mfuindia.com

15.12 Cut-Off Time

If a mutual fund sells new units at yesterday's NAV and invests the proceeds in the market today or tomorrow, there is a fear that the market would have changed during the interim. If the market falls before the fund manager invests the money, then the scheme (i.e., all unit holders in the scheme) benefits. If, on the other hand, the market gains before the fund manager can invest the money, then the unit holders in the scheme suffer.

This risk of gain / loss is obviated if instead of yesterday's NAV (historic NAV), the NAV as on the transaction date or a future date (forward NAV) is applied for the investment / redemption transaction. This, too, has its issues, as discussed earlier.

After considering all aspects, in particular the need to protect long-term investors from the machinations of short-term investors, SEBI has prescribed a cut-off time, to determine the applicable NAV. These are given in Table 15.2

For liquid schemes:

- Day(s) on which the money markets are closed, or otherwise not accessible, are not treated as business day(s).

- NAV is to be calculated for every calendar day, irrespective of whether or not it is a business day.

These cut-off regulations are applicable to all schemes, other than those that have substantial investment in foreign securities, whose valuation depends on time zones other than Indian Standard Time. Further, it is logical that this is not relevant for trades in listed mutual fund units between buyers and sellers in a recognised stock exchange. Cut-off timings mentioned in Table 15.2 are however applicable for transactions in open-end schemes that are merely routed (as distinct from traded) through the stock exchange broker.

Table 15.2

Application Time	*Cheque / DD*	*Applicable NAV*
Other than for liquid schemes		
Purchases less than ₹ 2 lakh: Up to 3 p.m.	Local cheque / DD payable at par at place of receipt of application	Closing NAV of application date
Purchases less than ₹ 2 lakh: after 3 p.m.	Local cheque / DD payable at par at place of receipt of application	Closing NAV of next business day
Purchases less than ₹ 2 lakh	Outstation cheque / DD	Closing NAV of date on which the payment instrument is credited in the bank
Purchase of units with amount equal to or more than ₹ 2 lakh, irrespective of the time of receipt of application		Closing NAV of the day on which the funds are available for utilization
Redemption requests received up to 3 p.m.		Closing NAV of same day
Redemption requests received after 3 p.m.		Closing NAV of next business day
Liquid schemes		
Purchase (up to 2 p.m.) and funds are available for utilization before the cut-off time without availing any credit facility, whether, intra-day or otherwise		Closing NAV of the day immediately preceding the day of receipt of application
Purchases (after 2 p.m.) and the funds are available for utilisation by the fund on the same day, without availing any credit facility, whether, intra-day or otherwise		Closing NAV of the day immediately previous to the next business day
Other Purchases		Closing NAV of the day immediately previous to the day on which funds are available for utilization
Redemption requests received up to 3 p.m.		Closing NAV of the day immediately previous to the next business day
Redemption requests received after 3 p.m.		Closing NAV of the next business day

The onus is on the AMC to deposit the investor's cheque / DD in the bank "with utmost expediency, prudently utilizing the appropriate banking facility". If an investor suffers a loss on account of lack of such prudence, then AMC will need to cover the investor for such loss.

As a further safeguard, SEBI has stipulated that:

- Application should be received before the cut-off time applicable.
- Money for the entire subscription / purchase should have been credited into the account of the scheme before the cut off time.
- The funds should be available for utilization before the cut-off time (3 pm) without availing any credit facility, whether intra-day or otherwise, by the respective scheme.
- The provisions regarding cut-off timing, receipt of application, credit to the account of the scheme and funds availability, are equally applicable in the case of switch-in to a scheme (by switching out of another scheme of the same mutual fund).

Despite such fine-tuning of cut-off times, a loophole still remains. Investors can bounce their cheque after seeing subsequent market performance. The provisions of the Negotiable Instruments Act, 1881 regarding imprisonment of signatories of a bounced cheque would not also apply to such cases because there is no prior flow of consideration from the fund to the investor.

Real Time Gross Settlement system of fund transfer by RBI has minimised the problem. Still, AMCs are best advised not to accept cheques from "habitual cheque bouncers". A mechanism for AMCs to share details of such investors would be useful for the industry.

15.13 Official Points of Acceptance

SEBI has designated official points of acceptance that can time-stamp documents for the purpose of determining the applicable NAV. These are:

- Offices of AMCs.
- ISCs of RTA.
- Stock exchange brokers authorised for the purpose.
- Clearing members of the stock exchange.
- Depository Participants (only for redemption of demat units).

Although distributors and branches of banks are permitted to accept applications, they are not designated as official points of acceptance for time-stamping purposes.

Mutual funds need to disclose "official" points of acceptance of transactions in their offer documents and web site. The "cut-off time" is to be reckoned at these official points. All purchase and redemption applications must be demonstrably received by the mutual fund at these "official" points of acceptance of transactions.

All these official points are required to have time stamping machine(s). For a given machine, the running serial number would be stamped from the first serial number of the machine and continue to be stamped up to its maximum capacity. Only, thereafter would the cycle be repeated.

Each and every application for the purchase and the corresponding payment instrument need to be stamped on the face and back respectively, indicating the date and time of receipt and running serial number. The running serial number on the application and the corresponding payment instrument need to be the same.

Each and every request / application for redemption has to be stamped on the request / application and on the investor's acknowledgement copy (or twice on the request / application if no separate acknowledgement is issued), on the face, indicating the date and time of receipt and running serial number.

Bunching of applications by giving single serial number is not permitted.

It is stipulated that the time stamping machine should have a tamper proof seal. For maintenance and repairs, the ability to open the seal must be limited to the vendor or nominated person(s) of the mutual fund, and a proper record of such repress, etc. has to be maintained. Any breakage of the seal and / or breakdown of the electronic time stamping process must be duly recorded by the mutual fund and reported to the trustees. There must be a process of verifying the accuracy of the time being stamped in such situations.

While every effort has to be made to ensure uninterrupted functioning of the time stamping machine, in case the machine develops a technical snag, the mutual fund has to take prompt action to rectify the situation. During such a period, a mutual fund is expected to adopt an alternative method of time stamping applications, which needs to be approved by both the Board of AMC and the trustees. An audit trail has to be available to check and ensure the accuracy of time stamping process during such a period.

Any alternate methods of transaction adopted by a mutual fund that are not paper based, or do not have an electronic trail, e.g. phone, SMS etc. have to be converted into a physical piece of instruction and time stamped in accordance with the above guidelines.

Mutual funds have to maintain and preserve all applications / requests, duly time stamped as aforesaid, so as to produce them as and when required by SEBI or auditors appointed by SEBI. No blank document shall be time stamped. Genuine errors, if any, during the time stamping shall be recorded with reasons and the corresponding applications / requests shall also be preserved as above.

The periodic reports of the trustees shall contain a declaration on the trustees are satisfied with the systems and procedures of the mutual fund in this regard.

15.14 Post-Investment Servicing

- Units need to be allotted, excess application money has to be refunded and e-mail / SMS has to be sent specifying the number of units allotted to the applicant as soon as possible but not later than five working days from the date of closure of the initial subscription list and/or from the date of receipt of the request from the unit holders.
- Mutual funds need to send consolidated (across all mutual funds in the country) statement of account for each calendar month, by the 10th of the following month, to the investors in whose folios transactions has taken place during that month.
- Mutual funds may dispatch the statement of accounts to the unit holders under SIP or STP or SWP, once every quarter ending March, June, September and December within 10 working days of the end of the respective quarter. The first statement of accounts should however be issued within 10 working days of the initial transaction.
- Mutual funds also need to provide statement of accounts to unit holders within 5 working days, without any charges, if specific requests are received from the investors. Further, if so mandated, a soft copy of the statement of accounts shall be emailed to the unit holders on a monthly basis.
- Mutual funds also have to provide statement of accounts to those unit holders who have not transacted during the last six months prior to the date of generation of the statement of accounts. In such cases, the statement of accounts may be issued along with the scheme's Portfolio Statement or Annual Report and should reflect the last closing balance and value of the units prior to the date of generation of the statement of accounts. Further, if so mandated, a soft copy of the statement of accounts shall be emailed to the unit holders instead of a physical statement.
- Scheme should be available for ongoing transactions / trading within 5 business days of allotment.
- Mutual funds are required to dispatch dividend warrants to the unit holders within 30 days of declaration of the dividend.
- Despatch of redemption or re-purchase proceeds has to be made within 10 working days from the date of receipt of request.

delayed payment, the AMC is liable to pay interest @ 15 per cent per 5 the unit holders. The AMC must ensure that the interest amount due for anriod of delay in dispatch of re-purchase or redemption and / or dividend is td to the proceeds when such payments are made to the investors. Such interest all be borne by the AMC(s).

The requirements regarding sharing of financial and portfolio information was discussed in Chapter 8.

15.15 Who Can Distribute Mutual Funds and Earn Brokerage

All persons engaged in sales and marketing of mutual funds need to pass the NISM Series V-A: Mutual Fund Distributors Certification Examination (www.nism.ac.in) (for which I have had the privilege of developing the official courseware).

People who are above 50 or have over 10 years of experience in mutual funds are exempted from passing the examination. (www.nism.ac.in). However, they need to attend the specified refresher course.

The examination is relevant for:

- Mutual fund distributors who are individuals;
- Employees of organisations engaged in sales and distribution of mutual funds;
- Stock exchange brokers desirous of handling mutual fund transactions;
- Employees of call centers involved in servicing mutual fund investors;
- Employees of asset management companies, especially persons engaged in sales and distribution of mutual funds.

After passing the examination, the person needs to register with AMFI for the AMFI Registration Number (ARN) before she can operate as an AMFI Registered Mutual Fund Adviser (ARMFA).

Intermediaries including the sales personnel of intermediaries engaged in sales / marketing need to obtain NISM certification and register themselves with AMFI and obtain an Employee Unique Identification Number (EUIN) from AMFI apart from AMFI Registration Number (ARN). The Intermediaries have to ensure that the employees quote the EUIN in the Application Form for investments.

Postal agents, retired government and semi-government officials (class III and above or equivalent), retired teachers and retired bank officers with a service of at least 10 years, and other similar persons (such as Bank correspondents) as may be notified by AMFI/ AMC from time to time are allowed to sell units of simple and performing mutual fund schemes subject to passing the Series V-B: Mutual Fund

Foundation Certification Examination (www.nism.ac.in) (for which, again I have had the privilege of developing the official courseware).

Diversified equity schemes, fixed maturity plans (FMPs) and index schemes that have returns equal to or better than their scheme benchmark returns during each of the last three years are treated as simple and performing mutual fund schemes.

SEBI has stipulated that mutual funds shall pay brokerage only to ARMFA or corporate intermediaries registered with AMFI and who have completed the Know Your Distributor (KYD) process (discussed in next section).

Further, distributors are not entitled to brokerage on their own investments. It is also stipulated that brokerage is not payable on investments made by the sponsor of a mutual fund in the schemes sponsored by fund.

SEBI has defined "brokerage" to include all amounts paid to an intermediary for selling the product of the mutual fund. This includes commissions on sale of mutual funds, incentives, consultancy fees, contest awards that have monetary value, gifts, as well as any lump sum payments.

Even ARMFAs earn a commission subject to their bringing in 12 investors in a year into the AMC whose schemes they want to market, failing which, they should bring in 25 investors in a year into the mutual fund industry (all AMCs together).

For corporate AMFI registered intermediaries, the qualifying criteria to earn commission from any AMC are:

- Bringing in 100 investors into the AMC in a year.
- Alternatively, the average assets under management during the year have to be in excess of ₹ 1 crore.

In either case, the applications need to be from investors other than "associates". If more than 75 per cent of the gross funds mobilized are from associates, then the agents needs to ensure that they service at least 200 investors who are not associates or employees of associates.

15.16 Know Your Distributor (KYD)

The KYD procedure consists of document verification and bio-metric process. The distributor is required to apply for KYD simultaneously along with application for registration of ARN. Separate forms are prescribed for individuals and non-individuals.

The documents to be submitted are given in Table 15.3.

Table 15.3

Category of ARN Holder	*Documents required to be submitted*	
	Identity Proof	*Address Proof (any one of following)*
Individuals, including Senior Citizens	Photo PAN Card	(i) Ration Card (Vernacular language) (ii) Passport (iii) Latest Demat/ Bank Account Statement ** (iv) Voter Identity Card (v) Latest Utility (Electricity / Municipal tax/ Water tax/ Land Line Telephone) Bill* (vi) Driving License (vii) Lease / Sale Agreement of Residence
Proprietory Concern	(i) PAN card of the Concern (if available) or (ii) Photo PAN card of the Proprietor	If the address of the proprietary concern and the proprietor is same, the following documents in the name of proprietor : (i) Ration Card (Vernacular language) (ii) Passport (iii) Latest Demat / Bank Account Statement ** (iv) Voter Identity Card (v) Latest Utility (Electricity/ Municipal tax/ Water-tax / Land Line Telephone) Bill* (vi) Driving License (vii) Lease / Sale Agreement of Residence In case location of concern is different, then the following documents in the name of proprietary concern: (i) Latest Bank Account Statement ** (ii) Latest Utility (Electricity/ Municipal tax/ Water-tax/ Land Line Telephone) Bill * (iii) Lease/ Sale Agreement of office
HUF	PAN Card of HUF	If the address of the HUF and the Karta of HUF are same, the following documents in the name of Karta: (i) Ration Card (Vernacular language) (ii) Passport (iii) Latest Demat/ Bank Account Statement ** (iv) Voter Identity Card (v) Latest Utility (Electricity/ Municipal tax/ Water-tax/ Land Line Telephone) Bill *

(Contd . . .)

Table 15.3 (contd.)

Category of ARN Holder	*Documents required to be submitted* *Identity Proof*	 *Address Proof (any one of following)*
		(vi) Driving License (vii) Lease / Sale Agreement of Residence In case location of HUF is different, then the following documents in the name of HUF: (i) Latest Bank Account Statement ** (ii) Latest Utility (Electricity/ Municipal tax/ Water-tax/ Land Line Telephone) Bill * (iii) Lease /Sale Agreement of Office
Partnership Firm / Society / Trust	PAN Card of Firm	(i) Latest Utility (Electricity/ Municipal tax/ Water-tax/ Landline Telephone) bill * (ii) Lease / Sale Agreement (iii) Latest Bank Account Statement / Bank Passbook **
Corporates (Pvt./ Public Ltd. Co., Banks, NBFC)	PAN Card of the Corporate Entity	(i) Latest Utility (Electricity/ Municipal tax/ Water-tax/ Landline Telephone) bill * (ii) Lease / Sale Agreement (iii) Latest Bank Account Statement / Bank Passbook **

* Not more than 2 months old.

** Where bank account statement is submitted as proof of address, the said bank account should have been opened at least six months prior to the submission of application and the statement should not be more than 2 months old.

AMFI has engaged the services of Computer Age Management Services Ltd. (CAMS) to carry out the KYD process through their centres referred as "CAMS POS".

KYD application along with the requisite documents could be submitted at any of the CAMS POS, a list of which is available at www.amfiindia.com or www.camsonline.com. The distributors are required to produce, in person, the original documents for over the counter verification at the time of submission of their applications along with self-attested photocopies of the same.

The bio-metric process involves taking impression of right hand index finger and registering the same for identification purpose. The said process is carried out at the CAMS POS at the time of submission of applications for registration or renewal of ARN along with the KYD application form.

- Individual and senior citizen category distributors are required to visit in person for biometric registration.
- In case of non-individual entities, bio-metric is required to be carried out for the authorised persons / officials as indicated in the Table 15.4.

Table 15.4

Category of ARN Holder	*Person to go through bio-metric process*
Proprietory concern	Proprietor
Partnership firm	All the partners
HUF	Karta of HUF and the signatory to the application (if the signatory is a person other than the Karta).
Society & Trust	Principal Officer/Chief Trustee and the signatory to the application (if the signatory is a person other than these officials).
Corporates (Pvt./ Public Ltd. Co., Banks, NBFC)	Authorized official who has signed KYD application

In case of non-individual entities, the persons who are required to undertake bio-metric process as indicated in the above table are also required to comply with the document verification process by submitting the required documents i.e. proof of identity and proof of address as applicable to individual applicants. However, they are not required to fill in their individual bank details/ furnish the documents in support thereof.

The ARN Holder has to obtain the acknowledgement from the CAMS POS confirming completion of KYD process. Existing ARN holders will have to send photocopy of the said acknowledgement to the AMCs with which they are empanelled.

SEBI has barred payment of commission / incentive to the distributors, who have not complied with KYD, with effect from 1 April 2011.

15.17 Brokerage, Commission and Transaction Charge

SEBI has been working towards a framework where the role of brokerage earning from the mutual fund is reduced. Initially, entry load was banned with a view to reduce the kitty that was available to pay brokerage. AMFI has also stipulated that brokerage which is paid upfront to the distributors should not exceed 1%, with effect from 1 April 2015.

Distributors are being encouraged to perform the role of investor adviser and recover a commission for their services directly from the investor through a separate cheque. The commission level is left to market forces. There is no statutory ceiling on the commission that an investment adviser can charge for the advisory services.

Mutual funds have also been permitted to pay a transaction charge to distributors (besides the brokerage / commission discussed above), subject to the following restrictions:

- For existing investors in a mutual fund, the distributor may be paid ₹ 100 as transaction charge per subscription of ₹ 10,000 and above.

- As an incentive to attract new investors, the distributor may be paid ₹ 150 as transaction charge for a first time investor in mutual funds.
- The terms and conditions relating to transaction charge have to be mentioned in the application form in bold print.
- The transaction charge, if any, shall be deducted by the AMC from the subscription amount and paid to the distributor; and the balance shall be invested.
- The statement of account shall clearly state that the net investment as gross subscription less transaction charge and give the number of units allotted against the net investment.
- Distributors can choose to opt out of charging the transaction charge. However, the "opt-out" shall be at distributor level and not investor level, i.e. a distributor shall either charge all investors (across mutual funds), or refrain from charging all investors. They can even choose to opt out of recovering the transaction charge for specific categories of schemes.
- As part of the "opt-in" application, the distributor has to commit to the following:
    - Agree to keep all investors informed of the applicable transaction charges.
    - Agree not to indulge in any kind of malpractice / mis-selling, including unwarranted splitting of investments and wrong declarations of a "new investor" for the purpose of receiving transaction charges.
    - Understand that no transaction charge will be levied for any transaction channelled through the stock exchange route.
- The AMCs is responsible for any malpractice / mis-selling by the distributor while charging transaction costs.
- There shall be no transaction charge on subscription below ₹ 10,000.
- In case of SIPs, the transaction charge is applicable only if the total commitment through SIPs amounts to ₹ 10,000 and above. In such cases the transaction charge shall be recovered in 3 to 4 instalments.
- There shall be no transaction charge on transactions other than purchases / subscriptions relating to new inflows.
- Mutual funds have been asked to institute systems to detect if a distributor is splitting investments in order to enhance the amount of transaction charges and take stringent action, including recommendations to AMFI to take appropriate action.

15.18 Supervision of Large Distributors

SEBI is keen that distributors operate within a self-regulatory framework. In the meanwhile, the responsibility for supervision has been passed on to the AMCs, through a due diligence process as follows:

- The due diligence process is initially applicable for distributors satisfying one or more of the following criteria:
    - Multiple point presence (more than 20 locations)
    - AUM raised over ₹ 100 crore across industry in the non-institutional category but including high net worth individuals (HNIs).
    - Commission received of over ₹ 1 crore p.a. across industry.
    - Commission received of over ₹ 50 lakh from a single mutual fund.

  SEBI clearly believes that stricter regulation of a few large distributors is more practical. Based on that, the rest of the industry will automatically fall in line.

- At the time of empanelling distributors, and on an ongoing basis, mutual funds / AMCs have to undertake a due diligence process to satisfy "fit and proper" criteria that incorporate, amongst others, the following factors:
    - Business model, experience and proficiency in the business.
    - Record of regulatory / statutory levies, fines and penalties, legal suits, customer compensations made; causes for these and resultant corrective actions taken.
    - Review of associates and subsidiaries on above factors.
    - Organizational controls to ensure that the following processes are delinked from sales and relationship management processes and personnel:
        - Customer risk / investment objective evaluation.
        - MF scheme evaluation and defining its appropriateness to various customer risk categories.
    - Customer relationship and transactions are to be categorized as:
        - Advisory — where a distributor represents to offer advice while distributing the product, it will be subject to the principle of "appropriateness" of products to that customer category. Appropriateness is defined as selling only that product categorization that is identified as best suited for investors within a defined upper ceiling of risk appetite. No exception shall be made.
        - Execution Only — in case of transactions that are not booked as "advisory", it shall still require:
            - If the distributor has information to believe that the transaction is not appropriate for the customer, a written communication has to be made to the investor regarding the unsuitability of the product. The communication shall have to be duly acknowledged and accepted by investor.

    - A customer confirmation to the effect that the transaction is "execution only" notwithstanding the advice of in-appropriateness from that distributor is obtained prior to the execution of the transaction.
    - On all such "execution only" transactions, the customer is not required to pay the distributor anything other than the standard flat transaction charge mentioned earlier.
  - No third categorization of customer relationship / transaction is permitted.
  - While selling mutual fund products of the distributors' group / affiliate / associates, the distributor has to make disclosure to the customer regarding the conflict of interest arising from the distributor selling of such products.

- ➢ Compliance and risk management functions of the distributor shall include review of defined management processes for:

  - The criteria to be used in review of products and the periodicity of such review.
  - The factors to be included in determining the risk appetite of the customer and the investment categorization and periodicity of such review.
  - Review of transactions, exceptions identification, escalation and resolution process by internal audit.
  - Recruitment, training, certification and performance review of all personnel engaged in this business.
  - Customer on boarding and relationship management process, servicing standards, enquiry / grievance handling mechanism.
  - Internal / external audit processes, their comments / observations as it relates to MF distribution business.
  - Findings of ongoing review from sample survey of investors

- ➢ Mutual funds / AMCs may implement additional measures as deemed appropriate to help achieve greater investor protection.

- Mutual funds / AMCs have to disclose on their respective websites the total commission and expenses paid to distributors covered by this due diligence process,

Clearly, the industry is moving to a regime where distributors need to be clear about their role:

- Executors of transactions will receive a small transaction charge from the AMC.
- Advisers who will receive a commission directly from the investor.

SEBI proposes to come out with stricter norms, where the mutual fund intermediary can either be a distributor (who will earn commission from the mutual fund) or an investment adviser (who will earn commission from the investor).

Those choosing to be distributor cannot provide advisory services even through immediate relatives, namely spouse, parent, brother, sister, child. Similarly companies cannot offer both distributor and advisory services through the same entity or even associates. SEBI has indicated that these provisions may become operational from 31 March 2019.

15.19 Investor Empowerment

Various measures taken to protect investors are detailed in the next chapter. Besides, investors have also been empowered in various ways.

15.19.1 Application Supported by Blocked Amount (ASBA)

ASBA is a facility, where the investor does not have to pay money to the scheme upfront. The money can remain in the investor's bank account. The banker will block the amount required to support the investor's mutual fund application. The amount for which units are allotted will be transferred by the bank to the scheme, on allotment. Until then, the investor continues to earn interest on the funds.

Mutual funds have been asked to make ASBA facility available for all NFOs. A list of bankers offering ASBA facility is available in SEBI's website www.sebi.gov.in.

15.19.2 Transfer of Units

SEBI has directed AMCs to ensure that demat units held by investors are freely transferable. Only in the case of ELSS, the transferability may be restricted, on account of the government's ELSS guidelines.

15.19.3 Change of Distributors

Investors are permitted to change their distributors or go direct. Mutual funds are not allowed to ask for a "No objection" from the existing distributor of the investor.

15.19.4 Direct Plan

Every mutual fund scheme has to offer a "Direct Plan" in which brokerage to distributor cannot be charged. The saving helps in boosting the returns for the investors who invest in the Direct Plan.

15.19.5 Investor Education

Several investor education programs are conducted by SEBI, AMFI, AMCs, distributors, stock exchanges and the media. Educative material is also made available in their websites. These efforts have increased the awareness about mutual funds, though much more needs to be done.

Annexure 15.1: SIP — NAV up 1%

Investment each month (₹) 1000

Movement in NAV each Month ->		*Scheme 1 1%*				
Month	*Cumulative Cost (₹)*	*NAV (₹)*	*New Units (Number)*	*Cumulative Units (Number)*	*Current Value of holding (₹)*	*Gain / Loss (₹)*
1.	1,000	10.000	100.000	100.000	1,000	0
2.	2,000	10.100	99.010	199.010	2,010	10
3.	3,000	10.201	98.030	297.040	3,030	30
4.	4,000	10.303	97.059	394.099	4,060	60
5.	5,000	10.406	96.098	498.197	5,101	101
6.	6,000	10.510	95.147	585.344	6,152	152
7.	7,000	10.615	94.206	679.550	7,213	213
8.	8,000	10.721	93.275	772.825	8,285	285
9.	9,000	10.828	92.353	865.178	9,368	368
10.	10,000	10.936	91.441	956.619	10,462	462
11.	11,000	11.045	90.539	1,047.158	11,566	566
12.	12,000	11.155	89.646	1,136.804	12,681	681

Total (Number)	1,136.804
Average (₹)	10.568
Total investment (₹)	12,000
Current Number of units	1,136.804
Average acquisition cost (₹)	10.556
Current NAV (₹)	11.155
Average acquisition cost (₹)	10.556
Gain / Loss (₹)	0.559
Gain / Loss (% to Current (NAV)	5.4%
Point to point NAV change in year	11.6%
Avg. acq cost (% to Avg NAV)	

Annexure 15.2: SIP — NAV down 1%

Movement in NAV each Month ->		*Scheme 2 – 1%*				
Month	*Cumulative Cost (₹)*	*NAV (₹)*	*New Units (Number)*	*Cumulative Units (Number)*	*Current Value of holding (₹)*	*Gain / Loss (₹)*
1.	1,000	10.000	100.000	100.000	1,000	0
2.	2,000	9.900	101.010	201.010	1,990	– 10
3.	3,000	9.801	102.030	303.040	2,970	– 30
4.	4,000	9.703	103.061	406.101	3,940	– 60
5.	5,000	9.606	104.102	510.203	4,901	– 99
6.	6,000	9.510	105.152	615.355	5,852	– 148
7.	7,000	9.415	106.213	721.568	6,794	– 206
8.	8,000	9.321	107.285	828.853	7,726	– 274
9.	9,000	9.228	108.366	937.219	8,649	– 351
10.	10,000	9.136	109.457	1,046.676	9,562	– 438
11.	11,000	9.045	110.558	1,157.234	10,467	– 533
12.	12,000	8.955	111.669	1,268.903	11,363	– 637

Total (Number)	1,268.903		
Average (₹)		9.468	
Total investment (₹)			12,000
Current Number of units			1,268.903
Average acquisition cost (₹)			9.457
Current NAV (₹)			8.955
Average acquisition cost (₹)			9.457
Gain / Loss (₹)			– 0.502
Gain / Loss (% to Current (NAV)			– 5.6%
Point to point NAV change in year			– 10.5%
Avg. acq cost (% to Avg NAV)			99.9%

Annexure 15.3: SIP — Random

Movement in NAV each Month ->		*Scheme 3 Random*				
Month	*Cumulative Cost (₹)*	*NAV (₹)*	*New Units (Number)*	*Cumulative Units (Number)*	*Current Value of holding (₹)*	*Gain / Loss (₹)*
1.	1,000	10.000	100.000	100.000	1,000	0
2.	2,000	9.000	111.111	211.111	1,900	– 100
3.	3,000	9.000	111.111	322.222	2,900	– 100
4.	4,000	10.000	95.238	417.222	4,383	383
5.	5,000	11.000	90.909	508.369	5,592	592
6.	6,000	11.500	86.957	595.326	6,846	846
7.	7,000	9.000	111.111	706.437	6,358	– 642
8.	8,000	8.000	125.000	831.437	6,651	– 1,349
9.	9,000	8.500	117.647	949.084	8,067	– 933
10.	10,000	12.500	80.000	1,029.084	12,864	2,864
11.	11,000	11.000	90.909	1,119.993	12,320	1,320
12.	12,000	10.00	100.000	1,219.993	12,200	200

Total (Number)	1,219.993
Average (₹)	10.000
Total investment (₹)	12,000
Current Number of units	1,219.993
Average acquisition cost (₹)	9.836
Current NAV (₹)	10.000
Average acquisition cost (₹)	9.836
Gain / Loss (₹)	0.164
Gain / Loss (% to Current (NAV)	1.6%
Point to point NAV change in year	0.0%
Avg. acq cost (% to Avg NAV)	98.4%

Chapter 16

Investor Protection

16.1 Structural Protection

In the case of other investment products such as bonds, fixed deposits and equities, the investor's funds go to an organization that uses the funds within the overall supervision of external regulatory authorities such as SEBI, RBI, etc.

With mutual funds, however, there is also an internal regulator in the form of a Board of Trustees, which as guardian for the unit holders,monitors the AMC. This additional layer of monitoring makes the structural framework of mutual fund operations sounder.

The structure has other in-built checks and balances. The custodian is responsible for custody of securities and ensuring that the schemes benefit from the corporate actions in investee companies. As discussed in Chapter 3, the custodian needs to be independent. A group company of the sponsor cannot be appointed custodian of its mutual fund, subject to some rigid exceptions.

The people who sell mutual funds (distributors, agents, AMC employees) or otherwise interact with mutual fund investors (investor service centers / call centers) need to pass the NISM Certification Examination. Therefore, investors can expect a certain minimum level of knowledge from these people. The distributors would also have gone through the KYD process — a further validation of the intermediary.

16.2 Role of AMFI

AMFI plays a proactive role in identifying the steps that need to be taken to protect investors and promote the mutual fund sector. Various regulatory measures taken by SEBI are on the basis of recommendations of committees constituted by AMFI. This approach is in the long-term interest of the mutual fund industry.

However, to clarify, AMFI is not a self-regulatory organization (SRO). Its recommendations are not binding on the industry participants. AMFI recommendations become mandatory only if and when SEBI incorporates any of them in the regulatory framework it stipulates for mutual funds.

In 1997, AMFI brought out the AMFI Code of Ethics (ACE) to promote investors' interest by defining and maintaining high ethical and professional standards in the mutual fund industry. It was produced by SEBI in association with Price Waterhouse LLP / FIRE Project funded by US Agency for International Development (USAID). Some of the standards prescribed by the code are:

- Members (i.e. the AMCs) and their key personnel, in the conduct of their business, shall observe high standards of integrity and fairness in all dealings with investors, issuers, market intermediaries, other members and regulatory and other government authorities.
- Mutual fund schemes shall be organized, operated, managed, and their portfolios of securities selected, in the interest of all classes of unit holders and not in the interest of:
    - sponsors;
    - directors of members;
    - members of Board of Trustees or directors of the Trustee company;
    - associates of the members; and
    - a special class selected from out of unit holders.
- Members shall not use any unethical means to sell, market or induce any investor to buy their products and schemes.
- Members shall not make any exaggerated statement regarding performance of any product or scheme.
- Members, in all their communications to investors and selling agents shall:
    - Not present a mutual fund scheme as if it were a new share issue;
    - Not create unrealistic expectations;
    - Not guarantee returns except as stated in the Offer Document of the scheme approved by SEBI, and in such case, the Members shall ensure that adequate resources will be made available and maintained to meet the guaranteed returns;
    - Convey in clear terms the market risk and the investment risks of any scheme being offered by the Members;
    - Not induce investors by offering benefits which are extraneous to the scheme; and
    - Not misrepresent either by stating information in a manner calculated to mislead or by omitting to state information which is material to making an informed investment decision.
- Members shall not, in respect to any securities, be party to:
    - Creating a false market;
    - Price rigging or manipulation; and

- Passing of price sensitive information to brokers, members of stock exchanges and other players in the capital markets or take action that is unethical or unfair to investors.

16.3 Rights of Unit Holders

Investors are expected to read the Offer Document before they apply for units of a scheme. The principle of *caveat emptor* — let the buyer beware — is applicable. Therefore, an investor cannot proceed against the trustees, the AMC or anyone else for something that is provided for in the Offer Document, merely on the grounds that she was not aware of it. An investor is deemed to have "constructive notice" of whatever is mentioned in the Offer Document.

Unit holders (but not prospective investors), however, have the following rights:

- Unit holders are entitled to the disclosures and other commitments outlined in Chapter 8.
- Unit holders are entitled to receive their account statement within 10 working days of the initial investment.
- They are entitled to account statements of their holdings and transactions, on an ongoing basis, as follows:
  - If there are no transactions, then once every 6 months. The AMC may:
    - Send it along with the Portfolio Statement or Annual Report of the scheme.
    - Send a soft copy, instead of hard copy, if investor has given such a mandate.
  - In the case of SIP / SWP / STP:
    - The AMC shall send it once every quarter ending March, June, September and December within 10 working days of the end of the respective quarter. (However, the first account statement under SIP/STP/SWP shall be issued within 10 working days of the initial investment).
    - The AMC shall provide it on Unit holders' request, within 5 working days, without any charges.
    - The AMC shall send a soft copy every month, if investor has given such a mandate.
- AMCs are to issue consolidated account statement (across all mutual funds) for each calendar month, by the 10th of the following month, to investors in whose folios transaction(s) has/have taken place during that month.
- Unit holders have a proportionate right in the beneficial ownership of the assets of any scheme and to the dividend declared, if any.
- Trustees are bound to make such disclosures to the unit holders as are essential in order to keep them informed about any relevant information, especially which may have an adverse bearing on their investments.

- With the prior approval of SEBI, the appointment of a fund's AMC may be terminated by 75 per cent of the unit holders, or by a majority of the Board of Trustees.
- Unit holders have the right to inspect all the documents listed under the heading "Documents available for inspection" in the Offer Document.
- 75 per cent of its unit holders can pass a resolution to wind-up a mutual fund scheme.
- The Trustee is obliged to convene a meeting on a requisition of 75 per cent of the unit holders of a scheme.
- The Trustee is obliged to obtain the consent of the unit holders:
  - Whenever required to do so by SEBI in the interest of the unit holders;
  - Whenever required to do so on the requisition made by three-fourths of the unit holders of any scheme;
  - When the majority of the Board of Trustees decides to wind up or prematurely redeem the units; and
  - When any change in the fundamental attributes (investment objective and term) of any scheme or the trust or the fees and expenses payable or any other change which would modify the scheme or affect the interest of the unit holders is proposed to be carried out.

    No such change can be carried out unless three-fourths of the unit holders have given their consent — and the unit holders who do not give their consent are allowed to redeem their holdings in the scheme at the prevailing NAV.

- At the time of closure / maturity, a mutual fund scheme may have some non-performing assets (NPAs). If such amount is realized within 2 years, and is in the opinion of Trustees substantial, then it needs to be distributed to the old investors. In other cases, the NPAs so recovered would need to be transferred to an Investor Education Fund, which is required to be maintained by each MF.
- The unit-holder has a right to nominate a person in whom the units held by her shall vest in the event of her death. Where the units are held by more than one person jointly, the nomination shall be done by the joint unit holders together. The format of the nomination form is given in Annexure 16.1.

16.4 Investor Relations Officer

Every AMC has an investor relations officer whom unit holders can approach for redressal of grievances.

The track record of the AMC in redressing investor complaints, including specifics of number of complaints and the time period when they were redressed needs to be disclosed in the Offer Document. This ensures that AMCs take an interest in sorting out investor complaints.

16.5 SEBI

To begin with, SEBI's approval is required to start a mutual fund operation. Thus there is a quality and credibility check on every one who enters the mutual fund business.

SEBI also seeks to ensure that only persons of integrity and reputation for fair dealings become trustees who, in turn, keep an eye on who is appointed a director in an asset management company. Various qualifications and disqualifications have been provided in the regulations to keep out people of disrepute.

If a unit holder is aggrieved by the actions of the AMC, and the grievance is not satisfactorily redressed by the investor relations officer, then the doors of SEBI would be a good place to knock. SEBI forwards the complaints to the AMC. This puts an additional pressure on the AMC to redress the grievance.

SEBI Complaints Redress System (SCORES) empowers investors to lodge online complaints against any listed entity or SEBI-registered intermediary.

16.6 Implications Under Various Other Statutes

16.6.1 Consumer Protection Act, 1986

Unit holders cannot approach consumer courts to redress their grievances against trustees because the nature of the relationship between unit holders and trustees is a fiduciary one. Unit holders themselves are beneficiary owners of the trust property. Being owners, they do not qualify as consumers under the Consumer Protection Act.

While this is the legal position, consumer courts have adjudicated on some mutual fund investor related cases.

16.6.2 Indian Trust Act, 1882

A legal technicality is that a trust is not a distinct or separate legal entity. A mutual fund trust is therefore in the nature of a "notional entity," which it is not distinct from the unit holders themselves. Therefore, its unit holders cannot sue a mutual fund.

However, since the trustees have a fiduciary responsibility to protect the interests of the beneficiaries (unit holders), the unit holders can sue the trustees for breach of faith if there are strong grounds to prove that the trustees were fraudulent or wilfully negligent in their role.

In case the trustees' breach of faith is proved and they need to personally pay damages, the Indian Trust Act provides that the trust cannot even compensate the trustees for such damages. The mutual fund regulations provide that neither the sponsor nor the AMC can compensate the trustees for such damages.

16.6.3 Companies Act, 2013

Investors in a fund are neither shareholders of the AMC nor depositors in the AMC. Therefore, the normal protection available to company depositors through agencies such as Department of Company Affairs and Company Law Board is not available to unit holders of a mutual fund.

The Companies Act provides for "piercing the corporate veil" in specific cases, including fraud. If fraud can, therefore, be proved, unit holders may then be able to pierce the corporate veil and hold the directors and management of the AMC responsible for such fraud.

16.7 The Role of Press

The press in India has performed a useful role in making people aware of the benefits of mutual funds. New fund offers, as well as NAV and other performance parameters are widely reported by the press. The press also takes up various investor protection issues. Several regulatory measures had their base on some press article on the subject. The press, like any industry, has its Achilles heel, as is evident from the following book extracts that describe the US context.

An anonymous journalist wrote a classic article in the 26 April 1999 issue of *Fortune*, called "Confessions of a Former Mutual Funds Reporter." A couple of excerpts from the story say it all:

> "Mutual funds reporters lead a secret investing life. By day, we write 'Six Funds to Buy NOW!'. . . By night, however, we invest in sensible index funds.
>
> I know because I was once one of those reporters — condemned to write a new fund story every day — when I covered funds for an online publication. I was ignorant. My only personal experience had been bumbling into a load fund until a colleague steered me to an S&P500 index fund. I worried I'd misdirect readers, but I was assured that in personal-finance journalism, it doesn't matter if the advice turns out to be right, as long as it is logical.
>
> Unfortunately, rational, pro-index-fund stories don't sell magazines, cause hits on Websites, or boost Nielsen ratings. So rest assured: You'll keep on seeing those enticing but worthless SIX FUNDS TO BUY NOW! headlines as long as there are personal-finance media."[84]
>
> "Experienced investors recognize Wall Street for what it is — a gigantic marketing machine that pumps out investment products by the truckloads. It is no coincidence that Madison Avenue, the hub of the advertising industry in the US, is only a few blocks away from the New York financial district. Madison Avenue and Wall Street are cut from the same fabric".[85]

Annexure 16.1

FORM FOR NOMINATION / CANCELLATION OF NOMINATION

(to be filled in by individual (s) applying singly or jointly)

I / We ___________ and ____________________ * do hereby nominate the person more particularly described hereunder/ and / cancel the nomination made by me / us on the ___________ day of ___________ in respect of the units bearing No. __________ .

(* strike out which is not applicable)

Name and Address of Nominee

Name: . . . .

Address: ....

Date of Birth : ....

(to be furnished in case the Nominee is a minor)

* The Nominee is a minor whose guardian is : ....

Address of the Guardian...

....

....

Signature of the guardian : ....

(* to be deleted if not applicable)

Unit holder (s) Signature : ....

Name : ....

Address : ....

Date : ....

Unit holder(s) Signature : ....

Name : ....

Address : ....

Date : ....

Contd . . .

Instructions

1. The nomination can be made only by individuals applying for / holding units on their own behalf singly or jointly. Non-individuals including society, trust, body corporate, partnership firm, Karta of Hindu Undivided Family, holder of Power of Attorney cannot nominate. If the units are held jointly, all joint holders will sign the nomination form. Space is provided as a specimen, if there are more joint holders more sheets can be added for signatures of holders of units and witnesses.
2. A minor can be nominated and in that event, the name and address of the guardian of the minor nominee shall be provided by the unit holder.
3. The Nominee shall not be a trust, society, body corporate, partnership firm, Karta of Hindu Undivided Family or a Power of Attorney holder. A non-resident Indian can be a Nominee subject to the exchange controls in force, from time to time.
4. Nomination in respect of the units stands rescinded upon the transfer of units.
5. Transfer of units in favour of a Nominee shall be valid discharge by the asset management company against the legal heir.
6. The cancellation of nomination can be made only by those individuals who hold units on their own behalf singly or jointly and who made the original nomination.
7. On cancellation of the nomination, the nomination shall stand rescinded and the asset management company shall not be under any obligation to transfer the units in favour of the Nominee.

Chapter 17

Taxation*

17.1 Asset Management Companies

As seen in Chapter 8, the financial statements of an AMC are distinct from the financials of each of its schemes. The AMC, like any other company, pays a tax on its profits and does not enjoy any special concessions or exemptions.

17.2 Mutual Fund

Section 10 (23D) of the Income Tax Act, 1961 provides that any mutual fund registered with SEBI or set up by a public sector bank or financial institution, or authorized by Reserve Bank of India is exempt from tax. The mutual fund trust that the sponsor constitutes through the trust deed is thus exempted from any tax on its income.

17.3 Schemes

The money that the AMC collects from investors on behalf of the mutual fund trust is managed under various schemes. As seen in Chapter 8, each scheme has both its own revenue account and balance sheet.

Since the schemes are managed for the benefit of investors, a scheme is essentially in the nature of a "pass through". Taxing the "pass through" would constitute double taxation. Given the exemption from taxation granted to the mutual funds, schemes are not liable to pay tax on interest, dividend, capital gains or any other income. As provided in Section 196 (iv) of the Income Tax Act, 1961, they will receive all their income without any deduction of tax at source. However, the taxes covered in the following sections are applicable.

17.3.1 Securities Transaction Tax (STT)

Mutual fund schemes need to incur this tax as shown in Table 17.1.

---

* The tax discussions in this chapter incorporate the changes in the Finance Act 2018, which are applicable from the Assessment Year 2019-20 (Previous Year 2018-19).

Table 17.1

Purchase of equity shares in a recognized stock exchange	0.1% of value of shares bought
Sale of equity shares in a recognized stock exchange	0.1% of value of shares sold
Sale of Derivatives (Futures) in a recognized stock exchange	0.01% of trade value
Sale of Derivatives (Options) in a recognized stock exchange	0.05% of the option premium
If the option is exercised, the purchaser would need to pay	0.125% of value of shares bought
Purchase of units of equity oriented scheme	Nil
Sale of units of equity oriented scheme to the mutual fund or in a recognised stock exchange	0.001% of the re-purchase price of the scheme, or trade value in the stock exchange

(STT is not applicable for investments in debt or debt oriented schemes or gold schemes.)

17.3.2 Additional Tax on Income Distributed (Dividend Distribution Tax)

Mutual funds are required to deduct "additional tax on income distributed" to unit holders. The incidence of such tax on income distribution (loosely referred to in the market as "dividend distribution tax"– DDT), under the provisions of Section 115R, is as follows:

Table 17.2

Income distribution to a unit holder of equity oriented funds of any AMC (Refer "Note" below table)	11.648% (10 per cent plus 12% surcharge plus 4% Health and Education Cess)
For other schemes (including debt schemes and gold schemes)	
■ If the unit holder is individual or HUF	29.12% (25 per cent plus 12% surcharge plus 4% Health and Education Cess)
■ Other Investors	34.944% (30 per cent plus 12% surcharge plus 4% Health and Education Cess)

Note — Equity oriented fund means schemes where the investible funds are invested in equity shares of domestic companies listed on a recognised stock exchange, to the extent of more than 65 per cent of the net assets of such scheme. The percentage is computed as the annual average of the monthly averages of the opening and closing figures each month.

A fund (source fund) investing in units of another fund (target fund) which is traded on a recognised stock exchange will be treated as an equity scheme for the purpose of DDT if:

- At least 90 per cent of the net assets of the source fund are invested in units of the target fund; and

- At least 90 per cent of the net assets of the target fund are invested in equity shares of domestic companies listed on a recognised stock exchange.

DDT is not in the nature of tax deducted at source (TDS). In the case of TDS, investors can seek exemption by furnishing specified forms. If tax is deducted at source, they can also claim credit for the same while filing their income tax returns. None of these options is available for investors when it comes to the additional tax on income distributed.

A point to be noted is that the tax is levied on income distribution — not on income earned by the scheme. Re-purchase transactions too are outside the ambit of this tax. The implications of these factors would be evident from some of the examples given later in this chapter.

17.3.3 Goods and Services Tax

GST is applicable at 18% on services rendered by mutual fund distributors to the mutual fund. Other service tax related to the scheme is charged to the investors, as discussed in Chapter 5.

17.4 Investors

17.4.1 Dividends

The dividend that the investor receives would be entirely tax-free, as provided in Section 10(35)(a) of the Act. Schemes are liable to pay tax on income distribution, as discussed earlier.

17.4.2 Securities Transaction Tax (STT)

Investors in equity schemes of mutual fund have to bear STT at 0.001% of the trade price at which they sell the units in a recognised stock exchange, or 0.001% of the re-purchase price at which they offer the units to the scheme. There is no STT on purchase of the units of equity oriented schemes.

STT is also not applicable to transactions in debt and gold schemes.

17.4.3 Business Profits / Capital Gains

Taxation of the gain on sale / transfer of mutual fund units may be treated by the income tax authorities as business profit or capital gain, on a case to case basis.

If treated as business profit, the following basic tax rates would apply:

- Individuals and HUFs — Depends on the income tax slab applicable to the investor;
- Domestic companies with turnover or gross receipts upto ₹ 250 crore — 25%
- Other companies and Partnership firms — 30%;
- Foreign companies — 40%.

In addition to the base-rate, surcharge would be applicable as follows:

- Individuals and HUF having taxable income in excess of ₹ 50 lakh but upto ₹ 1 crore — 10%
- Individuals and HUF having income in excess of ₹ 1 crore — 15%
- Partnership firms having income in excess of ₹ 1 crore — 12%
- Domestic companies having income in excess of ₹ 1 crore but upto ₹ 10 crore— 7%
- Indian companies having income in excess of ₹ 10 crore — 12%
- Foreign companies having income in excess of ₹ 1 crore but upto ₹ 10 crore — 2%
- Foreign companies having income in excess of ₹ 10 crore — 5%

Further, 4% will be added towards health and education cess on the amount of the basic tax and the surcharge.

The difference between cost of acquisition of units of a mutual fund and the amount realized on their sale or redemption is a capital gain (provided it is not treated as business profit). In case of investment in mutual fund equity schemes, it would be treated as:

- Short-term capital gains if the units are held for up to a year; or
- Long term capital gains if the investor holds on to the units for a period longer than a year.

  ELSS units are subject to a lock-in of 3 years. Accordingly, any sale of units after such lock-in will qualify as long-term capital gain.

In case of mutual fund schemes that do not qualify as equity schemes (including debt and gold schemes), it would be treated as:

- Short-term capital gains if the units are held for up to three years; or
- Long term capital gains if the investor holds on to the units for a period longer than 3 years.

The taxability of these gains further depends on the type of scheme, as detailed below.

17.4.3.1 Equity Schemes

- There is no tax on long term capital gains, provided the sale transaction is subject to securities transaction tax and the total long term capital gain earned by the investor from sale of equity shares or units of equity mutual fund schemes during the financial year is upto ₹ 1 lakh.
- If the total long term capital gain earned by the investor from sale of equity shares or units of equity mutual fund schemes during the financial year exceeds ₹ 1 lakh, then the excess is taxable at 10% plus surcharge and cess. Capital gains upto 31 January 2018 are exempt.
- If the sale transaction is not subject to securities transaction tax, then long term capital gains will be taxed as in the case of debt and gold schemes.

- Short term capital gains are taxable at 15%, provided the sale transaction is subject to securities transaction tax. Further, surcharge and cess will be applicable as per the rates discussed earlier.
- If the sale transaction is not subject to securities transaction tax, then short term capital gains will be added to regular income and taxed accordingly, as in the case of non-equity schemes.

In case of resident individuals, if the income from short term capital gains is less than the maximum amount not chargeable to tax, then no tax would be payable. Such maximum amount (including these capital gains as well as salary and other income of the assessee) is:

- ₹ 2,50,000 for individuals below 60 years of age and HUFs.
- ₹ 3,00,000 for senior citizens (60 years or more of age, but below 80 years of age).
- ₹ 5,00,000 for senior citizens aged 80 years or above.

17.4.3.2 Debt and Other non-Equity Schemes

Short-term capital gains are added to the other income of the investor for taxation purposes. Therefore, the investor would pay tax at her applicable marginal rate of taxation including surcharge, as applicable. The concept of marginal rate of taxation is elaborated later in this chapter.

In the case of long-term capital gains, the investor can take the benefit of indexation based on cost inflation index number.

The government declares a cost inflation index number each financial year. The change in index number between two financial years is an indicator of inflation during the period.

An investor is allowed to index her cost of acquisition for the purpose of calculating capital gain. The inflation adjusted cost of acquisition being higher than the basic cost of acquisition, indexation helps in reducing the capital gains.

Income tax on the post-indexation long-term capital gains is chargeable at the rate of 20 per cent, plus the applicable surcharge and cess. This is illustrated through an example given on next page.

Long term capital gain of Offshore Funds is taxable @ 10% plus applicable surcharge plus cess on the amount of tax and surcharge in terms of section 115AB of the Act.

Long term capital gain of Foreign Institutional Investors from is taxable @ 10% plus applicable surcharge plus cess on the amount of tax and surcharge in terms of section 115AD of the Act.

Transfer of mutual fund units (of any type) on consolidation of two or more plans of a scheme, or two or more schemes of a mutual fund, is exempt from capital gains tax.

Example 17.1

An investor purchased units worth ₹ 9,000 in the previous year 2014-15 and sold them in the previous year 2017-18 for ₹ 15,000 after a period of more than 3 years. Suppose the applicable index numbers are 240 for 2014-15 and 272 for 2017-18.

With indexation, the indexed cost of acquisition would be:

₹ 9,000 x 272 ÷240 = ₹ 10,200.

The capital gain would be:

₹ 15,000 – ₹ 10,200 = ₹ 4,800.

Tax on this income would be:

₹ 4,800 x 20% plus surcharge & EC = ₹ 960 plus surcharge & cess.

17.4.4 TDS and Withholding Tax

TDS is not applicable on re-purchase transactions and on income distributed to resident investors.

In certain cases, withholding tax is to be deducted at source by the mutual fund as follows:

- As provided in Section 196D of the Income Tax Act, 1961, withholding tax is not applicable in the case of capital gains (long term or short term) of FIIs.
- Withholding tax is not applicable on long term capital gains from equity oriented funds for non-resident unit holders, including Offshore fund unit holders.
- Withholding tax is to be deducted at 15% (plus applicable surcharge plus cess on the amount of tax and surcharge) on short term capital gains from equity oriented funds for non-resident unit holders, including Offshore fund unit holders.
- Under Section 196B of the Act, tax is to be deducted at source on the long term capital gains from non-equity oriented schemes for offshore fund unit holders at 10% (plus applicable surcharge plus cess on the amount of tax and surcharge).
- Under Section 196B of the Act, tax is to be deducted at source on the long term capital gains from non-equity oriented schemes for Non-Resident unit holders at 20% (plus applicable surcharge cess on the amount of tax and surcharge).
- In all other cases of investment by non-resident investors, tax is to be deducted from the capital gains at the rates specified in Section 195 of the Act plus applicable surcharge plus cess on the amount of tax and surcharge.
- The applicable surcharge rates and cess were discussed earlier in this chapter.

In the case of a non-resident unit holder who is a resident of a country with which India has signed a double taxation avoidance agreement (which is in force), the mutual fund is to deduct tax at the rate provided in the Finance Act of the relevant year or the rate provided in the said agreement, whichever is beneficial to such non-resident unit holder. (However, such a non-resident unit holder will be required to provide appropriate documents to the Fund, to be entitled to the beneficial rate provided under such agreement).

17.4.5 Tax Benefits on Investments

Section 80C

This benefit, applicable to individuals and HUFs, entitles them to reduce from total income, the value of specified investments they make during the previous year. Up to ₹ 1.5 lakh can be so deducted from total income. The following is a non-exhaustive list of investments covered:

- Subscription to specified mutual fund schemes (equity linked savings schemes);
- Life insurance premium (up to 20% of capital sum assured);
- Contribution to deferred annuity (up to 20% of salary);
- Contribution to specified provident and super annuation funds;
- Contribution to specified pension fund scheme of mutual funds;
- Tuition fees (but not donation or development fee) paid for a university, college, school or other education institution situated in India for the purpose of full time education of two children;
- Purchase of residential accommodation or repayment of loans taken for the purpose, from specified institutions;
- Specified deposits and issues of capital;
- Sukanya Samridhi Yojna; and
- Specified term deposits of 5 years or more with a scheduled bank.

Section 80CCC

This section offers a deduction from total income of individuals in any assessment year, for an amount of up to ₹ 1.5 lakh contributed to annuity plans of insurers for receiving pensions.

Section 80CCD

This section offers deduction from total income of any assessee who is an individual for amounts contributed to the government's pension scheme or any pension scheme notified by the central government.

Sec 80CCD(1) is applicable to contribution by the subscriber. It provides for a deduction upto 10% of salary in the case of assessees who are employees. In the case of other assessees who are individuals (e.g. self-employed) the deduction is available upto 20% of gross total income.Sec 80CCD(2) is applicable to contribution by the employer of the subscriber. It provides for a deduction for the subscriber upto 10% of salary.

Sec 80CCD(1B) provides for a deduction of ₹ 50,000, exclusively for contribution to the NPS. Thus, the exemption of ₹ 1.5 lakh can go up to ₹ 2 lakh if the investor contributes to NPS.

Section 80CCE

This section provides that the total benefit under Sections 80C, 80CCC and 80CCD(1) shall not exceed ₹ 1.5 lakh in any assessment year.

Section 54F

Long term capital gains arising to individuals and HUF from sale of mutual fund units (original asset) will be exempt from tax if the entire sale proceeds are invested in residential house property (new house). If only part of the sale proceeds are so invested, then a corresponding part of the capital gains would be exempt from tax.

The new house would need to be purchased within 1 year before or 2 years after (or constructed within 3 years after) the transfer of the mutual fund units.

On the date of transfer of the original asset, the person should not own more than one residential house (other than the new house). Also, the person should not buy another residential house (other than the new house) within 2 years after the transfer date, or construct another residential house within 3 years after the date of transfer.

The exemption will be withdrawn, if the person sells or transfers the new house within 3 years of its purchase or construction.

17.4.6 Setting Off Capital Gains and Losses, and Speculation Profits and Losses

The Income Tax Act provides for taxation of income under different heads of income, namely:

- Salaries;
- Income from House Property;
- Profits and Gains of Business or Profession;
- Capital Gains; and
- Income from Other Sources.

While calculating the tax payable, if the investor finds that she has a loss under the head "Income from House Property", then that loss, upto ₹ 2 lakh, can be adjusted against the income under the head "Salaries". This adjustment, technically called set off, helps her to reduce the tax which she would otherwise have had to pay on her salaries.

If such loss in an assessment year is more than the salary income, then she can even use the unadjusted loss to minimise her tax obligations in a subsequent assessment year. This process of taking the benefit in a subsequent year is technically called "carrying forward" the loss.

Where the assessee earns a capital gain on transfer of units of a mutual fund scheme, and the assessee has held the investment for more than a year (3 years for non-equity schemes), then the gain is treated as a long term capital gain. If a loss is incurred, where the assessee has held the mutual fund units for more than a year (3 years for non-equity schemes), it would be treated as a long term capital loss.

In the above scenarios, if the assessee's holding period of the mutual fund units is one year or less (three years or less in the case of non-equity schemes), then it would be treated as short term capital gain or short term capital loss as the case may be.

Section 28 of the Income Tax Act also provides that where speculative transactions carried on by an assessee are of such a nature as to constitute a business, the business (hereinafter referred to as "speculation business") shall be deemed to be distinct and separate from any other business.

All of us want to keep our tax obligations at the minimum. So, we would like a situation where any kind of loss can be set off against any kind of gain, while calculating the tax payable for a year. If loss is more than the gain in this year, then we would like the option of setting off the unabsorbed loss against the gains in a future year. However, the following provisions are applicable:

- Speculation loss can only be set off against speculation profit.
- If in any year, speculation loss is more than the speculation profit, then it can be carried forward for setting off against speculation profit in a future year. However, such carrying forward is permitted only for 4 years. Thus, speculation loss in the year 2014-15, can be adjusted against speculation profits in the same year, or against such profits in 2015-16, 2016-17, 2017-18 or 2018-19. After that, it lapses i.e. it would not be available for setting off against speculation profit in 2019-20 or later.
- Capital loss, short term or long term, cannot be set off against any other kind of income, like salary or business profits.
- Short term capital loss can be set off both against short term gain or long term gain
- Long term capital loss can be set off only against long term capital gain — not against short term capital gain
- If capital loss, long term or short term, is more than the capital gain in a year, then the unabsorbed capital loss can be carried forward for adjustment against the capital gains in a future year. Such carrying forward is permitted for 8 years, after which it lapses. Even in the case of such unabsorbed capital loss, the previous principles apply, viz. unabsorbed short term capital loss can be set off against short term capital gain or long term capital gain. However, unabsorbed long term capital loss (other than on equity mutual fund schemes) can only be set off against long term capital gain.

17.4.7 Dividend Stripping (Section 94)

If, an investor buys units within 3 months prior to the record date for a dividend, and sells those units within 9 months after the record date, the dividend would as such be exempt in the investor's hands. However, if there is a capital loss, then that would not be allowed to be set off against other capital gain of the investor, up to the value of the dividend income exempted.

For example, if record date for dividend of ₹ 3 payable to an investor is 1 April 2018. She buys the units at ₹ 12 and sells them at ₹ 8.

The dividend of ₹ 3 would be exempt from tax in the hands of the investor. Tax treatment of capital loss of ₹ 4 would depend on the dates of the transaction as follows:

- If the units were bought before 1 January 2018, or sold after 31 December 2018, then the entire capital loss of ₹ 4 would be available for set off against other capital gain of the investor (subject to the differences in set-off between long-term and short-term capital loss, as already discussed).
- If the units were bought after 1 January 2018, and sold before 31 December 2018, then the capital loss available for set off against other capital gain of the investor would be limited to ₹ 1, namely ₹ 4 capital loss *minus* ₹ 3 dividend that was exempt from tax.

17.4.8 Bonus Stripping (Section 94)

Suppose an investor buys units of a scheme at ₹ 22. Thereafter, the scheme declares a 1:1 bonus issue and the investor thus receives one new unit, for every unit that she bought earlier. Logically, the NAV of the scheme will halve, and it is likely that the units would now have a value of ₹ 11. At this stage, if the investor sells the original units at ₹ 11, then she would incur a loss of ₹ 11 [₹ 22 (original purchase price for the units) minus ₹ 11 (currently realised)].

However, such capital loss is not available for setting off against capital gains if the original units were bought within a period of 3 months prior to the record date for the bonus issue and sold off within a period of 9 months after the record date, and the investor continues to hold all or part of the bonus units.

Example 17.2

An investor purchased 100 units of a scheme at ₹ 22, on 1 February 2018. 1 March 2018 is the record date for a 1:1 bonus issue of the units. The investor sells her original holding of units at ₹ 13 per unit, on 30 March 2018.

The loss incurred by the investor is as follows:

Sale consideration on sale of the units = 100 units × ₹ 13 per unit	= ₹ 1,300
Less Cost of the units = 100 units × ₹ 22 per unit	= ₹ 2,200
Loss	**= ₹ 900**

In this case, the units were bought within 3 months prior to the record date, and sold within 9 months after the record date. Therefore, the loss — in this case it is a short term capital loss, because it is held for upto a year) will not be available for set off against any capital gain. Instead, the bonus units (which would otherwise have been treated as having no cost), would be treated as having been bought for ₹ 900.

In such cases, the capital loss will be treated as the cost of acquisition of the bonus units.

17.4.9 Marginal Rate of Taxation

As was mentioned earlier, any short term capital gain made by an investor from investment in a debt mutual fund scheme would be added to the investor's taxable income. Thus, the gain would be levied a tax at the investor's "marginal rate of taxation".

It would be pertinent to re-iterate here that even in the case of investment in an equity scheme, the benefit of concessional tax (10% for long term capital gain; 15% tax for short term capital gain) is applicable only if the sale transaction was subject to Securities Transaction Tax (STT). If STT was not applicable when the investor sold the equity mutual fund units, taxation would be the same as is applicable to debt mutual fund schemes, namely:

- any long term capital gain would be liable to tax at the rate of 20% (with indexation); and
- short term capital gain would be added to the investor's taxable income, and therefore would be liable to be taxed at the "marginal rate of taxation" for the investor.

What is "marginal rate of taxation"?

Suppose the basic tax rate prescribed for the assessee is 30%.

If the applicable surcharge is 12% (which is applied to the basic tax rate), then the effective tax would be calculated as 30% × (1 + 12%), i.e. 30% × (1 + 0.12), which is equal to 33.6%.

The government also levies 4% towards Health & Education Cess (which is applied to the basic rate plus surcharge).

We calculated the effective tax rate as 33.6%, for the person with basic tax of 30% and surcharge of 12%. Once we factor in the 4% Cess, the effective tax rate now becomes 33.6% × (1 + 4%), i.e. 33.6% × (1 + 0.04), which is equal to 34.944%. This becomes the effective tax rate for the assessee.

Marginal rate of taxation is the "effective" rate of taxation applicable for the assessee on his incremental income. In the above case it is 34.944%.

Where the income tax act stipulates different tax rates for different income levels (slabs), then the marginal rate of taxation would be the effective rate of taxation at the slab at which her highest income falls.

The marginal rate of taxation applicable for Assessment Year 2019-20 (i.e., Previous Year 2018-19) for various kinds of investors, calculated on the above basis, is shown in Table 17.3.

Table 17.3

Investor Type	*Taxable Income*		*Basic Rate*	*Surcharge*	*Health & Education Cess*	*Marginal Rate*
Individuals (Other than Specified Individuals) & HUF, Association of Persons, Body of Individuals, Artificial Juridical Persons	Upto	250,000	0%	0%	4%	0.00000%
	250,001	500,000	5%	0%	4%	5.20000%
	500,001	1,000,000	20%	0%	4%	20.80000%
	1,000,001	5,000,000	30%	0%	4%	31.20000%
	5,000,001	10,000,000	30%	10%	4%	34.32000%
	Over	10,000,000	30%	15%	4%	35.88000%
Specified Individuals — Indian Residents above 60 years of age, but less than 80 years of age at any time during the previous year	Upto	300,000	0%	0%	4%	0.00000%
	300,001	500,000	5%	0%	4%	5.20000%
	500,001	1,000,000	20%	0%	4%	20.80000%
	1,000,001	5,000,000	30%	0%	4%	31.20000%
	5,000,001	10,000,000	30%	10%	4%	34.32000%
	Over	10,000,000	30%	15%	4%	35.88000%
Specified Individuals — Indian Residents above 80 years of age at any time during the previous year	Upto	500,000	0%	0%	4%	0.00000%
	500,001	1,000,000	20%	0%	4%	20.80000%
	1,000,001	5,000,000	30%	0%	4%	31.20000%
	5,000,001	10,000,000	30%	10%	4%	34.32000%
	Over	10,000,000	30%	15%	4%	35.88000%
Partnership Firm and Local Authority	Upto	10,000,000	30%	0%	4%	31.20000%
	Over	10,000,000	30%	12%	4%	34.94400%
Co-operative Society	Upto	10,000	10%	0%	4%	10.40000%
	10,001	20,000	20%	0%	4%	20.80000%
	20,001	10,000,000	30%	0%	4%	31.20000%
	Above	10,000,000	30%	12%	4%	34.94400%
Domestic Company (Turnover or gross receipts upto ₹ 250 crore)	Upto	10,000,000	25%	0%	4%	26.00000%
	10,000,001	100,000,000	25%	7%	4%	27.82000%
	Over	100,000,000	25%	12%	4%	29.12000%
Domestic Company (Turnover or gross receipts exceeding ₹ 250 crore)	Upto	10,000,000	30%	0%	4%	31.20000%
	10,000,001	100,000,000	30%	7%	4%	33.38400%
	Over	100,000,000	30%	12%	4%	34.94400%
Foreign Company	Upto	10,000,000	40%	0%	4%	41.60000%
	10,000,001	100,000,000	40%	2%	4%	42.43200%
	Over	100,000,000	40%	5%	4%	43.68000%

In the case of foreign company, tax rate is 50% (instead of 40%) on specified royalty and technical service fees.

17.5 Tax in Specific Situations

Having covered the various elements that go into taxation, let us now consider a few typical issues given in example 17.3 and 17.4 that mutual fund distributors and intelligent investors face regularly.

Example 17.3

You have invested ₹ 10,000 each in the following investments for more than three years:

(a) Mutual Fund Liquid Scheme (Growth Option) — 1,000 units of ₹ 10 each, which has appreciated by 30%.
(b) Mutual Fund Liquid Scheme (Dividend Option) — 1,000 units of ₹ 10 each, which has appreciated by 30%.
(c) Mutual Fund Liquid Scheme (Dividend Re-Investment Option) — 1,000 units of ₹ 10 each, which has appreciated by 30%.

The dividend and dividend re-investment options in this mutual fund scheme operate on a mode that the maximum possible amount is paid as dividends at the end of 3 years, and the ex-dividend NAV is brought down to ₹ 10.

The government has declared cost-inflation index as 100, for the financial year in which you invested. The index is 130 for the current year.

You now need money to finance your holiday. What would be your post-tax return?

You can ignore the impact of loads and STT, if applicable. Make any other relevant assumptions.

(a) NAV has appreciated by 30% to ₹ 13. If 1,000 units are redeemed, you will receive 1,000 × ₹ 13 = ₹ 13,000

The appreciation is ₹ 3,000 (Sales realisation of ₹ 13,000 *less* Acquisition Cost of ₹ 10,000)

Since the holding period is more than three years, this would be a long term capital gain.

STT is not applicable because this is not an equity scheme. The taxation is as follows:

With indexation, at 20%

Indexed cost of acquisition would be cost of acquisition of ₹ 10,000 ×130 ÷100 = ₹ 13,000

Taxable Capital Gain would be Nil (Sales Realisation of ₹ 13,000 *less* Indexed Cost of Acquisition of ₹ 13,000).

So no tax is payable.

Your post tax return would be post-tax income of ₹ 3,000 ÷ Investment of ₹ 10,000, i.e. 30% over 3 years.

Here, you were able to save on tax because the appreciation matched the increase in cost inflation index.

(Contd . . .)

Example 17.3 *(contd.)*

In case tax were to become payable, then the Surcharge and Cess too would need to be paid, as discussed under "Marginal Rate of Taxation".

(b) Dividend can be paid only out of realised profits. Let us therefore assume that the entire ₹ 3 of appreciation represents realised profits. This amounts to ₹ 3,000 on 1,000 units.

Debt schemes, including Liquid schemes, need to bear income distribution tax of 25% (for individuals & HUFs) plus surcharge plus cess. This translates into an effective rate of 25% × (1 + 0.12) × (1 + 0.04), i.e. 29.12%. So you will receive 1 minus 0.2912, i.e. 70.88% of ₹ 3,000, i.e. ₹ 2,126.40. This is tax-free in your hands.

Your post-tax return is ₹ 2,126.40 ÷ ₹ 10,000, i.e. 21.264% over 3 years.

The marginal rate of taxation for individuals can go up to 35.88% (for those with taxable income in excess of ₹ 1 crore), which is higher than the rate of dividend distribution tax of 29.12% applicable for debt schemes.

For individuals who have overall taxable income below ₹ 10 lakh, the marginal tax rate is not more than 20.80%. For such investors, the higher dividend distribution tax on debt funds makes it tax inefficient.

(c) The dividend re-investment option would mean that you will receive new units equivalent to the dividend amount of ₹ 2,126.40 [as calculated in (b) above] ÷ Ex-dividend NAV of ₹ 10, i.e. 212.64 new units.

When you dispose the investment, you will realise ₹ 10 per unit on 1,212,64 units (1,000 original units plus 212.64 new units), i.e. ₹ 12,126.40. As compared to original investment of ₹ 10,000, the gain is ₹ 2,126.40

The realisation of ₹ 10 per unit is the same as the cost of acquisition (for the original 1,000 units, as well as the new 212.64 units). So, no capital gains tax is payable.

Your post tax return would be ₹ 2,126.40 ÷ ₹ 10,000, i.e. 21.264% over 3 years. This is the same return that was calculated in the case of dividend option.

The disadvantage of dividend re-investment option, as compared to growth option, is that the holding period (relevant for calculating the minimum 3 years requirement for treatment as long term capital gains) for the new units starts on the re-investment date. The new units will need to be held for a further period of 3 years, in order to become eligible for treatment as long term capital gains.

In order to minimise this problem, some schemes offer a daily dividend re-investment option. In such cases, subject to availability of realised profits, a dividend is declared every day, and re-invested in the scheme. Thus, the holding period for the new units starts much earlier, than is possible through the traditional mode of declaring a dividend at the end of a year. Further, the dividend declaration pulls down the ex-dividend NAV, and therefore the capital gains on re-purchase (which might be treated as gains from speculative business).

(Contd . . .)

Example 17.3 *(contd.)*

Tax on income distribution clearly made the dividend options inferior to the growth option, where indexation benefit associated with long-term capital asset helped in tax optimisation.

If the holding period were upto 3 years, then the marginal rate of taxation would be applicable on the gains. In that case, investors having taxable income over ₹ 10 lakh will find it more tax efficient to go for the dividend option.

Example 17.4

You have invested ₹ 10,000 each in the following investments for more than a year:

(a) Mutual Fund Equity Scheme — Growth Option — 1,000 units of ₹ 10 each, which has appreciated by 10%.

(b) Mutual Fund Equity Scheme — Dividend Option — 1,000 units of ₹ 10 each, which has appreciated by 10%.

(c) Mutual Fund Equity Scheme — Dividend Re-Investment Option — 1,000 units of ₹ 10 each, which has appreciated by 10%.

The dividend and dividend re-investment options of this mutual fund scheme operate on a mode that the maximum possible amount is paid as dividends, and the ex-dividend NAV is brought down to ₹ 10.

The government has declared cost-inflation index as 100, for the financial year in which you invested. The index is 110 for the current year.

You need money to finance your holiday.

What would be your post-tax return?

You can ignore the impact of loads and STT, if applicable. Make any other relevant assumptions.

(a) NAV would have appreciated by 10% to ₹ 11.

If 1,000 units are redeemed, you will receive 1,000 × ₹ 11 = ₹ 11,000
The appreciation is ₹ 1,000 (Sales realisation of ₹ 11,000 *less* acquisition cost of ₹ 10,000)

Since the holding period is more than a year, this would be a long term capital gain. STT would have been paid on the sale, and the capital gain would be taxable at 10% plus surcharge of 15% (assuming taxable income is in excess of ₹ 1 crore) plus cess of 4% on the tax and surcharge. The effective tax rate comes to 10% × 1.15 × 1.04 i.e. 11.96%. (If STT was not paid, taxation would be similar to the previous example on debt scheme).

(Contd . . .)

Example 17.4 *(contd.)*

The tax would thus be Capital Gain of ₹ 1,000 × 11.96% i.e. ₹ 119.60.

Net of tax, the capital gain would be ₹ 1,000 *less* ₹ 119.60 i.e. ₹ 880.40.

Post-tax return is ₹ 880.40 ÷ ₹ 10,000, i.e. 8.804%

If the investor's taxable income had been in excess of ₹ 50 lakh, but less than ₹ 1 crore, the effective tax rate would have been 10% × 1.10 × 1.04 i.e. 11.44%. The post-tax return would have been 8.856%.

On the same lines, investors having taxable income upto ₹ 50 lakh would have experienced an effective tax rate of 10.40% and post-tax return of 8.96%.

Cost Inflation Index number is irrelevant. Indexation benefit is not allowed in the case of long term capital gains on equity.

(b) Dividend can be paid only out of realised profits. Let us therefore assume that the entire ₹ 1 of appreciation represents realised profits.

Dividend distribution tax is 10% plus surcharge of 12% on the tax plus cess of 4% on the tax and surcharge. This works out to 10% × 1.12 × 1.04 i.e. 11.648%.

So you will receive 1 minus 0.11648, i.e. 88.352% of ₹ 1,000, i.e. ₹ 883.52. This is tax-free in your hands.

Post-tax return would be ₹ 883.52 ÷ ₹ 10,000, i.e. 8.8352%

The marginal rate of taxation for individuals can go up to 35.88% (for those with taxable income in excess of ₹ 1 crore), which is higher than the rate of dividend distribution tax of 11.648% applicable for equity schemes.

For individuals who have overall taxable income below ₹ 5 lakh, the marginal tax rate is not more than 5.20%. For such investors, the higher dividend distribution tax on equity funds makes it tax inefficient.

(c) Under the dividend re-investment option, you will receive new units equivalent to the dividend amount of ₹ 883.52 [as calculated in (b) above] ÷ ex-dividend NAV of ₹ 10, i.e. 88.352 new units.

When you dispose the investment, you will realise ₹ 10 per unit on 1,088.352 units (1,000 original units plus 88.352 new units), i.e. ₹ 10,883.52. As compared to original investment of ₹ 10,000, the gain is ₹ 883.52

The realisation of ₹ 10 per unit is the same as the cost of acquisition. So, no capital gains tax is payable.

Your post tax return would be ₹ 883.52 ÷ ₹ 10,000, i.e. 8.8352%, which is the same as in the case of dividend option.

(Contd . . .)

Example 17.4 *(contd.)*

The disadvantage of dividend re-investment option, as compared to growth option, is that the holding period (relevant for calculating the minimum 1 year requirement for treatment as long term capital gains) for the new units starts on the re-investment date. The new units will need to be held for a further period of 1 year, in order to become eligible for treatment as long term capital gains.

Unlike debt, equity portfolios do not earn an interest income every day. Therefore, daily dividend option is not feasible in equity schemes.

17.6 Tax in Summary

(a) Investors in equity schemes having taxable income in excess of ₹ 5 lakh would prefer the dividend option if their holding period is likely to be upto a year. The tax on income distribution at 10% is lower than the 15% capital gains tax on short-term capital gains.

If the holding period is more than a year, then the 10% capital gains tax is comparable to the 10% tax on income distribution. Investors having taxable income in excess of ₹ 5 lakh would prefer the dividend option, because the flexibility to sell within a year is retained.

Investors having taxable income upto ₹ 5 lakh will find the dividend option to be tax-inefficient, irrespective of holding period.

Dividend re-investment option increases the risk of having to book a short term capital gain (because the re-invested dividend would lead to new units being issued as of a current date, although the capital gain amount itself would be tempered by the dividend distribution).

Further, irrespective of whether it is a short term or long term capital gain, STT will be applicable on the re-purchase price.

(b) Investors in debt schemes who are clear that they will hold the investment for more than three years (and thereby make it eligible for long term capital gain) will find it more tax efficient to go for growth option on account of the indexation benefit, and the scope to avoid dividend distribution tax.

(c) Non-corporate investors in debt schemes, who are not sure if they will hold the investment for more than three years, would prefer the dividend option, if their taxable income is more than ₹ 10 lakh. The dividend distribution tax rate is lower than their marginal tax rate.

Daily dividend re-investment options minimise the risk of having to pay higher income tax on account of gains being treated as short term capital gains.

(d) The possibility of setting off capital gains against capital losses, or setting off speculative gains against speculative losses, might throw up tax efficient options for investors that are different from those stated above.

For instance, an investor who has short term capital losses available for set off against capital gains, might prefer a growth option in an equity or debt scheme, even if she is in a higher tax bracket. The short term capital loss already booked, offers a hedge against taxation of the capital gains (long term or short term), whereas the dividend option would impose a cost in terms of dividend distribution tax.

(g) Arbitrage funds (which seek to earn riskless profit, for example, by buying equity shares and selling equivalent future contracts on the same underlying equity shares) earn returns that are akin to debt market returns. However, because their investments are in equity, they would qualify as equity funds, with the incidental benefits of taxation. Thus, the investor combines the safety of debt with the tax benefits of equity. Eat your cake and have it too!

(h) Section 115JB of the Income Tax Act provides for "Minimum Alternate Tax" (MAT). This is a minimum tax which is payable by companies on the income they report in their accounts ("accounting profits"), even if the tax they otherwise need to pay (based on various tax provisions) is lower. The long term capital gains is included in the calculation of "accounting profits", on which the MAT becomes payable. Therefore, companies need to plan their tax well, lest the long term capital gains which they thought would be exempt from the tax, is caught under the mischief of MAT.

Good wealth managers assess the overall tax position of the investor and her family before making specific investment related recommendations.

Various suggestions made across this book are illustrative. Make sure you take appropriate advice. Please do not implement any of these suggestions blindly.

Chapter 18

Big Data, Artificial Intelligence, Block-chain and Mutual Funds

This chapter is not about a sectoral or thematic fund that invests in new technologies. The focus instead is to first understand the basics of these emerging technologies, and then envision how they might shape the mutual fund industry and affect unit-holders.

18.1 Big Data

The spread of internet at the turn of the century enabled tracking of browsing habits of people. Apps that we so freely download, have taken this tracking deep into any individual's private life. What you buy, where you go, who you spend time with, your appointments, your favourite sport, your political inclinations — nothing is a secret. Check the permissions you have granted to your favourite app. They might include access to the contacts in your handset, your messages, your e-mails, your phone calls, your calendar, your location based on Global Positioning System (GPS), etc. The standard justification that one sees in most apps for seeking such information is that it will help you enjoy a "customised experience".

An experiment for you. Browse the internet for a few minutes for information on an entirely off-beat country, say, Papua New Guinea. Soon you will receive offers for air tickets, hotels, visa services and tourist spots linked to that country. This is an example of "customised experience".

The foot-prints that we leave on the world wide web amount to a humongous volume of data. Hence, the term "big data". Declining data storage cost, falling internet access costs and advances in computing technology have made big data part of the sales strategy of most professional organisations.

Students of marketing know the concept of market segmentation — a strategy where the firm splits the market for a product into segments, e.g. high-income earner and low-income earner. Such segmentation ensures that the firm can adopt differentiated marketing and sales strategies for each segment. The higher end brand can be pushed to the high-income earner as a niche offering through sophisticated messaging platforms. The lower end brand can be pushed to the low-income earner as a value for money offering through "Buy one, get one free" type of conventional sales pitches.

Big data has made it possible to move from market segments to mass customisation and individualisation. A large mass of people can be offered individually customised experiences through application of technology on big data. Normally, customisation comes at a cost. This logic was given in Chapter 1 while comparing standardised mutual fund schemes with costlier portfolio management schemes. But with technology, customisation can reduce overall cost through sharper focus. Thus, both the manufacturer (mutual fund) and the consumer (investor) benefits.

The benefits of big data are clear. What are the issues with big data that mutual funds and unit-holders in India need to consider?

- Mutual funds appear to have focused their big data efforts on selling more of the same units. The potential to customise the offering or hand-hold current investors through market cycles is largely unexplored.
- Unrestrained use of big data to push the selling tactic in a specific system-determined direction could limit the human touch and hamper the development of employees and other investor-facing people. Normally, sales executives become seasoned professionals by learning from their past client management successes and failures. If they lose the habit of proactive application of mind, then there is little learning and growth. Are we emphasising machine learning (ML) over human learning?
- In some cases, big data efforts are leading to a prioritisation of tactics over strategy. Tactics can yield limited results if there is a fundamental problem with the strategy. Application of big data for strategy formulation and business process improvements are virgin territories for Indian mutual funds.
- The models that are used to translate big data into actionable insights are becoming black boxes. Mutual funds need to have a stronger grip on the insight generation process. Researchers know that data can be tortured into confessing to anything.
- As regard the investor, there needs to be awareness of the permissions she is granting to various apps. She will have to take an informed call on how much of her privacy she is prepared to surrender.
- The investor should also recognise the information asymmetry. The mutual fund knows a lot more about the investor as compared to what the investor knows about the mutual fund. In situations of information asymmetry there is greater scope for mis-selling, and hence the need to be cautious. Else, the investor might end up with lemons.

18.2 Artificial Intelligence

Intelligence of human beings and animals is natural intelligence. Intelligence that is attributed to computers and machines is artificial intelligence (AI) or machine intelligence. Limitations of human beings and expansion of computing capability have fostered an explosion in AI applications across industries.

Chess enthusiasts may recall IBM's "Big Blue", a super-computer that defeated Gary Kasparov who ruled the chess-world in the 1990s. Big Blue was obviously programmed with the rules of chess viz. the range and direction in which each piece on the board can be moved and the time limitations for making the moves in tournament conditions. The machine could think forward on the various moves that Kasparov might make, and the consequences thereof. This helped Big Blue out-think the "most intelligent" human being of the time and achieve its goal of defeating him.

With advances in technology, a computer playing chess is no longer considered a high-end application of AI. What sets apart the current wave of technology is ML viz. the ability of the machine to learn. A related concept is deep-learning, where the machine learns to replicate the human thought process.

Let us understand ML through the chess analogy. Suppose, the rules of chess were not fed into the machine. The machine learnt the game and mastered the tricks of winning by observing (using vision systems) the chess-moves in tens of thousands of games. That is ML. Achieving this at speed calls for an entirely new form of software architecture.

Have you tried talking to 'Siri' on your Apple device? Instruct Siri to remind you on the first of every month at 9 am to check if there is enough money in the bank for your SIP investment. Siri will seek your confirmation on what it has understood of your instruction. Once you confirm, see the magic. Until you cancel the instruction, it will remind you at 9 am on the first of every month that you need to check your bank balance. Siri is a chat-bot. Now visualise the power of a chat-bot that understands multiple Indian languages. More efficient and effective that your best secretary?!

A few years ago, the owner of a mum-and-pop shop in the US was killed. There was a fleeting image of the suspect with a gun in one of the surveillance cameras near the shop. Technology not only improved that image but also did pattern-matching of that image with the feeds from hundreds of surveillance cameras in the locality. Thus, the suspect could be quickly traced to his hideout. On the same lines, investigators have started using technology to conjure the appearance of the suspect in various disguises.

The next time you need a cab for your ride home during peak hours, ask a friend to book the ride on her mobile phone while you do the same on yours. The vastly different fares for the same ride on a similar vehicle at the same time should not shock you. Apps can create individual demand curves based on past behaviour.

Since the demand curve created for you is different from that created for your friend, the pricing offered by the app is different. The higher the surge fares you accept, the higher is likely to be the fare for your future rides. Differentiating extravagance from frugality is just an app away.

Cut back to the world of finance. Many investors would have encountered websites that assess their propensity to take risk. As mentioned in Chapter 14, a typical website will display a set of questions. The response to the questions would suggest a risk profile for the respondent. How reliable is the suggested risk profile? There could be problems with the design of the risk profiler itself. Were the questions formulated properly? Do the respondent and the person who formulated the profiler share the same understanding about the questions and the answer options? Was the respondent honest in answering those questions? Do the questions and the possible answers really measure the risk profile of an investor?

Now consider the possibility that a machine tracks the actual investment moves of the investor. Or, the investor is requested to play an investment game where market conditions are simulated. An intelligent agent — a software — will use the information to assess the investor's risk profile. Futuristically, the intelligent agent could communicate with a device that tracks the investor's blood pressure and heart beat on real-time basis. If your blood-pressure rises when the market falls, is advisable for you to have an equity-dominant portfolio? Doesn't this judge your risk profile better?

Academic researchers have started measuring psychological phenomena using sensors that are placed on the head of respondents. Eye-trackers can assess the effectiveness of advertisements. Carbon di-oxide measuring instruments in a theatre help assess the impact of various scenes in a movie. Footfalls in malls, and traffic in road-crossings can be accurately measured without any human involvement. Such are the mind-boggling capabilities of emerging technology.

Robo investment advisory firms have been in existence in India for a few years. These are digital platforms that provide automated investment advice. The benefit obviously is the low cost of service. These platforms may or may not be ML-based. When the algorithms are fed and remain relatively stable over time, they are unlikely to be ML-based. Programs (Robos) that keep learning from the responses of people are ML-based. The day the robo replicates the human investment advisor's thought process, "deep-learning" can be said to have arrived.

ML-based services are high-end in technology. But that does not mean that the core service offering (in this example, investment advisory) is superior. When models become black-boxes, there is danger lurking. The dictum shared by a professional — free investment advice is the costliest investment advice in the world — should not be forgotten.

Ideally, when mutual funds opt for AI, they should not try to replicate current business processes. Instead, business processes should be improved. Use the human for processes that AI cannot handle efficiently at the current level of technology. This will enhance the throughput of the human while maximising the service level for the client at an acceptable cost and risk.

18.3 Block-chain

Block-chain is a technology that facilitates storage of electronic ledgers in the web on a distributed basis. The ledger is open source, in the sense that many people can freely access it (subject to security protocols), but it cannot be copied. It can be used to store anything of value e.g. money, land, shares, documents, music and books. The distributed storage across multiple nodes ensures protection from hacking.

Consider your bank. It has a centralised repository of bank accounts of all its clients. Suppose you were to transfer money from your account to the account your husband maintains in the same bank. The bank, as an intermediary, will execute the transaction and send a confirmation to you and your husband. The banks records are centralised and liable to be hacked. If the transfer is between accounts in two different banks, then RBI as administrator of the payment system also is part of that transaction.

As an alternative, visualise a world where there is a ledger on the web with data distributed in blocks across millions of computers (nodes) in a fashion where a single node does not have adequate information. It cannot be hacked without disrupting the self-balancing nature of the whole system. In such an environment, when you transfer money to your husband, his account will be credited and yours debited without going through any intermediary like a bank. In a purely technological sense, people can have a block chain account to store their money without having a bank account! They can do purchase and sale transactions using the block-chain account. Where is the need for a bank or an RBI?! Extending the thought further, does a mutual fund really need a Custodian? Or an RTA? Think deeper — How does the mutual fund justify its existence in a block-chained world?

The person who conceptualised the block-chain technology used a pseudonym, Satoshi Nakamoto. He went further to create a new digital currency, "Bitcoin". Since regulators could not track it, Bitcoin became the favourite currency of kidnappers, smugglers and drug peddlers. Counterparties in the underworld no longer needed to match torn currency notes to confirm KYC. Subsequently, many others adopted the technology and created their own digital currencies. The common name for such digital currencies is "crypto-currency". The regulatory, economic and business model aspects of crypto-currency are not relevant for this discussion. But block-chain as a technology offers several interesting possibilities:

- The mutual fund investor in India has experienced the head-aches of complying with KYC requirements. Block-chain allows access to documents without copying. This can potentially simplify KYC processes while mitigating the risk of malpractices by the counter-party.

- Currently, SIP investors need to offer post-dated cheques or standing instructions to their mutual fund, besides the application form. Blockchain technology will enable regular money transfers based on just the application form maintained as a block-chain ledger.
- Your mutual fund scheme does well. The Board declares a dividend. The money can directly flow from the scheme to unit-holders like you. No need for the RTA.
- If you do not receive the dividend, you can send an e-mail. An automated intelligent agent can respond with the details instantaneously. No call-centre human interface required.

In this manner, a whole range of processes can be simplified. Transactions can flow through seamlessly without the need for many intermediaries. Or, the intermediaries could perform alternate roles that add value for the investor.

Most of these technologies remain at the back-end. The unit-holder may not see the technology, but she can experience the services that ride on the technology. How can mutual funds unleash the potential of such technologies? Some changes need to be implemented at the industry level, some others at the mutual fund level. Based on proof of concept and comforts with respect to risk and reliability, regulators too will need to buy-in and formulate facilitating rules and regulations.

Each mutual fund will have to take a call on how deep it wants to go. Do you want to test the waters or catalyse a shake-out in the industry? That is a senior management decision. Accordingly, the technology, and the features and processes where the technology will be used need to be finalised and prioritised. The scale of the technology vision will determine the organisation format for this new initiative.

As a thumb-rule, the more the number of software and hardware professionals in the design team, the more dangerous it gets. A good design team at each mutual fund will be led by a visionary who is equally comfortable with technology, financial markets, statistical tools and regulations. There should be a healthy mix of software professionals, hardware professionals, data scientists, financial market professionals and people who think with their heart. The last-mentioned skill is, unfortunately, the least recognised in the industry.

Further, an independent team should study the simulations and validate the models before offering them in the market place. If the gist of the working of the model cannot be explained in a few sentences, then chances are complexity has consumed reality.

The potential combined impact of big data, AI and block-chain is beyond imagination. Suppose you wake up one morning and ask your chatbot in English, "How much money do I have in my bank account?" It provides you the answer in English. Next you ask in Hindi, "What are the top three mutual fund schemes based on last 2 years' returns?" It lists the three schemes, now conversing in Hindi. Next, you instruct in Gujarati that you want to invest ₹ 5 lakh in Scheme X. It responds in Gujarati that "Scheme X is closed for subscription; Scheme Y is not suitable for you based on risk profile; Do you want to invest in Scheme Z?" You reply in Marathi that you are not sure. You would like to speak to the fund manager. Pronto, the Tamilian fund manager arrives in your drawing room. You ask him a few questions, gain comfort and inform the chatbot that you wish to proceed with the investment in Scheme Z. The chat-bot triggers the relevant actions. Your KYC and other formalities are done, money goes from your account to the scheme and you receive confirmation of the number of units allotted and the relevant NAV.

This is not science fiction — welcome to a new reality! Virtual Reality helps you immerse in an entirely artificial digital environment; Augmented Reality brings virtual objects (like the fund manager) into your real-world environment; Mixed Reality (also called "Hybrid Reality") offers superior levels of interaction between your real and virtual worlds.

If the vision is big enough, the entire world of finance and investments can be transformed. Who wants to take the lead?

List of Abbreviations and Acronyms

ACE	AMFI Code of Ethics
ADR	American Depository Receipt
AI	Artificial Intelligence
AIF	Alternate Investment Fund
AMC	Asset Management Company
AMFI	Association of Mutual Funds in India
ANOVA	Analysis of Variances
ARMFA	AMFI Registered Mutual Fund Adviser
ARN	AMFI Registration Number
ASBA	Application Supported by Blocked Amount
AUM	Assets Under Management
BSE	Bombay Stock Exchange
CAGR	Compounded Annual Growth Rate
CAN	Common Account Number
CBLO	Collateralised Borrowing & Lending Obligation
CCIL	Clearing Corporation of India Limited
CD	Certificate of Deposit
CDSC	Contingent Deferred Sales Charge
CDSL	Contingent Deferred Sales Load
CEPS	Cash Earnings Per Share
CII	Cost Inflation Index
CP	Commercial Paper
CPI	Consumer Price Index
CPPI	Constant Proportion Portfolio Insurance
CRR	Cash Reserve Ratio
DDT	Dividend Distribution Tax
DICGC	Deposit Insurance & Credit Guarantee Corporation
DTP	Dividend Transfer Plan

ELSS	Equity Linked Savings Scheme
EPS	Earnings Per Share
ETF	Exchange Traded Fund
EUIN	Employee Unique Identification Number
FATF	Financial Action Task Force
FII	Foreign Institutional Investor
FMP	Fixed Maturity Plan
FPI	Foreign Portfolio Investor
GARP	Growth at Reasonable Price
GDR	Global Depository Receipt
GMV	Gross Merchandise Value
GPS	Global Positioning System
GST	Goods and Services Tax
HFC	Housing Finance Company
HNI	High Networth Individuals
HUF	Hindu Undivided Family
IPO	Initial Public Offering
IRR	Internal Rate of Return
ISC	Investor Service Centre
ISIN	International Securities Identification Number
KAR	Know-your-client Registered Agency
KIM	Key Information Memorandum
KYC	Know Your Customer
KYD	Know Your Distributor
LLP	Limited Liability Partnership
LTCM	Long Term Capital Management
MAT	Minimum Alternate Tax
MF	Mutual Fund
MFU	Mutual Fund Utilities India Pvt. Ltd.
MIP	Monthly Income Plan
ML	Machine Learning
NAV	Net Asset Value
NEFT	National Electronic Fund Transfer
NFO	New Fund Offer
NHB	National Housing Bank
NPA	Non-Performing Asset
NPS	National Pension System
NRI	Non-Resident Indian
NSC	National Savings Certificate

NSE	National Stock Exchange
OBPI	Option-based Portfolio Insurance
OCI	Overseas Citizen of India
P/CE	Price to Cash Earnings (Ratio)
PD	Primary Dealer
PEG	Price-Earnings to Growth (Ratio)
PFM	Pension Fund Manager
PIO	Person of Indian Origin
PMS	Portfolio Management Scheme
PoA	Power of Attorney
PoA	Point of Acceptance
POP	Point of Presence
PPF	Public Provident Fund
PSU	Public Sector Undertaking
QFI	Qualified Foreign Investor
RBI	Reserve Bank of India
REIT	Real Estate Investment Trust
REMF	Real Estate Mutual Fund
RTA	Registrar & Transfer Agent
RTGS	Real Time Gross Settlement
SAI	Statement of Additional Information
SCORES	SEBI Complaints Redress System
SEBI	Securities and Exchange Board of India
SGL	Subsidiary General Ledger
SKU	Stock Keeping Unit
SID	Scheme Information Document
SIP	Systematic Investment Plan
SPV	Special Purpose Vehicle
STP	Systematic Transfer Plan
STT	Securities Transaction Tax
SWP	Systematic Withdrawal Plan
TDS	Tax Deducted at Source
TER	Total Expense Ratio
VAR	Value at Risk
YTC	Yield to Call
YTM	Yield to Maturity
YTP	Yield to Put

Glossary

Asset Management Company (AMC)	The company appointed by the mutual fund trust to handle the investments and other day-to-day activities of the schemes floated by the mutual fund.
Assets Under Management (AUM)	A measure of the size of business in the mutual fund industry. It is calculated for each scheme as "marked to market" valuation for the scheme investment portfolio plus all other assets of the scheme minus liabilities of the scheme to parties other than the unit holders. Alternatively, it can be measured as the unit capital plus reserves of the scheme.
Balanced Scheme	A mutual fund scheme that invests in a balanced mix of debt and equity securities.
Closed-end Scheme	A mutual fund scheme that receives money from unit holders only during the New Fund Offer period and has a fixed maturity.
Collateralised Borrowing and Lending Obligation (CBLO)	A product conceptualised by Clearing Corporation of India Limited, essentially to help non-bank entities to transact in the money market.
Continuous Offer Period	The period that commences a day after the inception date of an open-end scheme. Sale and re-purchase prices are announced from the date of commencement of continuous offer period.
Custodian	The agency appointed to have custody of the investments of mutual fund schemes.
Cut-off Timing	The time before which an investor's application for investment in new units or redemption of existing units should reach an Investor Service Centre, in order to be eligible for a particular day's NAV. Applications submitted after that time will be executed based on a later NAV.

Debt Scheme	A mutual fund scheme that invests primarily in debt securities.
Dividend Option	An option within a mutual fund scheme where a dividend is declared from time to time, subject to availability of profits.
Dividend Payout Option	A sub-option within Dividend Option, where the dividend that is declared is paid out to the unit-holder.
Dividend Re-investment Option	A sub-option within Dividend Option, where the dividend that is declared is not paid out to the unit-holder, but re-invested in the same scheme. Thus, the unit-holder receives new units in the scheme in lieu of the dividend declared but not paid.
Entry Load	The excess of the sale price over the Net Asset Value. Since entry load is not permitted under current regulations, the sale price is the same as the Net Asset Value.
Equity Scheme	A mutual fund scheme that invests primarily in equity shares and related securities.
Exchange Traded Funds (ETFs)	These are uniquely structured open-end index schemes that are listed in the stock exchange.
Exit Load	The excess of the Net Asset Value over the Re-purchase price. It is typically quoted as a percentage to Net Asset Value and is frozen when an investor buys those units.
Fact Sheet	Monthly publication brought out by AMCs to provide information about the portfolio and performance of each mutual fund scheme.
Fixed Maturity Plan (FMP)	A closed-end debt scheme that invests in debt securities whose maturity closely matches that of the scheme.
GARP stocks	Growth stocks that are available at a reasonable price.
Gilt	Government securities.
Gilt Schemes	Schemes that invest in only government securities.
Gold Scheme	A mutual fund scheme that invests primarily in gold and related securities.
Growth Option	An option within a mutual fund scheme where no dividend is declared.
Growth Scheme	A mutual fund scheme whose objective is to generate growth for the unit-holder through a portfolio that is oriented to growth assets like equity.
Growth stocks	Shares of companies whose earnings are rising faster than the economy.
Hybrid Scheme	A mutual fund scheme that invests significant amounts in more than one asset class.

Inception Date	The date of allotment of units after the New Fund Offer.
Income stocks	Shares of companies that offer an attractive return in the form of dividend yield.
Index Schemes	Schemes that maintain a portfolio which mirrors a pre-specified index, e.g. S&P BSE Sensex or CNX Nifty.
Interval Fund	A mutual fund scheme that is essentially closed-end, but becomes open-end during pre-specified periods of time, e.g. first 15 days of every quarter.
Interval Period	The period between two successive transaction periods in an interval fund is called interval period.
Liquid Schemes	A mutual fund debt scheme that invests only in short-term debt securities.
Load	Amount charged beyond the NAV for transactions that investors have with the scheme. See also "Entry Load" and "Exit Load."
Marked to Market (MTM)	Barring a few exceptional situations, all securities in the portfolio of a mutual fund scheme are valued at the market price in order to determine the NAV. Such valuation is called "marked to market."
Money market	The segment of the debt market where short-term debt securities (up to 1 year maturity) are traded.
Monthly Income Plan (MIP)	A mutual fund scheme that seeks to provide a monthly income by investing primarily in debt securities, but with a small exposure to equity. The monthly income is however not guaranteed.
Mutual Fund	The trust that floats various mutual fund schemes using the services of an Asset Management Company.
Mutual Fund Scheme	A mutual fund scheme is an investment vehicle in which unit holders invest. Each mutual fund scheme has a dedicated investment portfolio whose gains or losses belong to the unit holders in that scheme.
Net Asset Value (NAV)	The value of each unit of the scheme. This is determined based on "marked to market" valuation.
New Fund Offer (NFO)	When mutual fund schemes are offered to investors at large for the first time, it is called New Fund Offer.
Open-end Scheme	A mutual fund scheme that is open for investment and redemption on any working day. Such schemes do not have a fixed maturity.
Real Estate Investment Trust (REIT)	A vehicle for investors to take exposure to real estate which is structured differently from a Real Estate Mutual Fund scheme.

Real Estate Mutual Fund Scheme	A mutual fund scheme that invests primarily in real-estate exposures.
Registrar & Transfer Agent (RTA)	The agency that is responsible for maintaining records of unit holders and handling corporate actions such as dividends and issue of bonus units.
Re-purchase Price	The price at which an open-end scheme is prepared to buy its units from an investor.
Sale Price	The price at which an open-end scheme sells its units to an investor. Under current regulations, it is the same as the Net Asset Value.
Sponsor	The person who constitutes the mutual fund trust and promotes the asset management company.
Systematic Investment Plan (SIP)	An approach to investing, where constant amounts are invested in a mutual fund scheme periodically (mostly, every month).
Systematic Transfer Plan (STP)	An approach to mutual fund investing, where constant amounts are transferred from one scheme to another scheme periodically (mostly, every month). It is effectively a combination of a Systematic Withdrawal Plan in the scheme from which money is transferred, and a Systematic Investment Plan in the scheme into which money is transferred.
Systematic Withdrawal Plan (SWP)	An approach to dis-investing, where constant amounts are realised from a mutual fund scheme periodically (mostly, every month).
Transaction Period	The period during which an interval fund becomes open for transactions with investors.
Treasury Bills (T-Bills)	Short term debt securities (up to 364-days maturity) issued by the Reserve Bank of India to meet the short term borrowing requirements of the government.
Trustee	The mutual fund trust, being a notional entity, operates through individuals who are called "Trustees". Where a Trustee Company is appointed to handle the trusteeship activities, directors on the board of the Trustee Company operate as trustees. The trustees are primarily responsible for protecting the interests of unit holders.
Unit	Unit holders' investments in a mutual fund scheme is denominated in "Units". Most mutual fund units in India have a face value of ₹ 10 per unit.
Unit-holder	An investor in a mutual fund scheme.
Value stocks	Shares of companies that are fundamentally under-valued.

Further Learning

Websites

www.sebi.gov.in
www.rbi.org.in
www.amfiindia.com
www.irdaindia.org
www.nseindia.com
www.sebiedifar.nic.in
www.bseindia.com
www.valueresearchonline.com
www.crisil.com
www.econoview.info
www.myiris.com
www.moneycontrol.com
www. Timesofmoney.com
www.personalfn.com
www.morningstar.com
www.lipper.com
www.micropal.com
www.stanford.edu/~wfsharpe
www.financialengines.com
www.barra.com
www.marketguide.com
www.gold.org
www.Thebulliondesk.com
www.goldbulletin.org

Journals

Journal of Portfolio Management
Journal of Business (ceased Nov 2006)
Financial Analysts Journal
Journal of Investing
Journal of Finance
Journal of Financial Planning
Review of Economic Studies
Journal of Real Estate Portfolio Management
Journal of Financial Economics
Journal of Banking & Finance
Journal of Economics & Business
Review of Financial Studies
Journal of Financial & Quantitative Analysis
International Review of Economics & Finance
Journal of Behavioral Finance
Management Science

References

1. Bogle, John C., *Common Sense on Mutual Funds*, (John Wiley & Sons, Inc., 1999), p. 9.
2. Graham, Benjamin, *The Intelligent Investor*, Commentary by Jason Zweig, (Harper Business Essentials, 2003), p. 147.
3. Bogle, John C., *Common Sense on Mutual Funds*, (John Wiley & Sons, Inc., 1999), p. 61.
4. Hall, Alvin D., *Getting Started in Mutual Funds*, (John Wiley & Sons, Inc., 2000), pp. 58, 59.
5. Hall, Alvin D., *Getting Started in Mutual Funds*, (John Wiley & Sons, Inc., 2000), p. 63.
6. Faber, David, *The Faber Report*, (Little Brown & Company, 2002), p. 173.
7. Cunningham, Lawrence A., How to think like Benjamin Graham and Invest like Warren Buffett, (McGraw-Hill, 2001), p. 107.
8. Hall, Alvin D., *Getting Started in Mutual Funds*, (John Wiley & Sons, Inc., 2000), p. 36.
9. Lynch, Peter, *One Up on Wall Street*, (Fireside, 2000), p. 97.
10. Hall, Alvin D., *Getting Started in Mutual Funds*, (John Wiley & Sons, Inc., 2000), p. 138.
11. Lynch, Peter, *One Up on Wall Street*, (Fireside, 2000), pp. 110 – 129.
12. Lynch, Peter, *One Up on Wall Street*, (Fireside, 2000), p. 75.
13. Cunningham, Lawrence A., *How to think like Benjamin Graham and Invest like Warren Buffett*, (McGraw-Hill, 2001), p. 8.
14. Graham, Benjamin, *The Intelligent Investor*, Commentary by Jason Zweig, (Harper Business Essentials, 2003), p. 236.

15. Lynch, Peter, *One Up on Wall Street*, (Fireside, 2000), p. 22.

16. Graham, Benjamin, *The Intelligent Investor*, Commentary by Jason Zweig, (Harper Business Essentials, 2003), pp. 179-180.

17. Lynch, Peter, *One Up on Wall Street*, (Fireside, 2000), p. 186.

18. Graham, Benjamin, *The Intelligent Investor*, Commentary by Jason Zweig, (Harper Business Essentials, 2003), p. 516.

19. Lynch, Peter, *One Up on Wall Street*, (Fireside, 2000), p. 280.

20. Graham, Benjamin, *The Intelligent Investor*, Commentary by Jason Zweig, (Harper Business Essentials, 2003), pp. 529-530.

21. Graham, Benjamin, *The Intelligent Investor*, Commentary by Jason Zweig, (Harper Business Essentials, 2003), p. 76.

22. Graham, Benjamin, *The Intelligent Investor*, Commentary by Jason Zweig, (Harper Business Essentials, 2003), p. 364.

23. Graham, Benjamin, *The Intelligent Investor*, Commentary by Jason Zweig, (Harper Business Essentials, 2003), p. 365.

24. Graham, Benjamin, *The Intelligent Investor*, Commentary by Jason Zweig, (Harper Business Essentials, 2003), p. 365.

25. Damodaran, Aswath, *Investment Fables*, (Financial Times Prentice Hall, 2004), p. 60.

26. Damodaran, Aswath, *Investment Fables*, (Financial Times Prentice Hall, 2004), p. 62-63.

27. Cunningham, Lawrence A., *How to think like Benjamin Graham and Invest like Warren Buffett*, (McGraw-Hill, 2001), p. 144.

28. Graham, Benjamin, *The Intelligent Investor*, Commentary by Jason Zweig, (Harper Business Essentials, 2003), p. 570.

29. Graham, Benjamin, *The Intelligent Investor*, Commentary by Jason Zweig, (Harper Business Essentials, 2003), p. 3.

30. Cunningham, Lawrence A., *How to think like Benjamin Graham and Invest like Warren Buffett*, (McGraw-Hill, 2001), p. 64.

31. Cunningham, Lawrence A., *How to think like Benjamin Graham and Invest like Warren Buffett*, (McGraw-Hill, 2001), p. xv.

32. Cunningham, Lawrence A., *How to think like Benjamin Graham and Invest like Warren Buffett*, (McGraw-Hill, 2001), p. 143.

33. Bogle, John C., *Common Sense on Mutual Funds*, (John Wiley & Sons, Inc., 1999), p. 60.

34. Graham, Benjamin, *The Intelligent Investor*, Commentary by Jason Zweig, (Harper Business Essentials, 2003), p. 58.

35. *India Gold Report — India: Heart of Gold Revival*, World Gold Council.

36. Sankaran, Sundar, *Financial Planning & Wealth Creation*, (Indian Institute of Banking & Finance, 2003), pp. 5-24.

37. Source Unknown.

38. Business Standard, 14 June, 2005.

39. Sankaran, Sundar, *Workbook for NISM Series V-A*: Mutual Fund Distributors Certification Examination, May 2010, p. 4.

40. Hall, Alvin D., *Getting Started in Mutual Funds*, (John Wiley & Sons, Inc., 2000), p. 49.

41. Hall, Alvin D., *Getting Started in Mutual Funds*, (John Wiley & Sons, Inc., 2000), p. 168.

42. Ferri, Richard A., *Protecting Your Wealth in Good Times and Bad*, (McGraw Hill, 2003), pp. 175-176.

43. Source Unknown.

44. Mui, Ylan Q., *Blue Chip, White Cotton: What Underwear Says About the Economy*, The Washington Post, 31 August, 2009.

45. Cunningham, Lawrence A., *How to think like Benjamin Graham and Invest like Warren Buffett*, (McGraw-Hill, 2001).

46. Taleb, Nassim Nicholas, *The Black Swan: The Impart of the Highly Improbable,* (Penguin).

47. Ferri, Richard A., *Protecting Your Wealth in Good Times and Bad*, (McGraw Hill, 2003), p. 177.

48. Bogle, John C., *Common Sense on Mutual Funds*, (John Wiley & Sons, Inc., 1999), p. 150.

49. Sharpe, William, *Asset Allocation: Management Style & Performance Measurement*, (Journal of Portfolio Management), Winter 1992, pp. 7-19.

50. Cunningham, Lawrence A., *How to think like Benjamin Graham and Invest like Warren Buffett*, (McGraw-Hill, 2001), p. 168.

51. Faber, David, *The Faber Report*, (Little Brown & Company, 2002), pp. 52-53.

52. Cunningham, Lawrence A., *How to think like Benjamin Graham and Invest like Warren Buffett*, (McGraw-Hill, 2001), p. 193.

53. Cunningham, Lawrence A., *How to think like Benjamin Graham and Invest like Warren Buffett*, (McGraw-Hill, 2001), p. 200.

54. Faber, David, *The Faber Report*, (Little Brown & Company, 2002), pp. 52-53.

55. Source Unknown.

56. Bogle, John C., *Common Sense on Mutual Funds*, (John Wiley & Sons, Inc., 1999), p. 99.

57. Brinson & Fachler, *Measuring Non-US Equity Portfolio Performance,* (Journal of Portfolio Management), Spring 1985, pp. 73-76.

58. Sankaran, Sundar, Performance Attribution for Equity Mutual Fund Schemes, IIT Bombay, December 2013.

59. Sankaran, Sundar, *Performance Attribution for Debt Mutual Fund Schemes*, IIT Bombay, May 2014.

60. Campisi Stephen, *A Sector Based Approach to Fixed Income Performance Attribution*, (The Journal of Performance Measurement, Spring 2011), Vol. 15, No. 3, pp. 23-42.

61. Anson, Mark, *Institutional Portfolio Management,* (Journal of Portfolio Management), Summer 2005, pp. 33-43.

62. Leibowitz, Martin L., *Alpha Hunters and Beta Grazers,* (Financial Analysts' Journal), September / October 2005, pp. 32-39.

63. Source Unknown.

64. Ferri, Richard A., *Protecting Your Wealth in Good Times and Bad,* (McGraw Hill, 2003), p. 82.

65. Graham, Benjamin, *The Intelligent Investor,* Commentary by Jason Zweig, (Harper Business Essentials, 2003), p. 102.

66. Ferri Richard A., *Protecting Your Wealth in Good Times and Bad,* (McGraw Hill, 2003), pp. 209-210.

67. AMFI Mutual Fund Testing Programme — *Workbook*, 2nd edition, December 2001, p. 197.

68. Sankaran, Sundar, *Workbook for NISM Series V-A*: Mutual Fund Distributors Certification Examination, May 2010, pp. 289.

69. AMFI Mutual Fund Testing Programme — *Workbook*, 2nd edition, December 2001, p. 216.

70. Graham, Benjamin, *The Intelligent Investor,* Commentary by Jason Zweig, (Harper Business Essentials, 2003), pp. 114-115.

71. Graham, Benjamin, *The Intelligent Investor,* Commentary by Jason Zweig, (Harper Business Essentials, 2003), pp. 156.

72. Graham, Benjamin, *The Intelligent Investor,* Commentary by Jason Zweig, (Harper Business Essentials, 2003), pp. 176.

73. Graham, Benjamin, *The Intelligent Investor,* Commentary by Jason Zweig, (Harper Business Essentials, 2003), p. 124.

74. Ferri, Richard A., *Protecting Your Wealth in Good Times and Bad,* (McGraw Hill, 2003), p. 30.

75. Ferri, Richard A., *Protecting Your Wealth in Good Times and Bad,* (McGraw Hill, 2003), p. 31.

76. Ferri, Richard A., *Protecting Your Wealth in Good Times and Bad,* (McGraw Hill, 2003), pp. 34.

77. Bogle, John C., *Common Sense on Mutual Funds*, (John Wiley & Sons, Inc., 1999), p. 30.

78. Bogle, John C., *Common Sense on Mutual Funds*, (John Wiley & Sons, Inc., 1999), p. 104.

79. Hall, Alvin D., *Getting Started in Mutual Funds*, (John Wiley & Sons, Inc., 2000), p. 171.

80. Graham, Benjamin, *The Intelligent Investor*, Commentary by Jason Zweig, (Harper Business Essentials, 2003), p. 256.

81. Cunningham, Lawrence A., *How to think like Benjamin Graham and Invest like Warren Buffett*, (McGraw-Hill, 2001), p. 65.

82. Ferri, Richard A., *Protecting Your Wealth in Good Times and Bad,* (McGraw Hill, 2003), pp. 206-207.

83. Ferri, Richard A., *Protecting Your Wealth in Good Times and Bad,* (McGraw Hill, 2003), p. 272.

84. Ferri, Richard A., *Protecting Your Wealth in Good Times and Bad,* (McGraw Hill, 2003), p. 88.

85. Ferri, Richard A., *Protecting Your Wealth in Good Times and Bad,* (McGraw Hill, 2003), p. 98.

Index